D1221058
DUNSTABLE and LUTON DOWNS
Dunstable
Luton
Stevenage
Hemel Hempstead
Amersham
Rickmansworth
Enfield
THE RODINGS
CHELMSFORD
Witham
Maldon
Brentwood
Billericay
ESSEX
Rochford
MOU
HOUNSLOW HEATH
Tilbury Fort
ROCHESTER
EPSOM DOWNS
Croydon
CHALK HILLS OF SURRY and KENT
MEREWORTH WOODS
MAIDSTONE
GUILDFORD
HOLMSDALE
Tunbridge
WEALDS OF KENT
Goudhurst
Cranbrook
ASHDOWN FOREST
TILGATE FOREST
FOREST RIDGE
Burwash Down
Petworth
WEALDS OF SUSSEX
Battel
Hastings
SOUTH DOWNS
SUSSEX CHALK HILLS
Hailsham
PEVENSEY LEVEL
Eastbourne
BEACHY HEAD

THE OLD WAYS

By the same author

Mountains of the Mind: A History of a Fascination
The Wild Places

THE OLD WAYS

A Journey on Foot

Robert Macfarlane

HAMISH HAMILTON
an imprint of
PENGUIN BOOKS

HAMISH HAMILTON

Published by the Penguin Group
Penguin Books Ltd, 80 Strand, London WC2R 0RL, England
Penguin Group (USA) Inc., 375 Hudson Street, New York, New York 10014, USA
Penguin Group (Canada), 90 Eglinton Avenue East, Suite 700, Toronto, Ontario, Canada M4P 2Y3
(a division of Pearson Penguin Canada Inc.)
Penguin Ireland, 25 St Stephen's Green, Dublin 2, Ireland (a division of Penguin Books Ltd)
Penguin Group (Australia), 250 Camberwell Road, Camberwell, Victoria 3124, Australia
(a division of Pearson Australia Group Pty Ltd)
Penguin Books India Pvt Ltd, 11 Community Centre, Panchsheel Park, New Delhi – 110 017, India
Penguin Group (NZ), 67 Apollo Drive, Rosedale, Auckland 0632, New Zealand
(a division of Pearson New Zealand Ltd)
Penguin Books (South Africa) (Pty) Ltd, Block D, Rosebank Office Park,
181 Jan Smuts Avenue, Parktown North, Gauteng 2193, South Africa

Penguin Books Ltd, Registered Offices: 80 Strand, London WC2R 0RL, England

www.penguin.com

First published 2012
007

Set in Fournier MT Std 12.5/16pt
Typeset by Jouve (UK), Milton Keynes
Printed in Great Britain by Clays Ltd, St Ives plc

A CIP catalogue record for this book is available from the British Library

ISBN: 978–0–241–14381–0

www.greenpenguin.co.uk

Penguin Books is committed to a sustainable future for our business, our readers and our planet. This book is made from Forest Stewardship Council™ certified paper.

ALWAYS LEARNING PEARSON

For Julia, Lily and Tom,
and those who keep the paths open

Much has been written of travel, far less of the road.

Edward Thomas, *The Icknield Way* (1913)

My eyes were in my feet . . .

Nan Shepherd, *The Living Mountain* (1977)

CONTENTS

Author's Note xi

PART I TRACKING
(*England*)

1 Track 3
2 Path 11
3 Chalk 35
4 Silt 57

PART II FOLLOWING
(*Scotland*)

5 Water – South 85
6 Water – North 117
7 Peat 139
8 Gneiss 167
9 Granite 183

PART III ROAMING
(*Abroad*)

10 Limestone 209
11 Roots 233
12 Ice 259

PART IV HOMING
(*England*)

13	Snow	289
14	Flint	305
15	Ghost	331
16	Print	357
	Glossary	365
	Notes	375
	Select Bibliography	395
	Acknowledgements	409
	Index of Selected Topics	413

AUTHOR'S NOTE

This book could not have been written by sitting still. The relationship between paths, walking and the imagination is its subject, and much of its thinking was therefore done – was only possible – while on foot. Although it is the third book in a loose trilogy about landscape and the human heart, it need not be read after or in the company of its predecessors. It tells the story of walking a thousand miles or more along old ways in search of a route to the past, only to find myself delivered again and again to the contemporary. It is an exploration of the ghosts and voices that haunt ancient paths, of the tales that tracks keep and tell, of pilgrimage and trespass, of songlines and their singers and of the strange continents that exist within countries. Above all, this is a book about people and place: about walking as a reconnoitre inwards, and the subtle ways in which we are shaped by the landscapes through which we move.

PART I

TRACKING

(England)

1

TRACK

> All things are engaged in writing their history . . . Not a foot steps into the snow, or along the ground, but prints in characters more or less lasting, a map of its march. The ground is all memoranda and signatures; and every object covered over with hints. In nature, this self-registration is incessant, and the narrative is the print of the seal.
>
> Ralph Waldo Emerson (1850)

Two days short of the winter solstice; the turn of the year's tide. All that cold day, the city and the countryside around felt halted, paused. Five degrees below freezing and the earth battened down. Clouds held snow that would not fall. Out in the suburbs the schools were closed, people homebound, the pavements rinky and the roads black-iced. The sun ran a shallow arc across the sky. Then just before dusk the snow came – dropping straight for five hours and settling at a steady inch an hour.

I was at my desk that evening, trying to work but distracted by the weather. I kept stopping, standing, looking out of the window. The snow was sinking through the orange cone cast by a street light, the fat flakes showing like furnace sparks.

Around eight o'clock the snow ceased. An hour later I went for a walk with a flask of whisky to keep me warm. I walked for half a mile along dark back roads where the snow lay clean and unmarked. The houses began to thin out. A few undrawn curtains: family evenings underway, the flicker and burble of television sets. The cold like a wire in the nose. A slew of stars, the moon flooding everything with silver.

At the southerly fringe of the suburb, a last lamp post stands by a hawthorn hedge, and next to it is a hole in the hedge which leads down to a modest field path.

I followed the field path east-south-east towards a long chalk hilltop, visible as a whaleback in the darkness. Northwards was the glow of the city, and the red blip of aircraft warning lights from towers and cranes. Dry snow squeaked underfoot. A fox crossed the field to my west at a trot. The moonlight was so bright that everything cast a crisp moon-shadow: black on white, stark as woodcut. Wands of dogwood made zebra-hide of the path; hawthorn threw a lattice. The trees were frilled with snow, which lay to the depth of an inch or more on branches and twigs. The snow caused everything to exceed itself and the moonlight caused everything to double itself.

This is the path I've probably walked more often than any other in my life. It's a young way; maybe fifty years old, no more. Its easterly hedge is mostly hawthorn and around eight feet high; its westerly hedge is a younger mix of blackthorn, hawthorn, hazel and dogwood. It is not normally a beautiful place, but there's a feeling of secrecy to it that I appreciate, hedged in as it is on both sides, and running discreetly as it does between field and road. In summer I've seen small rolling clouds of goldfinches rising from teasel-heads and then curling ahead to settle again, retreating in the measure that I approach them.

That evening the path was a grey snow alley, and I followed it up to the hanger of beech trees that tops the whaleback hill, passing off the clay and onto the chalk proper. At the back brink of the beech wood I ducked through an ivy-trailed gap, and was into the forty-acre field that lies beyond.

At first sight the field seemed flawless; floe country. Then I set out across it and started to see the signs. The snow was densely printed with the tracks of birds and animals – archives of the hundreds of journeys made since the snow had stopped. There were neat deer slots, partridge prints like arrowheads pointing the way, and the pads of rabbits. Lines of tracks curved away from me across the field, disappearing into shadow or hedge. The moonlight, falling at a slant, deepened the dark in the nearer tracks so that they appeared full as inkwells. To all these marks I added my own.

The snow was overwhelmingly legible. Each print-trail seemed like a plot that could be read backwards in time; a series of allusions to events since ended. I found a line of fox pugs, which here and there had been swept across by the fox's brush, as if it had been trying to erase evidence of its own passage. I discovered what I supposed were the traces of a pheasant taking off: trenched footprints where it had pushed up, then spaced feather-presses either side of the tracks, becoming progressively lighter and then vanishing altogether.

I chose to follow a deer's trail, which angled tightly across a corner of the field. The slots led through a blackthorn hedge: I snagged my way after them, and emerged into a surreal landscape.

To my north, the land swooped smoothly away downhill for 300 yards or so. South and uphill of where I stood, big white humps surrounded what appeared to be a small neat lake with a flagstick in its centre. There were copses of beech and stands of pine, sudden drops and draws in the land, rounded hills and swathed valleys.

I walked over to the lake, stepped out onto its surface, and by its flagstick I sat down and took a drink of whisky. Edited of its golfers by the darkness, transformed by snowfall and moonlight, the county's most exclusive golf course had become a strange realm of open country. Murmuring insincere apologies to the club's members, I left the first green and set off to explore the course. I walked straight down the middle of fairway after fairway, my shadow falling undistorted by my side. In the bunkers snow lay calf-deep and sifted. On the fifth green I lay on my back and watched the stars' slow wheel.

Most of the animal tracks on the course had been left by rabbits. If you've seen rabbit prints in snow, you will know they resemble a Halloween ghost mask, or the face of Edvard Munch's screamer: the two rear feet are placed laterally to make elongated eyes, and between and behind them fall the forefeet in a slightly offset paired line, forming nose and oval mouth. Thousands of these faces peered at me from the snow.

Occasionally the headlights of cars on the road to the west showed as long yellow tunnels of light. On the twelfth fairway something large and dark ran from tree to scrub cover: it looked like a wolf, but must have been a deer or fox, and set needles of silly fear pricking in the backs of my hands.

At the far end of the course, I followed rabbit tracks through another blackthorn hedge and onto the Roman road that runs for miles over low chalk hills. The road looked magnificent in the snow – the white line of its route leading the eye far in either direction – and I walked it south-east. Vast fields were visible through the hedges to either side, throwing the moonlight back up in hard pale sheets. A bird moving in a tall ash tree sent snow dropping across the path ahead of me, falling like speckles on early film.

Distance stretched oddly, or perhaps time compressed, for it seemed that I had been moving for many miles or hours before I reached the point where the Roman road passed the end of a wide avenue of beeches that I recognized. I walked up the avenue, skirted the earthworks of a large Iron Age ring-fort, crossed a road and then entered a wide meadow that rises to the top of a chalk down, whose summit floats 250 feet above sea level. Charcoal trees, a taste of pewter in the mouth.

At the down's top, under the moon, near the outline of a Bronze Age burial barrow, I sat in the snow and drank whisky again. I looked back along the line of my own tracks leading up to the hilltop. Away to the north-west were dozens of other print-trails, spreading far and then further downhill. I picked a trail and set out along it, following those tracks to see where they might lead.

2

PATH

Foil — Trods & holloways — The blue & lucid ice — Utsi's Stone — A labyrinth of liberty — Consensual making — Desire lines — George Borrow — The Horrors — Ghost-lines — A territorial imperative — Cosmi-comic visions — Edward Thomas — 'Patient sublunary legs' — Hansel & Gretel — Hodology — Footfall as knowledge — Songlines — The Doomway & meteor showers — Biogeography — The pylon's lyric crackle.

Humans are animals and like all animals we leave tracks as we walk: signs of passage made in snow, sand, mud, grass, dew, earth or moss. The language of hunting has a luminous word for such mark-making: 'foil'. A creature's 'foil' is its track. We easily forget that we are track-makers, though, because most of our journeys now occur on asphalt and concrete – and these are substances not easily impressed.

'Always, everywhere, people have walked, veining the earth with paths visible and invisible, symmetrical or meandering,' writes Thomas Clark in his enduring prose-poem 'In Praise of Walking'. It's true that, once you begin to notice them, you see that the landscape is still webbed with paths and footways – shadowing the modern-day road network, or meeting it at a slant or perpendicular. Pilgrim paths, green roads, drove roads, corpse roads, trods, leys, dykes, drongs, sarns, snickets – say the names of paths out loud and at speed and they become a poem or rite – holloways, bostles, shutes, driftways, lichways, ridings, halterpaths, cartways, carneys, causeways, herepaths.

Many regions still have their old ways, connecting place to place, leading over passes or round mountains, to church or chapel, river or sea. Not all of their histories are happy. In Ireland there are hundreds of miles of famine roads, built by the starving during the 1840s to connect nothing with nothing in return for little, unregistered on

Ordnance Survey base maps. In the Netherlands there are *doodwegen* and *spookwegen* – death roads and ghost roads – which converge on medieval cemeteries. Spain has not only a vast and operational network of *cañada*, or drove roads, but also thousands of miles of the Camino de Santiago, the pilgrim routes that lead to the shrine of Santiago de Compostela. For pilgrims walking the Camino, every footfall is doubled, landing at once on the actual road and also on the path of faith. In Scotland there are *clachan* and *rathad* – cairned paths and shieling paths – and in Japan the slender farm tracks that the poet Bashō followed in 1689 when writing his *Narrow Road to the Far North*. The American prairies were traversed in the nineteenth century by broad 'bison roads', made by herds of buffalo moving several beasts abreast, and then used by early settlers as they pushed westwards across the Great Plains.

Paths of long usage exist on water as well as on land. The oceans are seamed with seaways – routes whose course is determined by prevailing winds and currents – and rivers are among the oldest ways of all. During the winter months, the only route in and out of the remote valley of Zanskar in the Indian Himalayas is along the ice-path formed by a frozen river. The river passes down through steep-sided valleys of shaley rock, on whose slopes snow leopards hunt. In its deeper pools, the ice is blue and lucid. The journey down the river is called the *chadar*, and parties undertaking the *chadar* are led by experienced walkers known as 'ice-pilots', who can tell where the dangers lie.

Different paths have different characteristics, depending on geology and purpose. Certain coffin paths in Cumbria have flat 'resting stones' on the uphill side, on which the bearers could place their load, shake out tired arms and roll stiff shoulders; certain coffin paths in the west of Ireland have recessed resting stones, in the alcoves of which each mourner would place a pebble. The prehistoric trackways of the English Downs can still be traced because on their close chalky soil, hard-packed by centuries of trampling, daisies flourish. Thousands of work paths crease the moorland of the Isle of Lewis in the Outer Hebrides, so that when seen from the air the moor has the appearance of chamois leather. I think also of the zigzag flexure of mountain paths in the Scottish Highlands, the flagged and bridged packhorse routes of Yorkshire and Mid Wales, and the sunken greensand paths of Hampshire on whose shady banks ferns emerge in spring, curled like crosiers.

The way-marking of old paths is an esoteric lore of its own, involving cairns, grey wethers, sarsens, hoarstones, longstones, milestones, cromlechs and other guide-signs. On boggy areas of Dartmoor, fragments of white china clay were placed to show safe paths at twilight, like Hansel and Gretel's pebble trail. In mountain country, boulders often indicate fording points over rivers: Utsi's Stone in the Cairngorms, for instance, which marks where the Allt Mor burn can be crossed to reach traditional grazing grounds, and onto which has been deftly incised the petroglyph of a reindeer that, when evening sunlight plays over the rock, seems to leap to life.

Paths and their markers have long worked on me like lures: drawing my sight up and on and over. The eye is enticed by a path, and the mind's eye also. The imagination cannot help but pursue a line in the land – onwards in space, but also backwards in time to the histories of a route and its previous followers. As I walk paths I often wonder about their origins, the impulses that have led to their creation, the records they yield of customary journeys, and the secrets they keep of adventures, meetings and departures. I would guess I have walked perhaps 7,000 or 8,000 miles on footpaths so far in my life: more than most, perhaps, but not nearly so many as others.

Thomas De Quincey estimated Wordsworth to have walked a total of 175,000–180,000 miles: Wordsworth's notoriously knobbly legs, 'pointedly condemned' – in De Quincey's catty phrase – 'by all . . . female connoisseurs', were magnificent shanks when it came to passage and bearing. I've covered thousands of foot-miles in my memory, because when – as most nights – I find myself insomniac, I send my mind out to re-walk paths I've followed, and in this way can sometimes pace myself into sleep.

'They give me joy as I proceed,' wrote John Clare of field paths, simply. Me too. 'My left hand hooks you round the waist,' declared Walt Whitman – companionably, erotically, coercively – in *Leaves of Grass* (1855), 'my right hand points to landscapes of continents, and a plain public road.' Footpaths are mundane in the best sense of that word: 'worldly', open to all. As rights of way determined and sustained by use, they constitute a labyrinth of liberty, a slender network of common land that still threads through our aggressively privatized world of barbed wire and gates, CCTV cameras and 'No Trespassing' signs. It is one of the significant differences between land use in Britain and in America that this labyrinth should exist. Americans have long envied the British system of footpaths and the freedoms it offers, as I in turn envy the Scandinavian customary right of *Allemansrätten* ('Everyman's right'). This convention – born of a region that did not pass through centuries of feudalism, and therefore has no inherited deference to a landowning class – allows a citizen to walk anywhere on uncultivated land provided that he or she cause no harm; to light fires; to sleep anywhere beyond the curtilage of a dwelling; to gather flowers, nuts and berries; and to swim in any watercourse (rights to which the newly enlightened access laws of Scotland increasingly approximate).

Paths are the habits of a landscape. They are acts of consensual making. It's hard to create a footpath on your own. The artist Richard Long did it once, treading a dead-straight line into desert sand by turning and turning about dozens of times. But this was a footmark not a footpath: it led nowhere except to its own end, and by walking it Long became a tiger pacing its cage or a swimmer doing lengths. With no promise of extension, his line was to a path what a snapped twig is to a tree. Paths connect. This is their first duty and their chief reason for being. They relate places in a literal sense, and by extension they relate people.

Paths are consensual, too, because without common care and common practice they disappear: overgrown by vegetation, ploughed up or built over (though they may persist in the memorious substance of land law). Like sea channels that require regular dredging to stay open, paths *need* walking. In nineteenth-century Suffolk small sickles called 'hooks' were hung on stiles and posts at the start of certain well-used paths: those running between villages, for instance, or byways to parish churches. A walker would pick up a hook and use it to lop off branches that were starting to impede passage. The hook would then be left at the other end of the path, for a walker coming in the opposite direction. In this manner the path was collectively maintained for general use.

By no means all interesting paths are old paths. In every town and city today, cutting across parks and waste ground, you'll see unofficial paths created by walkers who have abandoned the pavements and roads to take short cuts and make asides. Town planners call these improvised routes 'desire lines' or 'desire paths'. In Detroit – where areas of the city are overgrown by vegetation, where tens of thousands of homes have been abandoned, and where few can now afford cars – walkers and cyclists have created thousands of such elective easements.

~

I have walked paths for years, and for years I have read about them. The literature of wayfaring is long, existing as poems, songs, stories, treatises and route guides, maps, novels and essays. The compact between writing and walking is almost as old as literature – a walk is only a step away from a story, and every path *tells*.

The most charismatic of modern walker-writers is surely George Borrow, who inspired the surge in path-following and old-way romance that occurred in mid-nineteenth-century Europe and America, the effects of which are with us still. Borrow took to tramping in the 1820s, and he followed paths for thousands of miles through England and Wales, across the Channel into France, Spain, Portugal and Russia, as well as south to Morocco, coming to know the cultures and peoples of the road: the Romanies, the nomads, the tramps, the guildsmen, the shepherds, the farmers and the innkeepers. Over six feet tall, broad-framed, dressed typically in a black cloth suit with white stockings, his costume occasionally topped off by a sombrero, Borrow cut a distinctive figure on the path, and an even more distinctive figure in the sleepy East Anglian towns of Norwich and Great Yarmouth (where he could sometimes be seen riding bareback on his 'high-caste' black Arab stallion, Sidi Habismilk, also fondly known as 'My Lord the Sustainer of the Kingdom').

Borrow was a walker of awesome stamina and a linguist of almost inconceivable talent, who is said to have been able to speak twelve languages by the time he was eighteen and to have been competently acquainted with more than forty – including Nahuatl, Tibetan, Armenian and Malo-Russian – over the course of his life. In the winter of 1832–3 the British and Foreign Bible Society invited him at short notice to an interview in London, wanting to see if he could translate the Bible into a number of difficult languages. He walked to the interview from Norwich, covering 112 miles in 27 hours, sustained by a pint of ale, half a pint of milk, a bread roll and two apples. The society liked what they saw and commissioned Borrow to translate the New Testament into Manchu. What Borrow hadn't told them was that he did not have any Manchu. No problem. Once the job was landed, he acquired 'several books in the Manchu-Tartar dialect', and Amyot's Manchu–French (French!) dictionary. Then he travelled home (by coach, understandably) and shut himself up with the books. Three weeks later he could 'translate Manchu with no great difficulty', and fulfilled the society's commission.

Borrow spent more than forty years exploring England, Wales and Europe on foot. His temperament was steep-cambered, and like many long-distance walkers he was a depressive, pursued from a young age by what he referred to as 'the Horrors'. Walking became a means of out-striding his sadness. He was legendary for formulating – in his elaborate work of para-autobiography, *Lavengro* (1851) – the wayfarer's creed:

> There's night and day, brother, both sweet things; sun, moon, and stars, brother, all sweet things; there's likewise a wind on the heath. Life is very sweet, brother; who would wish to die?

Borrow knew the road's asperity as well as its sweetness. He was sensitive to the ethical difficulties involved in celebrating the life of the road when there were many who had no choice but to live abjectly upon it: the jobless and homeless, the tramps, hobos and bindle-skiffs, the dispossessed and the overworked.

But the Borrovian example – as reported in his tendrilled prose – proved wildly influential. The breeze on the face, the stars for a ceiling, the fire by the wayside, hedgerow philosophizing, open journeyings: Borrow set such images loose in the nineteenth-century imagination. Most of his emulators gained blisters rather than enlightenment as a result, but the cult of leisured vagabondage grew. By the end of the 1800s, walking clubs were being founded in number and a profuse literature of old-wayfaring had emerged. Pocket-sized books with titles like *The Open Road* or *On Foot*, bound in green buckram or red suede, became best-sellers. Robert Louis Stevenson wrote his dark and mystical *Songs of Travel* (1896) – which take their tempo from the rolling tread of the long-distance walker. The ornithologist W. H. Hudson pioneered a pastoral psychogeography, tramping for months along England's footpaths, waiting for what he called the 'charm of the unknown' to set his rods quivering (his journeys shaped in part by Borrow but also by earlier English mystics like Thomas Traherne, Henry Vaughan and Thomas Browne). At the turn of the century Hilaire Belloc strode from France to Italy, and wrote his bombastic pilgrim's tale *The Path to Rome* (1902). John Muir walked a thousand miles from Indianapolis to the Florida Keys in 1867, veering as he went between extremes of hunger and of ecstasy; seventeen years later a young man called Charles Lummis tramped across America from Ohio to California and claimed that he had made 'the longest walk for pure pleasure that is on record'. The Sierra Club was founded in 1892, inspired by Muir's convictions that the walker's bodily contact with the wild world benefited both walker and world, and that 'going out . . . was really going in'.

The shock of the Great War provoked intense British interest in the old ways. Some of the returning soldiers, wounded in body and mind, retreated to the English countryside, hoping that by recovering a sense of belonging rooted in nature and place they might dignify their damaged lives (the wish that it had all been *worth* something). Henry Williamson was one such casualty. Invalided home from France with gas injuries, he went to ground in rural Devon, where he paced out the paths of Dartmoor and tracked what he called its 'wildlings'. Out of those years he wrested his masterpiece *Tarka the Otter* (1927) – every word of which was, as he put it, 'chipped from the breastbone'.

Other people, traumatized into superstition by the war, took to the paths in search of ghosts – setting out on the tracks of the lost and the left-behind. Old paths became mediums in two senses: means of communion as well as means of motion. Interest built in the ghostliness of these ghost-lines. The convivial pilgrimages described by Chaucer became tinged with a morbid historicism: spectres stepped from the verge or hedge, offering brief address. The landscape was, John Masefield wrote, 'thronged by souls unseen, / Who knew the interest in me, and were keen / That man alive should understand man dead'.

I've read them all, these old-way wanderers, and often I've encountered versions of the same beguiling idea: that walking such paths might lead you – in Hudson's phrase – to 'slip back out of this modern world'. Repeatedly, these wanderers spoke of the tingle of connection, of walking as seance, of voices heard along the way. Bashō is said to have told a student that while wandering north he often spoke with long-dead poets of the past, including his twelfth-century forebear Saigyo: he therefore came to imagine his travels as conversations between a 'ghost and a ghost-to-be'. In Thomas

Hardy's novels, stretches of path can carry memories of a person, just as a person might of a path. Richard Jefferies, in a notebook entry from 1887, described reaching a Bronze Age tumulus in Gloucestershire and feeling '[a]s if I could look back and feel *then*; the sunshine of *then*, and their life'. Paths were figured as rifts within which time might exist as pure surface, prone to weird morphologies, uncanny origami.

It is true that one need not be a mystic to accept that certain old paths are linear only in a simple sense. Like trees they have branches, and like rivers they have tributaries. Seven years ago I travelled to Dorset, to explore the holloways of that green dairy county with a close friend of mine, Roger Deakin. 'Holloway' comes from the Anglo-Saxon *hol weg*, and refers to a sunken path that has been grooved into the earth over centuries by the passage of feet, wheels and weather. Dorset – like many of the soft-stone counties of England – is webbed with such paths, some of them twenty feet deep and most of them now overgrown by brambles and nettles. Roger and I spent days down in the gritty caramel sandstone around the little town of Chideock, following the holloways and discovering the stories associated with them: of sixteenth-century recusants taking refuge from persecution, of seventeenth-century priests holding Masses in the woods, of fugitive aristocrats seeking shelter from twentieth-century pursuers. In the dusk of the holloways, these pasts felt excitingly alive and coexistent – as if time had somehow pleated back on itself, bringing discontinuous moments into contact, and creating historical correspondences that survived as a territorial imperative to concealment and escape.

Two years after that visit, Roger died young and unexpectedly. Four years after his death I returned to Dorset to re-walk the same holloways, and found myself tracking our own earlier traces – the holly bush from which we'd cut sticks, the field selvedge where we'd camped for a night – and experiencing startlingly clear memory-glimpses of Roger himself, seen at the turn of a corner or ahead of me on the path.

~

Not all the early old-way walkers were savoury characters, nor were all their ideas appealing. The use of old paths to navigate terrains both real and imagined has attracted a rabble of delusionists, bigots and other unlovely maniacs. I've read with distaste the work of multi-purpose misanthropes, of nationalists peddling wrong-headed theories of race, and of nostalgists who demonstrate a preference for the biddable dead over the awkward living. I've read with bafflement the back-to-the-soilers for whom path-walking was (along with energetic morris dancing and long-term sandal-wearing) a means of cleansing the besmirched male soul.

But I've also met many walker-writers who avoided these thought traps and idiocies. Borrow danced gleefully around them all, weaving his cosmi-comic visions as he went. John Clare was fond of footpaths because they were 'rich & joyful to the mind': ways of walking that were also ways of thinking. To William Wordsworth, long-used paths were routes to adventure, leading into 'the recesses of the country'. William Hazlitt walked radically, making marches from chapel to chapel to hear Unitarian ministers preach, and acclaiming footpaths as 'lines of communication . . . by which the flame of civil and religious liberty is kept alive'.

The more I have looked, the more paths and tracks seem to thread their ways through the prose, poetry and art of Europe, America and – in particular – Britain over the past two centuries. They are there in Dorothy Wordsworth's journals, in Paul Nash's war-scapes, with their zigzagging duckboard walkways, in Michael Powell and Emeric Pressburger's 1942 film *A Canterbury Tale*, in which the ancient Pilgrim's Way is blithely churned up by tank brigades on manoeuvre, and in Bill Brandt's 1950 photograph of a narrow stretch of the same path, where the Way appears as a foot-worn crevasse into the underlying snow of the chalk – a gap down which one might slip not just to another time, but to another realm and climate. I have come to love Eric Ravilious's dreamy watercolours of the prehistoric tracks of the English Downs, and I have read and reread the Scottish writer Nan Shepherd's accounts of how she came to know the Cairngorm massif on foot, following its ridge lines and deer tracks for years until she found herself walking not 'up' but 'into' the mountains. These are the consequences of the old ways with which I feel easiest: walking as enabling sight and thought rather than encouraging retreat and escape; paths as offering not only means of traversing space, but also ways of feeling, being and knowing.

Above all, I have been affected by the life and work of Edward Thomas: essayist, soldier, singer, among the most significant of modern English poets – and the guiding spirit of this book. Thomas was born in London in 1878 to Welsh parents, and from a young age he was both a walker and a writer. After making his reputation with a series of travelogues, natural histories and biographies, he at last began writing poetry in the winter of 1914, at the age of thirty-six. In an astonishing late outpouring of art, he wrote 142 poems in just over two years: poems that changed the course of poetry and whose branch-lines are being followed still. On Easter Monday 1917, aged thirty-nine, he was killed on the opening dawn of the Battle of Arras.

I first read Thomas's poetry at school, in an anthology that included his best-known poems, 'Adlestrop' and 'As the Team's Head-Brass'. He seemed to me then an engagingly simple author, verging on the naïve: an elegist for a rural England of ploughmen, hayricks and meadowsweet that was vanishing even as he wrote. It would take me nearly twenty years to understand how drastically limited this account of Thomas was. He is still often thought of as a pastoral poet, celebrating place and belonging, but I now see that his true subjects are disconnection, discrepancy and unsettledness. His poems are thronged with ghosts, dark doubles, and deep forests in which paths peter out; his landscapes are often brittle surfaces, prone to sudden collapse. While he was drawn to the romantic figure of the self-confident solitary walker, he was more interestingly alert to how we are scattered, as well as affirmed, by the places through which we move.

Thomas possessed a pair of what Keats once called 'patient sublunary legs', and those legs carried him over thousands of miles of old paths, from the famous (Sarn Helen in Wales, the Icknield Way and the Ridgeway in southern England) to the local (Old Litton Lane and Harepath Lane, near his east Hampshire home). 'The earliest roads wandered like rivers through the land,' he wrote, 'having, like rivers, one necessity, to keep in motion.' Thomas used the old ways to keep himself in motion, for like Borrow – whose biography he wrote and with whom he closely identified – he was depressive. Like Borrow, too, walking was one of the few activities that could lift him from his depressions. He would cut a stick – holly was his favourite staff-wood – and set off along 'indelible old roads', 'worn by hoofs and the naked feet and the trailing staves of long-dead generations'. Ancient ways were 'potent, magic things', on which he could 'make time as nothing' while 'meandering over many centuries'. Hansel and Gretel being led into the wood, but dropping a trail of white stones behind them and finding their way back, came to his mind to be 'one of the great stories of the world'.

To Thomas, paths connected real places but they also led outwards to metaphysics, backwards to history and inwards to the self. These traverses – between the conceptual, the spectral and the personal – occur often without signage in his writing, and are among its most characteristic events. He imagined himself in topographical terms. Corners, junctions, stiles, fingerposts, forks, crossroads, trivia, beckoning over-the-hill paths, tracks that led to danger, death or bliss: he internalized the features of path-filled landscapes such that they gave form to his melancholy and his hopes. Walking was a means of personal myth-making, but it also shaped his everyday longings: he not only thought on paths and of them, but also *with* them.

For paths run through people as surely as they run through places. The American historian and geographer John Brinckerhoff Jackson – a man constitutionally wary of romanticism – puts it well. 'For untold thousands of years we travelled on foot over rough paths,' he notes, 'not simply as peddlers or commuters or tourists, but as men and women for whom the path and road stood for some intense experience: freedom, new human relationships, a new awareness of the landscape. The road offered a journey into the unknown that could end up allowing us to discover who we were.'

I have long been fascinated by how people understand themselves using landscape, by the topographies of self we carry within us and by the maps we make with which to navigate these interior terrains. We think in metaphors drawn from place and sometimes those metaphors do not only adorn our thought, but actively produce it. Landscape, to borrow George Eliot's phrase, can 'enlarge the imagined range for self to move in'.

As I envisage it, landscape projects into us not like a jetty or peninsula, finite and bounded in its volume and reach, but instead as a kind of sunlight, flickeringly unmappable in its plays yet often quickening and illuminating. We are adept, if occasionally embarrassed, at saying what we make of places – but we are far less good at saying what places make of us. For some time now it has seemed to me that the two questions we should ask of any strong landscape are these: firstly, what do I know when I am in this place that I can know nowhere else? And then, vainly, what does this place know of me that I cannot know of myself?

~

From my heel to my toe is a measured space of 29.7 centimetres or 11.7 inches. This is a unit of progress and it is also a unit of thought. 'I can only meditate when I am walking,' wrote Jean-Jacques Rousseau in the fourth book of his *Confessions*, 'when I stop I cease to think; my mind only works with my legs.' Søren Kierkegaard speculated that the mind might function optimally at the pedestrian pace of three miles per hour, and in a journal entry describes going out for a wander and finding himself 'so overwhelmed with ideas' that he 'could scarcely walk'. Christopher Morley wrote of Wordsworth as 'employ[ing] his legs as an instrument of philosophy' and Wordsworth of his own 'feeling intellect'. Nietzsche was typically absolute on the subject – 'Only those thoughts which come from *walking* have any value' – and Wallace Stevens typically tentative: 'Perhaps / The truth depends on a walk around a lake.' In all of these accounts, walking is not the action by which one arrives at knowledge; it is itself the means of knowing.

The proposition that cognition is both motion-sensitive and site-specific pre-dates Romanticism, though it was Rousseau who made it famous. It is now a familiar suggestion, and one which we are wise to be sceptical about when it is asserted as a rule. Sometimes walking is the mind's subtle accomplice; at other times its brutal antagonist. As you will know if you've ever walked long distances for day after day, fatigue on the path can annihilate all but the most basic brain functions. After twenty miles you're wall-eyed, inanely watching loops on what John Hillaby once called 'the skull cinema'.

In non-Western cultures, the ideas of footfall as knowledge and walking as a mode of thinking are widespread, often operating in particular as a metaphor for recollection – history as a region one walks back into. Keith Basso has written of how, for the Cibecue Apache, the past is figured as a path or trail (*'intin*), trodden by ancestors but largely invisible to the living, which has to be re-approached indirectly via the prompts of certain memorial traces. These traces – which include place names, stories, songs and relics – are sometimes called by the Apache *biké' goz'áá* – 'footprints', 'tracks'. To the Klinchon people of north-western Canada, walking and knowing are barely divisible activities: their term for 'knowledge' and their term for 'footprint' can be used interchangeably. A Tibetan Buddhist text from around 600 years ago uses the word *shul* to mean 'a mark that remains after that which has made it has passed by': footprints are *shul*, a path is *shul*, and such impressions draw one backwards into awareness of past events.

The ideas that walking might be thinking or that feet might *know* are, at first encounter, foreign and puzzling. We don't tend to imagine the foot as an expressive or perceptive appendage. The foot lacks the versatility of the hand. It has that irreversible big toe: the best it can do by way of grip is a clumsy scissor action with the second toe. The foot feels more of a prosthesis, there to carry us about, not to interpret or organize the world for us. The hand, surely, is always subtler than the foot – we speak of manipulation but never of pedipulation.

Yet Richard Long – who once walked thirty-three miles a day for thirty-three days, from the Lizard in Cornwall to Dunnet Head in northern Scotland – signs off his letters with a red-ink stamp that shows the outline of two feet with eyes embedded in their soles, gazing out at the looker. Footfall as a way of seeing the landscape; touch as sight – these are notions to which I can hold.

For Ludwig Wittgenstein, following lines of enquiry on foot as well as in the mind was integral to his philosophy. Studying in Cambridge under Bertrand Russell, he would stride up and down Russell's room in agitated silence, sometimes for hours, covering miles in a room of yards. 'Are you thinking about logic or your sins?' Russell asked once, half jokingly, of his striding student. 'Both!' answered Wittgenstein instantly. In 1913 Wittgenstein retreated to Skjolden, a tiny village on a remote Norwegian fjord, and spent a long dark winter there, contemplating logic and walking the paths that bordered the fjord and led up into the mountains. The landscape – ascetic, decisive – matched the thinking he undertook, and in the course of that winter he solved a major philosophical crux concerning the symbolism for truth functions. 'I can't imagine that I could have worked anywhere as I did there,' he wrote to his sister years later. 'It seems to me that I had given birth to new thoughts within me': '*Es kommt mir so vor, als hätte ich damals in mir neue Denkbewegungen geboren.*' The word Wittgenstein used for 'thought', *Denkbewegungen*, is a coinage that might be translated as 'thought movements', 'thought-ways' or 'paths of thought': ideas that have been brought into being by means of motion along a path (*Weg*).

In one of Thomas Clark's quiet poems, a walker along a seashore reaches a place where stone steps 'carved out of rock / go down to water' next to a mooring. The poem accepts their invitation to descend, and the walker imagines 'step[ping] down into the sea / into another knowledge / wild and cold'. The allusion is to Elizabeth Bishop's great poem 'At the Fishhouses', which passes into the 'clear gray icy water' of a Newfoundland harbour; water that is 'like what we imagine knowledge to be: / dark, salt, clear, moving, utterly free'. Bishop in turn casts backwards, I think, to Wordsworth in 1815 writing of how one accesses 'the depths of reason': a profound realm 'to which the mind cannot sink gently of itself – but to which it must descend by treading the steps of thought'. The three poems become restatements of each other – a print-trail or series of steps of their own.

The best-known connection between footfall, knowledge and memory is the Aboriginal Australian vision of the Songlines. According to this cosmogony, the world was created in an epoch known as the Dreamtime, when the Ancestors emerged to find the earth a black, flat, featureless terrain. They began to walk out across this non-place, and as they walked they broke through the crust of the earth and released the sleeping life beneath it, so that the landscape sprang up into being with each pace. As Bruce Chatwin explained in his flawed but influential account, 'each totemic ancestor, while travelling through the country, was thought to have scattered a trail of words and musical notes along the line of his footprints'. Depending on where they fell, these foot-notes became linked with particular features of the landscape. Thus the world was covered by 'Dreaming-tracks' that 'lay over the land as "ways" of communication', each track having its corresponding Song. The Australian continent, as Chatwin put it, could therefore be visualized as 'a spaghetti of Iliads and Odysseys, writhing this way and that, in which every "episode" was readable in terms of geology'. To sing out was – and still is, just about, for the Songs survive, though more and more of them slip away with each generation –

therefore to find one's way, and storytelling was indivisible from wayfaring.

The relationship between thinking and walking is also grained deep into language history, illuminated by perhaps the most wonderful etymology I know. The trail begins with our verb *to learn*, meaning 'to acquire knowledge'. Moving backwards in language time, we reach the Old English *leornian*, 'to get knowledge, to be cultivated'. From *leornian* the path leads further back, into the fricative thickets of Proto-Germanic, and to the word *liȥnojan*, which has a base sense of 'to follow or to find a track' (from the Proto-Indo-European prefix *leis-*, meaning 'track'). 'To learn' therefore means at root – at route – 'to follow a track'. Who knew? Not I, and I am grateful to the etymologist-explorers who uncovered those lost trails connecting 'learning' with 'path-following'.

~

In the months after my solstitial night-walk in the snow, I decided to make tracks of my own: to set out on foot along the old ways, and discover what might be learnt by following them. So on a late-May morning I left from my Cambridge home to walk what is often claimed to be the most ancient land route in Britain, the Icknield Way, which Edward Thomas had walked and bicycled a century earlier.

It was the first of my foot-journeys, most of which are recounted here, and they involved the traveller's usual mix of excitement, incompetence, ennui, adventure and epiphany. The Icknield Way was my entry to a network of old routes criss-crossing the British landscapes and waters, and connecting them to countries and continents beyond. Along the way – along the ways – I broke more bones than I had in two decades of mountaineering, drank too much gin with a sort-of shaman in the Outer Hebrides, walked stride for stride with a 5,000-year-old man near Liverpool, followed wadi paths through occupied Palestine, and found myself – like many English walkers before me – tramping an arid branch-line of the Camino in Spain, under a vulture-filled sky. I traced a tidal path nicknamed 'The Doomway', which is allegedly the deadliest path in Britain but which turned out to be a cakewalk, I admired the celestial bling of meteor showers over the North Atlantic, I traversed an arc of the winter Ridgeway on skis and saw, I'm fairly sure, a black panther in Wiltshire. I spent nights out in copses, fields and beehive shielings, and on the haunted summit of a chalk down in Sussex where I underwent heebie-jeebies at the hands of ghosts that I now suspect were probably only owls. And everywhere I met people – usual and unusual, quiet and voluble, everyday and eccentric – for whom landscape and walking were vital means of making sense of themselves and of the world. I met dawdlers, dreamers, striders, guides, pilgrims, wanderers, stravaigers, trespassers, cartographers – and a man who believed he was a tree and that trees were people.

Of the dozens of people who feature in this book, Edward Thomas is the most important. He ghosted my journeys and urged me on. I set out to walk my way back into intimacy with Thomas, using the paths as a route to his past, but ended up discovering much more about the living than about the dead. In his memoir *A Berlin Childhood around 1900* Walter Benjamin floats the idea of representing his own life cartographically: 'I have long, indeed for years,' writes Benjamin, 'played with the idea of setting out the sphere of life – *bios* – graphically on a map.' I have come to imagine Thomas's 'sphere of life' as a kind of way-map, and so I have retold it in this manner in the book's penultimate chapter: not an act of biography, exactly, but perhaps one of biogeography. That chapter is the convergence point of the book's various paths: the meeting of its ways.

The journeys told here take their bearings from the distant past, but also from the debris and phenomena of the present, for this is often a double insistence of old landscapes: that they be read in the *then* but felt in the *now*. The waymarkers of my walks were not only dolmens, tumuli and long barrows, but also last year's ash-leaf frails (brittle in the hand), last night's fox scat (rank in the nose), this minute's bird call (sharp in the ear), the pylon's lyric crackle and the crop-sprayer's hiss.

3

CHALK

An exultation of skylarks — Solid geology — Chalk dreams — The earliest paths — Departure — The accident — Bone for chalk — Path as direction of the spirit — Apocalypse & lockdown — A skylark's egg — Blind roads & shadow-sites — Aerial photography as resurrection — The long-barrow sleeping place — Trench art — A ghost sense of stride — The wallabies of Buckinghamshire — An illusion of infinity — Late-day light — A strange collection of votaries.

> . . . it is about a road which begins many miles before I could come on its traces and ends miles beyond where I had to stop.
>
> Edward Thomas (1913)

At four o'clock on a late-May morning, on a hilltop somewhere near Letchworth Garden City, I discovered one of the most effective alarm clocks in the world: a sky full of skylarks. Sleep is, I now know, impossible when skylarks are in song, and I now also know that skylarks don't sleep in. They sing until last light and then they start up again at crack of dawn.

I could have done with two more hours' sleep. I had walked thirty miles or so the previous day, and cycled seven more. I had broken at least one rib, cut up my left arm and damaged my right knee. I had blisters on my feet which needed draining by artesian well. My bed had been a patch of thistly grass. I *really* could have done with two more hours' sleep. But the skylark alarm clock had sounded. Once I had remembered where I was – on top of a chalk down, sleeping out beside a Neolithic long barrow – I cheered up. And once I'd limped to the top of the long barrow and looked down over the Bedfordshire landscape, to find it sunk in a slow-moving sea of white mist, I was in a positively good mood. All the while the skylarks sang on, readying me for the long day to come: another day on the Icknield Way, another day of walking the chalk.

~

Take a solid geology map of the British Isles and spread it out on the floor or tabletop. It is a document of great beauty, its patterns resembling the intricate marbling of an eighteenth-century endpaper. Each surface rock formation in the country is recorded on this map, and each is represented in a different colour. Granite is scarlet. Weald clay is a muddy military green. Lower Westphalian, one of the coal-bearing formations, is an inky purple. London clay is the pink of a hedge-fund manager's shirt. Significant towns and roads are marked on the map, but in a shadowy grey that only becomes visible if you peer through the colours.

The map shows around 130 different surface rock types in England and Wales alone. In the most geologically complicated areas, such as North Wales, the map looks like a Jackson Pollock canvas, all squirts and smears of colour. Central northern England is more ordered: stripes of rock run predominantly north to south, so that if you read the landscape west to east, from Oldham across to Grimsby, you encounter millstone grit (climbing country), Lower Westphalian and Upper Westphalian (coal country), magnesian limestone, Permian mudstones, Permian and Triassic sandstones, Triassic mudstones, Lower Lias, Middle Lias, Upper Lias, Inferior Oolite, Great Oolite, cornbrash, Oxford clay, Corallian, Ampthill and Kimmeridge clays and finally chalk. The names of the formations sound part epic, part nonsense; a Jabberwocky sprawl. It's tempting to lend them hypothetical definitions. Great Oolite (the honorific of the panjandrum of a non-existent kingdom). Cornbrash (a Midwest

American home-baked foodstuff). Permian mudstone (a health treatment for greasy hair). Inferior Oolite (the younger twin of Great Oolite, dispossessed of the kingdom by dint of being delivered a minute after his brother).

If you look at the southern England section of this map and part-close your eyes, so that your eyelashes haze out your vision, the formation that glows more brightly than any other is the chalk – coloured a shiny frog-green. This chalk was laid down on the bed of epicontinental seas at a rate of about 1mm per century over a period of about 35 million years. Where the chalk prevails, it does so almost without dispute, other rock types hardly extruding into it. It runs near-continuously in a vast zigzag swathe interrupted only by sea: from Yorkshire south-east down to Norfolk (zig), from Norfolk south-west to Dorset (zag) and from Dorset east to Kent and Sussex (zig again). Chalk is the dominant formation of south-eastern England, and it has influenced the industry, architecture and imagination of that region for thousands of years. It has conjured politically suspect dreams of belonging: chalk as the authentically English substance, pure and hallowed, the gleaming southern sea cliffs offering both blazon and bastion to those arriving from elsewhere. But it has also prompted less dubious localisms. Edward Thomas imagined the chalk counties of England to constitute a distinct bio-region he called the 'South Country', which was Cretaceous in origin and whose signature landscape was one of rolling downs, streams, beech hangers and wild-flower meadows. East and west across the South Country, Thomas wrote, 'go ranges of chalk hills, their sides smoothly hollowed by Nature . . . or sharply scored by old roads . . . their ridges make flowing but infinitely variable clear lines against the sky'. This was the landscape which, more than any other, shaped his imagination – as it did that of another twentieth-century artist of the path, Eric Ravilious.

The first foot-travellers to enter Britain almost certainly crossed over on chalk, which provided the land bridge with what is now Europe. At Boxgrove in the Sussex Downs, some of the earliest-known northern European remains of the *Homo* genus have been found, dated to around 500,000 years ago. These archaic humans are known to archaeologists as *Homo heidelbergensis*. The Boxgrove finds allow us – with an eerie clarity of historical sight – to know that half a million years ago 'Boxgrove Man' was drawn to the exposed chalk of those regions; that there he picked out cores of black glossy flint (perfect for making fine tools for butchery); that he knapped these cores into axes, cutting blades and spearheads; and that he then used these weapons to hunt and disarticulate prey: the horse, deer, bear, rhino and bovids that occupied the open grasslands. Later, the chalk is also likely to have carried the first significant hominin trails, which probably themselves followed the lines of game trails, and must count as being among the earliest acts of human landscaping. Later still, during the Neolithic, when warmer conditions had led to the growth of dense forest across southern England, the chalk ridges would have offered the obvious routes of travel. The high chalk was well drained, so the going was dry and the vegetation was less impeding than on the thicker lower clays. The ridges thus offered ease of navigation combined with ease of passage. So, over time, along their crests, the first real footpaths emerged.

During the nineteenth-century surge of old-wayfaring, walkers were drawn particularly to the paths of the English downlands: attracted by their involvement with prehistory and by the ideal of freedom they appeared to enact in their sinuous motion. A chalky mysticism established itself, a belief that it was a super-conductor of the sympathetic historical mind, allowing simultaneities and compassions to reach out across millennia. On 'the first // Inhabited heights of chalk', wrote Louis MacNeice – born in Belfast but educated at Marlborough, near the Downs – 'I could feel my mind / Crumble and dry like a fossil sponge, I could feel / My body curl like a foetus and the rind / Of a barrow harden round me, to reveal / Millennia hence some inkling of the ways / Of man before he invented plough or wheel'.

Arguably the oldest of these chalk paths is the Icknield Way, which rises somewhere on the heath and pine forests of south Norfolk and then runs west-south-west over chalk-land top-dressed with boulder clay, until it reaches the distinctive summit of Ivinghoe Beacon in Buckinghamshire. There it joins the Ridgeway, which leads on through Oxfordshire, Berkshire, Wiltshire – connecting Iron Age hill-forts, Bronze Age barrows and Neolithic burial chambers – and at last drops down to the sea at Dorset, thus linking the English Channel in the south to the Wash in the east.

The origins and history of the Icknield Way are shrouded in myth and confusion. It is now not thought ever to have been a single path, but instead a skein of parallel tracks, sometimes a mile from outer mark to outer mark, following a line of communication made easy by the trends of the landscape. It is possible that the entire route is post-Roman, confected into being by enthusiastic antiquarians. Despite these uncertainties the Icknield Way has long appealed to walkers hoping for communion with the prehistoric. It has cast its chalk-spell widely and keenly.

~

Within a mile of my home in Cambridge runs the grassy Roman road I had followed on my winter night-walk. In spring its wide verges are brocaded with flowers, and for much of its length it is bordered by hedgerows of briar, hawthorn and field maple. Seven miles south-east along it lies the village of Linton, through which passes the Icknield Way.

Just after dawn on a late May day I slipped out of the house while my family was asleep, got onto my bicycle and pedalled along quiet streets and paths – up onto the whaleback hill of chalk, past the great open field behind the beech wood – before turning onto the Roman road. The forecast was for warm dry weather extending unbroken for a week to come. There were sixteen or seventeen hours of sunlight each day. The scent of dog-rose sweetened the air. A crow flopped from an ash tree, its wings silver with sun. I felt filled with a boyish excitement. In my pack was a copy of Edward Thomas's *The Icknield Way*, his prose account of his journey along the Way.

I was cycling downhill along the Roman road, near the Iron Age ring-fort, when the accident happened. Happy to be on the move, I let the bicycle gather speed. The rutted path became rougher, my wheels juddered and bounced, I hit a hunk of hard soil the size of a fist, the front wheel bucked and twisted through ninety degrees, the bike folded in upon itself and I crashed onto it, the end of the left handlebar driving hard into my chest. The breath was bashed out of me. There was a sharp grating pain in my ribcage. My elbow was bleeding and my kneecap appeared to have grown a subsidiary purple kneecap. The severest injury appeared to be to my self-respect. What a fool I'd been, biking like a dizzy vicar down the road, too full of the romance of the way. I would have to limp home, not even two miles along my first path.

But after various diagnostic prods, it seemed that all might not be lost. The kneecap was injured but unbroken. I had cracked a rib, possibly two, but this seemed a minor impediment to walking. And the bicycle could, with some botched repairs, be just about persuaded to move. So I cycled on to Linton, slowly. A warning, I thought superstitiously, had been issued to me: that the going would not be easy, and that romanticism would be quickly punished. It was only a few miles later that I remembered the letter a friend had sent me when I told him about my plan to walk the Icknield Way. Take care as you pass the ring-fort, he had written back. When I mentioned the fall later, he was unamazed. 'This was an entry fee to the old ways, charged at one of the usual tollbooths,' he said. 'Now you can proceed. You're in. Bone for chalk: you've paid your due.' It was the first of several incidents along the old ways that I still find hard to explain away rationally.

~

Thomas followed the Icknield Way in 1911, in the depths of one of his worst depressions. He moved fast and then he wrote up the journey fast, in a matter of weeks. *The Icknield Way* is an unconventional book: partly a guide to the history and geography of the Way, partly a meditation on its metaphysics and partly a record of Thomas's own bleak unhappiness.

Surprisingly (given that it is a book set in an arid summer landscape far from the coast), but unsurprisingly (given that the geological origin of chalk is both submarine and morbid), *The Icknield Way* is preoccupied throughout with seas, drowning and islands. The chalk infiltrates Thomas's imagination, changes his mind, stirs deep-time dreams and bathyspheric descents. He dedicated the book to a recently dead friend, Harry Hooton, with whom Thomas had walked 'more miles . . . than with anyone else except myself', and the Icknield Way – with its uncertain history, its disputed route and its debatable limits – becomes in Thomas's hands a metaphor for the unknown domains that attend our beginnings and our ends.

In the 1890s a folklorist called John Emslie had walked the Icknield Way and collected the stories he heard told along the path. In many of these stories the Way – if followed far enough – passes out of the known and into the mythic, leading to kingdoms of great danger and reward. Emslie was told of one man who had 'travelled along this road till he came to the fiery mountains'. Another spoke of it as going 'round the world, so that if you keep along it and travel on you will come back to the place you started from'. 'All along my route', wrote Emslie, he had heard similar tales: that the path 'went all round the world, or all through the island . . . from sea to sea'. It was, in this respect, a path that stood as a prototype for all others, at last returning uroboros-like to engulf its own origin.

Thomas was compelled by the Way's existence as a braid of stories and memories. In one of his most enigmatic prose passages he suggested that paths were imprinted with the 'dreams' of each traveller who had walked it, and that his own experiences would 'in course of time [also] lie under men's feet'. The path's sediment comprised sentiment, and to follow a path might therefore be to walk up its earlier followers: this in the hunter's sense of 'walking up' – to disturb what lies hidden, to flush out what is concealed. In setting out along the Way I was turning Thomas's cryptic vision back on himself, hoping to summon him by walking where he had walked. It was to be miles and years before I understood the difficulties of such a recovery.

~

In Linton, I hid my damaged bike behind a hedge and walked my damaged body out of the village by its main street, under a rising sun. The cloud caul was breaking up and a lemony light pushed through the gaps. The path led me past Linton Zoo and from behind a high hedge came the grunts and calls of the inmates: zebras, lions, storks and cranes. I passed a thatched cottage with hollyhocks bobbing in the wind at its walls, and roses by its doors. The visuals were deep England but the soundtrack was Serengeti.

Quickly I was onto the chalky field-edge footpaths whose route corresponded roughly to that of the Way. I went through a narrow tunnel of spindle and hawthorn. A brown hare belted along the track, halted, regarded me briefly, then pivoted on its hind legs and dashed back off and away, as if committed to the path's pursuit. Within an hour the sun was fully out. Skylarks pelted their song down, lifting my spirit. Light pearled on barley. The shock of the crash began to fade away. Hawthorn hedges foamed white with flower and wood pigeons clattered from the ash canopies.

For the first eight miles of the day I saw no one at all, and had the peculiar feeling of occupying an evacuated landscape, post-apocalypse or in civil lockdown. So few people now labour on the land that the people one tends to meet on footpaths are walkers, not workers.

I followed a continuous line of bare white chalk, moving by hedge and field-edge bearing roughly west-south-west. I met a covey of French partridges with their barred sides and Tintin-like quiffs; three cock pheasants with their copper flank armour and white dog-collars (hoplite vicars); a grebe on a pond, punkishly tufted as Ziggy Stardust.

The landscape's emptiness spooked me, and it was an unexpected relief to hear the distant hum of the M11 motorway, growing to a roar as I neared it. The motorway occupied exactly the place in the landscape that a river might have done, running where two chalk ranges dipped down into a valley, and the sun-strikes off windscreen and paintwork lent it the distant dazzle of moving water. I approached it on high ground through the sage green of young cereal crops. Suddenly, above the roar of the cars, I heard someone singing. A ghostly high carolling, intermittent and tentative. It took a few seconds to understand that it was the song of the pylons, a long line of which marched away into the distance. I stood under one of them, listening to the spit and fizz of its energy, and the humming note that formed, with the other pylons nearby, a loose chord.

Great Chesterford was the town where I forded the motorway. In houses near the road's edge, bird fanciers kept parakeets which hopped around in their cages on faded St George's flags, chirruping to one another. I rested on the motorway bridge, arms hung over the railings, watching the rush of cars and the heat-waves rising from the asphalt. It was a perpendicular meeting of the Icknield Way (opened circa 4000 BC) and the M11 (opened 1975).

The middle hours of that day were also devoid of people. There was other company, though: family groups of roe deer which emerged from copses and rode their long legs off through the barley. I found a skylark's egg, baked dead on the ground, but intact, the green of its shell covered in brown jottings and scribblings. I curled my fingers round the egg and carried it in my hand for a mile or two, for luck and for its weight in the palm. In the villages through which I passed I saw deer skulls mounted on the flint walls, reassuring flickers of paganism in a landscape that might otherwise have been dreamed up by Enid Blyton. Greens smooth as snooker baize. Village ponds with yellow flag irises, in which carps burped and bubbled. Red phone boxes, freshly painted.

Around noon I neared the outskirts of Royston. Here, the path of the old Icknield Way aligned with the main A-road through the town. The hedges and field entrances were blocked with fly-tipped rubbish: computer monitors, inner tubes, carpet strips, a vacuum cleaner whose transparent body was filled with black flies. Dog-rose waterfalls cascaded from high hawthorn hedges. Shoals of starlings, dense and particulate, shifted above the rooftops.

The place names on the eastern fringe of Royston were pastoral throwbacks – Wheatfield Crescent, Poplar Drive, Icknield Walk – longing allusions to a time when this had been country, names settled on by developers to bump up the house prices or by a planner hoping to improve the town's mood at its margins. Starlings chattered on chimney pots and aerials – their feathers sleekly black as sheaves of photographic negatives – making their car-alarm trills, their aerosol-can rattles and their camera-shutter clicks. Their cheery urban rip-rap seemed to offer the ideal welcome to Royston as I walked the busy road, and there appeared to be nothing at all left of the Icknield Way.

~

Old paths rarely vanish, unless the sea eats them or Tarmac covers them. They survive as subtle landmarks, evident to those who know how to look – as Thomas did. 'Even when deserted,' he wrote, 'these old roads are kept in memory by many signs.' He called such lapsed ways 'ghostly . . . roads'; Walter Scott referred to them as 'blind roads'. Such paths also expressed themselves in custom, law and place names. 'It is one of the adventurous pleasures of a good map,' Thomas wrote, 'to trace the possible course of a known old road, or to discover one that was lost. A distinct chain of footpath, lane and road . . . leading across the country and corresponding in much of its course with boundaries is likely to be an ancient way.'

This was Thomas's wager: that the old persisted alongside and despite the new, surviving as echoes and shadows, detectable by an acute mind and eye. For him, map-reading approached mysticism: he described it as an 'old power', of which only a few people had the 'glimmerings'. He approached paths as not only solitary places but also sociable ones, where once-silenced voices might be heard. In his poem 'Aspens' he imagined that the wind-stirred trees at an old crossroads were giving whispered voice to a now-vanished village, and he eavesdropped on 'the clink, the hum, the roar, the random singing' of old smithies and inns. He liked to follow lines of white-beams, the tree most associated with paths in the chalk counties, and the tree's fallen leaves – which lie often with their silvery undersides uppermost, and can preserve their pallor until the following spring – reminded him of Hansel and Gretel's pebble trail.

Thomas was correct to think that long-term acts of wayfaring leave long-lived imprints. In the early twentieth century, much amateur energy was devoted to discovering and taxonomizing such marks: the furrows of forgotten tracks, the aligned scatters of eoliths (worked stones, dating from early phases of human occupation), the back-filled boundary ditches whose routes shimmered into view during rain or drought. Closely examined, the countryside revealed itself to be full of 'shadow-sites'. A shadow-site was the relic trace of a path, earthwork, post hole or ditch, hidden often in plain view but apparent only under certain circumstances – especially when the sun was low and bright, throwing its light at a slant and thereby lending revelatory shadows to the land.

The rise of aerial photography – developed first as a military technique but diverted after the First World War into archaeological research – also meant that these shadow-sites could be seen from above, from which perspective their patterns often stood out against the ground-level confusions. Landscape ghosts that had lain unseen for millennia suddenly reappeared. Aerial photography, as the historian Kitty Hauser has written, made possible 'innumerable queer resurrections', offering assurances that 'no site, however flattened out, is really lost to knowledge'. One such resurrection occurred thanks to Major George Allen, an early pioneer of aerial photography as an archaeological aid, who designed and constructed a large camera that he could manipulate while flying solo. In the winter of 1936, after heavy rain, Allen flew over the Icknield Way near Royston and took one of his best photographs. Horizontally across the image run a series of near-parallel lines. Uppermost of these is a railway track, upon which a train happens to be chuffing eastwards, trailing a long plume of steam. Below that is a road upon which a single car is driving westwards. Concealed to the passengers of either train or car, but clear to the bird's-eye view of the camera, are other lines in the landscape: the dark streaks of back-filled Iron Age ditches running north–south, medieval field boundaries, and – within a few yards of the Tarmac – the white rutted tracks of the Icknield Way itself. 'What is astonishing to the point of uncanniness,' writes Hauser finely of this image, 'is the way in which these ancient features . . . secretly share the landscape with the living, as they go about their business.'

I held Allen's photograph in my mind's eye as I walked the stretch of the Way between Royston and Baldock: the alignments of old path, new road and railway track, the co-present ghosts of the former and the future.

~

'A white snake on a green hillside' was one of Thomas's descriptions of a chalk path's motion through the land. The image is brilliantly compressive: a Zen koan. Emerging south out of Royston and onto Therfield Heath, I saw that its green slopes were alive with snakes. Chalk downs rise on both sides of the heath, leaving a cupped lower arena and lending to the whole space the air of an amphitheatre. The upper ridge is crinkled with broadleaf woods into which dozens of white paths disappear enticingly. Other paths lead to the crest of the heath, where the densest concentration of barrows in the Chilterns exists: ten Bronze Age round barrows and a Neolithic long barrow.

That bright afternoon it was instantly obvious, even across thousands of years, why prehistoric people had chosen to bury their dead in such a location. The heath was busy with people: walkers strolling up to see the barrows, children running and shouting. I stopped to eat and watch. The pleasure these people were taking in their landscape – and the feeling of company after the empty early miles of the day – gave me a burst of energy and lifted my legs.

Then came miles through the backstreets of Baldock and the industrial estates of Letchworth Garden City, where shipping containers – Maersk, Mitsui, Hamburg – were stacked high behind galvanized spike fences, ready to be lorried off again. Late in the day, my feet blazing, I rested in a churchyard in the village of Clothall. A wall of gold-green laurels leant forwards over the graves. I lay sleepily among the tombstones and late primroses, listening to the bees, watching the swifts hunting above the church tower. 'The eye that sees the things of today, and the ear that hears, the mind that contemplates or dreams,' Thomas had written, 'is itself an instrument of antiquity equal to whatever it is called upon to apprehend . . . and perhaps . . . we are aware of . . . time in ways too difficult and strange for the explanation of historian and zoologist and philosopher.' It was an idea to which he returned often in both his prose and poetry:

that there are certain kinds of knowledge which exceed the propositional and which can only be sensed, as it were, in passing.

~

I slept that night in a Neolithic dormitory on a seabed of chalk. I found my sleeping place just west of a medieval village called Pirton, through the centre of which the Way passed. I left Pirton at about nine o'clock by a wide and high-hedged path that was obviously of old use, its sides grown with dog-rose, yarrow, cherry plums and damsons. I'd developed the rolling hip-sway of a sailor on shore leave, brought about by fatigue and sore joints. The evening air was hot, still; the eastern sky an inky blue, orange in the west. The chalk of the path gathered the late light to itself, glowing whitely in the twilight. Pale trumpets of bindweed jumped forward to the eye. In the verge lay the part-eaten corpse of a blackbird, its scaly legs severed from its body and placed neatly alongside one another, like a knife and fork after a meal.

Near the top of the hill I found the long barrow I'd spotted on my map. Its tumulus had long ago been plundered and its roof had collapsed, but its contours were still apparent, and at that hour the long light lit it like a shadow-site. After I'd eaten some cheese and an apple, I unrolled my sleeping bag on a bank of grass to the south of the barrow and lay down. My limbs began to stiffen almost immediately, having been in motion for nearly sixteen hours, and I felt a kind of rigor mortis setting in. I had chalk all over me – my feet, face and hands powdered with it, my clothes pale with it – and I lay there, rigid and white, a ghost of the road.

A cuticle moon showed in the sky. A pheasant rattled in a far-off wood. Rooks flapped past on their roost flights. The sun dropped, reddened. What I thought was the first star turned out to be the night light for a plane coming into Luton.

~

At four o'clock the next morning the skylark alarm clock woke me. A slow mist had filled the valleys. The sky was white above but blue at the horizon line, as though it were a dome and the blueness had run down to its brinks. Looking from my long-barrow observatory I understood Thomas's comparison of the high grounds of Southern England to 'several chains . . . of islands or atolls . . . looming dimly through the snowy still mists of morning'. I was on one of the most easterly islands of this archipelago: away to the west, though I could not see them, rose dozens more of the chalk summits.

Those early-day miles were magical, up and down hills, through beech and coppice hazel woods, with a marine light in the beech woods that gave the feeling of walking in cool water. Among the trees, a taste of moss in the mouth; green silence.

Here and there people had used chunks of chalk to write on the grey bark of the trees: initials, stars, or squiggles like the looping signature Corporal Trim's walking stick leaves on the otherwise blank page in Laurence Sterne's *Tristram Shandy*. Chalk is a substance that marks and is easily marked – that writes and is written on. Areas of the Western Front, where Thomas would fight and die, were chalk landscapes, and one of the most affecting cultural outputs of the trench war was the land art that both German and British soldiers made there. These were men who knew their lives were likely to end soon, and the instinct to leave a trace was strong in them. Soldiers chipped out flat lumps of chalk and carved them into hand-sized plaques bearing memorial messages for dead comrades: 'Thiepval 1915, In Memory of Your Wilhelm'. British gunners used chalk nuggets to jot joke messages on the casing of the big shells: 'May It Be A Happy Ending', or 'To Fritz With Compliments'. Sappers on both sides created miles of tunnels through the chalk. Down in that troglodyte world they scored, in idle moments, hundreds of doodles, graffiti and messages into the walls. Many of these are now lost, but near Soissons there remain the outlines of fantastical female figures: cave drawings summoned from erotic dreams, there in the terrible dark.

By eight o'clock I was on a hilltop by a Bronze Age round barrow, looking onto Luton. I shambled through the town's outskirts, down Gooseberry Hill – a smart little street with neatly trimmed borders and bright bedding plants – past lime trees and health clinics. A postman rang a doorbell, nodded a greeting to me. Cars on the commuter cut-through raced past. Everyone else was starting their day, but I'd already walked ten miles and was tired. I envied them their eagerness. I left Luton's western outskirts along an alleyway between a cemetery and a row of houses.

Then the ground began to lift and I was soon on the summit ridge of Dunstable Downs, where scores of people were having fun. I sat and rested in a cooling wind and watched children flying kites. My legs preserved a ghost sense of stride, a muscle memory of repeated action, and twitched forwards even as I rested. My feet felt oddly dented in their soles, as if the terrain over which I had passed had imprinted its own profile into my foot, like a mark knuckled into soft clay. How had Flann O'Brien put it in *The Third Policeman*? When you walk, 'the continual cracking of your feet on the road makes a certain quantity of road come up into you'.

That day's walking was as hard and bright as the first. I passed through fewer built-up areas, and felt at times as if I were moving covertly from spinney to copse by means of hedgerows and green lanes. One of the woods through which I tramped was white with wild garlic, the air heady with its stink. I followed the perimeter of Whipsnade Zoo and saw five wallabies lolling in the shade of a hawthorn bush.

Thomas's many foot-miles on old chalk paths made him a connoisseur of their particularities. In summer, he walked overgrown lanes of hazel laced with white bryony, whose flowers were boiling with bees. He followed 'dark beech alley[s], paved with the gold and green of moss and walled by crumbling chalk'. He liked discovering neglected paths on the point of disappearance, 'buried under nettle and burdock and barricaded by thorns and traveller's joy and bryony bines'. He loved the border crossings that path-following enabled: the holloways that issue into hot fields of wheat, or the transition from tree-shade to the glint of meadow grass. But I doubt he ever saw a wallaby.

~

Towards evening, miles on from the hazel wood, my body settled into the rhythm of the walk and I felt, for an hour or so in that apparently endless day, as if the Way were endless too, ribboning whitely away across the land, and that if I kept to it there was no reason why I could not walk all the way to the Atlantic.

It wasn't until last light that I reached Ivinghoe Beacon, whose great chalk summit is crowned by an Iron Age hill-fort. I scrambled up to one of its grassed-up ramparts, sat facing westwards and let the setting sun soak me with its warmth. I took off my shoes and socks. My feet were puffy as rising dough. Across the land, millions of bindweed flowers completed their final revolutions of the day, buttercups returned their last lustre to the sun, the wallabies of Whipsnade settled to sleep and the day slowed to its close.

Sitting there in that buttery sunshine the many different names of the path – Yken, Ychen, Ycken, Ayken, Iceni, Icening, Ickeneld, Ikeneld, Ikenild, Icleton, Ickleton, Icknield – seemed to melt and combine, such that the Way seemed not like a two-dimensional track but part of a greater manifold, looping and weaving in time even as it appeared to run singularly onwards in space. *I could not find a beginning or an end of the Icknield Way . . .*

In the half-hour or so that I sat there, other walkers joined me on the hilltop for sunset: a man carrying a small dog bundled up in a tartan blanket; a middle-aged couple, laughing as they climbed and slipped up the steep side of the beacon; a man in a suit who had parked his car by the roadside and walked up the hill with his body held straight and upright; and an elderly woman who trailed up to one of the ramparts and then stood with her eyes closed, gazing blindly at the last sun. What a strange congregation of votaries we made, none known to the other, foreign as dark fish in ink.

I found my sleeping place at twilight, not far from the beacon's summit: a swathe of grass, the size of a double bed sheet, overhung by a spreading hawthorn tree and hidden from the path by a ramp of gorse whose yellow blossoms lent their coconut scent to the breeze. A green woodpecker yapped in the distance. Planes flew past every few minutes, dragging cones of noise. Lichen glimmered on the trees. Three deer, black-furred roe does, stepped from the wood. One looked across at me, its eyeshine gleaming gold with the last light, then all three moved off westwards along the chalk tracks. As I was falling asleep, the image rose in my mind of white path meeting white path, a webwork of tracks that ran to the shores of the land, and then on and out beyond them.

4

SILT

The silver ogee — The deadliest paths in England — Patrick Arnold — A causeway to the mirror-world — Crossing the border — The First Emperor Qin — The Colinda Point — Doggerland — A myriad of ogees — Our relieved discovery of the Maypole — Doublings — Thought as sensational — Landfall at Asplin Head — Shore-visions & rivers on the rise — Xenotopias — Cognitive dissonance in isotropic spaces — Danger at the outermost point — Mirage as authentic vision — The homewards channel.

Half a mile offshore, walking on silver water, we crossed a path that extended gracefully and without apparent end to our north and south. It was a shallow tidal channel and the water it held caught and pooled the sun, such that its route existed principally as flux; a phenomenon of light and currents. Its bright line curved away from us: an ogee whose origin we could not explain and whose invitation to follow we could not disobey, so we walked it northwards, along that glowing track made neither of water nor of land, which led us further and still further out to sea.

~

If you consult a large-scale map of the Essex coastline between the River Crouch and the River Thames, you will see a footpath – its route marked with a stitch-line of crosses and dashes – leaving the land at a place called Wakering Stairs and then heading due east, straight out to sea. Several hundred yards offshore, it curls north-east and runs in this direction for around three miles, still offshore, before cutting back to make landfall at Fisherman's Head, the uppermost tip of a large, low-lying and little-known marshy island called Foulness.

This is the Broomway, allegedly 'the deadliest' path in Britain and certainly the unearthliest path I have ever walked. The Broomway is thought to have killed more than a hundred people over the centuries; it seems likely that there were other victims whose fates went unrecorded. Sixty-six of its dead are buried in the little Foulness churchyard; the bodies of the other known dead were not recovered. If the Broomway hadn't existed, Wilkie Collins might have had to invent it. Edwardian newspapers, alert to its reputation, rechristened it 'The Doomway'. Even the Ordnance Survey map registers, in its sober fashion, the gothic atmosphere of the path. Printed in large pink lettering on the 1:25,000 map of that stretch of coast is the following message:

WARNING
Public Rights of Way across Maplin Sands
can be dangerous. Seek local guidance.

The Broomway is the less notorious of Britain's two great offshore footpaths, the other being the route that crosses the sands of Morecambe Bay from Hest Bank to Kents Bank by way of Priest Skear. As at Morecambe Bay, the Broomway traverses vast sand- and mud-flats that stretch almost unsloped for miles. When the tide goes out at Morecambe and Foulness, it goes out a great distance, revealing shires of sand packed hard enough to support the weight of a walker. When the tide comes back in, though, it comes fast – galloping over the sands quicker than a human can run. Disorientation is a danger as well as inundation: in mist, rain or fog, it is easy to lose direction in such self-similar terrain, with shining sand extending in all directions. Nor are all of the surfaces that you encounter reliable: there is mud that can trap you and quicksand that can swallow you. Morecambe is infamously treacherous, its worst tragedy being the death in February 2004 of at least twenty-one Chinese cockle-pickers, illegal immigrants who were inexperienced in the lore of the estuary and insufficiently aware of the danger of the tides, but who had been sent far out onto the sands to harvest cockles by their gangmaster.

Unlike the Morecambe Bay path, whose route fluctuates and whose walking therefore requires both improvisation and vigilance, the route of the Broomway seems to have been broadly consistent since at least 1419 (when it is referred to in a manorial record for Foulness). Conceptually, both the Morecambe crossing and the Broomway are close to paradox. They are rights of way and as such are inscribed on maps and in law, but they are also swept clean of the trace of passage twice daily by the tide. What do you call a path that is no path? A riddle? A sequence of compass bearings? A death-trap?

The geology and archaeology of the Broomway are disputed. Various theories have been proposed to explain its existence, including that it sits on top of a durable reef of chalk. Certainly, it takes its name from the 400 or so 'brooms' that were formerly placed at intervals of between thirty and sixty yards on either side of the track, thereby indicating the safe passage on the hard sand that lay between them.

Until 1932, the Broomway was the only means of getting to and from Foulness save by boat, for the island was isolated from the mainland by uncrossable creeks and stretches of mud known as the Black Grounds. For centuries, hazel wattles were bound and laid as floating causeways to enable safe passage over the Black Grounds and onto the sands (these causeways were analogous in technology and principle to the Sweet Track in Somerset).* At some point the wattles were replaced with jetties of rubble. During the eighteenth and nineteenth centuries, coach drivers would muster in the tavern at Wakering and drink while waiting for the tides to be right for the ride to Foulness. Several of them died on the job, befuddled by weather, or alcohol, or both. In the aftermath of the North Sea Storm of 1953, when floodwaters killed hundreds of people along the English east coast, the Broomway was the only reliable means of access to Foulness: army vehicles raced back and forth along its firm sand, evacuating the dead and the injured. The island is currently owned by the Ministry of Defence, which purchased it during the First World War for 'research purposes' and which continues to conduct artillery firing tests out over the sands.

~

I have for years wanted to walk the Broomway, but have for years been deterred from doing so by its reputation. Shortly after returning from the Icknield Way, however, a friend put me in contact with a man called Patrick Arnold, who had been born and raised on Foulness and who knew the Broomway better than anyone living. Patrick kindly offered to accompany me along it, and we agreed to walk the

* The Sweet Track is the wooden road laid across the spongy Somerset levels during the early Neolithic, to permit passage between areas of higher drier ground: the hills of the Mendips and the hummocks of Glastonbury. Astonishingly precise pollen-dating allows us to know that at Shapwick, near Westhay (place names which sound as if they should come from Shetland, not Somerset) in the spring of 3806 BC, rods of alder, hazel, holly, oak, ash and lime were bound and laid in a walkway across the levels.

path together on a Sunday, when the Ministry of Defence would not be firing and when the tide-times were right.

The Monday before that Sunday, a letter arrived. I recognized Patrick's handwriting on the envelope. 'With sadness,' the letter began stiffly, 'I must withdraw my offer to guide you along the "most dangerous road in England".' I felt a rush of disappointment. Patrick went on to explain that his elderly mother, for whom he cared, was too frail for him to leave her 'for many hours without being exceedingly anxious about her welfare'. However, he continued – and here my heart rose – he thought I might 'navigate the Broomway alone, without suffering any mischief'.

Along with the letter, Patrick had included the following documents: a hand-drawn map of the coastline between Wakering Stairs and Foulness showing the routes of the Broomway and its tributary causeways; a sequence of compass bearings and paced distances; a numbered list of observations concerning appropriate clothing to wear on the Broomway; and some points of advice as to how best to avoid dying on it.

Patrick owed his life to the Broomway. 'Let me tell you,' he explained to me the first time we spoke, 'there was a man called Mr William Harvey, and one day in 1857 he set out with a coach and horses to cross to Foulness. Well, he never arrived, and so they went looking for him. Of the horses no trace was found. The coach was discovered upside down in the sands, and there was William's drowned body lying dead on the flats.

'After she'd done with her grieving, William Harvey's widow went on to marry a Mr Lily, and of that congress was born my great-grandfather. So while the accident was Mrs Harvey's great loss – and indeed also Mr Harvey's – it was eventually my great gain. In this way, do you see, I am grateful to the Broomway, and so I have devoted myself to walking and researching it.'

Patrick spoke with precision, and with faint hints of Victoriana. He was a man of quiet honour and exactitude, punctilious with his facts. He had worked onshore as a form-maker and carpenter until his retirement, but he knew the sea well and held the speed record for rowing solo from London to Ostend. He told me stories about the Essex coast: about the fleets of collier-tugs that would assemble in the mouth of the Thames; about the dangers of easterlies blowing big ships onto the lee shore; and most often about the Broomway, of which he spoke respectfully but fondly as 'an old friend'.

Patrick had read almost every available account of walking the Broomway, and he relished the grisly melodrama of its past. Whenever we spoke he would have fresh tales for me, dredged from Broomway lore: a nineteenth-century coroner's account of the difficulty of identifying bodies once the crabs had been to work on faces and fingers, say; or a survivor who had written in a letter to a friend of the 'sheer panic' that he experienced as rain fell around him, and he wandered the sands in search of the right route.

'He was convinced he was walking towards the Mouse Lightship,' said Patrick, but 'in fact, he was walking out to sea, towards his death, and he was saved only by the accident of stumbling into a fish kettle – copper-nailed so as not to rust – which he knew had to have its closed point facing out to sea, and its open mouth gaping perpendicular to the shore, such that fish would become trapped in it during the retreat of the tide. This gave him the orientation he needed, and he made it back along the path. He was a lucky man.' Patrick sounded faintly disappointed that the death sentence of the Broomway had been, in this instance, commuted.

Until hand-held compasses became available to walkers, the safest way of navigating the Broomway in bad conditions, when it was impossible to see from broom to broom, was with stone and thread.

Walkers carried a 200-foot length of linen thread, with one end tied to a small stone. They would place the stone next to a broom and then walk away in what they believed to be the right direction, unspooling the thread as they went, until they could see the next broom. If they went astray, they could trace the thread back to the stone, and try again. If they went the right way, they hauled in the stone and repeated the action. It was slow and painstaking work, but in this way people could notionally follow the Broomway in safety, whatever the weather.

'It's a weird world out there on the flats,' said Patrick. 'Nothing looks the same as normal. Gulls can seem as big as eagles. Scale and distance change. It's very easy to lose your bearings, especially in dusk or dark. Then it's the lights on the Kent shore that often do it. People think they're walking back to the Essex coast, when in fact they're walking across towards Kent and so out into the tide. The mud's the thing to watch, too: step in the wrong places, and it'll bog you down and suck you in, ready for the tide to get you.'

Two days before I set off, my Alaskan friend James helpfully recommended that I take a small sharp hatchet with me: 'That way, if you get stuck in the mud with the tide coming in, you can cut your legs off at the ankles and escape.'

Patrick had a final warning: 'The Broomway will be there another day, but if you try to walk it in mist, you may not be. So if it's misty when you arrive at Wakering Stairs, turn around and go home.'

~

It was misty when I arrived at Wakering Stairs. Early on a Sunday morning, and the air was white. It wasn't a haar, a proper North Sea mist that blanked out the world. More of a dense sea haze. But visibility was poor enough that the foghorns were sounding, great bovine reverbs drifting up and down the coast. I stood on the sea wall, looking out into the mist, feeling the foghorns vibrating in my chest, and wondering if I could imaginatively re-categorize the weather conditions such that I could disregard Patrick's final warning. I felt mildly sick with anxiety, but eager to walk.

With me, also nervous, was my old friend David Quentin, who I had convinced to join me on the path. David is a former scholar of Renaissance literature, turned antiquarian-book dealer, turned barrister, turned tax lawyer. He is probably the only Marxist tax lawyer in London, possibly in the world. He likes wearing britches, likes walking barefoot, and hopes daily for the downfall of capitalism. He is 6' 7" tall, very thin, very clever, and has little interest in people who take it upon themselves to comment without invitation on his height and spindliness. We have covered a lot of miles together.

The air at Wakering Stairs was warm and close; thick like gel in the nose and mouth. The tide had recently turned, and just offshore the exposed Black Grounds were steaming: a brown mudscape of canyons and buttresses, turgid and gleaming, through which streams riddled. Sandpipers and oystercatchers strutted in search of breakfast. The surfaces of my body felt porous, absorbent. The creeks and channels bubbled and glistened. Two big gulls pottered the tideline, monitoring us with lackadaisical, violent eyes.

Where the road met the sea wall, there was a heavy metal stop-barrier, tagged with a jay-blue graffiti scrawl. A red firing flag drooped at the foot of a tall flagpole. Beyond the stop-barrier was a bank of signs in waspy yellow-and-black type and imperative grammar, detailing bye-laws, tautologically identifying themselves as warnings, indemnifying the MoD against drownings, explosions and mud-deaths, offering caveats to the walker, and grudgingly admitting that this was, indeed, the beginning of a public right of way:

Warning: The Broomway is unmarked
and very hazardous to pedestrians.

Warning: Do not approach or touch any object
as it may explode and kill you.

Away from the sea wall ran the causeway, perhaps five yards wide, formed of brick rubble and grey hardcore. It headed out to sea over the mud, before disappearing into water and mist. Poles had been driven into the mud to either side of the path, six feet tall, marking out its curling line. There were a few tussocks of eelgrass. The water's surface was sheened with greys and silvers, like the patina on old mirror-glass. Otherwise, the causeway appeared to lead into a textureless world of white.

Three oystercatchers flew overhead with quick-flick wing-strokes, piping as they passed. We climbed the ramp to the summit of the sea wall, stepped over a scatter of beer cans and walked down towards the start of the causeway. I stooped to gather a handful of white cockle shells from among the shore rocks. I subdued the alarm my brain was raising at the idea of walking out to sea fully clothed, as only suicides do.

We walked along the rubble and sea-cracked hardstanding, along the causeway and over the mud. A man with his dog paused on the sea wall to watch us go. Here and there we had to wait for the tide to recede, revealing more of the path before us. I peered over the edge of the causeway as if off a pier, though the water to either side was only a few inches deep. A goby in a pool wriggled its aspic body deeper into the sand.

After 300 yards the causeway ended for real, dipping beneath the sand like a river passing underground. Further out, a shallow sheen of water lay on top of the sand, stretching away. The diffused light made depth-perception impossible, so that it seemed as if we were simply going to walk onwards into ocean. We stopped at the end of the causeway, looking out across the pathless future.

'I think there's a sun somewhere up there, burning all this off,' said David brightly. 'I think we'll be in sunshine by the end of the day.'

It seemed hard to believe. But it was true that the light had sharpened slightly in the twenty minutes it had taken us to walk out to the end of the causeway. I glanced back at the sea wall, but it was barely visible now through the haze. A scorching band of low white light to seaward; a thin magnesium burn-line.

The sand was intricately ridged, its lines broken by millions of casts, noodly messes of black silt that had been squeezed up by ragworms and razor shells. The squid-ink colour of the casts was a reminder that just below the hard sand was the mud. I took my shoes off and placed them on a stand of eelgrass. For some reason, I couldn't overcome my sense of tides as volatile rather than fixed, capricious rather than regulated. What if the tides disobeyed the moon, on this day of all days?

'I'm worried that if we don't make it back in time, the tide will float off with my shoes,' I said to David.

'If we don't make it back in time, the tide will float off with your body,' he replied unconsolingly.

We stepped off the causeway. The water was warm on the skin, puddling to ankle depth. Underfoot I could feel the brain-like corrugations of the hard sand, so firmly packed that there was no give under the pressure of my step. Beyond us extended the sheer mirror-plane of the water, disrupted only here and there by shallow humps of sand and green slews of weed. I thought of the lake of mercury that allegedly surrounds the grave of the First Emperor Qin in the unexcavated imperial tombs at Xian in China, where the Emperor was buried in a grave complex a square mile in area, at the centre of which was his own tomb hall, a bronze vault designed to replicate in miniature the space of his empire. Jewels were embedded into the tomb's ceiling to symbolize the sky; the streams, wetlands and oceans were simulated by the lake and by the rivers of mercury that ran from it.

We walked on. I could hear the man whistling to his dog, now far away on the sea wall. Otherwise, there was nothing except bronze sand and mercury water, and so we continued walking through the lustrous air, out onto the flats and back into the Mesolithic.

~

In 1931 a trawler named the *Colinda* was night-fishing around twenty-five miles off the Norfolk coast, in the southern North Sea. When the men pulled in their nets and began to sort the fish from the flotsam and rubble that the nets had also trapped, one of the men found, part embedded in a hunk of peat, a curious object: sharp and shapely, about eight and a half inches long and unmistakably of human workmanship. The man handed it to the trawler captain, Pilgrim Lockwood. Lockwood passed it to the owner of the *Colinda*, who passed it to a friend, and in this roundabout way the object at last reached an archaeologist called Muir Evans who was able to identify it as a harpoon point, made from antler and with barbs carved on one side.

The Colinda Point, as it is now known, was one of the first archaeological clues to the existence of a vast, lost and once-inhabited landscape: a Mesolithic Atlantis that lies under the southern half of what is now the North Sea, and over which hunter-gatherers probably ranged. Even to conceive the possibility of such a landscape's existence – unaided by the technology that assists contemporary archaeologists – was in the 1930s an audacious thought-experiment. To imagine much of the North Sea drained away? To imagine what is now seabed as dry land? To imagine what is now the east coast of England as continuous with the north-west coasts of Germany, Denmark and Holland? To imagine a Mesolithic culture existing in this vanished world, rather than using it only for passage?

The drowned land that the Colinda Point – dated to between 10,000 and 4000 BC – helped bring back to light is now known as Doggerland, and thanks to the collaborative work of a remarkable group of archaeologists, geologists, palaeobotanists, and Dutch and East Anglian fisherman, our knowledge of the region is both extensive and detailed.

Around 12,000 years ago, during the most recent glaciation, so much water was locked up in the ice caps and glaciers that the sea levels around Britain were up to 400 feet lower than they are today. Doggerland, then exposed, would have been harsh tundra. But as global temperatures rose, melting ice sent freshwater rivers spinning through that tundra, irrigating and fertilizing it, such that it developed into a habitable, even hospitable, terrain. We know that there were trout in the rivers of Doggerland, wild boar and deer in its oak and ash woods, and that stinging nettles grew among its grasses. Using seismic-survey data of the seabed acquired from an oil company, archaeologists have been able to back-map an area of Doggerland around the size of Wales. Like early colonists, researchers have christened the features of this rediscovered world. The Spines is an area of steep dunes, probably running down to a river which, at its peak flow, was almost as big as the Rhine is today. The river has been named the Shotton River in honour of the Birmingham geologist Fred Shotton (who, among other distinctions, was dropped behind enemy lines to analyse the geology of the Normandy beachheads before the D-Day landings). Dogger Bank – a name familiar from shipping forecasts – is an upland area of plateaux in north Doggerland, and the Outer Silver Pit is a giant basin flanked by two huge sandbanks, almost sixty miles long, that resemble estuarine or lacustrine features.

As temperatures increased further and more land-ice melted, Doggerland was gradually inundated. Dogger Bank would have survived as a large island, before it too disappeared around 5000 BC, and the inundation of Doggerland was complete. The creep of the sea level across the land – up to one or two metres per century – would have been noticeable in a generation, but is unlikely to have taken people by surprise – even those who had established rudimentary settlements. The flooding was something that could be foreseen and adapted to, if not mitigated or resisted. As such, the Mesolithic retreat from Doggerland represents one of the earliest sustained human responses to climate change.

Considering Doggerland now, it is hard not to think forwards as well as backwards. To those living on the vulnerable east coast of England, drowned Doggerland offers a glimpse of the future. Around the coasts of Norfolk and Suffolk, the land is being bitten back by the ocean. Graveyards are shedding their bones and their headstones into the sea. Dwellings that were once miles inland are now cliff-edge, and on the point of abandonment. Eccles Church on the Norfolk coast collapsed into the waves in 1895. Anti-aircraft batteries and pillboxes built on cliffs in 1940 are slumped on beaches or sunk offshore. Roads end in mid-air. Footpaths that once ran along the coast have crumbled. Consulting historical maps of East

Anglia, you realize that substantial areas of the region have already joined Doggerland: coastlines have become ghost-lines. In places such as these the undertow of the past is strong – liable to take your legs from you and pull you down without warning.

At Dunwich, an entire town was swallowed by the sea over several centuries. Nothing of it is now left, though late-nineteenth-century photographs exist of its last towers standing crooked on the beach. Historical data about Dunwich is sufficiently profuse that maps have been made of the former outline of streets, buildings and churches, and their positions relative to the current shore. In this way, swimming off the shingle beach, you can float over invisible streets and buildings: the further out you go, the further back in history you've reached. Once, unaware of the ebb tide that was ripping round the coast, I crunched over the shingle and swam to around 1842, before I realized that I was being pulled rapidly out to sea, and struck out in panic for the present day.

It is likely that, thousands of years in the future, when the temperature cycles have turned again and the world's water is once more locked up in ice, Doggerland will be re-exposed; filled this time with the wreckage of an Anthropocene culture – a vast junkyard of beached derricks and stranded sea-forts, botched pipes and wiring, the concrete caltrops of anti-tank defences, fleets of grounded and upended boats, and the spoilheaps of former houses.

~

Out and on we walked, barefoot over and into the mirror-world. I glanced back at the coast. The air was grainy and flickering, like an old newsreel. The sea wall had hazed out to a thin black strip. Structures of unknown purpose – a white-beamed gantry, a low-slung barracks – showed on the shoreline. Every few hundred yards, I dropped a white cockle shell. The light had modified again, from nacreous to granular to dense. Sound travelled oddly. The muted pop-popping of gunfire was smudgy, but the call of a cuckoo from somewhere on the treeless shore rang sharply to us. A pale sun glared through the mist, its white eye multiplying in pools and ripples.

The miniature sandscapes of ridge and valley pressed into the soles of my feet, and for days after the walk I would feel a memory of that pressure and pattern. The ripple line of the ridges was recapitulated wherever I looked: in small bivalves between whose parted shells poked frilled lips, and in serpentine channels – apparent because they caught and returned the light differently to the shallower water. All these forms possessed the S-shaped double bend that William Hogarth in 1753 christened the 'ogee' or 'line of beauty', exquisite in its functionless and repetitive elegance; a line that drew the eye onwards.

With so few orientation points and so many beckoning paths, we were finding it hard to stay on course. I was experiencing a powerful desire to walk straight out to sea and explore the greater freedoms of this empty tidal world. But we were both still anxious about straying far from the notional path of the Broomway, and encountering the black muds or the quicksands.

Patrick's directions said that we should reach something called the Maypole, a sunken telegraph pole with cross-pieces that marked the south-eastern edge of a tidal channel named Havengore Creek. But scale behaved strangely, and we weren't paying sufficient attention to our pacings and distances. We became confused by other spars, sticking up from the mud here and there: relics of wrecks, perhaps, or more likely the mark-points of former channels long since silted up by the shifting sands. At last we found and reached what was surely the Maypole. It resembled the final yards of a galleon's topmast, the body of a ship long since sunk into those deep sands. At its base, currents had carved basins in whose warm water we wallowed our feet, sending shrimps scurrying. We took an onwards bearing and continued over the silver shield of the water.

My brain was beginning to move unusually, worked upon and changed by the mind-altering substances of this offshore world, and by the elation that arose from the counter-intuition of walking securely on water. Out there, nothing could be only itself. The eye fed on false colour-values. Similes and metaphors bred and budded. Mirages of scale occurred, and tricks of depth. Gull-eagles dipped and glided in the outer reaches of the mist. The sand served as the water's tain: 'tain', from the French for 'tin', being the lustreless backing of a mirror that makes reflection possible but limits the onward gaze, disallowing the view of a concept beyond that point.

Walking always with us were our reflections, our attentive ghost selves. For the water acted as a mirror-line, such that we both appeared joined at the ankles with our doubles, me more than twelve feet tall and David a foot taller still. If anyone had been able to look out from the shore, through the mist, they would have seen two giant walkers striding over the sea. That or a pair of long-shanked buffoons, traipsing to their foolish deaths.

Several years ago the sculptor Antony Gormley buried a full-size iron cast of his own body upside down in the grounds of Cambridge's Archaeological Research Institute. Only the undersides of the iron man's feet show on the surface. Two days before coming to walk the Broomway I'd slipped off my shoes and socks and stood barefoot in the rusty prints, sole to sole with that buried body. Now that act of doubling had itself been unexpectedly repeated out here on the sands. Everywhere I looked were pivot-points and fulcrums, symmetries and proliferations: the thorax points of a winged world. Sand mimicked water, water mimicked sand, and the air duplicated the textures of both. Hinged cuckoo-calls; razor shells and cockle shells; our own reflections; a profusion of suns; the glide of transparent over solid. When I think back to the outer miles of that walk, I now recall a strong disorder of perception that caused illusions of the spirit as well as of the eye. I recall thought becoming sensational; the substance of landscape so influencing mind that mind's own substance was altered.

~

You enter the mirror-world by a causeway and you leave it by one. From Asplin Head, a rubble jetty as wide as a farm track reaches out over the Black Grounds, offering safe passage to shore. As we approached the jetty the sand began to give way underfoot, and we broke through into sucking black mud. It was like striking oil – the glittering rich ooze gouting up around our feet. We slurped onwards to the causeway, the rubble of which had been colonized by a lurid green weed. Sea lavender and samphire thrived in the salt marsh.

I walked alongside the causeway rather than on it, finding that if I kept moving over the mud I didn't sink. I passed through miniature cactus forests of samphire and between torn chunks of ferroconcrete. The surface of the mud, a gritty curded paste, was intricately marked with the filigree of worm tracks and crab scrabbles. In the centre of the causeway, where the mud had dried and cracked into star patterns, there were many wader footprints – sandpipers, oystercatchers and gulls – and I remembered the printed snow of my night-walk back in Cambridge. The slithery clay offered pleasure to the foot, and mud curled up between my toes with each step, oily as butter. By the time we reached the sea wall, David and I both wore diving boots of clay. We washed them off in a puddle, and stepped up onto a boat ramp. We had made landfall.

We sat on the out-slope of the sea wall, eating sandwiches and talking. David took a photograph of an MoD sign that read 'Photography is Prohibited'. The sun was fully out now, and barely a wisp of the early-day mist survived. The clay dried fast on my legs, crisping the hairs and tightening my skin so that I felt kiln-fired – a mud man. To my joy three avocets rose from the salt marsh and flew screeching in circles above us, before rocketing back down into the sea lavender. I thought of the curlew I had seen in numbers out on this coast earlier in the year, and about how the paths of birds and animals were really the oldest ways of them all: aerial migration routes, bringing geese to this shore from Siberia, peregrines from Scandinavia, scored invisibly into the sky over millennia and signed by magnetic forces. Staggering recent research into avian navigation has revealed that, by means of retinal proteins called cryptochromes, birds can actually *see* magnetic fields. Magnetic force-structures are perceived as darker or lighter forms, which are superimposed on the conventionally visible landscape, and so help to guide the birds to their destinations.

Beyond the causeway's end, the shining sands stretched to a horizon line. One of Foulness's farmers, John Burroughs, has spoken wistfully of coming out onto the sands in late autumn to hunt wigeon: he brings a board to use as a shooting stick and, leaning against it, feels that he 'could be on the far side of the moon.' That felt exactly right: the walk out to sea as a soft lunacy, a passage beyond this world.

In his weird way-book of 1909, *Afoot in England*, W. H. Hudson described being on the Norfolk coast under similar conditions to the ones David and I had experienced that morning on the Broomway. The tide was low and Hudson was far out on the blonde sands watching herring gulls, when a 'soft bluish silvery haze' began to build, causing sky, sea and land to 'blend and interfuse', producing a 'new country' that was 'neither earth nor sea'. The haze also magnified the gulls until they seemed no longer 'familiar birds', but 'twice as big as gulls, and . . . of a dazzling whiteness and of no definite shape'. Hudson's prose registers the experience as mystical: a metaphysical hallucination brought about by material illusion. The gulls temporarily appeared to him as ghost gulls or spirit birds that merely 'lived in or were passing through the world', presences made briefly seeable by the haze. Then, in a scintillating reversal, he imagines that he himself – 'standing far out on the sparkling sands, with the sparkling sea on one side' – has also been dematerialized, 'a formless shining white being standing by the sea, and then perhaps as a winged shadow floating in the haze'. 'This,' he concludes, 'was the effect on my mind: this natural world was changed to a supernatural.'

Felt pressure, sensed texture and perceived space can work upon the body and so too upon the mind, altering the textures and inclinations of thought. The American farmer and writer Wendell Berry suggests this in a fine essay called 'The Rise', where he describes setting float in a canoe on a river in spate. 'No matter how deliberately we moved from the shore into the sudden violence of a river on the rise,' writes Berry, 'there would . . . be several uneasy minutes of transition. The river is another world, which means that one's senses and reflexes must begin to live another life.'

~

We lack – we need – a term for those places where one experiences a 'transition' from a known landscape onto John's 'far side of the moon', into Hudson's 'new country', into Berry's 'another world': somewhere we feel and think significantly differently. I have for some time been imagining such transitions as 'border crossings'. These borders do not correspond to national boundaries, and papers and documents are unrequired at them. Their traverse is generally unbiddable, and no reliable map exists of their routes and outlines. They exist even in familiar landscapes: there when you cross a certain watershed, treeline or snowline, or enter rain, storm or mist, or pass from boulder clay onto sand, or chalk onto greenstone. Such moments are rites of passage that reconfigure local geographies, leaving known places outlandish or quickened, revealing continents within counties.

What might we call such incidents and instances – or, rather, how to describe the lands that are found beyond these frontiers? 'Xenotopias', perhaps, meaning 'foreign places' or 'out-of-place places', a term to complement our 'utopias' and our 'dystopias'. Martin Martin, the traveller and writer who in the 1690s set sail to explore the Scottish coastline, knew that one does not need to displace oneself vastly in space in order to find difference. 'It is a piece of weakness and folly merely to value things because of their distance from the place where we are born,' he wrote in 1697, 'thus men have travelled far enough in the search of foreign plants and animals, and yet continue strangers to those produced in their own natural climate.' So did Roger Deakin: 'Why would anyone want to go to live abroad when they can live in several countries at once just by being in England?' he wondered in his journal. Likewise, Henry David Thoreau: 'An absolutely new prospect is a great happiness, and I can still get this any afternoon. Two or three hours' walking will carry me to as strange a country as I expect ever to see. A single farmhouse which I had not seen before is sometimes as good as the dominions of the King of Dahomey.'

The American artist William Fox has spent his career exploring what he calls 'cognitive dissonance in isotropic spaces', which might be more plainly translated as 'how we easily get lost in spaces that appear much the same in all directions'. Fox's thesis is that we are unable to orient ourselves in such landscapes because we evolved in the dense, close-hand environments of jungle and savannah. In repetitive, data-depleted landscapes with few sight-markers, 'our natural navigational abilities begin to fail catastrophically'. Fox had travelled to Antarctica, to the American deserts and to volcanic calderas in the Pacific to explore such monotone spaces – but David and I had stumbled into one a few hundred yards off the Essex coast.

~

We walked back along the causeway to the point where the Broomway supposedly began, and there we turned into the wind and returned along the route by which we had come. With the sun now fully out, each sand ridge carried its own line of light, running along its summit like an inlaid wire, and in each pool burnt a tiny version of the sun, a bright borehole to the earth's white core. Our shadows were with us now as well as our reflections: the two of us had been four on the way out to the island, and we were six on our return, at once solipsized and diffused by the proliferating versions of ourselves.

Perhaps halfway back to the Maypole, emboldened by the day, we could no longer resist the temptation to explore further across the sand-flats, and so we turned perpendicular to the line of the land and began walking straight out to sea, leaving the imagined safety of the Broomway behind us.

That hour, walking out – back – into Doggerland, was an hour I will never forget. We did not know where the sand would slacken to mud, and yet somehow it never felt dangerous or rash. The tide was out and the moon would hold it out, and we had two hours in which to discover this vast revealed world: no more than two hours, for sure, but surely also no less. The serenity of the space through which we were moving calmed me to the point of invulnerability, and thus we walked on. A mile out, the white mist still hovered, and in the haze I started to perceive impossible forms and shapes: a fleet of Viking longboats with high lug-rigged square sails; a squadron of feluccas, dhows and *sgoths*; cityscapes (the skyline of Istanbul, the profile of the Houses of Parliament). When I looked back, the coast-line was all but imperceptible, and it was apparent that our footprints had been erased behind us, and so we splashed tracelessly on out to the tidal limit. It felt at that moment unarguable that a horizon line might exert as potent a pull upon the mind as a mountain's summit.

Eventually, reluctantly, nearly two miles offshore, with the tide approaching its turn and our worries at last starting to rise through our calm – black mud through sand – we began a long slow arc back towards the coastline and the path of the Broomway, away from the outermost point. There was the return of bearings, the approach to land, a settling to recognizability. As we returned to shore, we laid plans to walk the Broomway again, later in the year, this time at night.

Mud-caked and silly with the sun and the miles, a pair of Mesolithic tramps, we left the sand where it met the causeway near Wakering Stairs. There at the causeway's frayed end, on the brink of the Black Grounds, were the marker poles, and there – perched on the top of their stand of eelgrass – were my faithful trainers, still waiting for me. I put them on and we walked out of Doggerland, or whichever country it was that we had discovered that day, off the mirror and onto the sea wall. For days afterwards I felt calm, level, shining, sand flat.

PART II

FOLLOWING

(Scotland)

5

WATER – SOUTH

Our cockle-shell — The sea roads — Land bias — Poetic log-books — Raiders & *peregrini* — *Immrama* — Dream islands — Boulder ballast — Sea stories & *astar mara* — A Stornoway crow's nest — 'The way one phrase talks to another' — The Hoil — In pursuit of the optimal — The Blue Men of the Minch — Shapes standing clear — Tide-turn — A riffle of puffins — Phosphorescence — Mafic glass — Islomania & the limits of knowledge — Surfing — A story-boat — The congress of substances — A voyage north.

The boat we sailed south down the sea roads was a century-old cockle-shell. I first saw her moored up alongside three other craft in Stornoway harbour on the Isle of Lewis in the Outer Hebrides. Nearest the quay was a rusting old fishing trawler, long since retired, its hulk secured by arm-thick hawsers. Moored against the trawler's side was an ocean-going yacht, toothpaste white, fifty feet long. Moored to the yacht's side was a thirty-three-foot cruiser with weathered teak deck-boards and a sharp bow point. And moored to the side of the cruiser was our little boat, her single mast unstepped, her terracotta sail folded in drapes along her thwarts, and from stem to stern measuring shorter than three men lying head to toe.

She looked like a dinghy or a dory, but she was *Broad Bay*, a lug-rigged open boat whose clinker hull was of Scottish larch. Her sides rode two feet above the water, she was two years short of her century, and two of us were going to sail her south through the Minch, the deep-water sea channel that separates Skye and the Outer Hebrides from the Scottish mainland. We would make first for the Shiant Islands, a mostly dolerite archipelago in the heart of the Minch, and then, wind and weather allowing, on further south to Harris and Uist, keeping to the routes of the sea roads – the *astar mara* in Gaelic – up and down which people, goods, gods, ideas and stories have moved for nearly ten millennia.

To my sea-fearful eye, *Broad Bay* was barely big enough to take a turn around the harbour, let alone head out into the fierce tidal waters of the Minch. We had no engine (instead, a pair of oars); we had no GPS (instead, a hand-held walker's compass); we had two people crewing a boat designed for a crew of four (and one of those two, being me, was an incompetent). It was to be the most basic form of sailing: a hull to hold the waves at bay and a sail to hold the wind for way.

~

In Old English the *hwael-weg* (the whale's way), the *swan-rād* (the swan's way); in Norse the *veger*; in Gaelic *rathad mara* or *astar mara*; in English the ocean roads, the sea lanes. There are thousands of them, and they include the *Rathad chun a' Bhaltaic* – the Road to the Baltic – that runs from Cape Wrath towards Russia by way of the Orkneys; the Brancaster Roads off the north Norfolk coast; and 'The Road', the channel that divides the islands of St Mary's and Tresco in the Scillies.* We think of paths as existing only on land, but the sea has its paths too, though water refuses to take and hold marks. Sections of the Icknield Way may have been first trodden into the chalk 5,000 years ago, but the sea will not record a journey made on it half an hour previously. Sea roads are dissolving paths whose passage leaves no trace beyond a wake, a brief turbulence astern. They survive as convention, tradition, as a sequence of coordinates, as a series of waymarks, as dotted lines on charts, and as stories and songs. '. . . as by Line upon the Ocean [we] go,' wrote

* Sometimes these 'roads' are sheltered expanses of water (the Carrick Roads at Falmouth, for instance, or those leading into the Mersey estuary).

John Dryden of English navigators in the 1660s, 'Whose paths shall be as familiar as the Land.' Along these sea paths for thousands of years have travelled ships, boats, people, objects and language: letters, folk tales, sea songs, shanties, poems, rumours, slang, jokes and visions. The sandy silt of the Broomway had been a transitional path, taking me half off land and half onto water. Now I had come to the Outer Hebrides to meet a man who knew the sea roads about as well as anyone living, and to sail these true waterways with him.

What you should first realize, to understand the sea roads, is how close the ocean brings far-apart places. In a pre-modern world, before cars and planes, the boat was the fastest means of long-distance travel. It is still surprisingly swift. Sailing a small craft in reasonable conditions, catching the right tides and the right winds, you can get from the Outer Hebrides to Orkney in a day, and you can reach the Faeroes in two or three. Estimates of the distances covered in a good sailing day by Viking ships range from 90 to 150 nautical miles, meaning that the trip from Bergen in Norway to the Shetlands could be done in two days, and Iceland could be reached in a week. A short commute to work, then, for first-millennial raiders: violence spread quickly over the water.

The second thing to know about sea roads is that they are not arbitrary. There are optimal routes to sail across open sea, as there are optimal routes to walk across open land. Sea roads are determined by the shape of the coastline (they bend out to avoid headlands, they dip towards significant ports, archipelagos and skerry guards) as well as by marine phenomena. Surface currents, tidal streams and prevailing winds all offer limits and opportunities for sea travel between certain places.

The existence of the ancient seaways, and their crucial role in shaping prehistory, were only recognized in the early twentieth century. Until then, pre-historians and historical geographers had demonstrated a 'land bias'; a perceptive error brought about by an over-reliance on Roman sources that tended to concentrate on the movement of troops, goods and ideas on foot and across countries. Certainly, the Roman Empire's road network transformed internal mobility in Europe and, unmistakably, Roman roads were the key to uniting the empire's dispersed territories, as well as generating its military and economic power. 'The sea divides and the land unites,' ran the Roman truism. But for millennia prior to the rise of Rome's empire, the reverse had been true. The classical sources misled subsequent historians – allied with the fact that the sea erases all records of its traverses, whereas the land preserves them.

It was the emergence of prehistoric archaeology as a defined discipline that revealed the significance of the sea roads. An early breakthrough was made in 1912 by a man called Osbert Crawford, who noticed that the distribution of Bronze Age gold lunulae of Irish origin suggested they had been transported by sea, and by what he called 'isthmus roads': overland routes used by early sailors who did not want to risk rounding stormy promontories – the boot of Cornwall, say, or St David's Head on the Welsh peninsula – and so unloaded their goods on one shore before portaging them to the opposite shore, where they loaded them into a different vessel. Advances quickly followed Crawford's breakthrough. During and shortly after the First World War, using distribution patterns of artefacts and technologies in Ireland, western and northern Britain, and the Atlantic shores of Spain and France, researchers began to reconstruct rudimentary maps of what became known as the Western Seaways.

The work was painstaking, but what it proved was astonishing: that there had been maritime traffic along the sea roads dating back at least to the Mesolithic, and intense activity for the three millennia before Rome built its roads. In 1932, Cyril Fox published a famous map showing a major seaway running from the Orkneys across the top of Scotland (the Pentland Firth), round the headland of Cape Wrath, down through the Minch, on south through the Irish Sea, around Wales and the Cornish peninsula, then heading south across the wide mouth of the Channel to Brittany, the Bay of Biscay and eventually north-western Spain. Off this main track came byways, tributaries and trans-peninsular routes.

More research followed, more mapping, and a web of short-haul journeys also emerged into view: an intricately laced network binding the coastal frontage of northern and western Europe. Fox described a shared Atlantic character belonging to the cultures of these conjoined seaboards, and conjured up a vision of prehistoric seas teeming with Neolithic argonauts afloat on their hide-hulled boats, moving by oar and sail, sometimes over great distances. There is proof, for instance, that around 5,000 years ago someone set sail northwards from Orkney – enticed perhaps by jetsam washing in from the north or by the northwards flights of birds towards the ends of days – and reached Shetland.

We can only surmise the navigational and boat-building technologies that permitted the earliest sailors of the sea roads to find their ways out and back. We have even less idea of why they travelled. In his superb work on Atlantic cultures, *Facing the Ocean*, Barry Cunliffe speculates that the 'restlessness of the ocean' might itself have been a prompt to travel, and more pragmatically points out that the pursuit of migrating fish and the uneven distribution of elite resources would have stimulated a need for reliable sea travel. The first sea-road mariners would have used natural navigation techniques: the direction of flight at dusk of land-roosting birds like fulmars, petrels or gannets; the Pole Star or the North Star, the fixed point of the celestial panorama about which all other stars appeared to rotate; the sighting of orographic clouds that signalled the existence of land over the horizon; the detection of swell patterns. Such methods would have allowed early navigators to keep close to a desired track, and would have contributed over time to a shared memory map of the coastline and the best sea routes, kept and passed on as story and drawing.

Such knowledge became codified over time in the form of rudimentary charts and *peripli*, and then as route books in which sea paths were recorded as narratives and poems: the catalogue of ships in the *Iliad* is a pilot's mnemonic, for instance, as is the *Massaliote Periplus* (possibly sixth-century BC). Word-maps of sea routes occur in skaldic poetry, and are also folded into the Icelandic sagas (some of which offer directions for sailing from Norway to Iceland, with details of way stations, sighting points and other key *landtoninger*, or landmarks), as well as into more functional medieval Icelandic texts such as the extraordinary fourteenth-century *Landnámabók* (*The Book of Settlements*) whose hundred chapters and five parts tell the story of the takeover of Iceland by the Vikings, and include guides to the *verstrveger* – the western roads of the Atlantic that led from Norway to the Orkneys, Scotland, the Hebrides and Ireland, as well as to the Faeroes, Iceland and Greenland. All of these documents are, in Kenneth White's resonant phrase, 'poetic logbooks, full of salt, wind and waves', and they eventually developed into the pilot books known variously as *routiers*, *rutters* and *portolani* (the latter offering directions for coastwise rather than trans-oceanic passage crossings, whereby progress was measured by marking off headlands).

The discovery of the sea roads necessitated a radical re-imagining of the history of Europe. Try it yourself, now. Invert the mental map you hold of Britain, Ireland and western Europe. Turn it inside out. Blank out the land interiors of these countries – consider them featureless, as you might previously have considered the sea. Instead, populate the western and northern waters with paths and tracks: a travel system that joins port to port, island to island, headland to headland, river mouth to river mouth. The sea has become the land, in that it is now the usual medium of transit: not barrier but corridor.*

Once you have carried out this thought-experiment, this photo-negative flip, many consequences follow. One is centrifugal. Matter and culture spin to the edges. The centre is emptied and the margins become central. The Atlantic fringe of Europe is no longer the brink of 'the Old World', but rather the interface with the New. The coastal settlements are places of departure and arrival, thriving crossroads: the Orcadian archipelago is not remote but a focal point, standing at the heart of a trade and pilgrimage network.

A second consequence is that today's national boundaries shiver and collapse. Instead of belonging to particular nations that happen to possess coastlines, these outward-facing coastal settlements – from the Shetlands and the Orkneys all the way round and down to Galicia in Spain – become a continuous territory of their own: Atlanticist in nature, sharing culture, technologies, crafts and languages. A dispersed occidental continent, if you like, whose

* When in 704 AD the Abbot Adomnán wrote the *Vita Columbae*, the first biography of St Columba – who in 563 AD had sailed from Ireland to Scotland to establish the monastery at Iona – the only journey he considers to be worthy of mention as in any way exceptional is a land journey, across Scotland from west coast to east.

constituent areas are united by their common frontage onto the same ocean. As Cunliffe argues, a shared cultural identity developed over ten millennia along this Atlantic facade, such that Galicians, Celts, Bretons and Hebrideans might be said to have had more in common with one another than with their 'inland kin'. Kenneth White proposes the recovery of 'lost wavelengths' and 'Atlantic sensations', the suggestion that there are ways of feeling and thinking that are inspired and conditioned by the fact of long-term living on an ocean edge. There are, White writes, 'events of the mind' that could have occurred only on these Atlantic coasts, where 'strange winds of the spirit blow': another version of the idea that so attracted Edward Thomas, of inner landscapes being powerfully shaped by outer.

Up and down these sea roads, from the Mesolithic era onwards, travelled people (raiders, devouts, migrants, traders, craftsmen) and their ideas (technologies, languages, dialects, beliefs and values). Along the seaways in the Neolithic moved beakers and battleaxes, oval pendants and stone beads, lance-heads of honey-coloured French flint, funerary practices and architectural techniques. Along them in the Bronze Age moved gold lunulae, pigments, jet, amber, copper, faience, bronze torcs and itinerant bronze-smiths (carrying their bags of scrap, their beeswax, their refractory clay). Along them in the Iron Age moved Cornish tin, art motifs, domesticated animals and precious metals. Along them in the Dark Ages moved the heavy freights of violence, trade and religion. Along them in the Middle Ages moved stone, lime, rope, pantiles, timber, wood-carving techniques, vernacular violin-playing, songs and airs (one of Robert Burns's most perfect songs, 'The Gallant Weaver', is set to a Scandinavian tune).

The growth of the Roman imperium and the consequent growth of the European road system transformed the political geography of

Europe, and for a time the importance of the seaways as routes of travel was diminished. But in the fifth century a new form of worship – physically demanding on the practitioner, and founded on an ideal of solitude, or *desertum* – spread from Gaul and arrived by means of the seaways into western and northern Britain. *Peregrini* – wandering devouts – travelled by boat on their pilgrimages, making landfall on distant islands and headlands (Iona, North Rona) long before the Norsemen reached such places. White has written well about this extraordinary moment in Christian history, when the monks – a-sail in search of their *desertum* – 'suddenly began to move further afield, flying in a great . . . migration, their heads full of grammar and geography, verb tenses and tempests, quick thinking and poetry'.

Some of the Celtic Christian literature that emerged from these centuries took the form of the *immram*, a word which might be translated perhaps as a 'wonder-voyage', a sea journey to an otherworld.* The *immrama* – *The Voyage of Mael Duin's Boat*, *The Adventure of Bran* and *The Voyage of Brendan* being among the best known – are set on the seaways. They are narratives of passage, which move easily from the recognizable to the supernatural, fading from known into imagined geographies with minimal indication of transition. In these tales, the actual territories of Scotland, Iceland, Orkney and Shetland are connected by the sea roads with fabled places such as the Hesperides, the Island of the Blessed, the Fortunate Isles (an archipelago that was still marked on charts of the west Atlantic into the fourteenth and fifteenth centuries), and Hy-Brazil,

* An *immram* is a 'rowing-about', from the Gaelic *ramh*, meaning 'oar', and can designate – like the Aboriginal Australian walkabout – either a pragmatic journey or a mystical spirit-voyage; an *iorram* is a rowing song that laments the dead.

the island of happiness off the west coast of Ireland, where sickness is impossible and contentment assured.*

These, then, were waters in which the geological and the theological mingled, zones in which 'metaphor and reality merged one into the other over time', as Cunliffe puts it, and they were the waters that I set out to sail with Ian Stephen.

~

Ian and I stood side by side on the Stornoway quay, looking across at the little boat he was proposing we take to sea. Ian, hands in pockets, relaxed. Me, hands on hips, apprehensive.

'The traditional ballast for boats such as *Broad Bay*,' Ian said, 'was boulders. She'd be laden with boulders of gneiss; folk would make a chain and pass the rocks along, and they'd be laid all along the keel like a clutch of heavy eggs.'

Ian's tone suggested that this was information I should find reassuring. I did not. Even though I was familiar with the logic of ballast, I simply could not find it sensible to load a boat with boulders before sailing her out into the open ocean.

I had first met Ian in Stornoway a year or so previously. He is – well, he is many things. A sailor before all else, determined by and for the sea, living mostly hand to mouth and with his eye always on the next adventure. His love of the sea is so keen that it might

* Cunliffe tells the charming story of the visions of T. J. Westropp, an antiquarian who in 1912 claimed to have seen Hy-Brazil three times in his life: 'it had two hills, one wooded; between them, from a low plain, rose towers and curls of smoke'. Mention of 'Brazil Rock' was not finally removed from all Atlantic charts until 1865.

seem like greed, but it is more imperative than greed. Born and brought up on the Isle of Lewis, he was a coastguard in Stornoway for fifteen years in the 1980s and 1990s, before he gave the job up because it bound him too much to the desk. He is now a sailor, an artist, a storyteller and a lyric poet of real worth. For much of his life he has been fascinated by the sea roads that lead to and from the Outer Hebrides, and he has spent years sailing them, and researching the tales and songs that have moved along them. 'There are stories you meet different versions of at different points up and down the Atlantic coast,' he told me. 'When you encounter them, you know well that this is a story that's travelled by the sea roads.'

Following the stories is for Ian a way of mapping the routes of the roads, and sailing the roads a way of mapping the routes of the stories. He has tracked mutations of sea tales – 'Three Knots of Wind', 'The Blue Men of the Minch', the 'Selkie' and the 'Fin-Men' legends – as they have been carried about over the centuries, making their landfalls here and there, finding retellings in different accents and different places. In 2007, he helped to sail three traditional boats along routes suggested by three Gaelic songs and stories, one of which was the 'Fraoch à Rònaigh', a song based on the air of a pibroch whose lyrics consisted mostly of the place names of the graveyards in North Uist. It was an exile's song, a lament that lists the places where the writer's ancestors lie. To Ian, traditional stories, like traditional songs, are closely kindred to the traditional seaways, in that they are highly contingent and yet broadly repeatable. 'A song is different every time it's sung,' he told me, 'and variations of wind, tide, vessel and crew mean that no voyage along a sea route will ever be the same.' Each sea route, planned in the mind, exists first as anticipation, then as dissolving wake and then finally as logbook data. Each is 'affected by isobars, // the stationing of satellites, recorded ephemera / hands on helms'. I liked that idea; it reminded me both of the Aboriginal Songlines, and of Thomas's vision of path as story, with each new walker adding a new note or plot-line to the way.

Ian in appearance: curly silver hair, a shallow white stubble, two thin silver earrings in his left ear, too fine to be piratical. Ian in manner: sharp, fox-like, generous, mischievous. Ian in voice: lilting, Gaelic-inflected. Ian in stature: small, almost boyish. He has an air of youthfulness to him, seems younger than me, though he's more than twenty years my senior. His physique, like his language, is compact and wiry, capable of reach and strength. Physically, he's whipped tight, made of hawser and halyard wire, but his character is full of flex. He passes in and out of moods of intense concentration, whose endings are marked by a quick grin, a register shift, an agile impiety. He doesn't take well to fools or frauds. The first time we met I felt gauged, appraised, quickly read. Eyes moved up and down me. I had the same sense of apprehension as when stepping through an airport scanner. Then – clear. Green light. No improper goods. Nothing falsely hidden. A test passed, for the time being at least.

Ian lives thirty feet from the quayside in Stornoway, in a former customs house that had been converted into a sail-loft, then a net-loft, then a gas depot, until it had fallen derelict for years, and eventually been restored. This is his dockside crow's nest.

When I first visited him there, one late-summer evening, I was shocked to see that he had just been burgled. The door was wide open, and objects spilled out from it as if from an overfull cupboard. Foot pumps, dry-bags, clothing, toolboxes, oars, a quiver of rigged fishing rods in a tube, down whose tight lines light ran in beads as we approached. Ian picked his way unconcernedly through the mess towards the open door. 'Don't mind that,' he said. 'That's the way it always looks round my front door. Come away in and meet whoever's around.'

That night we laid plans and plotted adventures up and down the sea roads. His house was, as I would later learn, run in a manner close to a commune. Financially, it survived mostly on barter and gift. People – sailors and fishermen in the main – passed in and out, sleeping in the loft, behind sofas, or paddling out to one of the boats that were moored in the harbour, and kipping in the berths there. Others would turn up in the kitchen, stopping by for an hour or two, for a coffee or dram. There was Michael 'The Boat', who turned up with a bucket of orange gurnard. There was Michael 'The Hat', who appeared wearing tweed and holding a monograph on the Scottish Enlightenment to his chest like a clipboard, as if he had come to inspect our intellects. There was an Englishman called Colin, who wouldn't tell me much about his life apart from that his business had taken him to many different countries ('import/export' – the old spy's alibi), and who worked cleverly with wood.

Ian lives on Lewis, but from there he has travelled far. He is an islander who's lived an international life. The Outer Hebrides are to him a crossroads, not a margin, and in that sense he is living proof of the surviving importance of the sea roads. The result of his ocean journeys is a knowledge and world view that are anchored in one place, but cosmopolitan in their range. His lines of connection are the dotted lines on the charts that run north and east from Stornoway to Norway, Orkney, Sula Sgeir and North Rona, the Baltic countries; or south down the Minch to Islay, Dublin, the Scillies and the Breton coast. He has friends and watch-mates from all over the Atlantic facade. 'If it's about anything, it's this,' he wrote in a poem:

the taste of the relations, out of town,
the watch-mates met again . . .

The way one phrase talks to another.
The history of your way through weather.
The touch of your people.

~

Mid-morning departure, Stornoway harbour, which is also known as the Hoil: hints of oil, hints of hooley. Sound of boatslip, reek of diesel. *Broad Bay*'s wake through the harbour – a tugged line through the fuel slicks on the water's surface, our keel slurring petrol-rainbows. Light quibbling on the swell. We nosed through the chowder of harbour water: kelp, oranges, plastic milk bottles, sea gunk. Big seals floating here and there, their nostrils and eyes just above the water, their blubbery backs looking like the puffed-up anoraks of murder victims. Nostrils up, *snort snort*, duck to rinse, and then dive with a final flip of the flukes. Out we went – by oar, sail and tow – past the drug-money pleasure-gardens and castle of James Matheson, who in 1844 used half a million pounds of the money he made pushing opium to the Chinese to buy the whole island of Lewis. Out past the lighthouse, out past the headlands, the sea opening like a cone into the Minch.

The sun above us, bright and high, but the sky darkening swiftly further out. Black sky-reefs of cloud to the east. The sea: graphite, lightly choppy, white-stippled. The wind: a near-southerly, Force 3 or 4, with just a touch of east in it. A good strength for a little boat like ours, but from the worst of directions. Our sea road led us south-south-east, but it's impossible to sail directly upwind: we would have to make long tacks. Two other boats left the Hoil with us: a full-size *sgoth Niseach*, called *An Sùlaire* (*The Gannet*), with a crew of five, and a sea-going yacht to keep watch over us in case of trouble. Ian and I were together in little *Broad Bay*.

'Let's get the sail up, show the people that we're leaving well,' said Ian. So I hoofed and hauled the big yard to the spar-top, the mainsheet was tightened and lightly jammed, the terracotta sail luffed then filled, *Broad Bay* surged southwards through the water, and my heart leapt in my chest. Our wake spooling white behind us, our track record. The water going past fast with a hiss like poured sand.

We would sail for nearly twelve hours that day, almost south into an almost-southerly. It was never certain until we reached the Shiants around dusk that we would make it to them at all. Our little boat with its two-man crew couldn't keep up with the other craft. Within a few miles of clearing the Stornoway headlands, the yacht and *An Sùlaire* were far ahead. We watched *An Sùlaire*'s swooping lugsail take a long tack out into the shining haze of the Minch, until she disappeared. Then it was just us, the water and the way. I felt no worry at being out there in that sea because I knew that I couldn't be with a more experienced sailor, and because this was a boat that had lasted a century and there was no good reason why she should founder now.

Those first hours were a time of quick learning for me, dredging back skills part-remembered from earlier weeks of sailing, suppressing my ineptitudes as best I could.

'Our deadline is the evening turn of the tide,' said Ian. 'I'd guess that we have a few hours of worthwhile struggle now against the tide, then six hours of good running, then an hour of slack, and then . . .' He clicked his fingers and jerked his thumb over his shoulder, back towards Stornoway, with a smile. '. . . then we'll be back in the Hoil before we know it.'

So every yard of way over ground counted. Ian had put me on the helm, traditional location for the landlubber, and I quickly learnt to steal from the wind, to pilfer a few yards here and a few there, by sailing as tight to the southerly as possible. If you turn too close to the wind, the sail empties, momentum is lost and the boat takes minutes to recover: a severe punishment on such a time-tight voyage.

We pursued our long and lonely tacks, like cross-stitches made over the direct line of the sea road, zigzagging south through the Minch towards the Shiants. Inland was the grey-green Lewis coastline, with its sumping sea lochs and high headlands. Eastwards, on the mainland, sun fell full on the Torridon Hills, gilding them such that I could discern peaks I'd known underfoot – Beinn Eighe, Beinn Alligin, Liathach – and whose paths I could remember well. Shifts in light changed the sea's substance. Clouds pulling over and the sea a sheeny steel; sunshine falling and the sea a clean malachite green.

The day before embarking, I'd been over on the west side of Lewis and had collected sixteen white pebbles of gneiss from an Atlantic beach – small ballast for our long journey – and as we sailed I slipped one over the stern for every mile over ground we made. The stones rocked down to the bed of the Minch, where about 1.2 billion years ago the biggest meteor ever to hit the land area now known as the British Isles struck. Iridium blast, liquefied rock, shock metamorphism, a vapour cloud dozens of miles wide, palling over the land, and rock cast by the slam up to fifteen miles from the impact site.

When Ian was at the helm and no rope-work was needed, I rested, lying in the stern along the line of the keel, my arms out, staring up the mast and sail to the sky, as if I were wearing the boat on my back as a beetle's shell. I could feel the sea thumping alarmingly at the wood, the fists of the Blue Men pounding at the hull, only an inch or two of larch away.

Otherwise I watched and tried to learn from Ian. He relished the challenge of making our destination. He was on high-alert: monitoring wind direction, checking our trim, watching our wake, fussing with the sails, refining our route. Only now and then, when satisfied we were making the best possible speed, would he tuck his hands back into his salopettes and settle briefly on a thwart. Then a shift in the wind or my helming would have him on his feet again, plucking and testing and changing.

This pursuit of the optimal way-speed was, I came to realize, in keeping with all that Ian does. In action and in speech, he is formidably exact. He exemplifies what Robert Lowell once called 'the grace of accuracy', and his poetry, too, is distinguished by its precision. Minimalist but not gnomic, it extends his commitments both to exactitude and communication. There is no surfeit to it. His poems are short and as taut as well-set sails. Poetry represents to him not a form of suggestive vagueness, but a medium which permits him to speak in ways otherwise unavailable. I had noticed how unquestioningly poetry was accepted as his work by the people with whom Ian lived – it was regarded a skill as vulnerable to failure or success as setting lobster pots, or navigating a passage along a lee shore. I had noticed, too, how often in his talk and poetry Ian represented himself to himself in the language of seafaring and wayfaring. When he had lost his way in life, it was to the sea that he had returned for clarification and reorientation. 'Leeway', 'mooring', 'making way', 'shifts of wind', 'casting off', 'being adrift': the language of the sea and its ways was also the language of Ian's self-understanding, his personal poetics of memory-making and wayfaring. In this respect, as in others, he reminded me strongly of Thomas: the same reciprocities between loved landscape and self-perception, the same sense of poetry as a means to express what exists at the cusp of consciousness.

~

Mostly, as a sailor, I did all right that day. Oh, admittedly, there was the moment during a tack when I dropped the yard – a twelve-foot pole of laminated pine – from ten feet up onto Ian's shoulders. Some disagreement still remains between us over the nature of the incident. I was adamant that the spar's descent had been controlled, if, undeniably, over-accelerated. Ian was adamant, once he'd stopped swearing, that it had been 'purely dropped'.

On a long tack, Ian told me the story of the Blue Men of the Minch. 'In poor weather or big seas,' he said, 'the Blue Men would come for your boat.' They would haul themselves – embodiments of storm and high water, malicious mermen – dripping onto the deck, ready to pull you down. 'But then,' he said, 'they give you a single chance. The leader of the Blue Men will cast you a rope. What he'll do is he'll throw you a line of verse and one by one, everyone on board, from the skipper down, needs to offer a reply in like rhythm and metre. If one man fails, well, then you've had your chance, and the vessel is pulled down to the seabed with all its men drowned. If by some chance all can answer poetically, well, then the ship is freed and the Blue Men, those slimy bastards, slide away to find another victim.' He grinned. 'So you see, it's eloquence that gets you out of trouble.'

Stories, like paths, relate in two senses: they recount and they connect. In Siberia, the Khanty word usually translated as 'story' also means 'way'. A disputed etymology suggests that our word 'book' derives from the High German *bok*, meaning 'beech' – the tree on whose smooth bark marks and signs were often incised in order to indicate routes and paths. Our verb 'to write' at one point in its history referred specifically to track-making: the Old English *writan* meant 'to incise runic letters in stone'; thus one would 'write' a line by drawing a sharp point over and into a surface – by harrowing a track.

As the pen rises from the page between words, so the walker's feet rise and fall between paces, and as the deer continues to run as it bounds from the earth, and the dolphin continues to swim even as it leaps again and again from the sea, so writing and wayfaring are continuous activities, a running stitch, a persistence of the same seam or stream.

~

Early afternoon: the Shiants at last starting to show as dark shapes glimpsed. Outline and texture slowly firming up: the islands and their guardian skerries seen as nibs, teeth, tables, gable ends, chapels. Geese coming over in lettersets.

When we were perhaps three miles distant, a band of rain swept in from the east, bringing with it a mist that occluded both coastlines and caused the illusion that the Shiants were receding in proportion to our approach. For half an hour or so we passed over the grey water and through that grey mist, and it felt as if we might be sailing towards a mythic archipelago, a scatter of Hy-Brazils: out of the real world and into a realm beyond verification. I recalled the clouds that so often enable the transition in the *immrama* from the known to the imagined, and I thought of the disorientations of the Broomway, and the sense of frontier crossing that the mist had brought that day. Then we sailed out of the southerly edge of the rain band, and there were the islands, sharp and true to the eye.

'Oh, you can see the shapes standing clear now!' Ian said, gazing ahead. Then, quietly to himself, 'What a life, what a life.' The tide fell slack just as we reached the outstretched arm of Eilean Mhuire, the most easterly of the Shiants, the wind fell light, and *Broad Bay* trembled almost to a halt.

All that paused water, unsure of its obligations, simmering, waiting for command. The lateral drive of the ebb tide canted to the vertical play of the slack tide. Gouts of water bulging up from deep down, polishing areas of ocean. Currents billowing and knotting.

The light flimsy, filmy. The earth open on its hinges, unsure of its swing. The day fathomable and still.

Suddenly the glossy black fin and back of a minke whale rose a hundred yards astern, two yellow-striped dolphins broke water and plunged cheerily down again, and then the flow of the turned tide could be seen as a chop on the water, small standing waves that indicated the whole Minch was reversing its direction – trillions of tons of brine, a mountain range of water turning in obedience to the invisible force of the moon, starting the long slop back north and carrying our little boat with it.

We almost made it under sail and oar, despite the tide, but at last Norman – the gentle and generous skipper of the safety yacht – motored his boat over and towed us the final half-mile to the anchorage. Relieved of the need to row, exhausted by the day-long sail, I could sit and enjoy entering the arena of the Shiants. The space braced by the island group is intensely dramatic. To the north and east was Eilean Mhuire, low-slung and grass-topped. To the west the massive shattered cliffs of Garbh Eilean, falling several hundred feet almost sheer to the sea. And joined to Garbh Eilean by a slender storm beach was the long and slender Eilean an Taighe.

We neared our anchorage under Garbh Eilean in dusk light. A cliff of dolerite columns rearing above the water, and shattered columns at its foot. Even in the twilight the rock was visibly glowing with orange lichen, like a low-burnt fire.

A sound came from above, an amplified riffle: banknotes being whirred through a telling machine. It was the compound wing-noise of puffins, thousands of puffins, criss-crossing the sky with their busy roosting flights. More distantly, I could make out the sound of sociable puffin chirrups: evening gossip from the birds in their nest-spots on the cliff. I watched them fly, their flight-paths so dense, and yet none of them colliding or even seeming to adjust their routes to avoid each other, living at busy cross-purposes but convivially. I thought of each towing a thread behind it and the weft they would make with their looming.

Anchored over the sand were *An Sùlaire*, who had flown there in two-thirds of the time we had, and two other yachts, both out of Stornoway. Ian knew everyone; of course he did. We moored up among that loose flotilla, and boat-hopped by dinghy. Down in the warm cabin fug of one of the yachts, we crowded round a table; hot food was served and whisky was passed about in a tin mug. Stories were told of the day, congratulations were extended to *Broad Bay* on her passage. 'We never thought you'd make it!' 'Only two of you, and Ian a raw novice!' Voices were raised in song, welcoming, happy. And a dog – no, two dogs – skittering about on the decks. After the long hours at sea, it all felt wonderfully hospitable: the sheltering arm of the island, the tittle-tattle of the birds, the good cheer in the cabin. I grinned and couldn't stop grinning. Outside, dark fell, and the forms of the islands shifted. Slope became undetectable, fall-lines sheered, the islands turned to silhouettes, then vanished altogether.

Around midnight, Ian rowed me to land in a dinghy. The black water seemed oily as paraffin, and gleamed with a green-gold phosphorescence. Each dip of the oars set loose a storm of light: a swarm of fireflies, a wind-curl of fire-leaves outlighting the vortices. Bright particles in ignition; apprehension taking form. Ian glided in to the storm beach. I stepped on shore, globes of dolerite rolling under my feet and knocking together with the hollow clicks of billiard balls. He pushed off with a hushed goodbye. I felt my way up the cliffs to the south until I found a patch of machair a few yards long and a few wide, where I pitched my tent and settled to sleep. The stars stood sharp above. It felt odd to be on rock again, not sea, to think of the ground on which I lay extending down to the floor of the Minch. Lying there, I could still feel the day at sea, blood and water slopping about in my bag of skin, the tidal churn of my liquid body, a roll and sway in the skull. My mind beat back north against the current, thinking of the puffins' flight, the lines we leave behind us, the spacious weave, our wake, then sleep.

~

The next day, my birthday, was one of the most charmed of my life. Blue-resin sky, coppery sun, a white wind. It passed with the deep, easy happiness of a castaway day; I had no imperative other than to spend it in the most enjoyable manner possible. All but one of the other boats sailed early, leaving the Shiants in a spray of routes. Ian and I, along with a kind couple called Rob and Karen on whose boat we had been made welcome the night before, decided to stay for at least another night. The winds were changing, and we wouldn't be able to push on south to Harris, so we wanted to make the most of the islands we had reached.

Walking, exploring, beachcombing, up and over the tops of the hills and along the shores, our small group drifting along together and then pulling apart. I scrambled down to a westerly headland and fished from rock slabs – grippy with barnacles, slippery with kelp – that slanted down into the water. I caught a big pollock, five or six pounds – bronze-on-silver flanks, coal-shovel tail – lured from the weed forests with a spinner. Where it was still, the water was jelly-clear. Between the rocks it chopped and sneezed. Under arches and overhangs, it was dark as mafic glass.

I climbed to the top of Eilean an Taighe and followed its south-eastern cliff-edges. Below me were wave-smashed theatres of rock: echoey sea caves, and bird-filled zawns. Here and there I flopped onto my belly and peered over the brink, looking down to where the sea shampooed the rocks, and listening to the yabber of the seabirds. Tiers of birds were in flight, dividing the air into strata: kittiwakes and fulmars, then puffins, then gannets. I felt a sensation of candour and amplitude, of the body and mind opened up, of thought diffusing at the body's edges rather than ending at the skin. *The light as a weir pouring over the edge of Europe.*

At the high point of Eilean an Taighe was a slung hammock of rock that had been heated by the sun. At noon or so I lay shirtless and shoeless in it, a comfortable Crusoe, looking eastwards over the main channel of the Minch. Tide and wave were writing their scripts upon the blue water: white wind glyphs, curled from the air in markings that reminded me of the patterns on the backs of spiders or of Arabic lettering.

Later in the afternoon, I sat facing west towards the dropping sun and read Adam Nicolson's fine book *Sea Room*, a study of the islands by one of their former 'owners', a copy of which I had found in the island's only current habitation, a whitewashed bothy. Nicolson had inherited the islands from his father, but had never considered himself anything other than their temporary paper-possessor. He had left them free for visitors, and kept the bothy hospitably maintained and open.

'The Shiants . . . are not really a lonely place,' Nicolson remarks in the first chapter of his book. 'That is a modern illusion . . . for most of their history . . . they were profoundly related to the world in which they were set.' Their position in the centre of the Atlantic seaways meant that they had been a stopping-off point for sea journeys for 5,000 years, a safe harbour in the mid-Minch. 'Our modern view of such [islands] as orphans or widows, drenched in a kind of Dickensian poignancy of abandonment, is, on the whole, wrong,' he continues. They are in fact:

> the hub for millions of bird and animal lives, as dynamic as any trading floor, a theatre of competition and enrichment. They are the centre of their own universe, the organising node in a web of connections, both human and natural, which extends first to the surrounding seas, then to the shores on all sides and beyond that, along the seaways that stretch for thousands of miles along the margins of the Atlantic and on into the heartlands of Europe.

I like that image of the 'web of connections': the seaways leading, like Thomas's land paths, 'from everywhere to everywhere', joining deep ocean to coastal shelf to estuary to river to back country. I also recognize Nicolson's account of having been chronically 'shaped' by his 'island times' on the Shiants. 'The place has entered me,' he wrote adoringly, 'it has coloured my life like a stain.'

Small islands have often inspired dreams of total knowledge in those who love them. I have read the work of several islomaniacs over the years – Tim Robinson's deep topographies of the Irish Aran islands, Nicolson on the Shiants and Lawrence Durrell on Corfu, as well as Nan Shepherd's study of her inland-island of the Cairngorm massif, and Gilbert White's record of his Hampshire parish of Selborne. All these people had been animated at first by the delusion of a comprehensive totality, the belief that they might come to know their chosen place utterly because of its boundedness. And all had, after long acquaintance, at last understood that familiarity with a place will lead not to absolute knowledge but only ever to further enquiry. For Shepherd, the Cairngorm massif was not a crossword to be cracked, full of encrypted ups and downs. Greater understanding of the mountain's interrelations served only to reveal other realms of incomprehension. She did not relish her discoveries so much as her ignorance: 'The mind cannot carry away all that the mountain has to give,' she wrote, 'nor does it always believe possible what it has carried away.'

Down on the storm beach, as dusk approached, I spent an hour building a small domed and chambered cairn out of dolerite, for the pleasure of the act of construction. It was two feet or so high, with corbelled sides curving up to a capstone roof, and its open doorway – lintel-topped and buttress-braced – faced due east, ready to be flooded by the rising sun. The smoothed dolerite boulders were shiny black when I brought them out of the sea, but they dried to a wolf grey. I found and kept a transom-ended stone of gneiss, fist-sized and coopered with a quartz band. Scouring the beach, I discovered a single white stone, the size and shape of an ostrich egg, and I placed that upright in the centre of the cairn. I was pleased when I'd finished the structure: it looked like a miniature Maes Howe, which would last until the next big tide or visitor's boot.

As the sun finally fell, I lay on the machair, hands behind my head. Time, briefly, felt not absent (the islander's dream of ahistory) but rather multiplied in its forms. Orange mites traversed boulders. *Xanthoria parietina* photosynthesized. Puffins shifted in their roosts, the tide gathered northwards pace. Rainwater that had fallen three days earlier filtered down inside the fissures of Eilean an Taighe, the body of the pollock stiffened in the black bucket by the bothy's door, and the sun loosed its summer light, as it had done for uncountable years, across the sea, the island and my body, a liquid so rich that I wanted to eat it, store it, make honey of it for when winter came.

That night Ian cooked the fish on the bothy stove. Whisky was passed around. A fire was lit, the wood spat. Ian spoke of a friend who had sailed a currach, the hull of which was made from hazel wicker and eight cow-hides, from County Mayo in Ireland across to Iona on the Scottish west coast, following the route taken by St Columba in the sixth century.

The fire died. Ash frosted the logs. The light dimmed. Late gold rip along the horizon line.

I slept again that night on the machair ledge and heard geese crying as they passed through the wind gap, over the storm beach.

~

Dolphins, a school of seventy or eighty of them, met us head-on as we sailed from the Shiants on the morning tide, a dozen or so breaking from purpose and coming to play, folding back on their set course to swim with us, swerving round and under the bow – briefly our outriders, our police escort.

We had rowed to *Broad Bay* not long after dawn, raised the sail, then at high water had sailed over the rock teeth that jag up in the northern gap between Eilean Mhuire and Garbh Eilean, the wind fluky, spooky in its sudden shifts. The weather had changed. Rain-squalls ahead, the wind higher but still from the south, so we reefed the sail and ran downwind, straight into the oncoming dolphins.

What a sail home it was! We made five knots, probably the top speed of *Broad Bay*, though in our little boat in that wind it felt far faster. Ian smiled proudly at the way she was taking the pace of hull on water. Our blue-white wake was brief behind us, broken quickly up in the chop. Ian taught me how to 'surf' a boat when running downwind in a decent swell. 'Just two slow little flicks of the tiller,' he said, '*this* way, to steer off the wind a touch – and then *this* way, to fill the sail again, so the boat boosts on and catches the wave that's passing under you. It's like a surfer kicking off to pick up a crest.'

I nodded, unsure.

'The only way to learn, really, is to do it.'

He was right, and once I'd learnt the trick of it I couldn't get enough. It felt as if a current or charge, the summoned energy of the ocean, were rushing along the helm, up my arm and down my spine. The feeling of connection to the water was immense, muscular, as if the Blue Men were lending their strength to my shoulder.

'Aye, we're cooking with gasoline now,' said Ian gladly. I surfed, and he started to tell me more old sea stories, bawdy and salty, well travelled along the sea roads.

By Kebock Head the rain set in. Hard rain plucking up the sea, and blistering on the creosoted thwarts. I shivered at the helm, and to keep my mind from the cold Ian talked me through *Broad Bay* as a boat, starting at the bow and ending at the tiller. He knew her biography as well as that of any long-term lover, and he told it to me as a story: how she had been built in Deerness in Orkney in 1912, and then registered in Kirkwall. How her hull was clinker-built, with ten overlapping planks of larch on each side of the keel, a method which has not changed since Viking days, and which suited the working boats of the northern and western Atlantic, making it possible for them to manage steep seas and strong tides while carrying substantial loads. How the port and starboard frames of *Broad Bay*'s hull were subtly different because of the builder's response to the particular qualities of each larch plank.

'*Broad Bay* was a 1912 boat; at least, she was made new in 1912,' said Ian, 'and as far as the insurance company is concerned she is just shy of her century, but in fact the only original part of her left is the keel, the spine of the boat running bow to stern; that and sections of the stem and stern posts.

'She's all made of opportunities,' he added. 'See the oak pieces near the bow, for taking the strain of the tack-hooks? They're laminated from oak taken from a house that stood along the route on which we're sailing, right over there.' He pointed westwards to the Lewis coast. 'That house was owned by Sopwith, so the oak from an English aeronautical baron from Kensington is now being used to keep the Hebridean maritime traditions going strong away up here! And the knees are salvage wood, ancient oak preserved by mud, which were found in the mud of the Hoil. They had a fine curve to them and are superbly strong; I think they came from an old herring drifter.'

He explained the sociology of boat construction, the importance of having neighbourly or kindred materials next to each other. 'You don't want to put galvanized on bronze,' he said, gesturing up at the bronze sheave in the lug-rig at the top of the mast. 'Stainless is closer, a first cousin in the metal family. You need to make sure that the woods, and above all the metals, are compatible.' I thought of how for Ian, objects and materials, like people and language, all had their fitness for purpose verified by use. Words and people, halyards and hawsers, they all got put under pressure. Some sheared, splintered and gave. Others held – and they were the ones to keep to hand.

Later, back into the Hoil. The tiller feeling like a bony extension of my arm. Slicks of fuel from the big boats making gneiss-patterns in the water. We helmed alongside the quay, and as we slid into the berth Ian was already talking about the next voyage, a voyage north.

6

WATER – NORTH

The men of Ness, the *guga* & the Rock — Green Rona, black Sula — 'At the hazard of their lives' — The dark arts — Map-reading as clairvoyance — Wind-histories — A weather window — Sailing from Port of Ness — Dilworth's kist — Placation vs sacrifice — Whalebacks, stramashes & clutters — 'Disturbances to the expected' — 'The face of the water' — The bird-bung — Roomy darkness — Steering by the North Star — A stately quadrille — Raising Sula Sgeir — Circumnavigation by oar & sail — The gannet in the gneiss — Heart-squeeze.

> In antiquity, Irish scholars were known . . . for their practice of '*navigatio*' . . . a journey undertaken by boat . . . a circular itinerary of exodus and return . . . The aim was to undergo an apprenticeship to signs of strangeness with a view to becoming more attentive to the meanings of one's own time and place – geographical, spiritual, intellectual.
>
> Richard Kearney (2006)

Listen now. Listen to the singing of the *guga* men on the bare rock of Sula Sgeir, hunched in a stone bothy on that little island far out in the North Atlantic, on an August morning nearly sixty years ago. If I could sing it or play it to you I would, but I cannot, so this will have to do. The scene: a rough hut, six feet high at its tallest, built out of blades of gneiss, its cracks plugged with rags. In its centre a peat fire, above which hangs a storm lantern that lends light to the space. Rough stone benches around the edges, on which the men are sitting, wearing tweed jackets and heavy wool jumpers. The mutter of the fire. The wind moving outside, testing the bothy.

The singing begins. First comes the leader, his voice low and rich, incanting the verses of the day in Gaelic – '*ach is e an gràdh as mò dhiubh so*', 'and the greatest of these is charity' – his voice dipping then rising at the end of each verse. The lesson ends. A pause. A cough to clear the throat. Then the leader offers a high line from a psalm, his voice gaining in volume: pure notes sung from the throat and chest. This is the 'throwing' of the line. The other men answer in song, the sound swelling to fill the bothy. Another line is thrown, followed, completed. Shades in the singing of cotton-field gospel, and hints too of the muezzin's call. These are fire-songs of worship, consolation and comradeship: song as devotion and as stay against the storm. These are the *guga* men of Ness, the gannet hunters, singing in the Year of Our Lord 1953.

Sula Sgeir sits around forty miles due north of the most northerly point of the Isle of Lewis; the same distance from the Outer Hebridean coast as St Kilda. Its form is geological-brutalist. It is a jaggy black peak of gneiss, the topmost summit of a submarine mountain, and it is home to around 10,000 pairs of gannets and – for a few years – the only black-browed albatross in the northern hemisphere.* The sea has bored clean through the southern part of the island to form a series of caves and tunnels. In big Atlantic storms, the waves break right over the top of Sula Sgeir.

Eleven miles to the east is its partner island of North Rona, *yang* to Sula Sgeir's *yin*: a tilted slab of green pasture which has been inhabited on and off for thousands of years by saints, farmers, shepherds and naturalists. St Ronan, one of the early Celtic Christian

* 'Albert Ross' the albatross first appeared on Bass Rock in the Firth of Forth in 1967, then relocated in 1972 to the vast gannetry at Hermaness on Unst in the Shetlands, to which island he returned annually for more than twenty years, before disappearing for a decade, and then visiting Sula Sgeir between 2005 and 2007. He seems to have been wandering the Scottish gannetries in search of a gannet partner, gannets bearing a passing resemblance to albatrosses as they do, and the 700,000 female members of Albert Ross's own species all residing, inconveniently, south of the equator.

monks who travelled by the seaways, is supposed to have been the first dweller on North Rona, arriving there as part of his search for 'a place of his own resurrection' (in the phrasing of the *peregrini*). Ruins of a chapel supposedly raised by him remain.

Journeys of varying purpose have been made for thousands of years on that northerly bearing, along that sea road leading up from the Butt of Lewis to Sula Sgeir and North Rona. On first sighting the two islands from the south, it feels as if you have sailed into a parable. There they are, forty or more miles out in the Atlantic and eleven miles apart. It's implausible enough that land should exist there, in the empty water between Scotland and Iceland, and then surprising that the contrast between them should be so strong: green fertile Rona, black hostile Sula Sgeir. At a distance they appear more allegorical than real: the Pasture and the Rock – a choice offered to the seafarer. The earliest seafarers understandably chose the Pasture. St Ronan's sister, Brenhilda, is alleged to have tried to live on Sula Sgeir: she was found dead with a seabird's nest built inside her ribcage. Lesson learnt. Since Brenhilda, Sula Sgeir has been mostly left to the seals, fulmars, puffins, gannets – and, briefly each summer, to the men of Ness in North Lewis who come to the island for a fortnight to hunt the *guga*, the gannet chicks.

The first record of the *guga* hunt dates to 1549, when the men rowed out in an open boat to cull the gannets and brought the bodies back as ballast. The tradition continues today, with very little change. Numbers vary: there are usually ten men, sometimes a dozen. But landfall is still made in the one possible landing place, in the main *geo* (bay) of Sula Sgeir, where the rock drops in a chute to the water. It's still a perilous landing, but it's the best on offer. When there's any swell the *geo* becomes a choppy mass of waves moving in cross-directions, bouncing off the walls and mashing together. These days the bothies are covered with plastic, then tarpaulins, then netting, then weighted down with more stones. But the men still share the bothies with the petrels who nest in the crannies (charcoal-coloured birds with white-flashed tails, who spend all day at sea and come ashore with high cries at night). The men still wrap rags around their heads at night to stop the earwigs that infest the bothies from crawling into their ears. The two weeks on the island itself are still dangerous; the Sabbath remains a rest day.

The first day on the Rock is spent setting up, and then the cull begins. The men are tasked with different jobs: there are catchers, killers, scorchers, scrubbers, pluckers and pilers. The cliff-men head down, roped, on ledges slippery with guano, with long nooses on poles and cudgels in hand. *Reach, noose, grab, crack*. The corpses are returned to the summit of Sula Sgeir, where 'the Factory' has been established. The birds are plucked, singed, seared. Then their wings are chopped off, they're scrubbed again, split open and emptied of their innards, and their evacuated bodies are placed on 'the Pile' – a great altar-cairn of *guga* corpses. So it proceeds. On the middle Sabbath comes rest, prayer and song. If summer storms blow in, the men sit them out in the bothies, for there's no working the Rock in big wind or big waves. Once the effort is over, they sail south again for Lewis. Crowds await their landfall at the Ness harbour, eager to buy and eat the birds. On a *guga* hunter's last visit to the Rock, before he becomes too old to return, he builds a cairn to mark his relationship with the island. Seen from the sea, Sula Sgeir's outline is prickly with these cairns.

The *guga* that survive the harvest will, eventually, stagger down the cliff ledges until they fall off and splash into the sea. They are water-bound for a couple of weeks, riding the waves and fasting, until they are light enough to take flight and make their maiden voyages: winging down the west coast of Britain, the north-west peninsulas of France, through the Bay of Biscay, along the Atlantic facade, following their own sea roads – their migration paths – until at last they reach their winter home off West Africa.

For centuries the men reached Sula Sgeir by open boat, rowing or sailing. 'There is in Ness a most venturous set of people who for a few years back, at the hazard of their lives, went [to the island] in an open six-oared boat without even the aid of a compass,' wrote the Reverend Donald McDonald in a 1797 census report. The last group of *guga* men to reach Sula Sgeir under sail did so in the summer of 1953. Since then they have travelled in fishing trawlers: still a hard five-hour journey. The precise time of the *guga* hunters' departure each year is, by tradition, a well-kept secret.

~

'Time for an hour or two of the dark arts,' said Ian, a few days after we had got back from the Shiants. He went upstairs and returned with three charts, a tidal atlas and what looked like a brass gannet's skull with a wine cork on the end of its beak. He unrolled the charts on the kitchen table, opened the tidal atlas, popped the wine cork off the gannet's beak and squeezed the skull's hinged circle, such that the points of the dividers – for this is what they were – first crossed and then became legs, with which he could stride across the charts.

Sea charts, even more than land maps, can lure you into hubris. All that featureless water – what could possibly go wrong? On maps of mountainous terrain there are warnings: the hachures showing cliffs, the bunched contours indicating steep ground and fall-lines. Charts record headlands, skerries and mean depths of water, but because most sea features are volatile – temporary functions of wind, tide and current – there is no way of reliably charting them. The act of chart-reading, even more than the act of map-reading, is part data-collection and part occultism. Sailors, like mountaineers, practise their map clairvoyance based on intuition and superstition as well as on yielded information.

I watched Ian run his fingertips over the chart, tracing possible paths of sail, fathoming the future conditions of the sea based on memory and inference. *Given this wind, this boat, this crew . . . given that tide, given this tack* . . . The further you get from land, the longer you get into the journey, the more rapidly the hypotheticals multiply. *If we've failed to make this channel, that headland, by still water, by the turn of tide, we would have fled for here, or perhaps for there* . . . He read down through his fingertips, the chart's flat blues and greens popping up into relief in his mind. *The waves here, at this time, in these conditions, will be unproblematic; but here they will stand up straight and hard like a wall.* Wind-histories as well as wind-futures need to be taken into account, for the sea can have a long memory for past agitations. If a wind has blown strongly from a certain quarter for days, the sea's motion will continue to register this even once the wind has dropped. It takes time to settle itself, to revise its inclinations.

The question preoccupying Ian was which sea road to follow next. The plan was, for sure, to sail out of Port of Ness on the far north of Lewis. From there, we would go either east round Cape Wrath and 'across the top' – the Pentland Firth – to Orkney: a thirty- to forty-hour continuous sail, one way. Or we would head due north, away up to Sula Sgeir and Rona. Ian placed one hand on top of the other and laid them on the chart, then looked off into mid-air. The shipping forecast murmured in the background: *Malin,*

Hebrides, Minch. Light southerly, 3 or 4. Cyclonic veering south-south-easterly for a time. 'Good wind strength for a small boat,' he said. 'Just a touch light, if anything.'

It took ninety minutes of assessing and second-guessing for him to arrive at a decision. Then he pinched the legs of the dividers together, pushed their sharp points back into the cork and laid them with a clunk across the chart.

North to Sula Sgeir, the Gannet Island, it was – and in *Jubilee*.

Jubilee was a *sgoth Niseach*: a class of Lewisian working open boat, lug-rigged, clinker-built and double-ended, designed for sturdy seaworthiness up there off the Butt of Lewis, where the Atlantic currents meet the currents of the Minch. Twenty-seven feet long, she had been built in 1935 by the MacLeod family from Ness and had remained a Ness boat for decades, before being re-registered to Stornoway. She was, really, a larger cousin of *Broad Bay*, and she was the boat in which the last *guga* hunters to reach Sula Sgeir under sail had travelled. 'I've spoken to one of the men who took *Jubilee* to Sula Sgeir,' my Lewis friend Finlay MacLeod told me before I left for Ness, 'and he described being in the *geo* there in bad weather, and seeing her sides literally squeezed inwards by the pressure of the waves bouncing around there.'

It was *Jubilee* that Ian wanted to sail to Sula Sgeir and back in this, her seventy-fifth year. He was eager to make this historic voyage, following the path of the *guga* men and the line of a gannet's flight, out to Sula Sgeir and back again.

~

We caught the afternoon tide from Port of Ness harbour. The aim was to sail without stopping through evening and night, and to raise

Sula Sgeir around dawn. The harbour: turquoise water over sand, the smell of diesel, sun hot on the concrete, rusted ladder rungs. Kelp popping, the squeak of buoys and fenders, old Ness men fishing off the pier.

As we loaded up the dry-bags and sea chests, people began to gather to see *Jubilee* safely away, for word had got round North Lewis that she would try for Sula Sgeir. *Jubilee* herself was beautiful, a gleaming red hull, with black-and-white checkerboard markings around the side and black-stained interior timbers. She was heavy, solid and loved as a craft. We stepped the mast, a pole of Douglas fir which took four people to lift and secure it. Then we slid out of the harbour by oar and engine, threading a series of breakwaters, through the mess of waves at the cliff's nose and into open sea.

Raise the sail, shake out the reefs, haul on the halyard, tighten the sheet. A little kick as the wind takes her northwards over high humping swells, lifting and dropping. People on the headland waving us off. Sun glint on blue water. Long fallows between the waves.

Ian had sailed out of Lewis for more than forty years, following his sea routes to and from St Kilda, the Orkneys, the Shetlands, Norway, the Baltic and Brittany. But he had never before got out to Sula Sgeir: the weather had always foxed him. He was excited, but wary. The forecast had showed a weather window – light airs, sunshine – but it was due to close in two days, with big westerlies blowing in. In a small open boat in big open seas, care needs to be taken. So another boat was sailing with us as our good shepherd: an ocean-going yacht called the *Hebridean*, which would keep a weather eye out for us.

On the morning of our departure, I'd met a friend of mine called Steve Dilworth in Stornoway. Steve lives on the south-east coast of the Isle of Harris, and is one of the most interesting sculptors currently at work in the world. He had something for me – an object to carry on the Sula Sgeir voyage. It came in a Tupperware box, was packaged in newspaper and bubble-wrap, and was shaped like a big flattened egg, which sharpened to a point at one end. Black in its centre and white-edged, it was the size of my fist and very heavy. It reminded me of a guillemot's head.

'It's a kist,' Steve said cheerily, 'a chest. Its main body is dolerite. I cored out the centre of the dolerite and put a glass phial in the hole. The phial contains seawater I gathered during a big storm twenty-five years ago. I used bronze wire to bind the phial in place, and then I capped the sides of the dolerite with some old ivory.' The surface of the kist was cool and smooth, even where the ivory met the dolerite.

It was, he explained, a votive offering: a storm charm. All maritime cultures have lore about objects and substances that are thrown into the seas to calm them when a craft is in danger. Ale, oil or blood are poured overboard to soothe the waves. Coins, bodies, swords, screeds of wool or gansey are yielded to sate the maelstrom. There are two kinds of offering: placatory and sacrificial. The placatory is assuaging (oil on troubled waters); the sacrificial is substitutionary – a minor loss sustained in the present (the object lost to the sea) replacing a future greater loss (the boat lost to the sea). Steve's kist was sacrificial in kind.

'I reckoned that these objects, these offerings, would have to be beautiful if they were to be offerings,' he said. 'Something it would pain you to lose to the waves.' I felt reassured to have the kist, and knew that if the seas rose I would have no hesitation in slipping it over the checkerboard side of the boat.

'Take care not to eat any *guga* if you're offered some,' Steve warned me just before we parted.

'Is it considered bad luck?' I asked.

'No', he said. 'It just tastes awful. Oily and chewy and acrid. I have no idea what all the fuss is about. I know a Lewisian crofter who, when I asked him whether he liked gannet meat, replied, "I gave a piece to the dog and it spent all week licking its arse to take away the taste." '

~

There were five of us in the crew. Ian. A young Lewisman, David, who had just joined the Merchant Navy at the age of sixteen. Colin, the shipwright from the Shiants trip. Diyanne, who sailed community boats over at Ullapool on the mainland. All of them loved the sea and loved old boats. Four highly able sailors – and me.

Another minke whale saw us off from near the Butt of Ness, feasting through a surface shoal of sand eels, gannets rocketing down around it to surface with bills full of silver. *Jubilee* wallowed northwards in light air, over high hills of swell. The sea resembled a shaken tablecloth, rippling humps of blue water up which the boat climbed and down which she ran. A sliding bump beneath the nearby water, raising it without breaking it, like a tongue moving under a cheek, then a sharp fin seen: a single dolphin.

Ian called the long waves 'whalebacks'. He was a connoisseur of waves, and I was starting to learn his vernacular for different kinds of water. A 'stramash' was the boiling effect where currents met and mixed. Where they clashed there was a 'clutter'. Small waves 'swithered'. Extremely disturbed water was either 'bouncy' or 'jabbly'. 'Long ones' were the big, fast, purposeful waves, smooth in profile but intent in action, that 'scratched their backs' on the keels of boats. 'Big bastard long ones' were problem causers: they offered what he called 'rough greeting', breaking over the stern or bow of low-beamed vessels. To me, the surface of the sea was the fluid equivalent of white noise or Classical Chinese. To Ian it was legible as a children's book.

I was realizing that Ian had two simultaneous states on the water. One was quietly and simply joyful to be at sea. The other, a background process humming away, was analytical: his mind gathering data from sources and of types that I barely knew existed; from subtleties of wind, wave, and waymark, from smells, from what he had called in a poem 'the bounce of light from incidental land' and the 'elaborate counter-physics' of tidal water. Each acquisition of information shifted the outline and position of the whole. He practised a pilot-poetics, and interpreted the sea with a rabbinical intensity of study. 'You need to look for disturbances to the expected,' he told me, 'be alert to unforeseen interactions.'

Watching Ian sail, I thought of Mark Twain, who studied as a river-pilot on the Mississippi. For Twain the river was a capricious text, which punished literalists and allegorists alike for the fixities of their interpretations. Horace Bixby, the veteran steamboat captain who apprenticed Twain, taught him the need to read surface for depth: how small perturbations might infer large submerged truths: the 'long slanting line' that suggested a reef which would 'knock the boat's brains out'. Under Bixby's tutelage, Twain learnt to steer his paddle steamer through the shifting sandbanks of the river, and to dodge snags and wrecks. Bixby gave the young Samuel Clemens his illustrious pen name ('Mark Twain' is a measurement of water depth, meaning 'two fathoms deep'), and forced him to learn the river 'by heart', standing in the prow for days, 'reading' the surface in silence. 'The face of the water,' wrote Twain, 'in time, became a wonderful book – a book that was a dead language to the uneducated passenger, but which told its mind to me without reserve . . . it was not a book to be read once and thrown aside, for it had a new story to tell every day.'

~

We settled into the patterns of a long sail in an open boat. Spells on the tiller: the course due north, a meridian bearing. Sandwiches and hot drinks when not helming. A watch-rota scribbled on the back of an envelope. 'That's the roster of the sleepless,' said Ian.

The sail flapping and gasping, sucking for air in the light breeze, bucking like a dying fish. Wildcat squeals of the outboard now and then. The land diminishing, details slipping away, Lewis thinning from cliff to band to line to nothing. *The boat, an open boat, has left the sight of known marks.* In a low wind on a single bearing in an open boat, time stretches, expands. There are hours for everything, it feels. An unhurriedness seeps into you. So we sailed happily on, into the long northern dusk, telling stories as we went, up and down the hills of water, past porpoises and under kittiwakes making their cat's cradles of flight, and at last into a darkness that seemed to lift from the sea rather than falling from the sky, starting as a black dye upon the surface and then wicking upwards into the cloudless air.

Ian told a story, an old one that I had encountered before. Versions of it exist near the gannetries of the Irish and Scottish west coasts, revised to freshness with each new telling. A small open boat is sailing out to St Kilda – or to Rona, or the Blaskets (choose your distant island) – when, far out of sight of land, it passes through a herring shoal so profuse that the surface of the sea seems firm enough to walk on. The herring brings the predators: whales, dolphins and gannets, gannets in their thousands, thumping down from the sky into the sea all around the boat.

'Suddenly,' said Ian, 'there comes a noise like a firearm being discharged. *Pack!*'

A gannet has dived by error into the open boat itself and there it is, up near the bow, stone dead, its body limp and its beak driven clean through the timber of the hull, its great wings, six feet for sure from tip to tip, splayed on the thwarts. Twenty miles from land in the big Atlantic waves and with a hole in the hull; well, that should have been death to the boat and its people. But then they realize that the gannet's impact has been so powerful that it has plugged the hole it made.

'So they sail anxiously on, with the head of the gannet buried like a bung in the hull.'

At last they reach the island, Hirta, in the Kilda group, with the weather worsening and the waves building. The islanders gather on the shore to help them in, and they see to their astonishment, as the boat's bow is lifted up by the last big wave, the black beak of the gannet sticking out like a short sharp keel.

I told a story about Tory Island, twelve miles off the Donegal coast, to which I had gone two summers previously. One night while I was on the island I heard a man shout, 'There's a dolphin in the harbour!' and I ran down to the jetty to find an astonishing sight. A Labrador dog was in the water, barking and paddling in circles, while around the dog played an eight-foot dolphin, blue in hue when on the surface but green-grey at depth. So I joined the two of them, stripping off to my shorts and then walking down the harbour steps and into the clear grey icy water of the sea. For fifteen minutes or so I swam with the two creatures. The dolphin was curious, familiar. It lay on its side beneath me, nuzzling my ankle, or bottled up to watch me with black cheeky eyes. Once it retreated to a distance of ten yards, then disappeared, before rising up sharkishly. Its skin felt blood-warm to the touch, and smooth as neoprene.

Later, an islander told me that the dolphin had been coming to the harbour for a year and a half, seeking company after the death of its mate, whose corpse had washed up on Tory's south shore. The dolphin had befriended the dog, with whom he now often swam. He also said that he had once seen 'upwards of a thousand dolphins' in Tory Sound, all heading westwards. The parents and their children leapt together in perfect synchrony, he said, 'as though each child were stuck to its mother's side'.

~

By nightfall we were in fully open ocean. The first stars showed, and then they came fast and then faster, speckling the cloudless sky, dozens more a minute. I cannot now describe the feeling of emptiness and remoteness that attended us then, the like of which I have only ever known when out at dusk in high mountains in winter, coming to the end of a long day's walk with the sun showing red on the snow, and a sleeping place still to find. *Jubilee* carried no lights. Ian would occasionally flick a torch-beam onto the sail, offering a glow to any unseen ship. Otherwise the dark and the sea extended about us with no implication of limit. We passed through what the philosopher William James once called '*roomy*' darkness.

My watch turn was at midnight. I groped along to the stern, over sleeping bodies. A whisper from the dark, Diyanne handing the tiller over to me: 'It's simpler to steer by the North Star than by the compass. Look for Polaris; it's easy to locate, though it's not the brightest star in the sky. Find the two stars on the far side of the Plough – see them? Now, follow to where they're pointing, keep going, one star, two stars, and there's Polaris, blazing away. Just hold the North Star steady between halyard and spar and sail on up.'

I felt glad to fulfil this oldest of celestial navigation techniques. The instruction rounded into a couplet – *Sail on up by the old North Star; hold it steady between halyard and spar* – and the lines rocked in my head as I steered. The water gurgled and slapped, as if it had thickened. I thought of Pytheas, the Greek voyager who had sailed north from France in 325 BC, following established trade routes to begin with – the 'tin road', the 'amber road' – and then just kept going, pausing on Lewis to erect his gnomon and take readings of sun height and day length, before sailing still further north, until he reached a latitude where the sea turned gelid with the cold and the air palled with freezing mists, such that the atmosphere resembled what Pytheas enigmatically called a 'sea-lung' (*pneumon thalassios*).

I have heard a sailor describe night-sailing in the busy waters of the English Channel as a deeply relaxing experience. At such times, he said, the world is reduced to code: the lights carried by the different vessels, the shared rules known by all participants as to who should give way to whom. The number of data-streams is minimized; inputs limited to night-murmurs on the VHF, blips on the radar and sequences of lights. Provided that the codes are correctly interpreted by all participants, tankers will slide darkly past dinghies, ship will pass ship, and so the arrangement will decorously proceed. What it most resembles, he said, is a quadrille – a stately dance of vast and mutual order. There is also, he added, a calming relationship of disproportion between the nature of the game played and the stakes wagered, in that proof of competence is derived only from absence of catastrophe.

That night, though, far out into the North Atlantic, there were no lights to be seen, for there was no shipping. The deep-water lanes that ducted the big freighters stayed much closer to the Lewis mainland. There was the *Hebridean*, 500 yards or so off our port stern, its green starboard lamp winking as it rose and fell in the waves. Otherwise, the only lights were celestial. The star-patterns, the grandiose slosh of the Milky Way. Jupiter, blazing low to the east, so brightly that it laid a lustrous track across the water, inviting us to step out onto its swaying surface. The moon, low, a waxing half, richly coloured – a red-butter moon, setting down its own path on the water. The sea was full of luminescent plankton, so behind us purled our wake, a phosphorescent line of green and yellow bees, as if the hull were setting a hive aswarm beneath us. We were at the convergence of many paths of light, which flexed and moved with us as we headed north.

At some point I handed over the helm, crept forward to the bows and tried to sleep while the boat slipped on into the night. I lay on my back, head on a fender, hands pocketed for warmth, gazing at the sky. That night was the last of the summer Perseid meteor showers, and shooting stars came most minutes: bright dashes, retinal scratches. I counted a hundred and then gave up.

I hadn't expected this of the night sail; the serenity it induced in me. Perhaps the cold, the fatigue of the early hours and the lulling chuckle of the water were involved with the effect. Stray images drifted into my mind, thoughts from other tides and oceans. Perhaps it was the mirroring of the sky's stars and the water's phosphorescence which made me experience the illusion of absent volume to our boat and its people, such that it seemed we were made of paper, laid flat like a model ship ready to pass through the mouth of a bottle before being sprung back upright by the tug of a thread, or as if we were sailing on through a narrow mineral seam between air and water, up that old and invisible sea road.

~

A hand on the shoulder, shaking me awake, and I sat up to find that I had woken into winter. There was Sula Sgeir, less than a mile away, surf sloshing about its foot, and it was covered in snow. Winter had come during that spellbound night; we had somehow sailed from August into January. No, of course, it wasn't snow – it was birds. Gannets, thousands of white gannets and their white guano and their white feathers, on every ledge of every cliff, and the air above the boat filled with flying gannets: their stout nicotine-yellow necks, their stiff-winged glides. Between the gannets, fulmars and kittiwakes were cutting the sky up in arcs and curves, leaving – to my night eyes – trails of light like the traces on an overexposed photograph. I looked up at the sky of birds, feeling vertiginous, unstable. Lines from one of Ian's poems came into my head: 'Wheeling flights / would drag you sky-high / if your wide feet failed / to suck the deck.'

Ian was pointing, saying, 'Look over there, look there!' A battered fishing trawler anchored a few hundred yards away: *The Heather Isle*. On her decks stood men, some facing us, others looking to the island. It was the *guga* hunters, ready to start their two weeks on the Rock, crashing into the *geo* to begin the work of unloading. We had by chance coincided with them to the hour.

Jubilee sloshed and rocked in the swell. Rona was a wedge of green to the east. Death and murder were everywhere underway. For Sula is a killing ground: a gathering point for predators and prey. Seals come for the big fish, gannets come for the herring and the sand eels, skuas come for the adult gannets, and the men come for the *gugas*. I watched gangs of skua pursue single gannets: their method was to fly above a gannet, drop onto its back, force it down onto the sea, smash its skull with their beaks until the gannet was dizzied, then paddle its head underwater with their feet until it vomited up the contents of its stomach, which the skua then ate. But other gannets were on their own hunts, slamming down into the water after fish invisible to me; you could see how they might pierce a hull. They came back out of the sea like white flowers unfurling. Fold, tuck, dive, unfurl: avian origami.

~

We boiled up black coffee in the galley bucket, then two of us set to the oars and rowed *Jubilee* once round Sula Sgeir; a circumnavigation under sail and oar. Ian was keen that we carry out this ritual circling to mark our passage.

It took us an hour to get round the island. Cormorants stood cruciform on low rocks, drying their wings. We turned the point of Pal a' Cheiteanaich, went through the narrow gap between the black skerries of Bogha Leathainn and Dà Bhogha Ramhacleit, sharp stacks over which the sea foamed, past An Sgor Mhòr, past Sròin na Lic on which the lighthouse stood, past the *geo* and Bealach an t-Suidhe. Sula Sgeir, a scrap of rock hardly ever inhabited, bears almost thirty toponyms.

As we rowed into the *geo*, we saw the *guga* men standing on the steep rock that slopes to the landing point. They had stopped their unloading and formed up in a group. They looked out at us, unsmiling. Their leader, Dodds, was in the centre. They knew the boat, and they knew Ian, but the implication was clear enough: *Keep away, this is our day, our rock*. Ian waved a greeting, they nodded back and we left the *geo*.

So we ended our circumnavigation near the southerly cliffs where the rock jutted out like the prow of a ship. A guillemot glided above, its sharp black head reminding me that I had carried Dilworth's kist with me and not needed it.

Suddenly Diyanne pointed. 'Look there,' she said, 'a cross in the rock!'

And there was, too: a rough cross twenty feet or so high made of pinkish rock, set into the dark gneiss prow of the headland: geology as theology.

Then she called out again: 'No, it's not a cross, it's a diving gannet.' And it was, too; we all saw it to be so. The downstroke of the cross tapering to a point was the bird's body and beak, and the cross-stroke was the bird's wings. It was as if, like the bird in Ian's story, a gannet had plunged down into the gneiss and crashed down through the rock to petrify right there on the prow of the island. Shock metamorphosis. I thought of a sentence I had read in a geological guide to the islands: *Garnets can sometimes be found within Lewisian gneiss.* I'd misread it first time through – *Gannets can sometimes be found within Lewisian gneiss* – and now my error had come true.*

~

Jubilee had made it safely to the Rock, but she had to make it safely back as well – and the gales were coming. So we set our bearing to 180 degrees, and began the day-long journey due south to Port of Ness, back down the sea road.

Our wake showed cream and mint. Sula Sgeir retreated behind us, from mountain to eave to thumbprint. The sea smelt silver. The day grew and the air thinned until we could see Suilven, Foinaven, Arkle and the other Sutherland hills away to the east.

* The cross/gannet is likely to have been a band of gneiss enriched by pink alkali feldspar, formed at some point in the Pre-Cambrian, and crumpled into its current shape by subsequent compression.

'The water ahead might be a wee bit jabbly,' said Ian as we came back into Port of Ness harbour that evening, and so it was: six- or seven-foot sharp peaks of wave where the cliff protruded, and then a big sloshing swell in the harbour itself. We ghosted in between the breakwaters in a manner that left me light-stomached and Ian exhilarated; David helming delicately, and Diyanne and I leaning out like twin figureheads from the bow, watching for depths and distances from the rock and the concrete, calling urgent nervous warnings – 'To starboard a touch!' 'Just over to port!' – until we nosed alongside the high quay, and threw out plump pink fenders that were squeezed like hearts between hull and quay, and so came at last to a halt.

I climbed the rusty-runged ladder of the breakwater and staggered along the quay. That night I lay in bed in Stornoway with a dream sea still rolling over and through me and gannets flying across the ceiling, while the real gales rose as promised outside over the north, from Iceland all across to Norway.

7

PEAT

An alley of stones — Cutting for sign — Route as rumour, route as folklore — Peat & gneiss — Manus's Stones — Finlay MacLeod — Libation & fornication — Functional land art — Holding eras in plain sight — Geography & history as consubstantial — Phobus — Place-learning & path-following — Disturbances to the expected — Anne Campbell & Bran — A swan's wishbone, a plover's egg — Toponymy & close-mapping — Songlines for the moor — Night on the *beirgh* — Seal-serenade — Jupiter & Griomabhal — Discovery — Decisive cairns — Quartz crystals — Barefoot walking — Beehive & moraine — *Tapetum lucidum*: the bright carpet — Paths to Geocrab.

A rainless gale rushing out of the east, deer tracks in moor mud, a black sky, gannets showing white as flares above the sea. Dawn on the Atlantic coast of the Isle of Lewis. Thin light, cold and watery. Burly clouds at 1,000 feet, the day forming from the dark. I left the little peninsula on which I'd slept the night and set off uphill and inland, onto the peat and into the wind, following the deer paths that laced the moor. The peat thinned as I gained height and rock began to show through the heather: Lewisian gneiss, the most ancient surface rock in Europe – 3.1 billion years old, zebra-striped, scarred and smoothed by multiple glaciations. The Pleistocene felt only a few weeks gone, the ice just recently retreated. The land dipped and cupped until I was walking up a mile-wide alley of rock, covered with fallen boulders and balanced glacial erratics. Ahead of me a great grey peak called Griomabhal lifted into the cloud. Half of its north face could be seen; the flank of a destroyer. A raven on a boulder croaked *gorack*, *gorack*; another rowed itself in high circles above my head. A grouse exploded away from the heather a yard from my feet, a drag-queen slur of red above each eye.

The path for which I was searching led up the alley of rock and underneath Griomabhal's face; these things I knew for certain. But I couldn't find its line. What was it I had been told? *You need to look for what shouldn't be there*. This path didn't exist as continuous track:

its route was indicated only by marker stones. But the terrain through which I was walking had hundreds of thousands of possible marker stones. Rock emerged from the moor in myriad forms: cannons and salmon, Levantine hats, bishops' mitres, monks' robes, mushrooms and fins. I cut for sign, making long zigzag sweeps, trying to pick up lines of stones. No success. I tried lying down flat to see if I could sight off an alignment. Nothing. It felt like an uncrackable riddle: *How do you find the stone in the alley of stones; the sign in the wilderness of signs?* I started to think that perhaps the path didn't exist at all.

~

I had come off the Hebridean seas and onto the Hebridean moors to find and follow a part-lost path. News of the path had reached me not as a drawn line on a map, but as a series of contradictory rumours and recollections. The path ran south-east from west Lewis obliquely down into Harris, and was to be navigated by moving from beehive shieling to beehive shieling in a Pictish dot-to-dot. Incorrect – it ran in fact up the coast from a peninsula called the Aird Bheag, over a high *bealach* and down to the west coast at the cleared village of Mealasta. It was marked by single standing stones. No, it was marked by ziggurat cairns placed on top of large boulders. No, it was marked by *rùdhan*, three narrow, long stones placed on end and leaning together at their tips, a cairn type whose structure was derived from the Hebridean method of arranging freshly cut peat bricks in order to encourage faster drying by wind and sun. The path had first been made in the 1850s. No, it was no older than the 1920s. Its architect was a crofter who had taught himself Greek to a high level, and who had kept a journal during the 1950s recording the passage of British military vessels up that apparently uninhabited coast. No, he spoke only Gaelic – but a woman in Uig had a photograph of him . . .

Yes, this was a path that existed as folklore before it existed as terrain, and I tracked it as a story before I tracked it on foot, moving from lead to lead as though from cairn to cairn. Like a folk song, oral poem or one of Ian's sea roads, its route altered subtly with each retelling.

The path's elusive nature was appropriate to the terrain through which it ran. For the two main surface substances of the Western Isles – black peat and pale gneiss – are differently hostile to path-making. The peat swallows paths, and the gneiss refuses them. The gneiss, tough enough to have withstood millions of years of geological tumult, is almost impossible to mark by footfall. The peat, springy and spongy, gulps down the paths that run across it unless they are kept in regular use. So it is that many of the thousands of footpaths that seam the Western Isles don't exist as continuous lines in the land, but instead as trails of intervisible cairns or standing stones.

Many of these stone trails indicate peat paths (leading to and from the worked peat-banks), crofting paths, and particularly shieling paths (leading from townships to the areas of the moor where each family kept its shieling, the stone-built shelter which would be used as a home during the summer grazing months). The journey to the shieling would be made by different family members at different times, and a key coming-of-age moment for a child was when he or she made the journey to the shieling alone. But bad weather could make navigation out there difficult, and the moor itself held the perils of bog and deep water. So it was that these routes became cairned onto the moor as guide-lines, designed to avoid *boglach* (general boggy areas), *blàr* (flat areas of the moor that can be very boggy) or, most dangerously, *breunlach* (sucking bog disguised by the alluringly bright green grass that covers it), and lead the walker safely to *tulach na h-àirigh* – the site of the shieling. Hansel and Gretel again: the stones that will guide you safely home. Instructions would accompany the departure for the path, a manual for use, stories for safe navigation: *Trust to the stones, keep them in sight, don't be tempted to walk lower down where the ground seems greener and flatter, for there it is also boggy and treacherous.* These practices have their parallels elsewhere in the country: in the line of white marker stones that used to run across Bodmin Moor from Watergate to Five Lanes, for instance, set there in the mid-1800s by a parson who wished to be able to traverse his trackless and often fog-bound parish without getting lost or enmired.

Most of the Hebridean footpaths are shown only on informal local maps, and in the memory maps that are carried in the minds of the people who walk them, their routes passed on by report and repute. But now that the shieling culture has almost vanished from the island, and now that peat-cutting is done primarily by machine, many of the paths are disappearing both from memory and from the land.

The path I wanted to find was imperceptible to the Ordnance Survey. It was known as *Clachan Mhànais*, 'Manus's Stones', and its cairns had been laid by a crofter called Manus MacLennan. This much I came to know for certain, and I had been told of the path by Finlay MacLeod, who was the reason I had first come to the Outer Hebrides, years previously.

~

Finlay MacLeod – naturalist, novelist, broadcaster, oral historian, occasional selkie-singer and seal-summoner, and an eloquent speaker in both English and Gaelic – is known throughout the Western Isles and the Scottish *gaeltacht* as one of the most eloquent and combative presences of the Atlantic coast. Courteous but unyielding in dispute, he is a keen celebrant of the Outer Hebridean landscape and a fierce opponent of those he considers his fierce opponents. He loathes as hypocritical and life-stifling the Calvinism that has held Lewis in its grip for so long. In the autumn of 2009 he and his wife Norma gladly boarded the first ever Sunday-sailing of a ferry from Stornoway. The event had outraged the Sabbatarians on the island (of whom there were many) and delighted the secular modernizers (of whom there were fewer, Finlay being one). As the ferry pulled heretically away into the Minch, bound for Ullapool, there were prayers and protests on the quay and there was champagne onboard ship.

Short, nimble and bright-eyed, there is more than a hint of faery to Finlay. He has a crinkled smile and his shoulders shake when he laughs, which is often. He is consistently impious, though that doesn't stop him from taking things seriously. The only Christianity of which he approves was that which flourished in the twelfth and thirteenth centuries on the island, a pre-Reformation worship in which pagan habits were mixed with Christian rites. 'In these places, and in the name of Christ,' he once told me with relish, as we stood in the ruins of a chapel on a remote headland, 'ale was libated to the sea to increase the fertility of the seaweed and the fish, there was new-moon worship, there was dancing and there was fornication!' He despises religious fundamentalism because it means, as he put it, 'the extinction of metaphor'; he wants to celebrate the Book of Genesis as folk tale, not doctrine.

Finlay's love for the landscape and histories of the Western Isles is intense but unsentimental. His filter for straining out romanticism is finely meshed. Born in Ness in the north of Lewis, he was brought up on a croft. As a child, he could hear the family cow moving about in the byre at the far end of the house. He used a bicycle pedal attached to a wheel-guard as the kettle rest on the peat fire which it was his task to tend. At seventeen, he joined the Merchant Navy and sailed to Australia and New Zealand. Later he was called up for national service and posted to an RAF base in Yorkshire. There, acutely homesick, he dreamt of the Western Isles. Within a month, he managed to arrange a reciprocal repatriation with a Yorkshireman who had been posted to the Isle of Lewis (where, acutely homesick, he had dreamt of Yorkshire).

He has devoted his life to the exploration, archiving and mapping of his archipelago, with a view to commending its protection to the wider world. He has mapped the locations and alignments of the healing wells of the Western Isles, their Norse mills, their blessing chapels. He has tracked down the benchmarks left by the Ordnance Survey during their work on the islands in the 1850s, walking the moor for miles in filthy weather to discover the incised stones. He has collected and curated scores of maps of the Outer Hebrides from the sixteenth century onwards.

Darwin is his hero, and there is much of Darwin's restless curiosity, of his accretive and probing brain, in Finlay. Like Darwin, Finlay is only interested in everything. He told me once about how Darwin had constructed a sandy path which looped through the woods and fields around his house at Downe, in Kent. It was while walking this path daily that Darwin did much of his thinking, and he came to refer to it as the 'Sandwalk' or 'the thinking path'. Sometimes he would pile a series of flints in a rough cairn at the start of the path, and knock one away with his walking stick after completing each circuit. He came to be able to anticipate, Finlay explained, a 'three-flint problem' or a 'four-flint problem', reliably quantifying the time it would take to solve an intellectual puzzle in terms of distance walked.

One of the many reasons I enjoy being with Finlay is his ability to read landscapes back into being, and to hold multiple eras of history in plain sight simultaneously. To each feature and place name he can attach a story – geological, folkloric, historical, gossipy. He moves easily between different knowledge systems and historical eras, in awareness of their discrepancies but stimulated by their overlaps and rhymes. Scatters of stones are summoned up and reconstituted in his descriptions into living crofts. He took me to a green knoll in Baile na Cille in mid-Lewis, and recalled for me the scene in 1827 when a Reverend Dr Macdonald had gathered 7,000 people around the knoll for a mass conversion to Calvinism. A crag-and-tail outcrop of gneiss in the moor drew him back into the Holocene and an explanation of how, after the glaciers had retreated from the Western Isles around 12,000 years ago, the peat began to deepen in the lees of the exposed rock-backs. To Finlay, geography and history are consubstantial. Placeless events are inconceivable, in that everything that happens must happen somewhere, and so history issues from geography in the same way that water issues from a spring: unpredictably but site-specifically.

One morning, a few days before I set out in search of Manus's path, Finlay invited me to walk a beach near his home in Shawbost and to meet what he mysteriously called his 'family'. The tide had recently gone out, and we walked across the wet sand leaving footprints precise as pastry-cuts. Gulls stomped and yapped. Finlay's 'family' turned out to be a colony of limpets that lived on the underside of a boulder which he had christened Phobus (the name of one of Mars's moons). He visited them almost every day, and had done so for a year, noting their relative positions on the boulder, their daily migrations and returns. He'd sketched and measured each limpet, and to each he had given a name. For months he'd been mapping the short journeys the limpets made across the surface of Phobus. He had become intrigued by their ability to find their way back to their 'home' positions on the rock, which they did with extraordinary diligence and accuracy, as if following an invisible path or trail.

This was perhaps the pre-eminent puzzle in limpet studies, Finlay said, smiling. Experiments had been done to try and discern how the homing instinct functioned in limpets. Researchers had set up physical barriers and chemical cordons on rocks to prevent limpets returning to their home positions by the same route as they had left it. Yet the limpets slowly moved around whatever impediment had been constructed, proving that not only could they navigate back to their home positions, but that they could do so without retracing their original track.

Limpets also practise a unique habitat adaptation, Finlay explained. The reason they stick so well to their rocks is that they create a seal between the rim of their shell and the surface of the rock to which they affix themselves. This seal prevents them from being pecked off their rocks by hungry gulls, or bashed off by waves; it also prevents them from drying out during low tide. 'They create this seal,' he said, 'by very slightly rotating their shells back and forth repeatedly. In this way the rock grinds its own outline into the rim of the shell.' Limpets abrade themselves to suit their chosen terrain, in an accelerated habituation to the specificities of place.

Place-learning and path-following are therefore the two remarkable skills of the limpet, Finlay said, and he did not need to add that these were among his own remarkable skills too.

~

With Finlay's help, I managed to confirm more facts about Manus's Stones and the man who had laid them. Manus had indeed lived as a crofter out on the south-western coast of Lewis. The Aird Bheag peninsula, whose steep sides ran straight into the Atlantic, had supported a small population of crofters for centuries and been constituted as a township shortly after the First World War. Manus had crofted there in the first half of the century, and in the 1920s he had marked out two paths along which he could leave his croft-home and return safely to it. One headed north-east from the Aird Bheag over the deep peat-lands south of a big estate house called Morsgail. The other headed north-west, then required a boat crossing of the often stormy mouth of Loch Hamnaway to Ceann Chùisil, then ran up and over a high pass, down beneath the north face of Griomabhal and along the mile-wide alley of stones to the west-coast village of Breanish. Fifteen miles on foot and by boat, and that just to reach a road-head: it was a hard life out on the Aird Bheag. The last crofter came in, reluctantly, from the peninsula in 1953.

In Stornoway, Finlay introduced me to Chrisella Ross, the great-great-niece of Manus. 'It was a track he created to guide people,' she told me of the path, 'rather more than to guide himself, as he knew every stone and turn.' She and her husband had walked the path, two decades earlier, from Mealasta up towards Griomabhal. 'We picked the path up at the edge of the cloud cover that day,' she said, 'and then we stepped into the mist under the mountain and the rest of the world was lost.' Chrisella had recently, barely, survived a battle with cancer. She was still recovering. If she was strong enough, she said, she would come to walk some of the path with me, to show me a little of the way before turning back.

Chrisella told me of another man who had walked it: Malky Maclean. 'It's a work of art, really,' said Malky when I met him.

'Like a Richard Long sculpture. When you're up there you need to look for what shouldn't be there: two or three pale stones aligned, the rock that has been displaced, that isn't where the ice and gravity should have left it. That's all Manus did, he just . . . recomposed the landscape a little.' I remembered Ian's advice about how to read the surface of the sea for danger: *You need to look for disturbances to the expected, be alert to unforeseen interactions.* I thought, too, of Edward Thomas training his eye to detect the 'disturbances' and imprints in the landscape which testified to the route of an almost-vanished path.

'It's ever so hard to find,' Malky warned me, 'for the whole area is filled with boulders, like great marbles. You're walking through a glen of stones.'

~

Out on the west coast of Lewis, in the township of Bragar, Finlay took me to spend an afternoon with an archaeologist and cartographer named Anne Campbell, who knew the path and who was engaged in a deep-mapping of the Bragar moorland. The front of her house was bermed with piles of pale gneiss pebbles, through which thrust the spear-like leaves and orange blossoms of montbretia.

Anne opened the door. She had dark hair and her eyes were set slightly wide, which gave her a look of mild surprise, though it soon became clear to me that she took the world very calmly indeed. On two walls of her sitting room were pinned large maps. Notebooks were open on a desk, with pencil sketches of stone-scatters, objects, coordinates and notes scribbled around them. Tacked above the fireplace were pages from a field guide, showing birds arranged vertically on the page in silhouettes, wings outstretched, reminding me of an aircraft recognition book I had studied as a child.

A wide pair of windows gave east out onto the moor of Lewis, the Brindled Moor. On the opposite wall was a big dresser whose back was entirely a mirror that reflected the moor it faced, doubling the room's space and giving it a feeling of transparency. On the mantelpiece and window ledges were dozens of found objects: bird's eggs, bones, antlers and pebbles. A swan's wishbone with no central join. A skua's egg from the Shiants. A pure-white golden plover's egg, fragile as a bubble. Dark-brown sea beans, floated in from the Caribbean, like little leather kidneys.

'Whenever I'm out walking on the moor, well, I tend to bring things back,' said Anne, waving a hand around the room. She pronounced 'moor' with the double 'oo' of zoo, and a roll of the final 'r'. She sat in a chair with her legs tucked up under her, beneath a spider plant whose trailing arms nagged at her hair and tapped her on the shoulder, until finally, as if settling a bothersome child, she tucked its arms away so they couldn't reach her. Behind the armchair, her sheepdog Bran yowled and scratched in his sleep.

'Bran's a busy sleeper', she said.

Fixed to the wall just beside the window was a big map, a cartographical version of the view over the moor. It was a conical wedge, extending from its narrow point at Bragar and the coast, backwards and outwards into the main space of the moor. It indicated, Anne explained, the agreed extent of the township's claim on the moor. I looked at the date: it was the 1853 Ordnance Survey map of the islands, carried out by British surveyors who had anglicized the Gaelic place names and diminished the density of toponyms on the landscape.

'I'm using the OS version of Bragar as my base map,' said Anne, 'but I'm trying to enrich it. I'm adding names again, where the sappers took them away. The pencil scribbles you can see are my additions.'

'Why are you close-mapping just the Bragar land?' I asked Anne.

She shrugged as though to indicate that this was not, to her, a question.

'It is the most interesting place in the world to me.' She paused. 'All I want, really, is to put stories to places and what joins them,' she said. 'So I spend most of my time walking shieling tracks, paths, and the streams and the walls that used to divide up the land. Then I talk to people and try to fix their memories to those particular places.'

Anne had been brought up in Bragar, and though she'd left the island to study archaeology on the mainland, she had been drawn back home. Her family had for several generations owned a shieling in the middle of the moor. They still gathered out there early each summer to spend several days cooking, walking and talking. When it wasn't too cold, and not so dry that the heather was sharp, Anne liked to walk barefoot on the moor. 'It takes about two weeks to get your feet toughened up so that it's no discomfort. And then it's bliss. You should try it when you're out there. Take those big boots of yours off!'

Anne's father had taught her the paths out to the shieling, and now she was walking further into the moor, noting and mapping its features. 'My father would tell me their routes, as we walked out looking for sheep,' she said. 'A lot of the paths are becoming lost now, disappearing from memory and from the moor. There's a stone track out by our shieling that has almost been sucked down into the peat, which my father made for the cattle to go to their water. It is still a beautiful thing.'

She had been making a series of walks with her friend and former partner, a man called Jon MacLeod. She and MacLeod had become fascinated by the trails that exist on the moor, each of them an archive of past habits and practices. So they began to create and record their own songlines, recording paths taken, events that occurred or were observed along the way. On a June day they walked between An Talamh Briste, Na Feadanan Gorma, Gleann Shuainagadail and Loch an Ois, and they saw along the way 'drifts of sparkling bog-cotton', 'scarlet damselflies', 'a long wind, carrying bird-calls'. They 'crossed a greenshank's territory' and 'disturbed a hind in long grass', before stopping 'at a shieling where an eagle had preened'. 'I merely walked and recorded what I saw in each place,' Anne said. 'A merlin flying by, a dragonfly laying its wings out to dry.' MacLeod delved further back, beyond the verifiable, making speculative reconstructions of atavistic memory maps 'of those who traversed this landscape before and after the peat grew, naming features to navigate their way around, or to commemorate stories and people'.

'I've walked back along Manus's path from the Aird Bheag,' she said. 'If you miss it at the start it's really difficult to pick it up but, once you've found it, it's really hard to lose it.' She took a map from a shelf, opened it like an accordion and spread it on a small table. She described the path, pointed out features and marks with her little finger. Way out in the deep space of the moor, she indicated a cluster of dots on the map.

'You could sleep here, if you manage to get this far on the first day from Mealasta. There are beehive shielings there; fine structures of Pictish design, small domed buildings with turf roofs. No one really knows when they were built. They're still intact. But you'll have to look hard to find them; they seem like part of the landscape. Only the deer use them now.'

Shortly before I left, Anne told me that her elderly father was in hospital, lost in the wilderness of Alzheimer's. 'He surprised a recent visitor, though,' she said, 'by suddenly reciting by heart, and unprompted, one of the Bragar songs that he had known.' The song was familiar ground, a track he could follow for a few minutes before he lost himself again.

~

Everywhere we went, people knew Finlay. They stopped their cars on the moor roads and scrolled down their windows to talk with him, or downed tools on peat-banks to raise hands of greeting. It was like travelling with the Queen. 'It must take you a long time to get anywhere,' I said.

Eventually, late on a windy sunlit day, he drove me down the thin west-coast road that leads from the great sands of Uig through the crofting township of Breanish to Mealasta, where the road petered out. All that survived of Mealasta was a ground-plan of stones, but it felt oddly like the blueprint of a future village, rather than the trace of a near-vanished one.

The road ended at a wide cove called Camus Mol Lìnis: the Bay of the Boulders of Linis. I hugged Finlay goodbye, and he drove off north, waving out of the window as he went. I walked onto the little peninsula that jutted south of the bay, and found a smear of grass on which to pitch my tent. The peninsula was a *beirgh*, or *a' bheirgh*, a loan-word from the Norse that designates 'a promontory or point with a bare, usually vertical rock-face, and often with a narrow neck'. Its cliffs were pinkish with feldspar. Inland, near Griomabhal, I could see a golden eagle, its primaries extended like delicate fingers, roaming on a late-day hunt. A tern beat upwind: scissory wings, its black head seemingly eyeless, its movement within the air veery and unpredictable as a pitcher's knuckle-ball. Creamy waves moshed and milked on the beach and rocks, making rafts of floating foam just offshore and sending spray shooting above the level of the tent. Wave-surged infralittoral rock, tide-swept circalittoral rock, micro-terrains of lichen and moss. Far out to sea there were breaches in the cloud through which sun fell.

I boiled up a cup of tea and sat drinking it and eating a slab of cake, glad to be alone and in such a place. A seal surfaced – a fine-featured female, ten yards to my north. I tried to sing a seal song that Finlay had taught me a year or two previously, but it turned out that I couldn't remember either the tune or the words, so I switched to early English folk music, a Vaughan Williams setting of one of Robert Louis Stevenson's 'Songs of Travel'. The seal ducked its head under water and out again three times, as if rinsing its ears clean of the noise. I changed to the only other song I could remember – 'Paradise City' by Guns N' Roses. The seal dived and never came back. I felt rather embarrassed.

The sun set over the Atlantic. The water a sea-silver that scorched the eye, and within the burn of the sea's metal the hard black back of an island, resilient in the fire, and through it all the sound of gull-cry and wave-suck, the sense of rock rough underhand, machair finely lined as needlepoint, and about the brinks other aspects of the moment of record: the iodine tang of seaweed, and a sense of peninsularity – of the land both sloping away and fading out at its edges.

A sea mist crept up the coast, cutting visibility to fifty yards, so that my narrow-necked cape of rock seemed to have become an island. It felt as if anything might be going on under the mist's cover, and soon I experienced the peculiar illusion, with a light westerly wind moving across my face from the sea, that I was on board a boat beating outwards into the ocean and that I would wake the next morning far out into the North Atlantic. Then in a meteorological magic trick – like whipping away the tablecloth and leaving the crockery standing – the mist dispersed to reveal a cloudless sky and the coastline still intact. Inland was the half-dome of Griomabhal, and near it hung Jupiter again, bright as a lantern, while clouds juddered westwards across the moon.

~

It was the next morning that I followed the deer tracks up into the glen of stones that ran beneath Griomabhal's north face, with the wind rushing from the east. I searched the glen for almost two hours, moving inland and uphill, losing hope of finding the path.

Right beneath the north face, where the rock dropped 500 feet sheer to the moor, was a pool called the Dubh Loch – the Black Lake – by whose shore I rested. Tar-black water, emerald reeds in the shallows. The surface of the loch was being stirred by the wind in vortical patterns, rotating in sympathy with the wind-shear flows coming down off the north face of Griomabhal. This was a miniature cyclone-alley. Griomabhal's summit was finally cloud-free, and looking up its face, with the clouds posting far overhead, the mountain seemed to be toppling onto me. The face was tracked laterally with seams of quartz, hundreds of yards long, standing out like the veins on a weightlifter's arms. I glanced uphill and into the wind to pick my next line – and there was Manus's path.

Click. Alignment. Blur resolving into comprehension. The pattern standing clear: a cairn sequence, subtle but evident, running up from near the Dubh Loch shore. The form of the cairns was the *rùdhan*, the three-bricked stack, though there were also single stones standing like fingers and pointing the way. I jumped up from my resting stone and followed Manus's path, eastwards over the slopes of gneiss.

Mostly, the cairns were thirty or fifty yards apart. But near the pass, where the ground flattened off, I found seventeen cairns, each no further than ten yards from the next. Malky had been right: Manus's path really was a Richard Long sculpture, created long before Long, and similar in form to his *A Line in the Himalayas*. I stepped into the path of the cairns and looked along it. One end pointed off towards the summit of the pass. The other ran towards Mealasta, dropping out of sight over a shoulder of gneiss. Above me, ravens muttered their hexes.

At last I reached the crest of the pass beneath Griomabhal's north face. I stopped to look out over one of the last great wild spaces of Britain – the deer forests of South Lewis and North Harris, hundreds of square miles of (privately owned) moor, river, loch and mountain. The cairn stones at the pass were decisive, and they led the eye and the foot down over the back of Griomabhal and towards the wilderness of the moor.

I was grateful to the *rùdhan* for their guidance, and followed them steeply down towards the head of Loch Hamnaway. The sun was breaking through the cloud, bringing a redness to the moor. I stopped to drink at a river pool, its water bronze and gold. In its shallows I could see several rough white pebbles of quartz, and I recalled a word that Finlay had taught me, one of the many poetically precise terms that Hebridean Gaelic possesses to designate the features of the moor landscape. '*Èig*' referred, Finlay said, to 'the quartz crystals on the beds of moorland stream-pools that catch and reflect moonlight, and therefore draw migrating salmon to them in the late summer and autumn'.

~

I walked for the rest of that day: happy hard miles over moor and rock, past loch and river. I stopped to fish here and there, catching small trout and carrying them with me, heading south-east towards the beehive shielings Anne had pointed out on the map. Once I saw a quick double flash of sunlight from the side of a distant hill: the binoculars of an estate watcher, checking me out, assessing whether I was a deer or salmon poacher. I didn't like being under surveillance in that open space, and moved into the cover of a rise of land.

When the day was at its warmest, and the peat at its spongiest, I took Anne's advice, tugged off my boots and socks, and walked barefoot for an hour or so. The peat was slippery and cool, and where I stepped on sphagnum it surged up and around my foot, damp as a poultice.

'Walking barefoot has gone out of fashion,' wrote Nan Shepherd in 1945, 'but sensible people are reviving the habit.' Such walking 'begins', she observed:

> with a burn that must be forded: once my shoes are off, I am loath to put them on again. If there are grassy flats beside my burn, I walk on over them, rejoicing in the feel of the grass to my feet; and when the grass gives place to the heather, I walk on still. Dried mud flats, sun-warmed, have a delicious touch, cushioned and smooth; so has long grass at morning, hot in the sun, but still cool and wet when the foot sinks into it, like food melting to a new flavour in the mouth.

I recognized from my own mountain days Nan's inclination not to put her shoes back on after a river crossing. Over the previous few years, I'd been experimenting with my own barefoot revival. I'd walked five miles across the White Peak in Derbyshire: over waterworn limestone that felt glassy as marble, up terraces of wiry grass littered with the striped shells of snails, over hilltops of thistly pasture and at last down on a warm footpath to a river, in one of whose bankside pools I gratefully bathed my feet.* In the Black Mountains of Wales I walked for most of a summer's day along paths of Old Red Sandstone, worn to an ultra-fine grade of dust that was soft as rouge powder. I spent half a day barefoot on the chalk downs and beech woods of south Cambridgeshire with Matt, an archaeologist friend. Early on, we both picked up on our feet a blackish tree-sap or resin, tar-like in texture. The resin acted as a sampler of the ground over which we walked – as the wax in the bottom of a lead-line samples the seabed – and we both acquired a layer of seeds, dust and leaf fragments on our soles. And in Essex's Epping Forest, wandering through glade and shade, I began to feel the changes of habitat underfoot: the different plants that populated each zone according to the available light, and the different temperatures of the leaf-litter. Then I trod on a holly leaf, and in trying to get away from the holly leaf I trod on a sprig of hawthorn, and so I spent five minutes tweezering bits of the forest from my heel.

It is true that I remember the terrains over which I have walked barefoot differently, if not necessarily better, than those I have walked shod. I recall them chiefly as textures, sensations, resistances, planes and slopes: the tactile details of a landscape that often pass unnoticed. They are durably imprinted memories, these footnotes, born of the skin of the walker meeting the skin of the land. I remember

* David, who was with me on that walk, tried tramping through patches of nettles and declared them to be 'like chilli for the foot', leaving it bracingly buzzing. I was insufficiently convinced by his recommendation to try this for myself.

a hot path across boulder clay: the earth smooth and star-cracked by sun, so that I walked with constellations and fault-lines underfoot. I remember crossing a freshly ploughed field, where the harrow had crushed the soil and the sun had warmed it, such that stepping into it was like treading ash from a fire several hours dead. Walking barefoot, you are freshly sensitive to the nap of a landscape. Grass suddenly feels wide and burnished: its blades flattened together to create a cool surface.

Not all of my barefoot walks have been pleasurable. Trying to cross a heat-baked ploughed field, with its rows of sun-hardened sillion, was like walking over a sea of swords. One August my friend Leo and I tried walking a stretch of Suffolk ling-land unshod. It looked like the most benign possible terrain for such activity: a dry sandy heath. But we were hopping in pain within five paces: the heather and moss concealed a widespread miniature gorse. Going on would have been like trying to stroll across pincushions or hedgehog backs.

The super-sensitivity of the bared foot is what has given rise to the 'Reek Sunday' climb of Croagh Patrick in Galway by Catholic pilgrims. That barefoot walk is founded upon the conviction that mortification of the sole leads to amelioration of the soul. This is barefootedness as penance, maceration, test: the stones cut the pilgrims' feet so badly that blood oozes up between their toes and stains the path.

Others have found a more benign connection between barefootedness and awareness. Between 1934 and 1936 the Scottish naturalist Frank Fraser Darling tracked a herd of several hundred red deer in Wester Ross, north-west Scotland. The breakthrough in Darling's understanding of their behaviour came when he decided to take his shoes off. 'During the summer of 1935,' he wrote in *A Herd of Red Deer* (1937), 'I went barefoot, and after a fortnight of discomfort

I had my reward. The whole threshold of awareness was raised, I was never fatigued, and stalking became much easier . . .' Darling's unconventional methods transformed modern ethology: instead of considering the deer as reflex creatures, displaying learnt but unversatile reactions to their environment, he proposed a dynamic model of the herd in which each deer's sensed experience of its landscape shiftingly informed their ways of living. Darling's contention, in short, was that deer 'were capable of *insight*', and his insight into *their* insight emerged from his decision to go sympathetically barefoot. What Darling's work proved was that there are kinds of knowing that only feet can enable, as there are memories of a place that only feet can recall.

Touch is a reciprocal action, a gesture of exchange with the world. To make an impression is also to receive one, and the soles of our feet, shaped by the surfaces they press upon, are landscapes themselves with their own worn channels and roving lines. They perhaps most closely resemble the patterns of ridge and swirl revealed when a tide has ebbed over flat sand. Our heels have marks that look like percussive shockwaves. The arch, where the foot's flex is greatest, is reticulated with shallow folds. The ball carries non-intersecting ripples. The whole foot is a document of motion, inscribed by repeated action. Babies – from those first foetal footfalls, the kneading of sole against womb-wall, turning themselves like astronauts in black space – have already creased their soles by the time they emerge into the world.

~

Anne had been right about the pleasures of the barefoot walk, and she was also right about the difficulty of finding the beehive shielings.

Just before dusk, with the weather worsening and my legs tiring, I stumbled up a valley to where the shielings were marked as black dots on the map.

But where the map told me I would find them, I could see only hummocky moraine: dozens of outsize grassy molehills or moguls, eight or ten feet high at most. I double-checked my map-work. This was definitely the right place.

Then I understood. The shielings *were* the hummocks, or rather were disguised as the hummocks. It was the doorways that gave them away. There were two dome-roofed rock huts next to one another, almost completely turfed over, but with low lintelled entrances at ground level, just large enough to admit me. Their form rhymed so closely with the hummocks that I couldn't believe they weren't influenced by them: architecture as camouflage and local vernacular.

I wriggled into the northerly shieling on hands and knees. It was dry inside, and quiet. It felt strange to be in shelter after the long day in the wind of the moor. I felt as if I had stumbled into Tolkien's Shire. I measured the shieling interior with my body: seven feet across at its widest point, and perhaps five feet high at its apex.

From inside, the simple but exquisite architecture of the shieling was more apparent. It was constructed of gneiss slabs that had neatly overlapped to create the corbelling. Turf had then been laid on top to act as windbreak, insulation and mortar: a living roof that grew together and bound the gneiss in place.

In the southerly shieling I cooked the trout. After supper, I crept out. No midges. A calmer wind, a massive sky; a sensation of extreme emptiness. Loch Reasort's magnesium-flare sheen, and the day's light lingering far into the night. In the last phase of twilight, three deer passed close by and upwind of me. One of them glanced at me, and its eyes flashed an alien silver. What was it that Nan Shepherd had wondered about glimpsing the eyes of creatures in the 'dark of woodland' at dusk: whether the 'watergreen' colour of their eyes was the 'green of some strange void one sees . . . the glint of an outer light reflected or of an inner light unveiled'.

Anatomically speaking, the reason that the eyes of birds and animals glow uncanny colours in low light is due to the presence of the *tapetum lucidum* (the 'bright carpet'), a mirror-like membrane of iridescent cells that sits behind the retina. Light passes first through the rod and cone cells of the retina, then strikes the membrane and rebounds back through the retina towards the light source. In this way any available light is used twice to see with. What we are witnessing when we perceive 'eyeshine' is the colour of the *tapetum lucidum* itself, which varies between species and according to light conditions, but is often red in owls, pale blue in cows and greenish-gold in felines. Even moths and spiders possess this membrane, and their eyes can sometimes be seen in darkness as tiny silver stars.

I slept in the northerly shieling, dry and warm in my den, grateful to have found these ancient shelters out in the moor's old expanse. I was woken only once that night, by a hoarse coughing close by; rasps of air from the lungs of a deer.

~

Dawn: two more golden eagles circling above. A big easterly wind meeting the sea wind from the west; the sky above the beehives full of crashing air. I walked on south-east all that day towards the Isle of Harris, following shieling path, croft path, drover's road and green way, stitching a route together. At some unmarked point I crossed the disputed border between Lewis and Harris, marked on a 1630 map of the Western Isles as 'a boundary between the two countries'. Around mid-morning a sharp sun burnt through the clouds and set cloud-shadows scooting across the moor: *Rionnach maoim* – another Hebridean Gaelic term of exquisite exactitude, meaning 'the shadows cast on the moorland by cumulus clouds moving across the sky on a bright and windy day'. Late that day, on a wet tarmacked road, by whose sides the rusty wrecks of cars and tractors were part sunk into the peat, I reached the peninsula village of Rhenigidale and slept in the youth hostel there, grateful for a bed.

The next morning I went west along the so-called 'green track' towards Tarbert, the main town on Harris. The track has been described as 'the most beautiful path in Britain', and that day it was hard to refute the boast. The track contoured above sea coves. Raised stripes of *feannagan*, or lazy beds, could still be seen on the hillsides; vestiges from the crofting years. After a mile the path dropped down into a sheltered coastal glen called Trollamaraig, and here, protected from the sea wind, I found a flourishing dwarf forest of willow and aspen, honeysuckle, foxglove and woodrush. Then it was up, zigzagging the east face of a hill called the Scrìob until the path eased and led due west between two pap-like peaks with Norse names, Trolamal and Beinn Tharsuinn.

And from that pass, the landscape of the Harris interior was suddenly visible to me – a maze of scarp, lochan and moor, laid out like a map to the eye, through which slender paths traced. I descended on shining tracks and under rainbows to Tarbert, and from there I went further south and east down the Harris coast, and eventually I knocked on the door of Steve Dilworth – artist, demi-magus, pathmaker – the man who had given me the kist to take north to Sula

Sgeir, and in whose house I stayed for several days, days which have in my memory taken on the texture of a fairy tale: the traveller on foot welcomed in off the path for a pause in his travels, to a house of dark wonders, the strangest energies and delight, and an apparently self-replenishing tumbler of gin.

8

GNEISS

The Hanging Figure — Beef as body, mane as hair — Skulls, skin, sperm, stone — Cryptozoology & shamanism — The aura of inner spaces — The hand-held, the held hand — Magus, murderer — Seal oil, baleen, cochlea — Unicorns? Hippogriffs? Dragons? — 'The stuff that the world is made of' — A mummified sparrowhawk — *Atticus atlas* — Swan-murder & pigskin mannequins — *Black Lamb and Grey Falcon* — Laputa, the gannetry — A path to the sacred landscape — Erratics — One hundred kilograms of best German lard — Frozen light — The last kist.

I find I incorporate gneiss & coal & long-threaded moss . . . & esculent roots.

Walt Whitman (1855)

On the south-eastern coast of the Isle of Harris, in a three-house village called Geocrab, behind a fuchsia hedge, in a chilly thin-walled workshop, hanging by a meat hook from a rafter is a human skeleton. Its 206 bones are held together by sinews of braided seagrass, which, as they pass through the vertebrae, are knotted alternately left over right and right over left. Stitched onto the bones are patches of meat cut from a dead calf, which together form a rough over-body. At the time of their first sewing – when they had been recently preserved using a solution of formaldehyde and sodium fluoride, administered with a horse syringe and prepared according to a mix-ratio perfected by the members of a mid-1920s zoological expedition to the Amazon – the meat patches were still plumply muscular. They have dried out over time, though, and wizened, their fibres bunching and separating such that their texture is now that of well-used hawser. Set within the hollows of the skeleton are a gnarled heart, a liver, two dried eyes and a windpipe, all also retrieved from the same calf. The skeleton is bound by seagrass ropes, and its trussed hands are outstretched before it, as if in a gesture of prayer or supplication. From its skull flares a fright wig of horsehair, black and blonde, the strands dropping down to the scapulae.

Steve Dilworth acquired the skeleton one day in 1978 when he contacted an anatomical suppliers in the well-named Gravesend and, posing as a professor of anatomy, bought the skeleton off them for £100, which was then more money than he could easily afford. The bones arrived in a box at the fifteenth-century cottage near Cirencester where he was then working part-time as a gardener. He spent weeks drilling and re-articulating the bones using marram and cords, and weeks more filling the skeleton with calf organs and clothing it in calf flesh, and weeks more noosing and binding it. The result – his sacrificial victim, his voodoo fetish, his Grauballe man, his friend – he named 'The Hanging Figure'.

As Steve and his wife Joan moved around the country, the Hanging Figure moved with them. Eventually in 1985 they washed up on the Isle of Harris, in the coastal township of Geocrab, where the three of them have lived happily ever since.

~

I knocked on Steve's door after my crossing of the Lewisian moor, footsore, sweaty and faintly apprehensive. There were shuffling and banging noises from inside the house. The door opened: a figure filled the frame. A hand of welcome was extended. Steve was wearing a *Matrix*-length coat, and slippers. Tall and fair-haired, with high cheekbones and bristling yellow eyebrows, he looks like a warlock or Viking raider. If you only knew Steve from his work and from his appearance, you'd be intimidated by him, imagine him severe and forbidding. In fact, he's good-natured and clownish, which is a relief. A shaman who took himself seriously would be insufferable.

Within a few minutes of arriving I was at the kitchen table with a coffee in one hand and a gin and tonic in the other, telling Steve and Joan about the night in the beehive shielings and the discovery of Manus's path. A stuffed guillemot regarded me quizzically from on top of a wall-mounted speaker. On a three-foot-deep southern windowsill sat what looked like the bronze skull of a praying mantis, two feet long and with bulging eyes. Stacked under the window were dozens of empty bird's-egg display cases: dark pine, glass-topped, segmented by fine wooden partitions, with cotton-wool nests ready to receive each blown dead egg, and copperplated name cards to identify the species: *Sardinian Goldfinch. Greenshank. Red-Billed Tern.*

The Dilworths came to the Outer Hebrides because it was one of the few places in Britain where they could afford to buy – beg, borrow, build – a house. It turned out that Harris also supplied Steve with the raw materials for his art. He found himself on a coast where he could walk the wrack-line each day to see what it held, and where he could live cheaply in a landscape of animal rituals, megaliths, weather dramas and excellent malt whiskies.

'When he first suggested we move to Harris, I thought he said Paris,' Joan remarked. 'So of course I agreed straight away. It took me a while to work out my mistake.'

The best description I have heard of Steve's art is his own: 'I have spent my life making ritual objects for a tribe that doesn't exist.' Among the materials that he uses in his work are the skulls, beaks, bodies, eyes, skins and wings of herons, wrens, guillemots, gannets, woodcock, fulmars, swans, owls, sparrowhawks, buzzards, black-backed gulls, hooded crows, puffin, sand eels, John Dories and dragonflies; tallow, lard, blubber, sperm; seawater collected during equinoctial gales, fresh water gathered from a deep well, still air gathered in a chapel, storm air gathered in the overhang of a boulder; the north wind, the south wind; the bone, baleen and teeth of whales; the vertebrae of porpoises and sheep; bronze, brass, nickel, copper; dolerite, gneiss, granite, soapstone, alabaster; 10,000-year-old bog oak, walnut, mulberry, rosewood; the prow of a fishing boat; hawking lures; sea beans, sand dollars, sea urchins; eggs, feathers and sand.

Among the objects he has made are the dolerite-and-ivory kist which I'd carried north to Sula Sgeir to placate the storm waves; a lead casket, barred with whalebone and bound with rope; a foot-long mulberry-wood chamber in the shape of a coffee bean, ribbed in steel and containing the body of a blackbird; a hollow case made of a shell of lignum vitae and a shield of whalebone, filled with loose dolphin teeth and the whole bound with fishing rope; a walnut sarcophagus, edged and locked with brass, in which lies a bird made of bog oak, beaked and tailed with bronze; a pair of herons, kills from a fish farm, locked into an embrace, their wings hung with hundreds of fish hooks, their legs bound with fine black cord (archaeopteryx fetish; an avian S&M dance). Crypts and chambers recur in his work; the aura of inner spaces, implied but not proven. The internal, often invisible, aspects of an object are considered equally with its palpable surfaces. One of the first of many hand-held objects Steve created was for a friend who was dying of cancer. He scooped seawater on a day of absolute calm, sealed the water inside a vial, sealed the vial inside a polished and hollowed piece of oak, bound the oak with rope and pressed the oak into her hand for her to hold, her own palm and fingers thus becoming the third layer or casing.

Paths and their markers fascinated Steve. After he had heard my description of Manus's path, he told me how he and his daughter Alexe had traced and then re-walked the routes of the old coffin trails which ran transways across Harris, from the townships on the east coast where the peat was too shallow to receive a corpse, over to the richer and deeper soil of the west coast where the bodies could successfully be laid to rest.

'Like Manus's track,' Steve said, 'these coffin paths don't exist as continuous lines on the land. They're marked by cairns. Some of the cairns are just stones leant up in a triangle, but some are huge, at least as tall as me and really finely made, properly sculptural. Sometimes you get three or four together on a high point, and when you see them from a distance they look spookily like a group of human figures, huddled out there on the moor.'

The journey from east to west could be six or seven miles over very rough ground. 'It was tough enough walking the path on a sunny day,' Steve said, 'with a rucksack on your back and a nice little picnic along the way. To have done it in a group, with a corpse in the coffin and the coffin on your shoulders, slipping on the peat and struggling over the boulders: well, it's almost unthinkable. But they had to put the bodies somewhere.'

He stood up from the kitchen table. 'Come into the workshop,' he said, creaking open a door at the back of the kitchen. I followed him, and found that I'd entered the lair of a murderer or resurrectionist. Dozens of corpses – birds, mostly – lay about in various states of decomposition, dismemberment and restraint.

On a chest freezer sat a human skull, the cheekbones of which had been partially built up with plaster and resin, but the nose of which was unreconstructed: just a blade of cartilage cutting out from the face. On a shelf was a wooden owl, with a glistening rope or cord of metal protruding from its open mouth. From a rafter, dangling from its meat hook, was the Hanging Figure.

Two of the walls were lined with workbenches. Barrels stood about as tables and desks. Every surface was cluttered with objects. Conical flasks, bell jars, retorts, syringes – the glassware of an apothecary or mad inventor. Cork-stoppered phials, film canisters. I found a jar containing an inch or so of a red unguent, which appeared to glow from within. I picked it up and rotated it so that I could read the sticker: SEAL OIL. The oil slunk around the jar's base, leaving a ruby tideline on the glass.

There were pots filled with feathers, mostly tail and wing, and separated roughly by species. On the benches were the tools of the job: clamps, pliers, calipers, gauntlets. A springy curl of minke baleen, a foot long, black and polished. The cochlea of a grey whale.

At waist level on a bench in the workshop was a basket filled with horns, teeth, bones and beaks from unidentifiable creatures. Unicorns? Hippogriffs? Dragons? I lifted the basket, and underneath it was a shallow crate containing perhaps fifty hollow sand dollars, little pods of white with their cryptic dot-markings. Nestled among them was an armadillo's shell, orangey in colour and delicately articulated, covered in pale wire-like hairs. I picked it out and held it. It sat like a bubble on my palm.

'Drop the armadillo back where you found it, close your eyes and put out your hands,' Steve said. I extended my hands towards him, palms upwards, arms touching at the wrists, as though I were submitting to being manacled or bound.

'Ready?'

I nodded. I felt a cool stone object being placed across my palms. My hands sank down under its weight.

'This is made of the stuff that the world is made of.'

It was a feather, a foot-and-a-half-long stone feather, made of a polished black rock with green flecks. Through the stone ran a curdy white spine that resembled ivory.

'The spine is whalebone, from a rib that I cut from a carcass I found washed up on the shore just there.' Steve pointed out of the window, over the fuchsia hedge, down towards the bay.

'The vanes and the rest of it are made of dolerite,' he said. 'I quarried it over to the west of the island, in what I'm told by an archaeologist was a Viking-era quarry, though what the hell the Vikings used to cut this stuff I can't imagine. I used a diamond-toothed cutter that I ran off a generator, and the dolerite all but knackered it.'

The feather was cool on my hands, and impossibly heavy. Its density seemed supernatural. It longed to fall, dragging my arms down. This was its brilliant contradiction as an object – it was a feather that yearned for the earth, a flight-object supercharged with gravity.

Steve took the feather back. I felt as if I'd been unchained.

I moved over to an oil barrel, on which was a see-through freezer bag, knotted shut. There was condensation on the inside of the plastic, but through the droplets I could make out black sharp objects. I picked it up, and the smell of rot roared in my nose. Stretching the plastic tight with my thumbs, I caught sight of stubby beaks and skulls with feathers and flesh still adhering, mulching in a humus of blood and loose meat.

'Guillemots,' said Steve, grinning. 'Still some way to go there. Back in a minute – I want to get something to show you.'

In a red plastic crate lay ten sparrowhawk corpses. An eleventh corpse had been mummified in masking tape. I picked one of the birds up. It was like picking up a seed husk or Airfix model, so light that it seemed to lift my hand. Nothing here weighed what it should. Everything had been hollowed by age or drill, or filled in with lead or stone. The hawk had a barred chest, honey-gold on grey, webbed laterally with wavery lines that resembled cardiogram patterns. The bird's old eyes were closed, and its head was turned to one side as if in embarrassment or to ward off a blow.

The spell of the room was beginning to work on me. I felt jittery. Fairy-tale stories rose up in my mind.

'This is one of the things I'm proudest of owning,' said Steve suddenly, startling me. I hadn't heard him come back in. He was carrying a red-and-blue cardboard box, a Woolworths Pick 'n' Mix container wrapped in cellophane.

'Last one!' he said, proudly.

'What's inside?' I asked, expecting him to say 'the tongue of a salamander' or 'a dodo's foot'.

Steve looked puzzled. 'Sweets,' he said. 'This was the last box of Pick 'n' Mix on the shelves on the last day of the Woolies' closing-down sale in Tarbert. That's a period piece now, that is.'

He put the box carefully on a shelf, in between an ivory tusk and a screw-top jar labelled '4000-Year-Old Storm Water'.

~

That evening, Joan, Steve and I sat round the table again while the late light faded out over the bay to a line of gleam. On the north wall of the kitchen was a glass box containing a white moth as big as a blackbird: *Atticus atlas*, from India. Its wings were linen-coloured and tightly stretched. In the corner a brindled kitten bullied an old white cat.

After supper, Steve pushed his chair back from the table, poured more drinks and began to talk. Most of his stories involved the killing and eating of wild creatures. Poverty, curiosity and a keenly carnivorous palate had led him to try most meats. He'd been a forager long before foraging was trendily rebranded as wild eating. When he was a student in art college he'd taken an air-rifle into the life-drawing class, sat by an open window that overlooked a stand of trees, and shot any squirrels that appeared. When he lived in the country, he used to carry a short-barrelled shotgun in his jacket in case he encountered moving foodstuffs.

'Have you eaten heron?' I asked.

'Oh yes. Best time to eat them is on the full moon, because they're fattest then. The flesh is very, very fishy. Fishier than guillemot. One of the fishiest birds I've eaten, in fact, except gannet.'

Had he eaten blackbirds? Of course, and in a pie. Curlew? Yes. More meat on them than you would imagine. Doves? Yes. Less meat on them than you would imagine. Eagle? No, not eagle, not yet. Swan? Steve's face lit up. Memories were whirring across his inner eye like an old home movie, and he told me a story that I can't repeat here – swan-murder still carrying a substantial penalty – involving a pigskin mannequin, an electric chair, two swans, a fireplace and an estate agent.

That night, waiting for sleep, my mind flocking with images of corpses and taxidermy, I remembered Rebecca West's description in *Black Lamb and Grey Falcon* of the assassination of the Archduke Franz Ferdinand, an avid hunter who was said to have killed half a million creatures in his life. On the day of his death the Duke was in a reception hall in his palace in Sarajevo – even as Princip and the other assassins were taking up their positions along the line of the cavalcade – and the walls of that reception hall, wrote West, were:

> stuffed all the way up to the crimson and gold vaults and stalactites with the furred and feathered ghosts, set close, because there were so many of them: stags with the air between their antlers stuffed with woodcock, quail, pheasant, partridge, capercailzie, and the like; boars standing bristling flank to flank, the breadth under their broad bellies packed with layer upon layer of hares and rabbits.
>
> Their animal eyes, clear and dark as water, would brightly watch the approach of their slayer to an end that exactly resembled their own.

I thought of how, once the *guga*-hunting party had departed from Sula Sgeir each year, the amputated wings of the dead gannets – 4,000 wings from 2,000 birds – were left lying on the summit, so that when the next big autumn storm came and the next big wind blew from the south or the west, thousands of these severed wings would lift from the surfaces of the island, such that it seemed, when seen from the sea, that the rock itself were trying to lift off in flight – an entire island rising into the air, like Swift's Laputa.

~

On the Sunday, Steve took me on a pilgrimage to his most sacred landscape.

I was sitting in a Victorian dentist's chair in Steve's front room, reading. The chair was set on a pole on a massive base. It was upholstered in pink corduroy, with a narrow chintzy trim. There was a cast-iron grille for the patient's feet to rest on, with the word

AUSTRAL woven into it in iron, surrounded by a floral leaf design. The dark-stained pine of the chair arms was worn blonde by decades of anxious fingers. Levers and foot pedals offered a variety of operating positions. It was very sinister and very comfortable.

I heard Steve approach behind me. 'I've got the instruments to go with the chair, you know,' he said, reassuringly.

Then: 'Shall we go for a Sabbath walk? Come on, let's annoy Calvin. You can take a fishing rod, try one of the lochs in the interior. And I'll show you the path I've made, and the place where the Hanging Figure's eventually going to end up.'

We left by the workshop door, and followed a stream that led uphill and inland, by the side of which ran a faint track that Steve had created and maintained himself. It was afternoon. The sky was black trimmed with grey: rain on the way. A lapwing turned and tumbled overhead, making for the coast, letting out wireless bleeps and twiddles.

'Lapwings have got those lovely spoon-shaped wings,' I said. 'They're one of my favourite birds.'

'Not much flesh on them,' said Steve.

After half a mile, we cut up from the bottom of the stream to a high rock ridge. Steve's path continued, loosely written into the heather. From the ridge a view of the Harris interior opened up: thousands of hectares of lochans, streams, glacier-scraped crags, moor and bog. The standing water was collecting and returning the light, so that it resembled ice. It was a terrain that readily abstracted to pure form. The road and the houses of Geocrab were already closed out, only minutes after leaving them. The wind was now hectic, roaring. It was hard to hear or speak. Looking back I could see a big swell breaking on the easterly points of land, sending up smoke-plumes of spray, so that it looked as if the coastline were on fire.

We reached a smooth platform of gneiss, blazed with a lightning strike of quartz. Steve leant close to my ear and shouted over the wind. 'Look! Follow my finger.' He pointed out and across, his finger panning over the landscape. 'There. There. There. There, and . . . there.'

My eyes were rheumy from the gale, but I could see that he was marking off a series of massive boulders, distinctive even in that wilderness of rock. Each was balanced on a high point of land, each was whiter in tone than the surrounding surface rock, and together they seemed to be arranged in a rough circle, perhaps 300 or 400 yards in diameter. At the noon-point of the circle was the whitest boulder, and at the circle's heart was the biggest boulder.

It was a ring of megaliths. But these boulders hadn't been brought here and raised by human effort. They were erratics, carried to these positions by the glaciers that had carved Harris during the Pleistocene. As the glaciers melted, the boulders would have been lowered gently into their present positions: a line of dropped stones, marking the route. We walked the circle, following the thin track that threaded from boulder to boulder.

Steve had worked each of the stones in some way. Several years previously he had set fire to one of them, caking its surface with jelly-turps and then lighting it at dusk: boulder as fire-cairn, beacon. In homage to Joseph Beuys, he had coated the noon-point rock in fat: 'One hundred kilograms of best German lard!' The lard had drawn seagulls to the boulder, and they had flocked about it for days, picking and pecking at the lard. 'It looked as if they were trying to lift the rock into the air!'

At last we reached the great central rock, about which this chance structure of megaliths had organized itself. It was eight feet or so tall at its highest point, roughly rhomboid in outline, and poised on one of its vertices. Steve bent down and picked up a shard of quartz from its base. 'Sami shamans call quartz "frozen light",' he said. 'Here, take this.' I took it, glad of the talisman. Its crystal planes were large, and it was shaped like a shark's tooth or a mountain's peak.

I hauled myself up the side of the boulder and onto its sloping summit. It was a raptor perch, well used. Buzzard or eagle or both. There were big black and white turds, and dozens of excreted bird and animal bones. It had a miniature forest of lichens, foliose and squamulose. I scrambled down and we took shelter in the lee of the boulder, under its steepest overhang.

'Nine tons, I estimate!' he shouted, touching the boulder's flank. 'I'm going to slice its top off,' he said. 'Then I'm going to remove a cylinder from its centre, like coring an apple. Then I'm going to put the Hanging Figure inside that space. And then I'm going to put the top back on. None of this will be easy. But the incision line will be so fine it will be nearly invisible, and it will soon heal over with lichen and weathering, and then almost no one will ever know where the Figure is, except for me, you and a few others.'

He paused. 'This will be its last kist. And this, for me, will be coming full circle. It will be the most important thing that I've ever done.'

I felt the stone's tilted weight above us, charging the air. We were sitting in space that should have been filled, and briefly I imagined the wind unbalancing the boulder and the stone crushing us, sealing us in. Steve's affection for the boulder and its world was cold and hard and tender, a longing simultaneously for distance and for enclosure: a paradox understandable to anyone who has ever been in a certain kind of love.

We completed our walk around the circle, returning to our

starting point on the platform of gneiss. Then Steve strode home, and I fished one of the high dark lochans to see what it held. A rainstorm hit me, soaking me for an hour, which I took to be God's sign that I was behaving badly by fishing on the Sabbath. But then I was rewarded with two trout, which I took to be God's sign that Calvin had behaved badly by forbidding fishing on the Sabbath. As I fished I thought about Steve's landscape: how each of the great rocks here held a story, with his path threading them together in a ritual circumambulation. The Harris interior was his consecrated terrain, invested with belief and dedicated to a tribe that had never existed, as mysterious and moving in its way to me as the monuments of Callanish or Avebury.

When I got back to the house, following the little path down and out of the wilderness, it was six o'clock and nearly dark. It was too early for dinner, so Steve, Joan and I sat on the sofa together, drinking wine and watching *Antiques Roadshow*, while the Figure hung on in the workshop.

9

GRANITE

A ritual walk — My grandfather — 'Interesting times' — Miracle upon the water — The first crossing — *Via viridis* — Drovers & the streams of beasts — Britain's Arctic — Hyper-ordered, chance-made — 'A traffic of love' — Onto the granite — The Lairig Ghru — Crossing a border, passing a portal — Permanent snows — Plutonic rock — Landscapes we carry with us — That the compass is not the index of the heart — Approaching the pass — The eyes of the mountain — Walking the flesh transparent — Fire at the watershed — Funeral — The final walk.

> Since to follow a trail is to remember how it goes, making one's way in the present is itself a recollection of the past . . . onward movement is itself a return.
>
> Tim Ingold and Jo Lee Vergunst (2008)

It was a ritual walk across the Cairngorm massif from south to north, and these were the things we met with in its course: grey glacial erratics, river sand, siskins, pine cones, midges, white pebbles, the skeleton of a raven, footpaths, drove paths, deer paths, dead trees, sadness, rounded mountains and fire; and these were the many rock types over which we passed in its course: limestone, diorite, quartzite, granulite, granite, slate, phyolite and mica-schist. The fire? Oh, the fire came in the late-day gloom on the summit of the pass itself – an episode of combustion in the gathering dark – and the fire, like the walk, was made in memory of my grandfather who had died on the far side of the mountains, and to whose funeral I was walking as commemoration and as recollection, following the old ways up across a watershed, over the great pass of the Lairig Ghru, and then down through the pine forest on the northern slopes of the massif.

~

Wherever my grandfather had gone in his remarkable life, he had walked. He had been a diplomat and a mountaineer who spent fifty years travelling the world, and in every posting he had sought out high ground, open space and paths. In Bulgaria in 1940, only a few weeks before the country joined the Axis and banished its British diplomats, he was busy exploring the Rila mountains. In 1943 he and a climber-friend called Robin Hodgkin reached the summit of Demirkazik (12,323 feet) in the Turkish Ala Dag. They thought themselves the first summiteers – but then found a tattered swastika flag left there by an Austrian party several years earlier (ever alert to propaganda opportunities, my grandfather carried it down to prove to local villagers that the Nazis had plans to annex their mountain). The posting he longed for but never got was to Tehran: the politics of Iran fascinated him, but its mountains, rearing snowbound over the city, fascinated him even more. Politics and wild landscape were the two strands of his unusual life. Now he had died, only a few months after my grandmother, in a house at the foot of the mountain range they had both come to know better than anywhere else, and having walked from north to south across the Isles of Lewis and Harris, I was now setting out to walk from south to north across the inland-island of the Cairngorm massif.

My grandfather, whose name was Edward Peck, had a habit of turning up in history at what Eric Hobsbawm called 'interesting times'. He was in Vienna for the Anschluss in March 1938 and saw Hitler being driven up Mariahilferstrasse in celebration of the union. He watched Jews in Leopoldstadt hurriedly packing suitcases before fleeing for the Czechoslovakian border at Bratislava. In the late spring of the same year, he saw the little figure of the Emperor Haile Selassie being escorted into the headquarters of the League of Nations to plead his case against Italy's invasion of Ethiopia. His first official posting was to Barcelona in the last months of the Civil War; he added Spanish to his languages, and Franco's propaganda agents led him into torture chambers with blood-soaked walls which they claimed had been used by the Republicans, but which the Republicans claimed had been used by Franco's men. In wartime Turkey he came very close to the so-called 'Cicero Affair', an espionage incident involving an ambassador's valet; in Berlin he dealt with the arrest of Russian spies outside the zoo, and with the successful British and American 'listening tunnels' leading into East Germany (later betrayed by George Blake). In 1947 he was denounced as a 'fascist dog' by *Pravda* and blacklisted by the KGB from ever entering the Soviet Union, much to his relief. He picked up languages like stones and dropped them like feathers; they left him only slowly. I think that, at the height of his powers, he spoke twelve languages. He once advised me to learn Turkish because, he said, you get at least six other Turkic tongues almost for free if you do.*

He loved landscapes passionately, but he wasn't a landscape mystic. His considerable analytical powers were directed outwards, to the explanation of geopolitics and historical tectonics. This was somewhere we differed; I have always been more interested in the relationship between landscape and individual lives, and how the places we inhabit shape the people we are. Certainly, my grandfather would have been hard pushed to express exactly why certain landscapes meant to him what they did. Not because he was incapable of such analysis, but because to him it was all so self-evident: the beauty of high country in particular; the companionship provoked by passage through certain landscapes; the fortifying power of hardship experienced at nature's hands; and the dignified tradition of the

* I've failed to do so.

scholar-mountaineer, to which he made a significant addition himself. He cherished wild country for all these reasons and wherever in the world he found it. He moved through mountains with the minimum of fuss, carrying with him an immense and weightless load of cultural-historical knowledge. He covered vast distances, his steady legs and his six-foot wooden skis taking him to summits in the Himalayas, the Alps, up Kilimanjaro and Kinabalu, and all over the British ranges.

After retirement, he and my grandmother settled in a former forestry cottage near the village of Tomintoul just to the north-east of the Cairngorms proper. The house – which they named Torrans – was set amid pine forestry above the River Avon, which has its source under the Cairngorms themselves. Until his last few years, when failing sight and lameness kept him from the mountains, he walked the paths that led around his home and through the mountains. On one wall of the house hung a large 1:50,000 map of the massif on which the footpaths were marked in Ordnance Survey candy-pink, whose lines we would trace with our fingertips while planning expeditions.* It was the influence of my grandfather and my parents which had drawn me to mountains as a child; it was my grandfather who had helped high country and wild places to cast their strong spells over me.

~

I started my crossing of the Cairngorms at Blair Atholl, an hour after dawn. Still air, hot and yellow, tepid with moisture. Dark rain-clouds to our north. David was with me again, and we walked

* As described in the fifth chapter of *Mountains of the Mind*. My grandparents and their world began that first book; it is appropriate that they recur in this one.

together up the valley of Glen Tilt, which runs almost exactly due north-east, cutting up into the lower southern hills of the Cairngorms. The first miles were wooded; the River Tilt incised down into the rock, the path keeping well up the valley side. Siskins flashed yellow between the green. Small birds cheeped busily in the canopies. There was just enough wind to stir the loose skin on the pine trunks. Midges clouded the air, encouraging us onwards. The river was glimpsed through evergreens and birch. I saw a dipper in his pianist's white bib hunting where water poured onto other water, heard the crash of rapids into plunge-pots. There were wide still pools where the water ran so deep that only the spin and glide of pine needles proved the current's movement.

The sound of an engine behind us, then the honk of a horn: an estate Land Rover bounced past, hardly slowing to let us leave the track. The back of the vehicle was open but caged. Two glum-faced young men in flat caps gazed out at us without changing their expressions as they trundled on up the valley. Apprentice ghillies, I guessed, but they looked like inmates being transported between penitentiaries. A mile further on we passed the estate shooting lodge. Four men, presumably clients, stood talking a hundred yards away under a larch. I raised a hand, called a brief greeting. They paused their conversation, looked blankly at us, resumed talking. It felt as if we had stumbled into an episode of *The Prisoner*, and I was glad to get away from the estate roads and out onto the unmetalled footpaths and former drove paths of the upper Tilt.

We stopped to rest by a long river-pool among the dotted ruins of former shielings. A big salmon leapt from the water and flopped back with a splash like a dropped log. Another dipper whirred upstream from rock to rock, then dived, and I watched its dark form digging along underwater. David stripped and bathed in the pool, letting the river rinse away the morning's miles. He swam out to a flat boulder that lay just beneath the water, and assumed the lotus position upon it, perched miraculously on the water's surface like a yogi, grinning. But soon the midges moved us on. They were there in their thousands, and they rose like smoke from the heather as we passed: a robust encouragement to all-day walking.

So it was on again, the valley curling round to the north, over a rickety bridge past the vast Pools of Tarf, where a small plaque was raised in memory of a boy who had drowned there a century before. On north-north-east, and then after three further miles, suddenly we were into the open ground of a high flat pass, the first of the day's two great watersheds. It was a wide valley of yellow moor grass through which wandered a footpath, following the route of the old drove road. Seen at distance, the colour of the mountains was generalized and subdued; the purples and greys of the heather, the bleached grass. But locally, at our feet, the moor was a carpet of colour: the gold of tormentil, the greens and pinks of sphagnum, bright stars of butterwort and sundew, the sage of bog myrtle.

That open ground would have been one of the 'stances' of the drovers: the resting places – not too far from water and on level ground – where the men could sleep and the cattle could graze. There are few Highland glens that were not used at one point as a route for the drovers, whose work was a major feature of Highland and Island life between the Act of Union in 1707 and the trade's decline in the second quarter of the nineteenth century. Illegal droving, mostly by reavers (cattle thieves) dated as far back as the sixteenth century, and charters from as early as the fourteenth century refer to *via viridis*, which seem to have been green roads wide and soft enough to move herds along, but it was the agricultural revolution and the subjugation of the Highlands by General Wade after the rebellion of 1745 that greatly extended the licensed droving industry. Cattle were the chief form of movable wealth in the Highlands, and they had to be transported from the grazing grounds of the Highlands and Islands down to the markets and purchasers in the Lowlands and the Borders. A complex network of tracks, paths and practices came into existence to enable this movement.

A. R. B. Haldane, in his classic work on the subject, *The Drove Roads of Scotland* (1952), describes how during the Second World War, intrigued by 'a lonely grass-grown track crossing the hills' behind his home in Perthshire, he became drawn into the history of the droving centuries. He determined to map the main drove-ways as best he could, even as they were disappearing, and set out to re-walk many of their routes, reading and pacing his way back into an understanding of the era. His book – though wary of nostalgia and rigorous in its historiography – has a finely managed tinge of elegy to it. In his account the drovers, while resilient in the face of hardship, were by no means impervious to beauty. They relished – some of them at least – what he called a 'love of movement and adventure', and they left behind them the landmarks of a fascinating age:

> The brown sails of the cattle boats have gone from The Minch. On slipways and jetties from Skye to Kintyre, thrift grows undisturbed in the crannies of stones once smooth and polished with the tread of hooves. Lonely saltings where the Uist droves once grazed, and throughout the Highlands in hill pass and moorland, as in the minds of men, the passing years increasingly dim and obscure the mark and the memory of the men and beasts that once travelled the drove roads of Scotland.

~

The Cairngorms are a landscape on which both history and snow – perhaps the two substances my grandfather loved most – lay thickly. Climatically speaking, the Cairngorms are Britain's Arctic. In winter, storm winds of up to 170 miles per hour rasp the upper shires of the range, and avalanches scour its lee slopes. My grandparents saw the tremble of the aurora borealis from the north windows of their house: billowing curtains of green or, more rarely, red light. In places on the summit plateaux of the massif, the wind blows so hard and insistently that vegetation exists in bonsai form: pine trees grow to just a few inches high; there are dwarf willows; and a miniature creeping azalea called *Loiseleuria procumbens* – which became one of my grandfather's favourite alpine plants – forms mats barely an inch high among the pebbles, keeping its head down, staying prostrate (*procumbens*). The massif is a terrain shaped by what Nan Shepherd once called 'the elementals'. Mountain landscapes appear chaotic in their jumbledness, but they are in fact ultra-logical landscapes, organized by the climatic extremes and severe expressions of gravity: so hyper-ordered as to seem chance-made.

Anna 'Nan' Shepherd was born in Aberdeen in 1893 and died there in 1981, and during her long life she, like my grandparents, spent hundreds of days and covered thousands of miles exploring the Cairngorms on foot. Her reputation as a writer rests on the three modernist novels she published between 1928 and 1933 (*The Quarry Wood*, *The Weatherhouse*, *A Pass in the Grampians*), but to my mind her most important work is her least known – an eighty-page prose meditation on the Cairngorms, and more generally on our relationship with landscape – called *The Living Mountain*, written in the 1940s but not published until 1977. It is a difficult work to characterize. A celebratory prose-poem? A geo-poetic quest? A philosophical enquiry into the nature of knowledge? None of these quite fits, though it is all of them in part. Shepherd herself called it 'a traffic of love' between herself and the mountains – with 'traffic' implying 'exchange' and 'mutuality' rather than 'congestion' or 'blockage'.

The book's prose is both exhilaratingly materialist – thrilled by the alterity of the Cairngorm granite, by a mountain-world which 'does nothing, absolutely nothing, but be itself' – and almost animist in its account of how mind and mountain interact. What Shepherd understood – like Edward Thomas, and like so many of the other people in this book – was that landscape has long offered us keen ways of figuring ourselves to ourselves, strong means of shaping memories and giving form to thought. Like Thomas, she thought topographically, and like Thomas she understood herself to be in some way thought *by* place. On the mountain, she wrote, moments occur at which 'something moves between me and it. Place and a mind may interpenetrate till the nature of both is altered. I cannot tell what this movement is except by recounting it.'

Better than anyone else I have read, Shepherd 'recounted' the power of the Highland landscape to draw people into intimacy with it, and showed how particular places might make possible particular thoughts. Slowly and effortfully, my grandparents acquired an intimacy with the Cairngorms. Torrans and its fields became a compact between the wildness of the uplands and the civilization of the valleys. Striking accommodations and compromises were often arrived at with the terrain. Where she encountered erratics so heavy they couldn't be shifted, my grandmother built rock gardens around them and grew alpine succulents between them. They had an acre of land behind the house that ran up to the treeline of the forestry, and seventeen acres of rough marshy pasture. On one side the pasture sloped down to a stream gorge with three waterfalls, by the sides of which grew geans. On the other it fell to the banks of the River Avon itself, whose waters in spring spated with snow-melt from the Cairngorms, and in whose summer pools the salmon, following their migration routes up to the source, would hang and flicker. When the water was warm enough, which was almost never, my brother and I would float downstream, goggled and snorkelled, our heads under the water, looking for the shadows of the fish. On the shoulder of moor that faced Torrans from the south, gorse showed yellow and ling showed purple, and curlew would sometimes settle there in number, setting high curved cries adrift across the valley.

The house and the pasture stood on an unusual upsurge of Scottish limestone, which sits above the hard-wearing mica-schists of the Avon valley and beneath the great granite batholith of the Cairngorms themselves. The calcium in the soil made it fairly good grazing land, and so sheep and cattle were brought onto the pasture in summer. My grandparents also planted their land up with trees, both those native to Scotland, and exotics which stood in memory of the countries where they had lived. They planted willows, cherries, alders and birches in number, as well as special singletons: a *Nothofagus antarctica*, a *Metasequoia glyptostroboides* (the coelacanth of trees, thought long extinct, then discovered alive in China in 1950), a Western Hemlock, a Korean Fir, a Noble Fir, and a red-barked Tibetan *Prunus*. Gradually, they named their land into being: 'The Torrans Burn', 'The Crocodile', 'Alison's Folly', 'The Avon Express'. Small acts of verbal landscaping, a temporary habitation. It was, though, always a struggle to manage the incursions of the wild: the snow that drifted to ten feet against the sides of the house in deep winter, the deer and rabbits that ate the seedlings, the family of pine martens that one year nested in the roof and liked to play in my grandmother's underwear drawer.

~

Somewhere on the moorland of the first watershed, we crossed over from the schists onto the Cairngorm granite proper: a medley of quartz, feldspar and tiny sheets of dark glinting mica, which weathers over time to a grey brown but which, when cracked open or scarred, reveals a rock the pinkish colour of flesh. It was on the granite that we entered the Lairig Ghru.

The Lairig Ghru is the great glacier-gouged valley that divides the Cairngorm massif from north to south, and whose highest point – at over 2,600 feet – is higher than the summits of most British mountains. It is also among the most affecting places I know. Entering the Ghru from north or south, I have always had the feeling of crossing a portal or border. People have died in the Lairig Ghru, and more have died on the summits to either side of it. One of Shepherd's own students perished in a blizzard, 'far out of her path', her body found months after her death – once the drifts had thawed – with abrasions to her knees and hands where she had crawled over rough granite boulders, battered to the ground by exhaustion, snow and wind.

Through the droving centuries, the Lairig Ghru was the main route across the massif, taking cattle down through Glen Lui and then on south to Braemar. Sheep coming from Skye would occasionally be driven across the pass, and its last recorded use as a drove route was in 1873. It posed problems to the drovers, however, in terms of distance, severity of weather and ground underfoot. Each winter brought fresh stone-fall from the surrounding crags, and the upper reaches of the pass became strewn with leg-breaking boulders, ill-suited to the hooves and long legs of cattle. So late each spring, men were sent up to the high pass to shift the boulders and open the path.

David and I entered the Lairig Ghru from the south, moving up and over the pink flat steps of granite down which the young River Dee split and tripped. We passed between the gatekeeper peaks of the valley: Devil's Point to the west, with its diagonal flashings of scree, and the black flank of Carn a' Mhaim to the east, down which a thin line of white water was crashing, thousands of feet above us. Both peaks loomed, close and intimidating, and I felt the signal prickle of entering a wild space.

Then we were over the border, and into the pass proper. On the valley floor flourished a fragrant and complex ground cover: bog myrtle, bog asphodel, juniper with its ginny scent, the creeping azalea, dwarf pine trees, saxifrages, bilberry and ling. I began to gather bunches of Cairngorm flora; one to place on my grandfather's coffin, and one to burn on the summit pass. Where the river swung close to the path, we stopped and bathed our feet in its pools. The midges still smoked the air, still maddened us.

So it was up and on for another four or five miles, towards the high point of the Ghru, the pass itself. David walked ahead and, left alone, I was struck suddenly by a hammer blow of sadness. Looking west, I saw the snows of Braeriarch. In the shaded north-east-facing corries and crags of that great mountain, old snow often lies all year round, sintering slowly into ice, sitting in cold stagnancy, the snow breeding its own little ice age. It's a reminder that winter never really leaves the Cairngorms, or rather that this is the point from which the cold musters itself again each year, and out of which it pours. A reminder, too, that the summit of the Lairig Ghru was, 12,000 years ago, not a watershed but an ice-shed: the point from which glaciers crept seawards to north and south, scouring out the shape of the Highland landscape we now know, scavenging into the granite.

Granite was my grandfather's best-loved rock. He shared his liking of granite with one of his heroes, Goethe, to whose writing he had been introduced when studying at Oxford in the mid-1930s under Walter Ettinghausen, who later went on to found the Israeli Foreign Service. As a young man, Goethe wrote an essay entitled 'Über der Granit': an essay on (*über*, 'concerning') the subject of granite, but also an essay about literally being on (*über*, 'over') granite. Granite – that igneous rock of upsurges and plugs – satisfied Goethe for its connection to the earth's hot core. Shepherd valued granite for similar reasons. One October night she slept out on the granite of the plateau in air that was as 'bland as silk', and while half asleep felt herself become stone-like, 'rooted . . . in . . . immobility'. On a hot summer day she lay down and sensed under her 'the central core of fire from which was thrust this grumbling grinding mass of plutonic rock, over me blue air, and between the fire of the rock and the fire of the sun, scree, soil and water, moss, grass, flower and tree, insect, bird and beast, wind, rain and snow – the total mountain'.

Over the course of his eighties, my grandfather got less and less often to the granite, felt less often the fire of the rock and the fire of the sun. He gave up the summits for the passes, then the passes for the valleys, and at last the valleys for the limestone land around the house. His mobility decreased, and his eyesight lessened. He could only walk in memory the routes in the Cairngorms that he knew so well underfoot. Balustrades were fixed on the path down to the gorge to prevent slips and falls. Stiles became difficult to negotiate. Even in his nineties, however, he was occasionally to be found on his old cross-country skis – long heavy wooden skis, made in Austria in the 1930s – sliding up and down the driveway. As his legs weakened and his sight failed, his desire for the hills – for the bend in the path, for the hill after this one – remained undiminished. Unable to reach the mountains himself, he began to live through stories told to him by his children and grandchildren, nourished on accounts of walks taken by others, or by the recollections of his own climbs and treks. Even in the furthest depths of his age, when he was increasingly mentally confused, brief periods of intense clarity would occur, lucid river-pools in the mind, and he would offer topographically accurate accounts of turns in certain Himalayan valleys, or the summits which were viewable from a particular Scottish peak.

We tend to think of landscapes as affecting us most strongly when we are in them or on them, when they offer us the primary sensations of touch and sight. But there are also the landscapes we bear with us in absentia, those places that live on in memory long after they have withdrawn in actuality, and such places – retreated to most often when we are most remote from them – are among the most important landscapes we possess. Adam Nicolson has written of the 'powerful absence[s]' that remembered landscapes exert upon us, but they exist as powerful presences too, with which we maintain deep and abiding attachments. These, perhaps, are the landscapes in which we live the longest, warped though they are by time and abraded though they are by distance. The consolation of recollected places finds its expression frequently in the accounts of those – exiles, prisoners, the ill, the elderly – who can no longer physically reach the places that sustain them. When Edward Thomas travelled to fight on the Western Front, the memories of his 'South Country' were among the things he carried. 'When standing at the entrance of his dugout,' wrote his widow, Helen, after his death:

> he looked north and saw, or dreamed he saw, Sussex, with her gentle downs scattered with sheeplike grey boulders, and thorn trees bent and wracked by the wind, and the sheltering folds where the wind never came; and Kent, the Weald of Kent, whose clay oaks and hops and apples love, whose copses the nightingale seeks; Hampshire, with her hangers of beech and yew, merry tree, and white beam, and the cottage at the foot of the hill.

Kenn, the young hero of Neil Gunn's novel *Highland River* (1937), grows up by the side of the Dunbeath river in the Highland region of Caithness. He comes to know the river so well that when he is sent to the trenches to fight in the First World War he can 'more readily picture the parts of it he knew than the trench systems he floundered amongst. In zero moments it could rise before him with the clearness of a chart showing the main current of his nervous system and its principal tributaries.' John McGahern has written of how the Irishmen who were imprisoned by the British during the War of Independence fought off the boredoms and humiliations of jail by sharing their memories of the River Shannon, 'walking together in their imagination up one bank of the Shannon in the morning, returning down the opposite bank in the evening, each man picking out what others had missed on the way.' 'They knew,' concludes McGahern, 'the river stretches like their own lives.' When the painter John Nash was in the trenches of the Western Front with a Romany friend from Buckinghamshire, they discussed the old ways and green lanes of England, telling stories to each other that were guided by the paths they had walked, and they promised each other that, if they escaped the mud alive, they would travel them together.

~

As we approached the Lairig Ghru's summit, the beaten-earth track narrowed to a slender thread and disappeared altogether into the wilderness of a boulder field. Then – as when Manus's path became apparent in the glen of stones on Lewis – I suddenly learnt to see the path: now a faint line of rosy granite, scoured from the brown patina of the boulders by the passage of feet and crampons. Shepherd had noticed the same phenomenon of the granite 'shin[ing] as red as new-made rock' where feet had fallen.

We followed that track of new-made rock and it led us to the Pools of Dee, two tiny lochans whose water falls as rain and snow and is filtered by the granite of the pass. I have seen the Pools many times, and except once in winter when they were frozen solid, their water has always been miraculously limpid. To my mind the Pools possess a near-supernatural presence, recalling the dust-free mirrors of Buddhist symbolism or the 'well at the world's end' in Neil Gunn's novel of the same name, which contains water so clear that it is invisible to the eye but palpable to the hand.

That day, amid the confusion of boulders, the silver sheets of the Pools' surfaces were a surprise, and the lucidity of their waters once more an astonishment. Transparent and reflective, they appeared like the mountain's own eyes, gazing skywards. I stood by the edge of the first one. The stones in its shallows seemed set beneath glass. Green weed on its floor caught the light and sent it back. I stooped and dipped a hand through the mirror, the water binding cold to my fingers.

'A mountain has an inside,' Shepherd had written. It is a superbly counter-intuitive proposition, for we customarily imagine mountains in terms of their external surfaces and outward-facing forms: cliffs, plateaux, pinnacles, ridges and scarps. But mountains are also defined by their interiors: their corries, caves, hollows and valleys, and by the depths of their rivers, lochs and lochans. Once our eyes have learnt to see that mountains are composed of absent space as well as massy presence, then we might also come to imagine walking not 'up' a mountain but 'into' a mountain. Shepherd was always looking *into* the mountain landscape; again and again she pries through surfaces: into cracks in rocks, into the luminous interior of lochs or rivers. She stepped naked into the shallows of Loch Avon, she poked fingers down mouse-holes into the snowpack, and she recalled how as a child she would play in waterfall-pools by 'pitching into them the tiniest white stones I can find, and watching through the appreciable time they take to sway downwards to the bottom'. 'Into', in *The Living Mountain*, is a preposition that gains – by means of repeated use – the power of a verb. She went into the mountains searching not for the great outdoors but instead for profound 'interiors', deep 'recesses'.

On foot for hour after hour, wrote Shepherd, one 'walks the flesh transparent'. 'On the mountain,' she remarks in the closing sentences of *The Living Mountain*, 'I am beyond desire. It is not ecstasy . . . I am not out of myself, but in myself. I am. That is the final grace accorded from the mountain.' This was her version of Descartes's *cogito*: *I walk therefore I am*. She celebrated the metaphysical rhythm of the pedestrian, the iamb of the 'I am', the beat of the placed and lifted foot.

~

The final half-mile up to the watershed. Heavy legs, slow feet. A blue dusk starting to haze the air. The terrain narrowing, funnelling down. Perception gradually squeezed, sightlines narrowed, vision diminished . . . and then suddenly the pass was reached and the world yawned open ahead, pine-forested northern lands spread out ahead and below us. I placed my handful of bog myrtle, azalea, juniper and dry heather on a natural ortholith of granite, and set them alight: a brief flare of orange in the dusk, a beacon-fire at the pass.

We walked on in the gathering gloom, down the great north slope of the massif, telling stories to each other to sustain ourselves, down through the vast pine forest of Rothiemurchus, which in that dusk had become a fairy-tale wood of shadows and toadstools, through which the path picked its way, moonlight shimmering off the pine needles and pooling in the tears of resin wept by the pines to either side, and in this way we made the descent to the north, the sky above us still blue and incredible, our legs tiring and our pace slowing.

~

Towards the very end of his life, even the walk down to the stream gorge became impossible for my grandfather. His legs – which had carried him so far over so many countries – lost their vigour, his centre of gravity rose and his stability diminished. Stride shortened to shuffle, shuffle to dodder, dodder to step. The walking sticks that he and my grandmother had for years kept by the back door, used for whacking down nettles or for pointing out landscape features, became crucial auxiliaries to movement.

During the same years that my grandfather was losing the ability to walk, my children – his two first great-grandchildren – were gaining it. Step lengthened to dodder, dodder to shuffle, shuffle to stride. Five days after my grandfather died, my three-year-old son and my five-year-old daughter reached the summit of their first true hill, Darling Fell, near Loweswater in the Lake District. The final slopes of that fell are sheep-cropped grass, into which previous walkers have imprinted a series of deep and distinct footmarks. My children went on ahead of me to climb that last slope, fitting their feet into the marks, following the invitation of the print-trail. I watched them go, and thought of having been one of those children myself, watched by my parents, and of my mother having been one of those children in turn, watched over in turn by my grandparents. When the summit had been reached, we all sat together, drank cups of sugary tea and looked across at the mountain ridges receding into the distance, too many to count.

~

My grandfather's funeral occurred in the modest church in the village of Tomintoul. I stood with my brother and our cousins by the door. There were murmurs and handshakes with people we did not know, or knew but could not name. A procession of dark suits, respectful comments. The coffin-bearers wore black gloves on their thin arms, and reminded me of Mickey Mouse. The organist struck up. Mourners moved up the aisles and into the dark-wood pews. High in the north-east Cairngorms, the quartz of the granite shone in the light, and the mica of the granite flashed. Foam in the pools of the Avon, and alder leaves turning in eddies. I walked to the front of the church where the coffin was waiting, an arrangement of gentians, heather and delphiniums on its pine lid, and tucked a sprig of creeping azalea into the heart of the bouquet.

The service began. The minister said, 'What will survive of us is love.' Scree shifts slightly in Lurchers Gully in the Northern Corries of the Cairngorm. A stone falls and then comes to rest. 'What will survive of Edward and Alison is love,' said the minister. 'Knowing another is endless,' Shepherd had written; 'The thing to be known grows with the knowing.' I nearly cried, and could not tell why I did not.

As we filed out of the church, the organist struck up with 'The Road to the Isles'. It's a well-known Scottish folk song of nineteenth-century music-hall origin – rife with pseudo-Gaelicisms and tinged with remembered Jacobitism – about dreamed-of western landscapes, the open road that leads to them and the foot-travel by which they will be reached. It plays with the walk west to the Hebrides as a walk in the direction of loss, a journey towards the setting sun. My mother's mother had sung it to her, and she in turn had sung it to me as a lullaby and as a walking song, in her high voice.

A far croonin' is pullin' me away
As take I wi' my cromack to the road.
The far Coolins are puttin' love on me
As step I wi' the sunlight for my load.

The organist duffed note after note, but the song was still recognizable, and the old words ran through my head in time to the music. We moved onto the pavement and into the sunlight. More murmurs, more handshakes. Sunlight, pebbledash, car-noise, woodsmoke. People were bustling and talking, louder now, while the organist played boldly on. The hearse gleamed. The congregation was reflected in its polished side doors. The bearers emerged, wheeling the coffin on its carriage. A whispered *one, two, three, heave* and the coffin was off the carriage and into the back of the hearse. It shifted a few millimetres each way, nudging the rubber buffers which held it like a parent guarding a young child from harm.

Sure by Tummel and Loch Rannoch and Lochaber I will go
By heather tracks wi' heaven in their wiles.
If it's thinkin' in your inner heart the braggart's in my step,
You've never smelled the tangle o' the Isles.

One of the coffin-bearers stepped into the middle of the road, and raised a flat hand to stop the traffic with all the authority vested in him by death and dark clothes. The cars slowed, stopped, began to back up into a queue. From inside the church the final verse of 'The Road to the Isles' drifted out.

The blue islands are pullin' me away
Their laughter puts the leap upon the lame;
The blue islands from the Skerries to the Lewis
Wi' heather honey taste upon each name.

The hearse starts off up the road, and in front of it, a few yards ahead of it, leading the way, clearing the path, goes the chief coffin-bearer, stepping slowly and measuredly up the road, a respectful stiffness to his gait and his body. Sun glints on the dark road, the hearse creeps forwards, the undertaker makes my grandfather's final walk for him, his journey marked by the beat of each carefully placed and lifted foot.

PART III

ROAMING

(Abroad)

10

LIMESTONE

Raja Shehadeh — Claustrophobia & conflict — The *sarha* — Walking as resistance — Depressions of the land, depressions of the spirit — Reaching Ramallah — The basketball match of the Martyrs — A strange pattern of lights — Down Wadi 'qda — Bullet-holes & bullet-casings — *Natsch* — Land-zones — *Qasr* & dog fox — A wadi path — 'Encrustations of curses', 'bones of rock' — The imam's sermon — The Zalatimos — *Taboun* pebbles — Clemens Messerschmid — Preferential pathways — Chert eyes & amorous chameleons — Contact springs & generosity — Walk, Don't Walk.

The month after my grandfather's funeral, my friend Raja Shehadeh, a former human-rights lawyer and passionate path-follower, travelled to Cambridge from his home in Ramallah in Palestine to walk with me. For two days we tramped footpaths and old ways through the late-summer East Anglian countryside: along the Anglo-Saxon earthwork of Fleam Dyke, which runs like a raised and linear wildwood across the chalk valley to the south of Cambridge, through ripe fields of corn and barley, our arms raised up above the crops as though in surrender, along cliff paths out on the crumbling Suffolk coast, and at last onto the great shingle spit of Orford Ness, formerly a nuclear weapons testing site, where the buildings and debris of the Cold War decades now dilapidate in the salt air. 'I look forward to a time,' said Raja, 'when the landscape of my own country has been demilitarized in this way, and we in Palestine are able to regard the artefacts of war as museum objects, rather than as live threats.'

As we went we talked about the differences between walking in Britain and walking in Palestine. I told Raja about my crossing of Lewis and Harris, about the ritual circlings of Sula Sgeir (by boat) and Steve's ring of megaliths (on foot), about the beehive shielings in which I'd slept, about the watcher on the shore with his binoculars who had monitored my progress, the walk to my grandfather's funeral, and looking into the Pools of Dee.

Raja told me in turn about claustrophobia, restricted movement and conflict. He said that as a Palestinian it was unadvisable to walk outside the main cities, and that if you chose to do so it was unadvisable to carry a map, a camera or a compass, in case you met an Israeli patrol, for all were items that would provoke suspicion, confiscation and even detention. A friend of Raja's had been imprisoned for eleven days for taking photographs while walking in Northern Israel, up near the Golan Heights.

Raja had been walking the hills and paths of the Ramallah region for more than forty years. When he began walking, before the Six-Day War of 1967, the appearance of the hills was largely unchanged from the time of the Roman occupation, and it was possible for him to move more or less unimpededly among them: to conduct what in Arabic is known as a *sarha*. In its original verb-form, *sarha* meant 'to let the cattle out to pasture early in the morning, allowing them to wander and graze freely'. It was subsequently humanized to suggest the action of a walker who went roaming without constraint or fixed plan. One might think the English equivalent to be a 'stroll', an 'amble' or a 'ramble', but these words don't quite catch the implications of escape, delight and improvisation that are carried by *sarha*. 'Wander' comes close, with its word-shadow of 'wonder', as does the Scots word 'stravaig', meaning to ramble without set goals or destination, but best of all perhaps is 'saunter', from the French *sans terre*, which is a contraction of *à la sainte terre*, meaning 'to the sacred place'; i.e. 'a walking pilgrimage'. Saunter and *sarha* both have surface connotations of aimlessness, and smuggled connotations of the spiritual.

Since the occupation of the Palestinian territories by Israel in 1967, Raja had watched the open landscape around Ramallah increase in hazard and diminish in size. It had become gradually more difficult for him to find paths near his home that weren't cut across by a settlers' bypass road, or that didn't lead too close to a militia training area or an Israeli army post. The Israeli settlement policy in the West Bank has brought with it a lavish road-building project, with the use of the new roads usually restricted to Israelis and their routes secured by the army. Ramallah, too, had sprawled as a city, its planning restrictions lax, eating up more of the countryside around it.

So Raja's *sarha* had become almost impossible. Hills that had once for him connoted freedom had come to feel endangered and endangering. Nevertheless, Raja still walked: a minimum of once a week, usually more. Sometimes only a couple of miles, sometimes ten or twelve if routes could be found that avoided difficulties. Paths that had connected village to village or village to town for many centuries had been closed by the Israelis; long diversions were often necessary. As walking had become less easy, it had become correspondingly more important to him – a way of defeating the compression of space of the Occupation; a small but repeated act of civil disobedience.

Occasionally, Raja told me, walking allowed him briefly to forget the situation on the ground. He spoke of the pleasure he felt at being out beyond checkpoints, walls and barriers, of feeling 'giddy with joy' under a wide-open sky. Sometimes the evidence of the spans of geological history, the knowledge that he was walking on limestone which had formed as the bed of an ancestral sea, crushed his frustrations at the Palestinian predicament to a wafer. He had written a book about life in the West Bank called *Palestinian Walks* (2007), in which path-following figured as an explicitly political act and walking as a means of resistance. But walking was also, for Raja, the means for inner voyages, and the passage through landscape was a hugely private as well as intensely political experience. The landscape – the depressions of the Dead Sea and the Rift Valley, the elevations of the Ramallah hills – were both cause and correlate of profound shifts in his own spirit.

Not long after Raja walked in East Anglia with me, I travelled out to the West Bank to join him on a *sarha*.

~

I reached Ramallah as dark fell. Winding terraced hills of limestone, ceding to marly chalk. Piles of rubble and rubbish in the city outskirts. Jasmine, lemon and bougainvillea lining the streets, scenting the air. Hooded crows scavenging in trash-heaps, making two-footed hops. Posters on telephone poles advertised 'The 29th Basketball Match of the Martyrs'. The walls were tagged with green, red and black spray-can graffiti. The bougainvillea were on the turn, and had shed hundreds of thousands of white petals, like vellum pages, which gathered on the pavements in flocks.

I sat in a chair by a lemon tree in the courtyard of Raja's house, recovering from the journey. The square of sky above, framed by the courtyard walls, was pricked with stars. I had not had an easy border crossing at Tel Aviv airport. My passport had been confiscated and my luggage searched. I had been questioned for an hour and a half by a series of officials in a series of rooms of diminishing size: airport entrance hall, side room, back room, booth. My questioners had been especially suspicious of the flints I had brought as gifts for Raja and others in the West Bank (I would later discover why). At last I'd been allowed to go, and my final questioner had escorted me back to the entrance hall, murmuring apologies for the mild inconvenience. He hoped that I understood the situation, the necessity. He hoped that I would have a good stay in Israel.

I left him, trying to walk confidently, truthfully, on my jelly legs across the hall: like a drunk driver attempting to pace off the road-dashes to prove his sobriety. I imagined that there was a path ahead of me on the glossy tiled floor, to which I had to keep, and this steadied my gait a little.

Raj and his wife Penny had heard many versions of this story, many times before. They calmed me, set my minor difficulties in context.

Later that evening, Raja drove me up to an unlit road that ran along the high ground on the south-west of Ramallah. From the road edge, the land fell steeply away in terraces. We got out, and stood looking across the landscape.

'This is where we will walk from tomorrow,' Raja said.

The valley at our feet was in darkness. Beyond it was a strange pattern of lights. Nearest to us, at our altitude, were squashed ellipses with ribbons of paired lights swooping up to them. Between the ellipses, but lower, were untidy neon scatters. Further away, in the distance, a curve of sodium orange, then pure blackness. I recalled an account I'd read of certain Aboriginal Australian dream-runners who were exceptionally fluent in the Songlines, and whose knowledge allowed them to move across the land at great speed in the dark, for they saw the glow of the song as vividly as if they were running along great lighted pathways.

'Twelve in that direction alone,' said Raja.

'Twelve?'

'Settlements. The rings of light are the Jewish settlements on the hilltops, with the well-lit roads leading up to them. The smaller lights, lower down, are the Palestinian villages. The curve beyond them is the coast of what is now Israel. The darkness is the Mediterranean. Over there is Jaffa, where my family lived before the *Nakba*.'

It was all so small in scale, absurdly small. You can see from the middle of the West Bank right across Israel to the Mediterranean. It felt as if I could have thrown a stone from where I was standing into the nearest settlement.

'It will be necessary to be vigilant tomorrow,' Raja said, as we looked out over the darkness and the light. 'Down there' – he gestured into the valley – 'is where Penny and I were pinned down by gunfire, behind a boulder.' They had been walking during the wild early years of the second intifada when bullets suddenly struck the rock above their heads. They sheltered while ricochets and limestone splinters hissed around them. Not Israeli settlers, but Palestinian militia – practising their aim, choosing live targets.

There had been other alarming encounters: Palestinian villagers who thought Raja was an Israeli settler; Israeli settlers who thought Raja was a Palestinian villager. Three years ago, while out walking with an English friend, Louisa Waugh, he had been confronted by two young Palestinian men, unrecognizable beneath their *kaffiyehs*. They were carrying cudgels. 'Except for you,' they had said, 'we would slaughter her immediately,' pointing to Louisa. 'It is *halal* for us to kill the guilty English.'

~

The next morning, not long after dawn, we left from Raja's house to begin the first of our walks, down a long curling valley, Wadi 'qda, which trends westwards towards the coast and through which runs an ancient right of way that follows the wadi line. The sides of the valley were formed of hundreds of receding terraces of limestone, scrubbed with olive and oak and streaked beige, cream and ivory by the heavy marl that mixed with the limestone. I felt very nervous.

We dropped off the edge of the high road and down a poorly tarmacked hairpin track. Almost immediately we met with a bad omen. A thin breeze-block wall, plastered with cement, which had been turned into a firing range. Targets were scratched onto the plaster: concentric circles plugged by bullet-holes. Green glass bottles were lined up along the top of the wall. Most had had their tops shot off. I started humming 'Ten Green Bottles' to myself; the song would buzz like a fat fly, like a greenbottle, in my brain for the rest of the day.

'Militia or police?' I asked Raja.

'It could be either. Most probably police.' It was only over the past three years or so that an effective Palestinian police force had been established, reclaiming most of the West Bank towns from armed gangs. They needed somewhere to train.

A hundred yards further on, the road ran out, dribbling to a stop next to a part-completed villa. We moved onto rough ground and picked up a path that descended the terracing, towards the wadi bed. The heat of the day was building but a big westerly wind was also blowing. At the base of an olive tree was a scatter of big bullet-casings. They looked like the spoor of a creature: AK-47 droppings.

The sunlight fell hard as timber. Big holm oaks grew here and there among the olives. Bryony with its baroque-heart leaves snaked up stands of teasel: unexpected botanical rhymes with the chalklands of Thomas's English South Country. Marjoram, sage, thyme and hyssop. Everywhere was *natsch*, a scrubby spiny thistle that grows to ankle height throughout the West Bank. The existence of *natsch* has been used by Israeli land-lawyers as a floral shorthand for waste ground – evidence that an area of land is not being farmed or maintained. Once designated as unused, the area of land can be reclassified as 'public' land and then more easily requisitioned when necessary for Israeli purposes. Everything here, including botany, is political.

Land in the West Bank is zoned by the Israelis into three areas: A, B and C. A is for the major Palestinian towns and cities. B is for the villages. The rest of the West Bank, the open country, is C, and is out of bounds to Palestinians. Raja told me this with some pleasure when we crossed into Zone C and became trespassers according to Israeli law.

A big dog fox broke cover on the other side of the valley, vaulted downhill, disappeared into rocks, bringing the barren slope to life. After a mile or so of moving along the terraces, we came to a tower made out of limestone that had been tanned by the marl to a yellowish brown. It was a *qasr*, a traditional building used as a base by farmers and shepherds. *Qasrs* dot the hills of the West Bank; most are ruined. This one was intact and corbelled, and reminded me instantly of the beehive shielings. I went in through the narrow doorway on hands and knees. Raja followed.

'Actually, it is a good idea to offer warning of coming,' he said, his voice echoey in the cool space. 'Throw a stone in first, so that any snakes or scorpions will retreat. You can think of it as a gesture of politeness, like knocking on a door.'

Raja is precise in his movements and his speech. Physically, he is small, bird-like. When he's looking for the right word, he rubs his forefinger and thumb together as if crumbling something friable, reducing it to finer units. When he's thinking about something, he tilts his head a little to one side. A comment which requires no response from him is met with none. It took me some time to interpret his silence not as a reprimand but merely as an efficiency. His humility is uncontrived. He has none of the English modesty which knowingly depresses evidence of achievement in order that it might spring out more forcefully at some future point. His modesty is a function of the sense that his own life will always remain subservient to the larger questions of his region.

Raja is also a good route-finder. Over the decades of *sarha* he has gained, as he put it, 'an eye for the tracks that criss-cross the hills, like catwalks'. Near the *qasr* he picked up an obviously old path which led down to the floor of the valley, the dry wadi bed. There, the path merged with the wadi, following the natural line in the landscape for both walkers and water. We passed coils of barbed wire, snaking out of the wadi-floor silt. There were more bullet-casings: reminders that this valley was fought over in 1967; that Ramallah was besieged and bombarded as recently as 2003.

As we walked the wadi path, Raja told me stories. He talked about the people he had brought walking in this valley here, and the ways in which the landscape had affected them. He talked about the different seasons of colour in the valley, which that day was yellow and purple. He pointed out a stand of dark, finger-like cypresses perhaps two miles away, rare strong verticals in this lateral landscape.

'For years it was impossible to come into this valley because the army was stationed where those cypresses are,' he said. 'They surveyed the valley and would intercept anyone walking here. Now they've moved closer to Dolev, so we are able to walk here again.'

A westerly wind blew hard up the wadi, filling it with air. We were walking in a wind-river, against the flow. A pair of kestrels cried and roamed above the far side of the valley, following their kill paths. Then a pair of gazelles – the same browns and tans as the hillside – appeared below the kestrels, flowing uphill seemingly without using their legs, like a counter-gravitational fluid. Then – men were watching us. Palestinian men, from a roadside, perhaps half a mile away. They had turned towards us, were talking. Raja watched them watching us, but didn't say anything to me. He just altered our route slightly, heading further up and away from them. I felt exposed, scrutinized, filled with the ridiculous worry that I might lose my footing and accidentally fall.

~

Travellers to the Holy Lands have always moved through a landscape of their imagination. The land itself has been easily forgotten (scurfed off as inconvenient or irrelevant) or dismissed (as lifeless and repugnant). Western pilgrims, surveyors and cartographers found the same qualities in the Palestinian hills: barrenness, the macabre. William Thackeray came to Palestine in the 1840s and rebuked the countryside as 'parched', 'savage', 'unspeakably ghastly and desolate', a place marked only by 'fear and blood, crime and punishment', a terrain of sustained sanguinary rites: 'There is not a spot at which you look but some violent deed has been done there, or some massacre has been committed.' To Herman Melville, a decade later, the limestone resembled an ossuary spread over thousands of square miles. He dashed down an appalled stream of impressions in his journal: the hills were 'bleached', reminded him of 'leprosy', of 'encrustations of curses – old cheese – bones of rocks – crunched, gnawed & mumbled'.

For Raja, walking and wayfaring offered a means to refute such illiterate readings of his hills, a method of telling and discovering stories other than those of murder and sterility. Like Finlay on Lewis, Raja was a map collector, who had built up a substantial library of historical maps of the West Bank and the Holy Land. But he disliked using maps when he walked – partly because map-reading could be mistaken for a suspicious action, but also because each official map (Israeli, or British Mandate) had its own colonial biases of self-interest and misreading. Raja had preferred to develop what he called his 'map in the head', signposted by personal memories and references. He showed me a map he had drawn of the Ramallah hills and wadis. It was marked with doodles, Arabic place names denoting escarpments, outcrops or wadi outfalls, and little captions in English recording events: 'Where Penny and Raja came under gunfire'; 'Where Aziz [Raja's nephew] picked up the unexploded missile'; 'Where I encountered the Israeli settler with a gun'; 'Where I found the dinosaur footprint'. It reminded me of Anne Campbell's songlines on the Lewis moor: 'Where the dragonfly had laid its wings out to dry'; 'Where the eagle had preened'.

To walk between such places was, for Raja, a way to join events up into stories. He discovered on his walks and marked on his maps the locations of Palestinian villages erased by Israeli forces during the *Nakba* of 1948, whose former existences were sometimes indicated only by the presence of almond trees: shadow-sites of a kind. In recording his walks, Raja was seeking to archive in language what was vanishing, or to recreate in language what had already gone.

~

Miles further on, we left Wadi 'qda and entered another valley called Wadi Kalb. The Palestinian village of A'yn Qenya was to our north-west, and beyond that, on a hilltop, half a mile further on, the Israeli settlement of Dolev, with an army post and watchtower guarding its main entrance.

The sky had become heavy with unseasonal rain. The air was close, tense. So was the landscape. Suddenly there was a crackle. A boom echoed across the valley. I thought, *That was a peal of thunder*, then I thought, *That was a bomb*. No, a feedback screech followed. It was the static of the loudspeakers from the A'yn Qenya mosque being turned on. Silence, and then a voice, furiously emphatic, began to shout. *God is Great! God is Great! Muhamad is his prophet! Allahu Akbar!*

It was the Friday sermon. Eight loudspeakers mounted on the mosque tower, two in each window, pointing to each cardinal point. Raja sighed neatly.

'There did not use to be this zealousness to the sermons. But now, of course, as there is so little pleasure in this life, the only hope is in the next. People have become disaffected, and as they have done so, the sermons have become angrier.'

We stepped over two dead dogs, flattened into the ground. I stopped to look at them, distracted by the fabulous mycelial landscape of mould that had sprung up on their pelts.

'In Ramallah now, Penny and I cannot sleep through the 4 a.m. sermon. The imam becomes crazier and crazier, and then everyone complains, and he calms down for a while, and then he forgets and becomes crazy again.'

We picked our way up through terraces of prickly pears. Terrace-walking is like upwards pachinko. You move along, and then where the land offers you an option – a slope-spill of soil from one terrace down to the next; a protruding boulder – you ascend. Along, up, left and along, up, right and along, making for the next ascent point.

Terraces of olive, lemon, orange and pomegranate, the pomegranates over-ripe, splitting lavishly on the branch, and around the foot of the trunks were scattered plastic bottles, food wrappers and human turds.

The imam ranted and raved. *Of the best deeds are the unity of Moslems in general and of Palestinians in particular! Do not be like those who thrive in disputes for they will be severely punished!*

Rain began to fall. The droplets were the biggest I had ever seen, leaving splash-marks on the limestone the size of two-pound coins. Because of the westerly wind, the splash-marks were elliptical rather than circular. The drops also seemed to fall in interlocking squares, as if the rain were leaving corridors down which we could walk without getting struck.

The rain made the marly soil sticky as treacle. Raja and I soon both had bulbous cakes of yellow mud on the soles of our shoes, our feet heavy as a deep-sea diver's boots. The rain woke the scent of the sage, but also the smell of decaying animal flesh and human waste, which almost overpowered the sage.

'Let's run for the villa,' Raja said, beginning to march smartly up the path. I came on more slowly. The villa was perhaps a hundred yards up the slope, and it was one of the waypoints of our walk. Until 1967, Raja had told me earlier in the day, the villa had belonged to the Zalatimo family, well known in Palestine as pastry-makers. A big terrace blocked my view of the villa, but I knew roughly where it was. The rain was pummelling down, so I thought I'd take a short cut. I crossed a small field, scrambled up a limestone buttress of the big terrace – and froze.

A man was running across the open ground in front of the house, making for cover. He was not Raja. Inside the villa I saw another man. He was wearing some sort of webbing and strapping. Something metal was slung across his front, glinting. The doorway and windows of the villa were black like eyeholes.

I dropped back down behind the limestone terrace. *They must be either settlers or soldiers*, I thought. Then I thought, *I have to stop Raja*. I ran uphill after him, past a holm oak, only to see him already moving along the path to the house.

He had almost reached the front door. I thought, *He can't have seen that there are people inside*. He opened the door. There was a shout. One of the men moved quickly towards Raja – and embraced him. I heard Raja exclaim, 'Basel!' Then, 'What luck!'

The first thing I saw when I entered the villa was a white horse. The back double-doors of the house were wide open, and a white horse was standing centred in the threshold, looking over its shoulder at me. There were also five people. Three men, two women. One of the men, who was obviously Raja's friend, had a baby slung on his front in a carrier, the metal buckles of which glinted.

It was the Zalatimo family themselves, back to see their ancestral villa. 'I try to come here once a month or so,' said Basel, Raja's friend, who now lived in Jerusalem. 'This is my mother, who hasn't been back for many years,' Basel said, 'and this is my aunt, making her last visit.' A look passed between Basel and his mother. The aunt smiled broadly and nodded a greeting to Raja and me. Outside, the thunder gave its first rumbles.

The family had been forced to abandon the villa in 1967 after the Six-Day War. It was now a ruin. There were fangs of glass in the windows, the floor was strewn with pine needles and acorns, and the walls were dense with graffiti. The villa, visited both by settlers from Dolev and villagers from A'yn Qenya, had become a site of textual dispute. There were crude black drawings of AK-47s spitting out bullets at a spray-painted Star of David, a swastika, a heart dripping black blood, as well as many Romanized names that meant nothing to me, and Arabic and Hebrew texts that I couldn't read.

The big central hall gave onto two domed-roof rooms. I scuffed away the dust from a section of the floor with my foot, feeling a glossy surface beneath, and exposed intact floor-tiles, marked with interlocking black diagonals. Basel's mother came over.

'These are a very special surface,' she said apologetically, as though the tiles had been left dirty for a day rather than for forty-two years. 'You need only to wipe them with a mop and – they gleam as though they've been waxed!' She told me that she had left Palestine in 1959 for Kuwait, and then for America, rarely returning to the West Bank. Then she steered me back inside, and gave me a tour of the house, as if I were the first visitor since a recent refurbishment.

'This is where we piled the sacks of flour,' gesturing to one corner of the hall, 'and here where we piled the sacks of rice.'

She stepped close to me and opened her hand to show two knobbly brown pebbles sat in her palm, like a magician revealing a palmed coin.

'I could not resist it, I have taken two more.'

'Not *more*, mother,' said Basel from the other room.

'You would like to come and see the bread-oven my father and uncle built?' She led me out of the back door of the house, past the horse, in the rain, along a muddy path.

'Come, come, and here it is.' I was expecting a vast stone oven; a blast-furnace built into the hillside. In fact, it was a small rusty carcass, barely recognizable as an oven, with an L-shaped mouth.

'This is how it opens,' she said, creaking open the bent door. The interior was filled with brown pebbles.

'This is where the pebbles come from?'

'Yes, many from here – a whole bag. I took other stones from Hebron, Haifa, Jericho, Jerusalem, one or more from every part of Palestine. I took these stones home and laid them on the belly of my oven in America, and I bake my bread on them, so that when I lift the loaf up once it is baked, Palestine has left its mark on the belly of the bread. You can get this kind of bread in Ramallah; it is called *taboun*. I recommend it!'

Her brow furrowed. 'The Israelis have stolen this land from us, they are thieves. I once wrote a letter to Ronald Reagan, I knew it would go in the waste-paper basket, but I needed to get it off my chest. "Dear President Reagan," it began . . .'

I stopped listening. Down in the valley, a covey of partridges broke from cover and whirred, churring, across the far flank of the valley. A man came out of a house on the lower side of the village and hurled a bucketful of rubbish down the hillside. I thought of John Berger's word 'landswept', coined to describe the regions of conflict zones, meaning 'a place or places where everything, both material and immaterial, has been brushed aside, purloined, swept away, blown down, irrigated off, everything except the touchable earth'.

'My aunt remembers this place and that is good,' Basel said to me as we were about to leave. 'At the border crossing at King Hussein Bridge they gave her one week on her visa. We've outstayed the visa by two weeks. It doesn't matter. Her Alzheimer's is too bad.'

The aunt smiled at me. The thunder crashed. A donkey brayed. The imam ranted. The rain poured. A drill thumped like gunfire. Somewhere higher up the valley, the wadi started to run with water, and the old path we had walked became a new river.

~

The following day, Raja and I walked again, on another long Zone C trespass, starting this time from the village of Ras Karkar. Our route followed old paths and wadi beds from Ras Karkar up to a hill-top refugee camp, then down a long sine-wavey valley, Wadi Zarqa, which was fed by scores of springs. Ras Karkar was well known for having resisted the British in the early years of the mandate. It had a history of wealth and respect, but it was now extremely poor. Plastic drinks bottles had been embedded into the walls to save on concrete. A fence had been constructed out of beer crates, broken chairs and thorn branches.

We left Ras Karkar by its western slope, which was its slum slope. Weird limestone sculptures had been carved by the rain, standing out from the slope like ghouls and hoodoos. Around their bases were children's shorts, dead dogs, flip-flops and thousands of nappies, flung dirty from the balconies of the houses. Most of the nappies had split and rotted, and the absorbent gel with which nappies are packed had spilled out in grey crystalline slews.

Raja and I were accompanied by a German geologist called Clemens Messerschmid. Truly, that was his name. Messerschmid was tall. His hair was grey and long. Hanks of it fell across his face, and he used his little fingers to tuck them back behind his ears. He walked with a hungry bouncing lope. His passion was geology, and he barely talked about anything else. For years, he had been studying the flow-rates of the springs and rivers in Wadi Zarqa. The Israelis didn't want him working in the West Bank, but he had developed methods of avoiding their attentions when he travelled in and out of the country, and thwarting their attempts to hinder his research.

Messerschmid seemed to know everything about the region through which we were walking. He was familiar with every foot-path and every side valley, and graded each according to the relative likelihoods of meeting settlers or soldiers. He liked to describe the geomorphology of each new area, and his language was unselfconsciously lyrical. He drew explanatory diagrams for me in quick black ink. I loved listening to him. He told me patiently about the 'anticline cross-section' of the West Bank and the location of the two vast and crucial aquifers which hydrate the dry land. He explained the colours of the landscape; how the loose iron in the soil is mobilized by the dry climate, such that it rusts the earth orange and brown. He pointed out the three main surface rock formations of the area: the plated limestone and marl horizons of the 'Bethlehem' formation, the marl of the 'Yatta' formation, and the karstified limestone of the 'Hebron' formation, with its Swiss-cheese holes, which Melville had disparaged.

Geologists describe the solvent action of rainwater on limestone as creating 'preferential pathways'. With each rainfall, water-drops are sent wandering across the surfaces of the limestone, etching the track of their passage with carbonic acid as they go. These first traverses create shallow channels, which in turn attract the flow of subsequent water, such that they become more deeply scored into the rock. Through the action of water, a hairline crack over time therefore becomes a runnel, which becomes a fracture site, which becomes an escarpment edge.

In a landscape where the limestone is a major surface formation, like the West Bank, these larger-scale fissures are often decisive in the development of terracing and footpaths. Humans and animals, seeking a route, are guided by the pre-configured habits of the terrain. These pedestrians create preferential pathways, which in turn attract the flow of subsequent pedestrians, all of whom etch the track of their passage with their feet as they go. In this way the path of a raindrop hundreds of thousands of years ago may determine the route of a modern-day walker.

Later, we were walking up a wadi bed towards a refugee camp. The stones of the wadi had been rinsed, turned and graded by its intermittent flow, so it was like walking a cobbled street.

'These are the most natural paths of the landscape, and certainly the oldest,' said Messerschmid.

I saw a rounded lump of chert; bent down and picked it up. It resembled a white eyeball wrapped in layers of brown linen. Messerschmid took the stone from my hand, eyed it back and weighed it thoughtfully.

'A nice piece of chert, this.'

I told him about the questioning I had received at Tel Aviv concerning my flints. He smiled.

'Ah, well, you know that chert, a flint, is the favourite stone of the intifada!'

He tossed up the eyeball and caught it again.

'The young Palestinians have told me that chert is their favourite throwing stone, that it makes the best missile. It's sharp, hard, and heavy in the hand.'

Toss. Catch.

'During the first intifada the young ones who took on the Israeli military with chert became known as the "children of the stones".'

Messerschmid tucked a hank of hair behind his ears. Raja walked on down the path with careful steps. A bulbul fluttered out from a gum tree. Yesterday's rain soaked down through the karstic pipes into the aquifer 40 million years beneath our feet.

'Not far from here,' said Messerschmid, 'I once came across two chameleons making love in a fig tree. One of them had turned black, the other had turned red. It was unclear which one was enjoying itself.'

~

Miles later, down in Wadi Zarqa, we stopped at a trough chiselled into a limestone cliff, into which spring water trickled. Messerschmid bent over and drank from the spring with two cupped hands.

'They call these the bleeding hills, or the crying hills,' said Messerschmid, pointing to the spring, 'because they weep water. In January, February, when the proper rainfall happens here, many springs run. They are the consequence of the meeting of geological layers: where karstic limestone encounters marl, the Hebron meeting the Yatta, the water can't descend further and so it emerges as a spring. The springs run, and the hills weep.'

He indicated a dark slur of stain on the limestone with his little finger.

'We call such springs "contact springs". They occur when two different kinds of rock formation encounter one another. Permeable and impermeable combine, and the result is a kind of generosity.'

We left the spring and walked west through hot, still air, past a freshly ploughed field. Sweat beaded on my eyebrows. Mosquitoes buzzed around my head. We passed stands of eucalyptus with their peeling bark, a species introduced by the British, and then among irrigated terraces of aubergine and chilli plants, cages of netting draped with vines, the vegetation startling against the tan soil. I remembered that British army snipers were taught to glance at something bright green just before firing, as the best way to clear the eyes.

Figures appeared on the western skyline, backlit, silhouettes. A ripple of concern passed between Raja and Messerschmid. Settlers? Then a sheep moved onto the skyline to join the figures. Bedouin. Raja relaxed.

~

Back in Ramallah that night, I walked the streets, enjoying the cool air and the feeling of enclosure that the city and the darkness brought, after the exposure of the day. On waste ground by the side of a busy four-lane road, I passed a skip whose contents had been set on fire, and out of which rose and shifted a column of black smoke. A single trainer hung over the outside of the skip, hitched by its laces to its unseen partner on the inside. I waited to cross the road, while the pedestrian crossing flashed its orders: WALK, DON'T WALK; WALK, DON'T WALK.

11

ROOTS

On pilgrimage — 'Bees of the Invisible' — The Rule of Resonance — The Library of the Forest — A demonstration of dominion — *The Mask of Henry Moore* — A winter storm — *Zarzamora virgen* — *Senderismo, cañadas & caminos* — The survival of the old ways — The witches of Galicia — Valley as heartland — A gentle Green Man — Eternal light, resinous air — Miguel's observatory — Moss-pillows — Black vulture — A miracle of levitation — Magical Zen garden — Prometheus unbound — Under a hot-coin sun — River-bathing — The pollen shower — A vulture feather across the path — Into Segovia — City of birds — North-west into the heat haze.

‘We have been,’ wrote the poet Edmund Blunden in 1942, ‘increasingly *on* pilgrimage.’ We are once again increasingly *on* pilgrimage. In Spain, medieval hostelries on the roads to Santiago, closed for centuries, are reopening to cater to the volume of new custom along the Camino. Across Europe a revival is underway, with pilgrimage numbers steadily increasing even as churchgoing figures steadily fall. Shortly after I returned from Palestine, I came across a beautiful short essay by a Czech writer called Václav Cilek, entitled ‘Bees of the Invisible’. ‘The number of quiet pilgrims is rising,’ it began. ‘Places are starting to move. On stones and in forests one comes across small offerings – a posy made from wheat, a feather in a bunch of heather, a circle from snail shells.’ I recognized these insignia of passage – minor rearrangements of the world, serving as temporary waymarkers – having encountered them often on my walks. Indeed, it seemed that every month I had been walking the old ways, I had met or heard tell of someone else setting out on a walk whose purposes exceeded the purely transportational or the simply recreational, and whose destination was in some sense sacred. Thousands of these improvised pilgrimages seemed to be occurring, often unguided by the principles of a major world religion, and of varying levels of seriousness and sanctity. The hinterlands were filling with eccentrics, making their odd journeys in the belief that certain voyages out might become voyages in.

The words 'pilgrim' and 'pilgrimage' have become, at least to secular ears, tainted with a tiresome piety. But the people I was meeting on my walks were inspiring and modest improvisers. All were using walking to make meaning for themselves – some simply, some elaborately; some briefly, some life-dominatingly – and I couldn't find a better name for them than pilgrims: Raja out on his *sarhas*, Finlay MacLeod and Anne Campbell on the moor paths of Lewis, Steve treading his track between his circle of stones, Ian sailing his sea roads through storm and sunshine, even Clemens Messerschmid, trying to understand politics by means of geology. Back among the dead were Thomas, Shepherd and dozens more.

Stories reached me of other such 'quiet pilgrims', undertaking their slow travels. A young man, influenced by George Borrow, had set off and walked from Cambridge to St David's in Pembrokeshire, following only footpaths and green ways across the country. Three folk singers called Ed, Will and Ginger had sold their possessions, left their homes and taken to the paths of England, sleeping in woods and earning their food by singing folk songs they learnt along the way. A woman had walked from Paris to Jerusalem over the course of a year, and met her husband en route. A man had walked the boundaries and footpaths of the county of Northamptonshire (home of Britain's boot industry), sleeping in barns and church porches as he went. One day, in conversation with a friend who walks, I noticed that tattooed in a continuous circle around his bicep was probably the best-known line in Spanish poetry: Antonio Machado's '*No hay camino, se hace camino al andar*' – 'there is no road, the road is made by walking'.

A man I'd never met wrote from Dorset to tell me of a long walk he had made along the Ridgeway, with a close friend who had been released after four years in prison. He sent me blurred photographs, taken through heat hazes, showing chalk paths disappearing over green hills into the uncertain distance. 'Once walked,' he wrote, 'the old ways inhabit us. Even here, now, in the green and low south-west, I often find myself looking high for a beaten chalk path, and recalling those days of strange liberation.' I didn't dare ask what the friend's crime had been that had brought such a sentence with it. One day I walked twenty-five miles with a young man called Bram Thomas Arnold who, after the death of his father, had set out from London and walked to St Gallen in Switzerland (where he had lived as a child), carrying his father's ashes with him, sleeping in a small tent by the sides of vast alfalfa prairies and cropfields in northern France, making camp after dark and striking camp before first light in order to avoid farmers and police.

There was also Cilek himself, a geologist specializing in rare minerals, who was born in a country he chose to refer to as 'Bohemia'. Thirty years previously Cilek had started to wander across his own country, feeling inexplicably compelled by the desire to explore what he called 'underground empires'. He did not do so with any purpose in mind, in terms of the acquisition of understanding or of experience: he was 'a pilgrim, not a conqueror'. Over the last ten years, however, his curious compulsion had sharpened into an obsession, and he had taken to walking as often as he could through hallowed places, castle sites, cloisters and churches. He had spent a week walking the thirty-mile-long maze of subterranea at Monkton Farleigh Quarry near Corsham. 'I find I understand much better those landscapes and places where I can get underground, or at least sleep in nature,' he wrote. Cilek proposed a series of what he called 'pilgrim rules'. Of these, the two most memorable were the 'Rule of Resonance': 'A smaller place with which we resonate is more important than a place of great pilgrimage'; and the 'Rule of Correspondence': 'A place within a landscape corresponds to a place within the heart.'

I read Cilek's rules not long after returning from Palestine, and soon afterwards I travelled to Madrid to walk a branch-line of the most famous pilgrimage route of them all, the Camino de Santiago, from Madrid north up through the pine forests of the Guadarrama mountains, then down to the medieval city of Segovia and out onto the scorched yellow *meseta* – the high tablelands – towards Santiago. I also wanted to meet a man called Miguel Angel Blanco, who has created one of the most astonishing libraries in existence, dedicated to the archiving and documenting of his many hundreds of quiet pilgrimages.

~

'Choose three books from the library,' said Miguel, gesturing around the hot room. 'The first will tell your past, the next knows your present and the last will see your future.'

A basement in Madrid: its walls lined from ceiling to floor with shelves. On the shelves: hundreds of wooden boxes, ranging in size from narrow cigar case to shallow treasure chest. The boxes were all open at their outwards-facing end, and the mouth of each box had an identifying number burnt into it. Held in each mouth was the plain linen-covered spine of what appeared to be a book, though some of these spines were thicker than the spines of any book I had ever seen before. Pinch-holes had been cut into the boxes so that the books they contained could be gripped and slid out, as one might pull a loose brick from a wall. The spines of the books were unmarked by text and were of different colours: orange, mulberry, taupe, black, scarlet. The effect was postmodern baroque: Pompidou colours for a vast *Wunderkammer*.

'You don't need to take much care,' said Elena, Miguel's wife, smiling, 'because the books will choose you, not the other way round.'

The library of Miguel Angel Blanco is no ordinary library. It is not arranged according to topic and subject, nor is it navigated by means of the Dewey Decimal system. Its full name is the Library of the Forest, *La Biblioteca del Bosque*. It has so far been a quarter of a century in the making, and at last count it consisted of more than 1,100 books – though its books are not only books, but also reliquaries. Each book records a journey made by walking, and each contains the natural objects and substances gathered along that particular path: seaweed, snakeskin, mica flakes, crystals of quartz, sea beans, lightning-scorched pine timber, the wing of a grey partridge, pillows of moss, worked flint, cubes of pyrite, pollen, resin, acorn cups, the leaves of holm oak, beech, elm. Over the many years of its making, the library has increased in volume and spread in space. It now occupies the entire ground floor and basement of an apartment building in the north of Madrid. Entering the rooms in which it exists feels like stepping into the pages of a Jorge Luis Borges story: 'The Library of Babel' crossed with 'The Garden of Forking Paths', perhaps.

In the Museum of the Botanical Gardens of Lisbon, there is a wooden chest of fifty-six drawers presented in 1560 to King Pedro V of Portugal by Vasco da Gama. Each of the drawers of the chest was made of a different species of tropical hardwood, and each of these fifty-six species was at the time to be found growing somewhere in the colonies of Portugal. Though the chest's form is analogous to the library, its purpose is drastically different. Da Gama's chest treats trees as colonial subjects whose acquisition and arrangement was a means of demonstrating dominion – proof of plural worlds under a singular control. Miguel's library, by contrast, disperses its maker's self into nature.

I slid the first book, my 'past', from its snug wooden box. It was small, about the size of a paperback novel, and its identifying number was 95. Miguel took it from me. 'Ah!' he said. '*La Máscara de Henry Moore*!' He and Elena glanced at each other. Miguel carried the book over to a desk, placed it in a pool of light from an angle-poise and opened its cover. At first, it resembled a conventional book. There were four pages of shiny paper, with bold black hand-writing on them. 'These are made of vegetable paper,' Miguel said, running his fingers over their rough grain as he turned them.

Then he turned the fourth page and the book became a box. There was a glass window and beneath it a cabinet-like space resembling a specimen drawer in a Victorian natural history museum. Under the glass was a strip of rusted metal with two rhomboidal eye-holes punched into it, pieces of broken white pottery and two shards of white quartz. These objects sat on a bed of what looked like sand and resin. I looked at Miguel and Elena for interpretation, but Miguel showed his palms, as if to say, *Only you can know what this means*. I thought of the many trails of white stones I'd met, and of the fragment of quartz that Steve had found for me beneath his boulder.

The Library of the Forest owes its existence to storm and snow. Between 30 December 1984 and New Year's Day 1985 a severe winter gale struck the Guadarrama mountains, the sierra of granite and gneiss that slashes from north-east to south-west across the high plains of Castille, separating Madrid (to the south) from Segovia (to the north). Thousands of the Scots pines that forest the Guadarrama were toppled. For those tempestuous days, Miguel was trapped in his small house in Fuenfría, a southern Guadarraman valley. When at last the storm stopped and the thaw came, he walked up into the valley, following a familiar path but encountering a new world: fifteen-foot-deep drifts of snow, craters and root boles where trees had been felled, sudden clearings in the forest. As he walked, he gathered objects he found along the way: pine branches, resin, cones, curls of bark, a black draughts piece and a white draughts piece. When he returned to his house he placed the gathered items in a small pine box, lidded the box with glass, sealed the glazing with tar, bound pages to the box with tape and gave the whole a cover of card-backed linen.

In this way the first book of the library was made. Miguel called that original book-box *Deshielo*, 'Thaw', and it became the source from which a stream of works began to flow. His manufacturing method is unchanged in its fundamentals. All his book-boxes contain objects he has collected while walking; the results of chance encounters or conscious quests. The found objects are held in place within each box by wire and thread, or pressed into fixing beds of soil, resin, paraffin or wax. Thus mutely arranged, each book-box symbolically records a walk made, a path followed, a foot-journey and its encounters. And the library exists as multidimensional atlas – an ever-growing root-map, and the peculiar chronicle of a journey with no respite.

I carried *La Máscara de Henry Moore*, the book of my past, back to its host box, feeling the displaced air rush out around my fingers as I slid it home.

'Now for the box of your present! Let the oracle speak!' said Miguel. I chose a bigger box, backed with purple linen: No. 588. I opened it on the desk, in the pool of light. The title page read '*Zarzamora virgen*'. I leafed through the pages and reached the glass.

The bed of the box was covered in a curdy yellow substance that resembled congealed fat. Protruding through the fat were thirty or forty curved thorns, like the dorsal fins of sharks swimming in a lipid sea. Like my first box, it was sharp on the eye, full of aggression and darkness, compelling but obscene. Miguel frowned. 'I'm not sure what you call these,' he said, pointing to the thorns, which looked to me like very large bramble thorns, 'but we will see much of this sharp plant, this *Zarzamora*, in the next few days, when we go to the Guadarrama to walk.'

For all the atmosphere of fairground clairvoyancy that surrounded the choosing, I felt somehow *known* by these boxes, this vast mute library, these books which I appeared to open but which actually opened me.

Miguel and I had been corresponding for several years, but this was the first time I had come to Spain to see him and his library. I wanted to find out more about Miguel's obsession with walking and wayfaring, and his unconventional means of recording his journeys, as well as about Spanish practices of *senderismo*, or 'path-following'. There is an exceptional richness and variety of old paths in Spain. A network of *cañadas* or drove roads crosses Spain for nearly 80,000 miles, occupying almost a million acres of public land, shaping land-holding patterns across the country (especially on the plains), and still used for the transportation of livestock. It includes routes such as the Cañada Real, which runs from León to Extremadura, curls round to the west of the Guadarrama and then takes a near-perfect north-easterly bearing up towards the Basque country. In parts of Asturias, the red cows of the north – the *vacas rojas* – roam in free-grazing herds, trampling wide and persistent paths into the landscape as they search for shade and pasture. The pilgrimage to Santiago has its local and profane versions in the *romeria*, the traditional village community walk that originated in the pilgrimage to Rome, but which is now usually made from the village centre to a nearby sacred site, with drinking and eating en route to celebrate the revival of the land after winter. In the Cantabrian mountains, where bears and wolves survive, different rural relics can be found: nomadic shepherds moving their flocks and herds along pathways thought to date from the Bronze Age. Paths snake in their tens of thousands out of the coastal mountain ranges to make landfall at ports and bays, connecting the interior with the sea. As the valleys down from the mountains drained the snow-melt, so the paths have over the centuries ducted the flow of pilgrims, traders, merchants and other travellers.

The profusion of paths, the reputation of the Santiago pilgrimage and the picaresque tradition of wandering in search of adventure made famous by Don Quixote have attracted many English and Irish walkers to Spain since the end of the Peninsular Wars. George Borrow of course, but also Laurie Lee, V. S. Pritchett, Walter Starkie, Richard Ford, Gerald Brenan and, more recently, the walking artist Hamish Fulton, who, in a campaign of chronic athleticism, has walked across Spain dozens of times, clocking up tens of thousands of miles and inscribing his routes in black marker-pen on a large-scale road atlas of the country. A former student of mine, Matt Lloyd, had walked the full Camino route one autumn, with a knapsack and a ukulele, like a latter-day Lee living off his musical skills and the hedgerows: 'Forty days westering across the breadth of Spain,' he wrote in a letter to me after he had returned, 'feeling a whole country turn beneath my feet, beginning in the French mountains and ending in the Spanish sea, singing for my supper as I went.'

The concept of the path animated Miguel's library. 'Each of my books,' he said, 'records an actual journey but also a *camino interior*, an interior path.' He had once walked the Camino Francés – the traditional route through the Pyrenees and across the Castilian plains – and collected moss from the facade of the cathedral in Compostela, which he had used to make Book No. 632. In the late 1990s he had lived in the village of Brion in Galicia, around ten miles from Compostela. There he had met and walked with the *meigas* of Galicia, the wise women known pejoratively as 'witches' and admiringly as 'herbalists'. The *meigas* quickly accepted Miguel into their world and began to teach him their knowledge of medicinal herbs. He began to use these 'witches' plants' in the boxes he was making there, creating what he called a 'shadow herbarium'. Over the course of several months he also established an alternative, pagan *camino*, which he named the Camino de Santa Minia. This path began and ended in an old wood where a great oak stood as altarpiece within the cathedral of the grove itself. Miguel first walked the route on the day of the full moon, 17 April 1998, and then repeated it daily until he had inscribed his own path.

Miguel's true heartland, though, is the Guadarrama range. He has devoted hundreds of books to the mountains, gathering objects from its summits, creeks, paths, steep slopes and secret sites. He has known the Fuenfría valley since the age of two, and walking the forest's paths has become to him a means of metaphysical as well as actual wayfaring, much as sailing the sea roads has helped Ian Stephen to navigate and steer himself within the world.

'My life,' Miguel noted, 'has been united with trees, which I have considered as my equals, and in them I have seen my destiny.' He once described himself to me as having 'roots' in Fuenfría, of becoming 'part tree' when he was there. Such utterances are as natural to Miguel as offering a cup of tea or commenting on the weather. There is no silliness to him because there is no pomposity. He mentions these matters with none of the ostentation of someone unveiling a carefully nurtured eccentricity. His animism is so unabashed as to exceed naïvety. He is a gentle Green Man and I have been fortunate to know him.

Miguel also possesses an air of great and influential calm, secure in the knowledge that he has consecrated his life to a worthwhile proceeding. The library structures his life past and his life to come. His belief in the worth of his ongoing task is absolute and modest. Money seems uninteresting to him, and he long ago stopped selling his work to galleries. It has become more important to perpetuate the library and preserve its integrity. The library's melancholy grandeur lies in Miguel's total commitment to his project, and in his disinterest in himself. Its artistry exists not in the detail, not in the individual boxes – exquisite though they are – but in the overall gesture. He has created a memoir utterly devoid of egotism, an autobiography with only nature at its heart. 'This is my life, my memory store,' he said to me. 'It will be here when my memory is gone.'

'Finally, then, your future!' called Elena. I chose No. 818. Its title was *Pizarras, Espejo de los Alpes* ('Slates, Mirror of the Alps'), and it was the most conventionally attractive of the three books. I was glad to have picked it after the sinister jags and angles of the first two. The opening pages were of a lightweight and translucent vegetable paper that bore the imprint of rock forms and fossils. Strands of seaweed were strewn under the glass. The book commemorated a walk in the Alps in 2001, and played with the fact that the summits of Alpine peaks had once been seabeds: the coccoliths represented in the paper alluded to this deep-time conversion of the submarine into the aerial.

I browsed the library for another two hours. The day lessened outside. The noise of cicadas bristled from nearby trees. Elena and

Miguel sat, talked quietly with each other, watched me. They had seen the magic of the library work on people before.

The last box I looked at was entitled *Luz Eterna*, 'Eternal Light'. It was arrestingly beautiful. The inside of the book was covered in gold leaf, over which had been poured a layer of pine resin, tapped from a Guadarraman pine and honeyish in lustre. The gold acted like the *tapetum lucidum* of an animal's eye, doubling the passage of light through the resin. The gold reflected and the resin magnified, such that the box seemed to brighten the dim room. I closed the book, like turning off a light, and we left the library.

~

Early the next morning, Miguel and I went to the mountains. We drove north out of Madrid, whose suburbs give way abruptly to holm-oak scrub. We crossed parched-earth plains for miles. The land became disturbed by teeth and fingers of granite. Stone walls divided the landscape where previously there had been wire fences. The Guadarrama stood sharp on the hazy horizon, fine-ridged and implausible: born in the Tertiary and far older than both the Pyrenees and the Alps. Scots pines stood about in ones and twos, then groups, then groves: blue-green needles, orangey bark. We passed a junction where a drove road, the Cañada Real, crossed the highway: its route was marked out as a crossing point with barriers and signs, our new way respectful of the old way that met it at a slant.

Finally we reached the village of Cercedilla, at the mouth of the Fuenfría valley, and from there we set off on foot up into the pines and the high ground. Miguel was obviously delighted to be out, and so was I. The sun was already high and hot. The forest air smelt musky, antiseptic. 'I have to walk each day, or else I feel lame,' said

Miguel. He stepped lightly, with a bounce to his stride. I had a heavy pack, and plodded.

We wandered through the valley, following routes that at times were perceptible only to Miguel. He led me along side-streams that fed the main river. One year he had walked and mapped the course of every waterway in the valley.

Mostly Miguel talked about trees, introducing me to individual specimens as if to old friends: to a white cedar, a pair of vast hollies, an infrequent oak subspecies, *Quercus petraea*, which was a relic of the oaks that once grew on the range. By an old stone bridge he dropped down to the riverside to show me where two yews had grown into one another. Their joint foliage was covered with translucent red berries, like half-sucked cherry drops. 'These are the oldest living beings of the Guadarrama, along with the lichens,' he said, patting the trunk of one of the yews. I remembered what Thoreau had written in his journal about thinking nothing of walking eight miles to greet a tree.

Miguel's favourite trees were the pines. 'There is *pino piñero*. Over there is *Pinus nigra*, the black pine. There is *Pinus pinaster*, the maritime pine. *Pino vigía*, the sentry pine, the oldest wild pine of the Fuenfría, with its branches twisted. Also of course *Pinus sylvestris*, the Scots pine, which grows so straight that Columbus asked for them to make the masts of his caravels. Up on the high ground there you can see the *pino carrasco*, which grows like a cloud. The *carrascos* are dotted across the forest, and sometimes I walk from *carrasco* to *carrasco*.'

Later, we emerged out of the shade of the forest into a high pasture area grazed by patient cows with long blunt tongues. Their bells tolled an idle music. The turf, dried yellow by the sun, was starred with pink autumn crocuses, between which butterflies were picking paths. Miguel led me across the pasture and over granite boulders to a rock outcrop that ended in a small cliff. A dead pine leant away over the drop, stripped of its bark by wind and sun, down to pewter cambium. He reached out and grasped one of the pine's low limbs, as though shaking hands. Then he rested companionably against its trunk.

'This is my observatory,' Miguel said. 'I knew this pine when he was green, and still now he is . . . *seco*, dry; he's one of my oldest friends.' We looked out over the wooded bowl of the Fuenfría valley, its north-eastern rim jagged with seven bare granite peaks. Miguel didn't seem to notice, or didn't mind, the graffiti penis that had been scrawled in black aerosol on a nearby boulder, or the forty-foot-high television transmission aerial inside its barbed-wire cage that hummed a few yards away from us. The pine's underskin was a fluid silver, currents of grain with ripples and eddies, the knotholes standing as rocks in the stream about which the grain-lines flowed. Wood beetles had been at work, and the tree was riddled with tunnels that extended and interconnected invisibly within the timber.

~

The Fuenfría valley gathers towards a high pass over the Guadarrama – the Puerta de Fuenfría – which for centuries has been a key crossing point of the range. As a result, the valley is woven with old paths from different eras. There is a Roman road, the Calzada Romano, whose building was commissioned by the Emperor Vespasian between 69 and 79 AD. There is a branch-line of the Camino leading from Madrid to Compostela, which largely follows the route of the Roman road. And there is the Calzada Borbónico, constructed in the eighteenth century to transport the Spanish monarchs from their hunting palace on the north side of the Guadarrama down to Madrid. The two main paths meander uphill like partnered streams, crossing and recrossing. The cobbles of the Bourbon way have been heavily polished by the traffic of centuries, like the shining steps of the Via Dolorosa in Jerusalem.

Miguel and I picked up the Roman road at the valley floor and followed it up towards the Puerta in diminishing shade and among pines of diminishing height. The path wandered like no Roman road I'd ever before known, drifting back and forth over the riverbed, passing among granite boulders fleeced with green and grey moss that was as soft to the touch as jewellery-box velvet.

'The monks of the nearby monasteries would gather pillows of this moss,' said Miguel, pressing it with his fingertips, 'and sleep with their heads on them. The moss drew away bad thoughts from the mind, and soaked up dark dreams.' I liked the sound of that: moss as nightmare-proofing absorbent, a dabbing cloth for ill feelings.

Minutes later, upon the path, I found what looked like a large jay feather, far bigger than any I had ever seen in England, bar-coded in lapis and black along its upper edge.* 'You see, I don't need to walk thirty miles to find things out,' Miguel said, suddenly. 'Six paces will do well for me. There's a Spanish saying,' he added with a broad smile, ' "*Caminar es atesorar!*": "To walk is to gather treasure!" '

~

Miguel left me at a crook in the track, an hour or so short of the pass, walking back downhill with his quick step until the path folded him out of sight. I sat for a while in the shade, drank water, then

* I later discovered that it had come from an azure-winged magpie.

shouldered my pack and walked on up. The heat was drowsying. I was already looking forward to finding somewhere to sleep the night, and perhaps before then a good siesta site. For the night, I had in mind some sun-baked outcrop, which – like a stone left in the fire to heat – would then release its day's warmth into me once dark had fallen.

I was now into the pine forests of the upper range. The cherries and oaks that dotted the lower reaches of the valley had disappeared. Through a gap in the canopy I glimpsed an eagle with white wings; far above it in the blue, the glint of an aeroplane. I felt happy there among the trees, glad to have had Miguel's company but glad also now to be alone in the forest. My feet crunched through drifts of red-gold bark. Great tits and crested tits made quick flits between branches.

From a clearing I looked across to the hill slope on the facing side of the valley, two miles or more away. Gliding above the canopy was a bird so big that its shadow slipped over the treetops beneath it. Light glanced from its mantle and wings. It was a black vulture, the emblematic bird of the Guadarrama. The big females easily reach a nine-foot wingspan; the biggest, ten feet. Among birds of prey, only the Andean condor has a greater wingspan than the black vulture. It was to the Guadarraman pine forests that the soldier and egg collector Willoughby Verner had travelled in the late nineteenth century to take eggs from the nest on the summit of a Scots pine (a near-legendary feat in bird-lore, possessing something of the epic quality of Sinbad's ascent to the Roc's nest).

I reached the Puerta de Fuenfría around two in the afternoon, and rested in hot shade. I ate the smoked ham, fresh bread and ewe's cheese that Miguel and Elena had packed as provisions for me; drew cool water from a spring and drank deeply. Then from the pass I pushed north-east up through steeply forested ground, towards the summits I'd spotted from Miguel's observatory – the Siete Picos; the Seven Peaks. The path zigzagged, its route marked by little cairns of white granite which were perched anywhere available – on the ground, on flat-topped boulders and even in the crooks of young trees: a path-marking method I hadn't ever seen before. As I climbed, the pines thinned in number and then failed altogether, having reached the limit of their range.

I passed from their care out into open granite fields. Shattered boulder heaps, sparse scrub, the sun pressing down like armour on the head. Juniper bushes grown into arrowhead shapes; *jara*, a scented and sticky scrub bush. Groups of little birds burst apart like shrapnel when I approached, then regrouped again several yards ahead of me. Miles away on a high peak was an industrial ski centre; it looked like a lunar station, with a vast rocket identical to the red-and-white one in which Tintin blasts off in *Destination Moon*.

To the north, over pine-forested slopes, I could see the *mesa* – ochre plains stretching to the horizon – and rising out of the *mesa* was Segovia, standing like an imaginary city, complete and close-knit within its high medieval walls, illuminated by the orange sun. There was a low heat haze on the plains, shivering out of the base of the walls, and briefly but intensely I experienced the illusion that the city was itself floating aloft from the plain. It made perfect sense when I later discovered that Segovia's best-known miracle is one of levitation: on a November day in 1602, a bright light was seen shining over the convent of Santa Cruz, and the crowd that hurried to its source found a Dominican theologian called Melchor Cano, 'lost in prayer upon his knees, but suspended a good four feet above the ground'.

I reached the first of the seven peaks, and found that I'd stepped into a Zen rock garden. The ground was covered in a fine white quartz gravel, out of which emerged wind-stunted juniper, thigh-high pine trees and granite boulders. Alpine succulents, plump-leaved and audacious, crammed the rock cracks. And from the gravel also reared the peak itself, a granite castle sixty or seventy feet high. The rock had been rounded by water erosion into a tumbling drapery of swathes and ruches, fulsome and pillowish – pure Henry Moore.

Although it was only late afternoon, I was already sure that I wanted to spend the rest of the day and night here, up in this magical ridge-garden with Madrid glinting far to the south and Segovia orange to the north. I slipped off my rucksack, socks and shoes, left them all in the shadow of the first peak, and set off to investigate the ridge and scramble its rocks. I followed the white-quartz paths that curled between the boulders and trees. The second peak from the west was a castle of granite even bigger than the first. I climbed its slopes to its summit. Lizards skittered away in sudden darts and stops, pausing face down on overhangs as if to show off their adhesion.

I found a wide grooved channel in the rock, like the gutter of a bowling alley, and lay back in it, my shoulders comfortably cupped, the soles of my feet buzzing from the rough hot stone. The granite extended thousands of years below me, and thousands of feet above me two black vultures gyred slowly on the peak's thermal. The warmth of the granite soaked up through my body, and I dozed off.

I woke to find a vulture about fifty feet away from me, flying inquisitively past. It was the size of a hang-glider, and had a tortoise-like neck and head, baggy with skin. It passed on creaking wings. It appeared to be trying to decide if I was carrion, or at the least some version of Prometheus, chained to the rock and vulnerable to inquisition. I sat upright, making vigorous signs of life and freedom, and it veered away. I don't need any help damaging my liver.

Late in the afternoon, between the first and second peaks as counted from the west and the sixth and seventh as counted from the east, I came across a natural cave in a subsidiary granite outcrop, big enough to hold two people lying side by side. It had been part adapted as a shelter. One end had been blocked up with piled stones. There were two tea-light candles, and a half-full water bottle. I couldn't have asked for better accommodation, combining as it did shelter and remoteness. I moved my belongings to the cave, and when dusk came I lit the candles, and my shadows flickered off the rock interior.

The night: a milk-white half-moon, cool air. Owls in the forests below, their hoots pushing through the dusk. The light soughing of wind in the pines. Sound drifting, two shooting stars.

~

Dawn was dewless and dry. When the sun came it was a storm of gold, rich on the face, Miguel's *luz eterna* pouring through the air. I ate apples, bread and cheese, and watched the light flood the land. Where it reached the dark pines across the valley they appeared to shake. I felt uncomplicatedly happy to be in that place and at that time.

Those good spirits stayed with me all that long and lazy day, which was spent tramping some of the forest's many paths under a slice-of-lemon daytime moon and a hot-coin sun. A shiny cricket sat in a patch of shade by the path's side. An owl hunched high in a pine, brown and round-shouldered as a beehive. I found the ruin of a royal palace in which kings and queens would spend the night when crossing the range. A female falcon rose on a gyre, then fell away on a shallow stoop; I tracked her as she dropped, and as she passed from sky-backed to tree-backed she took colour and became brown.

Many dead pines interspersed the living in the forest. Barkless, they gleamed: ghosts among the green. For an hour or so I used them as path-markers or path-makers, walking between them. Silver and twisted, they resembled frozen columns of water, as if they had been poured from beneath the earth. As on the Broomway, I felt that I might be walking on the world's underside and not on its surface.

That afternoon, when the sun was at its hottest and the flies at their most sedulous, I dropped a thousand feet off a ridge, down to where Miguel had told me I would find bathing pools in a river. It seemed impossible that there would be water here, but soon I heard its chortle and there was a blue stream, leaping its way between boulders. I followed it as it built in volume, and soon discovered a series of small deep pools. I stripped and bathed, hoo-ing and hah-ing at the water's coldness, then lay on a flat riverside rock and let the heat run into me from the sun and the stone.

I spent that night in a dense part of the forest, surrounded by an untuned orchestra of crickets. At sunset the day's light came amber and slantwise through the pines, and I saw millions of particles of pollen ticking down through it, gilded by the light, a steady shower of tree dust that settled on my skin and set the air seething.

'As I watch [the world],' wrote Nan Shepherd in 1945, 'it arches its back, and each layer of landscape bristles.' It is a brilliant observation about observation. Shepherd knew that 'landscape' is not something to be viewed and appraised from a distance, as if it were a panel in a frieze or a canvas in a frame. It is not the passive object of our gaze, but rather a volatile participant – a fellow subject which arches and bristles at us, bristles into us. Landscape is still often understood as a noun connoting fixity, scenery, an immobile painterly decorum.* I prefer to think of the word as a noun containing a hidden verb: landscape scapes, it is dynamic and commotion causing, it sculpts and shapes us not only over the courses of our lives but also instant by instant, incident by incident. I prefer to take 'landscape' as a collective term for the temperature and pressure of the air, the fall of light and its rebounds, the textures and surfaces of rock, soil and building, the sounds (cricket screech, bird cry, wind through trees), the scents (pine resin, hot stone, crushed thyme) and the uncountable other transitory phenomena and atmospheres that together comprise the *bristling* presence of a particular place at a particular moment.

Later that night, from the deeper shadows of the pine forest, two pairs of animal eyes glowed orange and green.

~

I woke powdered in pollen. The sky above the mesa was blue-brown. From dawn it was down on switchbacks through the pines for several hours, then out into open ground and scrub. 'Santiago: 587 KM' read one of the signposts I passed, marked with the scallop-shell motif of the Camino. Too far for me.

* 'Landscape' is a late-sixteenth-century (1598) anglicization of the Dutch word *landschap*, which had originally meant a 'unit or tract of land', but which in the course of the 1500s had become so strongly associated with the Dutch school of landscape painting that at the point of its anglicization its primary meaning was 'a painterly depiction of scenery': it was not used to mean physical landscape until 1725.

At a turn in the path I found a great brown feather a foot and a half long, with sticky spots of blood on its quill. It was from either the tail or wing of a vulture. When I picked it up it weighed almost nothing: an inverse echo of Dilworth's dolerite and whalebone sculpture. The upper vanes were rough and the brown of a monk's habit, but near the quill the vanes became a tousled white down, each strand so delicate that I couldn't feel them brush my fingers.

I approached Segovia across baking plains, dust puffing up with every footfall, dust in the mouth, dust in the eyes. Red kites with notched tails turned watchfully overhead. Segovia has long since sprawled from its medieval walls, and to its south there are warehouse complexes and a glinting new rail terminal. Yet it still seems to sail upon the flatlands that surround it, as Ely does upon the Fens, and as I neared the city it felt like an allegorical journey: to have crossed a pine-forested mountain range on a series of ancient paths, sleeping out by the wayside, under a vulture-filled sky, and then to be entering on foot a walled medieval city seen first from a mountain summit, levitating from the baking plains.

The cathedral was still my guide and sighting mark, though now I could also see the pinnacles of the Alcázar, the castle that clings to the northern edge of the old city. I passed elderly Spanish men, shirtless in the noon heat. One man, who wore braces over his bare brown belly, asked me if I was walking to Santiago. I said I'd come over the mountains from Madrid and Cercedilla, and was walking on northwest, but was unlikely to reach Santiago. He nodded his approval, and walked companionably but silently alongside me for a while, before turning off, nudging a swing-gate open with his hip, and stepping into a cropless field.

Late in the afternoon I reached the cathedral plaza in Segovia's heart. I sat in the shade, rested, watched the square. Pigeons rose applauding in small crowds with echoey wing-claps. Hook-beaked stone gargoyles of vultures protruded from the cathedral's exterior walls. Scattered upon the surface of its main dome were hundreds of pigeons, starlings and crows, looking as if they were preparing to carry the building aloft.

That night, from the southerly ramparts of the city, the Guadarrama showed as a long, low-slung silhouette, above which a red moon hung.

I slipped out of Segovia just before dawn and walked out along the Camino to the north-west, onto the *meseta* proper. There was a haze in the air again, the land was shivering up into the sky, and I imagined pilgrims all over Spain and France converging on the sacred point of Santiago de Compostela, passing over landscape that was both real to the foot and mirageous to the mind.

12

ICE

Kailash & Minya Konka — Pilgrims & summiteers — Panda-hunting — Jon Miceler — The death of Charlie — Peter-Panism — Sunlessness — Karim's game theory of driving —Up the Dadu — The 1932 expedition — *Darshan!* — Kangding's missionary — The sacredness of quartz — At Jatso's stockade — Pyramidal mountains & their power to enchant — To the river — An ice armoury — Altitude sickness — Kiln-fired by cold — *Gomchen* & *tumo* — Milarepa & his songlines — A sacralized landscape — Completing the *kora* — 'The traffic of love' — Death on the mountain — The tenderness of glaciers — An arrow-shower of choughs — Footplinths — Encounters with an earlier self — The ghost path.

Of the many sacred mountains of Buddhism, the holiest is Mount Kailash in Western Tibet, where the Ganges, the Brahmaputra, the Indus and the Sutlej all have their source, and around whose base pilgrims have been walking circuits of notorious arduousness for thousands of years. The most extreme form of this *kora* – the Tibetan-Buddhist term for the form of pilgrimage in which the walker circumambulates, clockwise, the holy site – involves the pilgrim making body-length prostrations over the entire length of the circumambulation: *bend, kneel, lie face down, mark the earth with the fingers, rise, pray, shuffle forwards to the finger-marks, bend, kneel . . .* for thirty-two miles of rough rocky path, over the 18,000-foot Drölma pass.

Kailash is the most famous of the sacred peaks, but it is not – to my eye at least – the most graceful. That honour would go to Minya Konka, 'The White Snow Peak of the Kingdom of Minyak', a pyramidal mountain that rises in easterly isolation as the last great upsurge of the Central Asian ranges. Minya Konka is vast: 24,790 feet high, more than 1,500 feet higher than Kailash. From its sharp summit, the land plunges four vertical miles to the floodplain of the Sichuan Basin. Seen from the Basin, through rare breaks in the cloud, the peak rears up as if footless on the earth.

Since the 1200s, Buddhist pilgrims have been walking and riding to Minya Konka. Some have made the lengthy *kora* of the entire massif, a journey that takes several weeks. Others come to visit the monastery that faces the peak from the west, which is reputed to be the home of the reincarnated living Buddhas of Minya Konka, and was destroyed by Red Guards during the Cultural Revolution. Others come just to see the mountain. 'The power of such mountains,' the Buddhist scholar Lama Govinda wrote of the peaks of Himalayan Buddhism:

> is so great [that] people are drawn to them from near and far, as if by the force of some invisible magnet; and they will undergo untold hardships and privations in their inexplicable urge to approach . . . the centre of this sacred power. This worshipful . . . attitude is not impressed by scientific facts, like figures of altitude, which are foremost in the mind of modern man, nor is it motivated by an urge to 'conquer' the mountain.

Minya Konka has also drawn another kind of worshipper. Since the 1920s – when the mountain was first seen by two of Teddy Roosevelt's sons, who were in Sichuan to prove their manhood by shooting pandas – mountaineers have also travelled to Minya Konka, pulled 'as if by the force of some invisible magnet' to try and reach the mountain's sharp and ice-fluted summit. Many of them have died in the attempt, for Minya Konka is formidably difficult to ascend. Until 1999, more people had been killed climbing it than had reached its summit.

These two kinds of mountain-worshipper stand in strong contrast to one another. There is a humility to the act of the *kora*, which stands as a corrective to the self-exaltation of the mountaineer's hunger for an utmost point. Circle and circuit, potentially endless, stand against the symbolic finality of the summit. The pilgrim on the *kora* contents himself always with looking up and inwards to mystery, where the mountaineer longs to look down and outwards onto knowledge.

~

In early winter, my friend Jon Miceler called to ask if I wanted to join him on a short expedition to Minya Konka, following the trails that once connected the tea-growing regions of Sichuan with Nepal and Tibet, and then the pilgrimage routes – some of them more than 700 years old – that converged on the peak. My interest in pilgrimage was growing increasingly strong, and my hunger for high mountains has long been unseemly. I couldn't think of anything I'd rather do, so I travelled to Chengdu, the capital of Sichuan Province in western China, and met Jon at his apartment there. He'd just returned from an attempted three-week vehicular traverse of the Burma Road.

'Failed,' he said ruefully. 'Gumbo mud. Permit trouble. And way too many leeches.'

Jon is a Tibetologist, a polymath and an explorer. He's also both a pilgrim and a mountaineer. American by birth, he was raised by a Buddhist mother and a physician father. For nearly twenty years he has been exploring the cultures and landscapes of the Eastern Himalaya: as a guide, historian and latterly as a regional director for the World Wildlife Fund. That remarkable fold of the world – the Burma–China–Tibet–India border – is his fascination; in particular its natural histories and spiritualities. He speaks Chinese fluently and Tibetan serviceably and his learning in Buddhism, especially Himalayan Buddhism, is near lifelong.

I couldn't have asked for a better companion in that region. Jon is a formidably fit as well as erudite man. He is 6' 3" tall, thin and strong, with a freckled and sun-polished face, rimless glasses and a mop of curly dark hair. On the flat he moves with a bouncy lope that eats up the miles, and on the steep he moves with a steady herring-boned tread that eats up the yards. He has circumambulated Kailash four times, and he has made scores of what ecologists call 'foot transects': data-gathering treks, which in Jon's case sometimes lasted months. Foot transects make possible an otherwise unattainable acquaintance with a region: the walker records and locates what he or she sees – species, scat, scrapes, weather, erosion – and the accidental encounters born of the transect's line are part of its virtue as a method. Walking Himalayan paths again and again over twenty years has given Jon an exceptional first-hand knowledge – what in Greek might be termed *metis*, or in Chinese *nei heng*, both terms suggesting a 'knowing through experience' – but he wears it lightly and gives of it generously.

Jon's heroes are the plant-hunter Frank Kingdon-Ward, the poet Gary Snyder and the legendary field biologist George B. Schaller, with whom Jon had become friends. It was Schaller who had taken the writer Peter Matthiessen into the north-west Nepal Himalaya in the 1970s in search of the *bharal*, the Himalayan blue sheep: that journey had issued into Matthiessen's classic work *The Snow Leopard* (1978). Schaller's walking powers and single-minded pursuit of field data were infamous. 'I should warn you,' a friend of Matthiessen had written to him on learning that he was to accompany Schaller into the high mountains, 'the last friend I had who went walking with George in Asia came back – or more properly *turned* back – when his boots were full of blood . . .' Matthiessen had passed the Schaller test, though, and so had Jon, who in 2001 accompanied

Schaller up onto the area of northern Tibetan plateau known as the Chang Tang, where they discovered the birthing grounds of the endangered Tibetan antelope, the *chiru*.* But I was anxious about my ability to pass the Miceler test.

~

Jon's plan for our expedition was simple but fallible. We would travel light, and count on good weather. 'Sometimes, weather windows open up in the depths of the Himalayan winter,' he said. 'If we're lucky, it'll be dry and bright and fearsomely cold. If we're unlucky, it'll be blizzarding and overcast and fearsomely cold.'

We'd take the paths as we found them, but always with the aim of curling up and round to the western face of Minya Konka and the monastery that watches it. Climbing the mountain was out of the question, but I began to wonder if this might become a reconnaissance trip for a later summit expedition. Jon quickly scotched such thoughts. 'You'll never get up Minya Konka, and you wouldn't want to try. When we've set eyes on the mountain, I'll tell you a story that will absolutely convince you of this.'

There would be two tents, two ponies and four people. Jon, me, a Tibetan horseman, plus a young Canadian climber, Erik. Erik was rigging-thin and taller even than Jon. At just under 6' 2", I was the

* On another expedition, Schaller and Miceler travelled to Arunachal Pradesh in north-east India, to make a survey line through a previously unsurveyed region. Up in the far north-west of the region, they met the first ever recorded snow leopard in Arunachal Pradesh, coming down a mountain path towards them. It was swinging by its bound feet from a pole, carried by four men, having been clubbed to death that afternoon. Schaller and Miceler accompanied the party down to a nearby village, and watched in silence as the leopard was skinned.

shortest member of our trio. I felt like a Scots pine who had entered a grove of redwoods. Erik's obvious potential for physical action contrasted appealingly with his air of languor and sweet temper. He was only twenty-four years old but already a well-known climber on rock and ice. He had grown up on the Canadian plains, and had cut his teeth putting new routes up frozen waterfalls near Lake Ontario. Some of his friends were into climbing the sides of icebergs floating in Baffin Bay. His dream was to summit an ultra-hard mountain such as Minya Konka.

Jon had been a tough climber in his day, leading multi-pitch big-wall routes in Yosemite and pioneering climbs of Himalayan peaks. He had also lost several friends to the mountains. 'One of them,' he told me as he stuffed gear into rubberized bags in a corner of the apartment, 'disappeared only a few months ago, killed by an avalanche not far from where we're going. I heard the news, and after the initial shock and sadness, I understood that it was exactly how Charlie would have wanted to die. He couldn't ever have been happy growing old, I don't think.'

So many mountaineers and explorers have Peter Pan fixations, a desire never to age, and a dark fulfilment of those desires can come when death occurs in high altitudes or high latitudes. Extreme cold slows the process of decay and confers a cryogenic immortality on the body – George Mallory's corpse found seventy-five years after his death on the upper terraces of Everest, the skin and muscles of his back still standing strong as those of a marble sculpture; Captain Scott, scribbling one of his last letters to J. M. Barrie as he froze in his little tent on the Antarctic plateau, a few miles short of food, safety and warmth; and the bodies of the Franklin crew at Beechey Island, exhumed from the ice 138 years after their deaths, their glassy eyeballs and grinning, startled faces looking as if they had just been roused from a deep sleep. Barrie himself, lecturing on the theme of 'Courage' in 1922, explicitly connected Peter Pan, Scott and the eerily preservative powers of ice. 'When I think of Scott,' he told his audience, 'I remember the strange Alpine story of the youth who fell down a glacier and was lost, and of how a scientific companion computed how the body would again appear . . . many years afterwards. Some of the survivors returned to the glacier to see if the prediction would be fulfilled; all old men now; and the body reappeared as young as on the day he left them. So Scott and his companions emerge out of the white immensities, always young.'

~

We drove west from Chengdu under a dishwater sky of low cloud, out along the flatlands of the Sichuan Basin.

'The sun almost never shines on the Sichuan plain,' said Jon. Erik, who had lived on the Sichuan plain for the past year, nodded feelingly.

'There's a missionary-explorer's account from the 1870s,' Jon continued, 'in which he describes how, when the sun did come out around here, the dogs all barked at it because they didn't know what the hell it was.'

Karim, our driver, wore a black leather jacket with an Eagles escutcheon embroidered onto its breast, and sang Tibeto-pop in a heliated voice. The landscape streamed past us. Terraced rice fields with intricate irrigation channels. Bamboo groves with individual stems spindling up like antennae. Tea bushes in rows as neatly managed as the box-hedging in a Renaissance garden. Karim drove exceptionally dangerously, playing chicken with oncoming lorries and passing slower vehicles on the inside, bouncing along the rough verges of the road. His game-theory logic of driving, when questioned on the matter by Jon, was that he hadn't yet died and this fact was proof of his ability behind the wheel. He explained this to us at some length while glancing back over his shoulder, and gesturing with both hands to underline his subtler points. Eventually, my heart thrumming as yet another lorry dopplered past, its horn blaring, I took to looking backwards, out over the hump of the spare wheel. There was never any trouble to be seen out of the rear window.

So we peeled off the miles towards the mountains. Fat flies smacked like spit on the windscreen. The roadside poplars *sha-sha-shaed* through the open window. Grey road, grey sky. The ground rose and the road fell into line with the Dadu river, a tributary of the Yangtze. Its silty waters had carved a gorge into the sandstone. The gorge sides blocked out the sun and we drove in damp shadow, looking up to the hammer beams of sunlight that roofed it.

'When the first American expedition came in to try and climb Minya Konka in 1932, they rafted *up* the Dadu,' said Jon. 'They were shot at from the banks. Warlordism was rife here. There were no casualties. But to come under fire before they'd even reached the mountain . . .' He gazed out of the window and blinked happily, imagining a time when such adventure was still possible.

Images flashed past us. A pig hung by its ankles from a tree branch while a man drew a knife down its belly and yards of blue intestines slithered over his arm. A woman moved through a rare shaft of sunlight, a baby slung on her front. After five hours' driving we entered a tunnel from which we emerged, several miles later, into flaring sunshine and ringing skies, and there was Minya Konka, roaring white on the horizon, far higher than I had imagined. Karim pulled to a halt on the verge, and we got out. A plume of ice crystals and cloud unfurled from the summit like a silk blessing-scarf.

The tunnel had taken us through the weathershed into a new

world. It was as if we had stepped into Kodachrome from sepia. I thought of what E. M. Forster had said about railway termini: they are 'our gates to the glorious and the unknown. Through them we pass out into adventure and sunshine.' The tunnel felt like that: a gateway into a brilliant realm, entirely unimaginable from the other side. The light that fell here was hard and silvery – what Matthiessen called the 'sword-light of the Himalayas'.

'There's a Sanskrit word, *darshan*,' Jon said as we gazed up at Konka. 'It suggests a face-to-face encounter with the sacred on earth; with a physical manifestation of the holy.' I hadn't known the word, but I was glad to have learnt it. *Darshan* seemed a good alternative to the *wow!* that I usually emitted on seeing a striking mountain.

We drove on and up along switchback roads, through valleys whose steep slopes were forested with pines. The sun burning through the frozen air; a bright halo of ice crystals; pine needles glinting in the sword-light.

At six that evening we reached the town of Kangding, a centuries-old hub-town for the tea routes to Lhasa. Tea grown across Yunnan and Sichuan would converge there and proceed by armed caravan to Batang, Chamdo and at last Lhasa.

Jon met a Taiwanese climber who told us which passes were still viable at this stage of winter. He also told us to head for a remote village called Yulongxi, and look for a man called Batso. Batso had good horses and was trustworthy. Later, we ate noodles with a young man called Kris who had lived in Kangding for a couple of years, running a Christian guest house. Born in Sri Lanka and schooled in the Indian Himalayas, he had eyes as wet as a seal's. He spoke Sinhalese, Hindi, Chinese and Tibetan, as well as English.

'I'm not a missionary,' Kris said softly, 'but my faith informs everything that I do here.'

'He's a missionary,' said Jon as we left the noodle shop.

The next morning we drove again. Hairpins from Kangding to the pass of Zheduo, at nearly 16,500 feet. A *chorten*, and prayer flags lashing in the wind. Porcelain snow. Beyond us to the west was a wide river valley, dry and lunar, through which ran a river of white ice and blue water. Long hours through bare brown land. Snow lying in lines in fields, thawed from the summits of the plough-lines but holding white in the trenches. Groups of dung-tailed yaks. The distant hollow sound of boulders being rolled by the current along the riverbed. Solid stone-built Tibetan houses with elaborately painted eaves. Patties of ice on the river's surface. Prayer flags twined around bridges and gateways, bright against the landscape's close tones.

For seven hours we drove, as our route dwindled from road to track to path almost to nothing. Once, down in that seemingly endless valley, we stopped at a holy site: a low, lozenge-like mound, the size of a small croft, layered and tiled with hundreds of *mani* stones: slabs of rock with prayers chiselled into them. Several tall wooden lances spiked out of the *mani* heap, from which fluttered prayer flags printed with more texts. At one end was a cairn of white stones several feet high.

'White stones have a particular force to the Qiang people of Northern Sichuan,' said Jon. 'They gather up white quartz and marble shards and heap them up in these cairns, some of which are vast! I've seen ones dozens of metres in diameter. The cairns mark the landscape's most sacred points.' I took two of the white stones, both triangular blades of white quartz laced with pink.

For the last two hours of the light we searched the valley for Batso. 'A bit further up' was always the answer. A nod of the head or wave of the hand north. Just as dusk was settling, we found him. He was Jatso, not Batso, and he lived in a clutch of houses beneath a flash of red rock at over 13,000 feet. He sauntered down a beaten earth track to meet us, entirely unsurprised at our appearance in his valley. He was younger than me and preposterously good-looking in a Johnny Deppish way. A stockade of thorns marked out his arable field, and his family's homestead faced Minya Konka, the peak itself hidden by a high range to the east.

The five buildings of Jatso's settlement were wide-walled and heavy-tiled, hunkered close to the ground, ready to see out winter after winter. Lines of prayer flags flapped from the ridges of the house. Each of the wooden shutters that covered the small windows had been intricately carved and coloured with blues, golds and reds. Decorative lines of orange rock had been built into the walls like strata. The late-day light gleamed as gold on the edges of the roof tiles, and shone as silver on the tall grasses that shook in the wind. A bird I couldn't name flew across the valley to the south. Two lenticular clouds hung above snowfields to the west.

That night we pitched our tents in Jatso's yard, just out of reach of his leashed dog. The sky was cloudless and speckled with more stars than I had ever seen. The laughter of children came from inside a building. I gazed up, neck cricked back and mouth bashed open by the beauty of it all. The snow-topped summits caught and returned the moon's tint. Jatso's dog barked and barked through the night.

~

Horse bells, the crunch of feet, my own ragged breathing: pedestrian life at 15,000 feet. Pace after pace, patiently, exhaustingly, following the bare trace of a path. The world dwindled to the next step, then opened out at an upwards glance. The sun gold in the sky, pouring down its heatless light; hard snow, high albedo.

We'd left Jatso's house early, as two ravens wandered the blue air above the stockade. We crossed a river by an unsteady wooden bridge, the water frozen at the river's margins, flowing deep and green in the centre. Up through a trackless rising valley, scrubbed with juniper, with vultures wheeling overhead, and unclimbed peaks – triangular mostly, granite all – lining the northern sky. The snow over which we passed bore the slot marks of fine-footed ungulates, as well as fox fonts and the scat of unknown creatures. Bird-feet printed it like tiny arrows or route-markers: *this way, this way!*

Four hours' work brought us to a pass. And there before us – two miles away and nearly two miles up – was Minya Konka, far closer than I had expected. *Darshan!* I sat down in the snow under a rope of weathered prayer flags, gulping for breath, astonished by the mountain, trying to make sense of its architecture.

The summit split away into three main ridges, each branching into subsidiary ridges with crenellated peaks, each of which then branched again. This dendritic principle created a structure of immense complexity. The flanks of the main ridges were heavily serrated, the fluting visible even at this distance, and from the vast south-western face a white glacier cantilevered out. Simple at the heart of this maze was the main summit, sharp as a shark's tooth, biting into the sky.

Seen from the west, from that pass, Minya Konka resembles a child's sketch of a mountain: a pyramid of white ice and black rock. In this respect, it is familial with the world's other great pyramidal mountains: Ama Dablam in the Nepal Himalaya; Mount Assiniboine in the Canadian Rockies, which my brother had climbed, returning with the arches of both feet broken; the Matterhorn – up which my grandfather had been in a tweed jacket and hobnailed boots – and Khan Tengri in the Tian Shan mountains of Kyrgyzstan, a 23,000-foot pink marble peak that glows mauve in certain evening lights. Pyramidal mountains fulfil a Platonic vision of a mountain, a dream of what one should resemble. Their purity of form heightens the encounter. Approaching such mountains, you feel as though you are stepping into a fable or an epic poem. 'The effect of this strange Matterhorn upon the imagination is indeed so great,' John Ruskin wrote in 1856, 'that even the gravest philosophers cannot resist it.' Historically, these have been the mountains that have compelled the most votaries and claimed the most lives.

Sitting there on the pass, the summit of Minya Konka seemed implausibly easy to ascend. I could tell Erik was thinking the same thing: as if we might just step across the space that separated us from it, dance up its avalanche slopes, teeter along its ridges, float over its cream-puff glaciers, and touch its enchanted summit . . . I shook my head to rid it of such nonsense. The pass was wind-scoured, and no place to loiter long. Far below us was the river gorge that separated our range from the Konka massif. We had miles to go before we slept, somewhere in that valley.

So it was down, steeply down, across shale slopes, the stones of the path flowing in the sunlight, the horses skidding on their front hooves, braking with their back hooves, deerskin bags lurching forwards on their flanks, their bells tolling rapid alarm. We came on behind, tracing a stream-cut as it plunged off the pass, following it between saplings of pine and Himalayan oak and through bushes of rhododendron, stumbling in powder snow that reached knee-deep in places. The stream was part frozen: halted mid-leap in elaborate forms of yearning – chandeliers, ink-flicks and hat feathers. On the west side of the valley, the tops of distant oaks shone like brass in the sunlight. A small bright bird flew to a gnarled pine. We rested in a clearing at a shepherd's hut. I sat with my back against the warm wall, facing the sun and the mountain, narrowing my eyes.

Hours later, we emerged from the forest at the main river. Just downstream of us was a frozen waterfall, hundreds of feet high and a hundred across, hanging off the vertical side of the gorge. Racked spears and lances of ice, glittering in the late light: an armoury. The moon was showing in the sky. We found a little flood-flattened shore of rock-sand knitted over with grass, big enough for two tents. Jatso hobbled the horses and scavenged dead wood to build a fire, while we pitched the tents. Oak leaves spun slowly out in the river's centre as the current raced them away.

Once the first chores had been done I worked my way upstream through brush until I was out of sight of the camp, stripped off, cracked the ice away from the river's edge and bathed briefly, sluicing off the day's sweat. 'You Brits are all the same,' said Jon when I returned, faintly blue around the mouth and lips, but happy. 'Always looking for a mountain bath. Tillman never thought a day was done until he'd had his bath.' Jon had made a rough fire pit out of flat rocks and got a wood fire going. In the centre he'd stacked three rocks into a trivet, on which he set a big metal kettle boiling. We sat on stones and warmed our bare feet against the flames.

Half an hour later, altitude sickness struck me like a blow from the back of an axe. If you've ever suffered from altitude sickness, you'll know how debilitating it is. Nausea, bone-hurt and skull-ache. A medieval pain-helmet of pig-iron jammed down over the head. A bad attack can kill you. A mild attack leaves you mute as a fish and sick as a dog. Each time I come to altitude and fall sick, I vow that I won't return. Once, in a hut in the French Alps, I wrote that vow down and signed it – an affidavit to a future self – but then became so disoriented that I lost the piece of paper. At 21,000 feet in the Nepal Himalaya, I walked a snow-path spattered to either side with the blood and vomit of previous trekkers, their bodies wrecked by the arduousness of the height. Old remedies for altitude sickness include soaking a cloth or sponge in urine and holding it to the nose and mouth. This is not something I've tried.

Two hours later, I was able to speak again. We sat around the fire in the bitter darkness while the kettle spat water at the flames and the flames hissed back. From the night came the cold clink of the horses' bells. 'What was it Kerouac said?' asked Jon just before we all headed to our tents. '"Let us sleep by rivers and purify our ears."'

Of the nights I spent out while following my paths, that one was by far the coldest. At its lowest, it reached -20°C: a dry cold, but a cold that stole to the bone. None of us really slept except for Jatso, with whom I shared a tent and who snored inspiringly from beneath a heap of blankets for ten hours. At one point I crawled out of the tent to try and shake warmth back into my limbs. The sky was framed by the black valley sides. There was a shooting star and then a satellite, winking across the darkness. A gold-grey flutter of light from the fire. A curd-yellow moon. Old land, high crags, silence, the moon, the fire, and a feeling of deep calm and connection.

When I came out again in the dawn half-light, everything in the valley was edged with frost. When I pulled my sleeping bag out, I found it had frozen into a rigid cocoon. I propped it up against a tree. I looked for my trousers, but they'd also frozen. I stood them beside the sleeping bag. It was so cold that even Jatso wrapped a scarf around his nose and mouth, and tucked his trousers into his socks.

But to wake up in that wild place, in such weather, on such a morning? Sleeplessness and core-temperature loss felt like minor costs. Jon cajoled the fire back into life. We sat around its flames, roasting our bared feet from ice back to flesh. The diesel in our fuel bottles had congealed into jelly, so Erik laid the cylinder in the fire to warm it back into useful life. Sunlight tipped off the high peaks to our west, then the sun itself flashed over the eastern summits, and warmth and light came flooding down.

I asked Jon about the lives of the early Buddhist saints: men who lived up in these fastnesses, in such conditions, for almost their whole lives. How could they have stood it?

'But this was what they came here for,' he replied. 'Deeply forested valleys, the roar of the river, the silence of the skies. That's what these *gomchen* – these great meditators – needed to reach their levels of concentration. Men like Milarepa, the eleventh-century hermit who set his spiritual peregrinations to verse, writing a vast and complex web of songlines for the high Himalayas which are still sung today.

'Milarepa taught a form of tantric yoga called *tumo*. Practitioners of *tumo* were, at their most powerful, able to generate an extreme body heat. Milarepa's sect of Tantric Buddhism was famous, in fact, because they only ever wore one layer of white cotton cloth. It was supposedly this inner heat of *tumo* which allowed them to sit out in these landscapes and meditate, even in the harshest conditions.

'I remember once,' Jon continued, 'when I was in north-west India with a group of Ladakhi hermits, cave-dwellers who practised a similar form of Buddhism. These men became renowned for displaying – to a few select foreigners, not including myself – a certain trick. At about 4,000 metres they would soak their robes in water, then sit outside in the winter wind and *steam* their cloaks dry. Get that! Their *tumo* was an inner furnace, so hot that it turned water to steam.'

'I could have done with some *tumo* last night,' I said.

That morning's ascent, on a subtle path up through sparkling oak and pine woods, was among the finest forest hours I have ever spent. Sunlight, sifted by foliage, cross-hatched the path. The lower head of the valley was lost in haze. Another unidentifiable snow range rose above it. We might have been walking through a Chinese scroll painting. The understorey of the forest was thickened with rhododendron, whose leaves shone bronze where the full light caught them. Up through the trees we went, crossing iced streams and passing through tunnels of leaning oaks, following a leaf-and-dirt path. Cairns marked its route, some with niches filled with flower heads, leaves and feathers.

'We've joined the pilgrim trails now,' said Jon.

Up and on for hours, until finally our path cut sharply back north and its uphill bank began to show further eye-catching evidence of pilgrimage – prayers scrawled on paper and weighted down with stones; articles of clothing shed in obeisance; strings of flags. Like a stream flowing into a river our subsidiary path was absorbed into the main pilgrim route, and like a river, too, this new path divided as it encountered obstacles, finding various ways around boulders, trees, stupas and *mani* stone walls, about which pilgrims had performed miniature *koras*, beating circular paths into the dry earth. I was surprised at how busy the route to Minya Konka seemed to be, for the Chinese colonization of Tibet in the 1950s, and the subsequent violent suppression of traditional Tibetan Buddhism, had made pilgrimage much more difficult, especially for ordinary Tibetans. The numbers undertaking the *kora* had dropped drastically.

I felt excited to be walking these paths, which so many pilgrims had followed over centuries, drawn to this great and sacred mountain and others like it. Running through my brain, falling into a rhythm to which I set my pace, was a Spanish palindrome on the subject of pilgrimage: '*La ruta nos aportó otro paso natural*' – 'The path provides the natural next step'. Its chiasmic form cleverly acknowledged the transformative consequences of the foot-pilgrimage, which returns the traveller to his origin and turns the mind back upon itself, leaving the pilgrim both ostensibly unchanged and profoundly redirected. It recalled Thomas's method of making one-day walks in the design of 'a rough circle', trusting that he might 'by taking a series of turnings to the left or a series to the right . . . take much beauty by surprise and . . . return at last to my starting-point'.

The clean tinkle of a bell – and round the corner came a man riding a chestnut horse, magnificently dressed in brocades and silks of river-green, red and blue, stitched and patterned into dragons and interlacings. The silk rang in the sunlight like armour. He took the reins in his left hand, raised his right hand in greeting and then passed on around a bend in the path, back or forwards to whatever time he had come from, his appearance entirely in keeping with that magical forest.

Finally we emerged from an arch in the trees and there right upon us was the Minya Konka monastery, perched on the brink of a ravine, and right upon the monastery, it seemed, was the mountain itself, hidden from us all morning by the slope and the trees.

I hadn't ever before reached a mountain landscape so wholly sacralized, in which almost every human mark was either an expression of devotion or a marker of hierophany. Everything was oriented towards the peak. On the west-facing slopes were stands of white wooden lances, ten or fifteen feet tall, each pennanted with white prayer flags that snapped in the wind, dispersing *om mani padme hums* to every direction. Wide stones marked with crosses or footprints showed places where lamas had self-arisen, creating images of themselves through intense meditation. There were stupas, and *mani* stone piles, and there was the monastery itself, its windows and doorways gazing up at Minya Konka.

'*Nayri*,' said Jon. '*Nayri* is the Tibetan term for a sacred place such as this: *ri* means "mountain", and you'll find it everywhere in Tibet; *nay* means something like "embodiment of the sacred". *Nay* could be found in a series of rocks, or a tree, but it's most usually present in a mountain.'

We dropped our packs, tethered the horses and sat quietly on a grass bank near the monastery in the sunlight. Dirty grey moraine slopes led the eye up to Minya Konka's south ridge, which rose finely towards its summit. Ravens flew north in the ravine beneath us. The earth of the path was terracotta. Sunlight curled and pooled on the shell of a blue-black beetle dragging and bumping itself towards the monastery. Racks of incense sticks smouldered, rings of orange fire creeping down them, blue smoke coiling up into the still air. A monk walked back and forth along the front of the monastery, rumbling a line of heavy bronze prayer wheels with his fingertips. I felt a familiar tingle in my stomach, the mixture of fear and something like lust that high mountains have often provoked in me.

In *The Living Mountain*, Nan Shepherd described the conversion in her relationship with mountains that she experienced in the course of her life. As a young woman, she had been prone to a longing for 'the tang of height', and had approached the Cairngorms egocentrically, apprising them only for their 'effect upon me'. Over time, however, she learnt to go into the hills aimlessly, 'to be with the mountain as one visits a friend, with no intention but to be with him', or to 'go round' the mountain 'in circles to see if it is a good place'. Circumambulation came to replace summit-fever for Shepherd; plateau substituted for peak. 'I believe that I now understand,' she wrote in the last paragraph of the last chapter of her book, 'in some small measure why the Buddhist goes on pilgrimage to a mountain.' She had come to practise her own *kora*, and the Cairngorms had become sacred to her in the materialist sense of being consistently marvellous but also partially explicable. Sitting there in the sun, looking up at Minya Konka, I thought that I had undergone a similar conversion; pushing when young for the summits of mountains, longing to get into unmapped and unexplored territory, but now happier on the beaten track, following the footsteps of others.

A man and a woman plodded towards us, leading a horse between them on which a young boy sat, swaddled in fur and quilted blankets. They stopped to speak with us. The horse cropped the thin winter grass of the bank. The man held a gold-braided halter rope loosely in his hand. His wife smiled, her hands clasped in front of her. Their boots were very worn and dusty. They were farmers from a hundred miles or so away, and they had just that day completed, the man explained to Jon, the full *kora* of Minya Konka. There was no pride or self-acclaim apparent in his explanation, just a calm recording of a fact and an air of weary gladness.

'Let me tell you the story I promised you,' Jon said, gesturing up at Minya Konka, after the pilgrims had walked on, 'the one that'll put you off a summit attempt for ever. For you must be assured that every route on this mountain has one foot in the grave. In 1980, China opened its doors to Western mountaineers for the first time since 1949, and there was a rush among climbers in the know to get to the gems. Although at that time there were many unclimbed mountains, Minya Konka was one of the great challenges. It had been climbed, epically, by the American team in 1932–3, then by a Chinese team in 1956, but that was it. So in 1980, a friend of mine called Rick Ridgeway – the first American to summit K2 – along with a guide called Kim Schmitz, a man called Yvon Chouinard, who founded Patagonia, and a young mountain photographer called Jonathan Wright came here to make an attempt on Minya Konka. They arrived at the monastery in wrathful weather, and after establishing a low camp up on the moraine, they began the hard mixed climbing that is necessary just to access Konka's north-west ridge. You can see the difficulty of ascent from here.' Jon pointed up at the ridge: bulging snowfields, desperate fall-lines.

'Well, they'd only reached the lower walls of the lower ridge when the group was hit by a massive avalanche. The damage done to them by the snow was terrible. Kim broke his back in several places. Rick broke several ribs. Yvon escaped significant injury. But Jonathan Wright suffered a broken neck. Rick managed to crawl over to him, and Jonathan died in Rick's arms, high up on the wall there.

'Somehow, they got Jonathan's body down. And they buried him in a crevasse on the glacier, lowering his body deep into the ice, the burial point within eyeshot of the summit. They marked the site with a cairn. Then, of course, they abandoned the expedition. Kim managed to walk out with a multiply broken back, and eventually made a total recovery.

'In 1999, Rick contacted me, and I helped him to set up an expedition back into Konka. But this time ascent wasn't the aim. It was a pilgrimage of a very different kind. Rick was accompanying Jonathan Wright's daughter, Asia – who had been a baby at the time of her father's death – back to the place where he had died. She wanted to understand why her father had risked his life and eventually died for these mountains, and Rick wanted to help her with that, so she came here on foot.

'They had a hell of a time even getting close to the mountain. The weather conditions were terrible – blizzard, lightning, thunder – but at last they reached the monastery, and from there Rick and Asia made it up onto the glacier. And eventually Rick guided Asia to the point where he remembered burying her father.

'To their horror and fascination, Rick found the cairn but he also discovered a flap of Gore-tex showing beneath the stones. He understood straight away what had happened. The glacier had shifted, and the cairn had shifted with it, but – in the surprisingly tender way of glaciers – Jonathan's frozen body had been pushed to the surface.'

Jon paused. 'Rick told Asia to wait at a distance, and he made her confirm that she wanted to see her father. She did, and so she approached, and there her father was, not returned from the grave but returned by it. She was able to see him in the flesh, preserved almost as well as the day he died. She could touch his face, and she did so. She cut a lock of his hair. Shortly afterwards, they reburied Jonathan, twenty years on from his death.'

~

That afternoon Erik and I walked on up onto the westerly moraine of Minya Konka, towards the grave of Jonathan Wright. It was pathless terrain, a maze of boulders and melt-streams, its topography constantly shifted by the movements of ice beneath it. We rock-hopped between lumps of white rock as large as desks, and crossed the bigger streams by wading, or improvising bridges from tree trunks. We saw the pug marks left in grey silt by what looked like a large feline. I watched five musk deer crest the main Konka moraine, pick their way over its lip, then move down at a graceful diagonal over the steep rubble slope.

We followed the route of the biggest river, up past boulders covered with ivory-coloured ice, dripped like the wax from church candles. A flock of finches gusted up from the river-shore with shrill cries.

At the highest point we reached, we could see more closely the hazardous beauty of the north-west ridge: the brittle flutings, the ice bulge, hundreds of yards across, on which Wright had been killed. I felt no desire at all to climb the mountain, glad only to have seen it in such weather and such light. I made a pair of cairns: each of stones of diminishing size, balanced on top of one another, to mark that sighting of the peak.

Days later, we left the Minya Konka region by another pass. Toiling upwards, we startled a big flock of snow pigeons, which rose with snapping wings. As they turned, the sun flashed from their ice-coloured bellies. Three hard hours' climb to reach the pass. Jagged rows of rock and snow peaks ranked away to the south. The snow there had drifted, melted, then frozen again, so that it was hard and shiny as white vinyl. An arrow-shower of choughs, bright-beaked and solid-bodied, chattered overhead, leading my eye back down the valley. The snow pigeon flock could still be seen, rising and wheeling in front of Minya Konka like thrown quartz chips. Jatso muttered mantras to himself, *om mani padme hum, om mani padme hum*, as we crossed the pass and began the descent back to earth.

Coming up the snowfield on the far side was a long trail of footprints, left by a single walker. These footprints were not pressed down into the snow, though, but raised above it: a series of low snow pedestals, each perhaps three or four inches high. They weren't footprints but footplinths, and they were the print-trail of an unknown earlier walker, entering the sacred space of the Minya Konka massif.

~

A foot falls in the snow – human or animal – and the downwards pressure of the foot compacts the snow beneath it into the form of the print. The sun melts the looser-lying snow surrounding the print, or the wind scours that snow away, and gradually the snow level erodes down to the print, and then below it, so that the compressed snow of the footprint stands out in relief. Such footprints are counter-intuitive, for the downwards pressure of a footfall appears to have *grown* a structure upwards from the ground, rebuking gravity. They are palindromic in form: that which was depressed becomes elevated, and impression is reversed into expression.

A few times, coming down a winter mountain on the same path by which I ascended it, I have met my own earlier footprints, raised up as footplinths. The uncanniness of such moments has its source in the encounter with the altered traces of an earlier self. The world has been slightly but importantly shifted between your first passage and your return, and this feeling accords with the more familiar experience of having been changed by the upper world of the mountains, and by the hours and miles that intervene between ascent and descent. Sometimes these protruding prints have appeared to me like the footmarks of an unseen walker, and the surface of the earth nothing more than a flexible film through which the walker's ghostly feet are pressing, leaving these raised marks on our side of the world: an inverted spectral presence striding through the solid earth as easily as we stride through solid air.

After I returned from Minya Konka, I went with David and three other friends to Scotland, to a range east of Ben Nevis called the Grey Corries, to spend three days following an old drove road into the mountains, and walking the peaks and ridges of the range. The conditions were astonishing: a heavy fresh snowfall, bright winter sunlight, and a howling wind that shook the snow alive. We passed through a white-out so pure and even that it abolished all directions except those proved by gravity. We saw plumes of spindrift sixty yards long streaming northwards from the sharp summit of a mountain called Stob Coire Easain, like the blessing-scarf of ice crystals that had furled out from the summit of Minya Konka. In an eastern corrie, where the wind was given a spin by the form of the land, it whipped up small snow cyclones, fifty feet or more high, that roamed and roved across the mountainside. Once or twice the path of one of these cyclones crossed ours: there was the rising hum of its approach, the fierce hiss of snow grains in the nose and eyes, the silence after it had gone. It felt as if we had been passed through by a ghost.

On the last day, coming off the last shoulder of the final mountain, I found and followed a trail of footprints, and I now wish I hadn't, for they led us into grave trouble. These prints began in the centre of an open snowfield, as if their maker had stepped down from air onto land, and they weren't dinted into the snow but raised above it.

I shouldn't have followed the footplinth trail down off that shoulder, onto steepening ground, but of course I did, because when you are unsure of a route it is natural to put your trust in precedent. So I followed the prints and the others followed me.

Beneath the snow there was heather, whose wiry pale stems gave no grip, and there was slick, sheeny moor grass. Soon the incline was at forty degrees to the horizontal, then fifty, then sixty. The rocks that jagged from it were iced, and shucked off our hands and feet. Everything sloped away beneath us, and yet the footprints proceeded, calmly, across the hillside, the stride-length unvarying, leading us out and down and on.

I shouldn't have continued to follow them, but I did, and on they still led, now along a narrow terrace in the heather that might have been a deer track. That track led to the top of a ten-foot chute of hard ice, which stopped abruptly on another narrow terrace above a seventy-foot drop to rocks. Down the ice chute led the prints.

I shouldn't have gone down the chute, but I did. Skid, thump, a dig of the heels to stop rocking over the lip and down the drop. The others came down in turn, and we shuffled further out along the terrace. I kept on moving, facing inwards now, though the terrace was thinning to little more than a ledge. The wind tore and ripped across the slope. Veers of the brain; needles of sun on snow. Boulders pushing at us. The suck and draw of the drop beneath; blood-thump in the ears.

Then the ledge narrowed to no ledge at all; just heather and rock, perhaps twenty degrees off the vertical. By now we had stopped speaking, concentrating on each handhold and foothold. Below us was the fall, behind us an almost irreversible route, and ahead of us apparently untraversable ground – across which the footprints padded; the same regular spacing, the same enticing trail. I stopped. The others stopped in turn behind me. I felt sick. The slop and douse of adrenalin, panic spliced with moments of hovering calm, pinpricks of fright in my temples. In the valley below us I could see normal life continuing: the flash of sun from a car's windscreen as it moved along the road, a walker on the loch-side path, a gull banking over birch trees.

We clung to that terrace for perhaps three minutes of stalled horrible time, not wanting to go on or retreat. I remembered what real fear in the hills felt like, and how little I liked it. Then at last I decided that death looked more likely ahead than it did behind and so, step by step, we climbed our way back out of trouble, chipping hands into holes in the ice chute, following our own footprints back up that steep ground to the summit of the ridge where it had all begun. When we reached safe ground again, I lay flat on the snow for a while. We laughed and shook hands, and David started singing a Blondie song, and we followed another set of prints away to the west. I still can't work out how those footplinths had been made, floating their way down that impassable terrain.

PART IV

HOMING

(England)

13

SNOW

Prehistoric land art — Sacred architecture — Landscape theatre & the drama of perception — Black horses, white horse — Wiltshire as Antarctica — Illusions of flying — Eric Ravilious — Out-of-kilterness — Engraving as track-making — Flattening light, beckoning path — A bleak glitter of sun — An airborne island — Northwards — Life at frost point — Narwhal horn — Turbulence, disappearance — The tobogganers — A pair of glowing eyes.

RIDGEWAY

Not long after we had followed the ghostly footprints in Scotland, snow fell across southern England, and David and I set out to traverse that arc of the Ridgeway which curves over the Marlborough Downs in Wiltshire, from the White Horse at Uffington past mysterious Silbury Hill and Avebury. The Ridgeway is the name usually given to the hundreds of miles of chalk-down trackway of Neolithic origin, of which – depending on your version of prehistory – the Icknield Way is either a constituent section or a later extension.

The Wiltshire section of the Ridgeway passes through arguably the most sacralized terrain in England. Between 3,000 and 4,000 years ago, vast devotional interventions were made in the landscape here. Megaliths and henges were raised, sarsens were organized in avenues, earthworks were dug, and the cryptically simple edifice of Silbury Hill – a huge truncated cone of tamped chalk – was somehow constructed. At Avebury and Silbury, as at Minya Konka, an ease of relation is expressed between topography and belief. And paths, tracks and cursuses were intricately involved with this Neolithic landscape theatre. The archaeologist Christopher Tilley, in his pioneering work *The Phenomenology of Landscape*, argues that to understand many of the sacred landscapes of Neolithic Britain we need first to understand the importance of the ancient paths that both link and bypass them. Walking, both as approach and traverse, was crucial to the dramas of perception: what Tilley calls 'the strong paths' of this region were used to 'pattern' the relationship 'between sites and their settings'.

David and I decided to follow the Ridgeway that winter day not on foot, but by the decidedly unprehistoric means of cross-country skiing. Cross-country skiing shares nothing with downhill skiing save a basic principle of motion. There are no lifts, no chalets, no snow machines and no trust funds. Cross-country skiing involves moving through landscapes that haven't been prepared for that purpose save by snowfall. On cross-country skis you can ski up and over hills as well as down them. They bestow an exhilarating freedom and mobility.

We left London shortly after dawn in David's white van, trucking west along the A40. Heaps of old black oily snow by the sides of the roads; the sky low and overcast; a hidden sun shedding a weak and eely light. Somewhere near Swindon, we left the van in a snowed-up side lane and took to our skis, following a wide old sunken track over which black hawthorns bent from either side, up towards the summits of the chalk downs where the Ridgeway ran.

On the ridge it was five degrees below zero; even colder in the wind, which shivered the hedges from the east. Three black horses stood statue-still in the middle of a snow-covered field, so flattened by contrast and distance that they resembled paper-cuts. Near them was a white horse, showing grey against the snow. The sounds of gunshots reached us from the west, the noise rippled by the land over which it passed. We settled to the rhythm of the skiing: *glide, hiss, flick, step, slide*.

Low light, saturating the landscape with a dull glow that never thickened to a shine but still drew blues from the long-lying snow. Where the chalk showed, it was the yellow of polar-bear fur or an old man's knees. I found it all bleakly beautiful: the air battened down, the light at its slant. It felt both absurd and wonderful to be moving on skis over this ancient path.

We saw no one for the first two hours. The cold and the gloom had emptied the landscape of people. We had stepped into another xenotopia: Wiltshire as Antarctica, the crossing of a border brought about by the strangeness of the weather. The air felt charged with the static of imminent snowfall, though the snow never came. Beech plantations stood to either side of the path. On the uphills and plateaux the skis gave an extra two yards for every pace we took, and it seemed at times, moving along those high ridges, as if we were flying, the snow beneath us figuring as white air and strengthening the fantasy.

This is, I now know, a well-documented illusion of England's downlands – one of the common conjurings that this landscape can make upon the mind – and it comes upon the walker as well as the skier. Virginia Woolf compared striding the crest of the Downs to flying through the air. Thomas found his imagination borne aloft as he watched kestrels hunt high above him. W. H. Hudson wrote in 1900 of how on the Downs' ridges he felt his mind 'become more aerial, less conscious of gravity', and that the 'desire for flight' came to him 'most often . . . on these great green hills'. At times, he wrote, it seemed that he might 'lift great heron-like wings and fly with little effort to other points of view'.

That day it was apparent to me why this dream of flight is so forceful on chalk downs. The lines of the landscape are both bare and continuous, a wave of dips and rises. There is little to impede the free movement of the eye or the presumed free movement of the body: no ravine or cliff that might detain you, few forests to tangle your sight. The repetition of the down-form suggests infinite distance and unlimited regress. The downland turf also contributes: a cocoa-matting of plant life whose natural springiness exceeds even that of peat, such that your foot bounds up from contact with it. And there are the birds of the Downs, its true gliders and soarers: buzzards, owls, kestrels, skylarks, rooks and swifts, tracking always overhead.

Flight-filled, the chalk hills have long attracted wingless walkers, would-be aeronauts, aerial dreamers and other devotees of the elevated view. Most fascinating to me among these people was Eric Ravilious (1903–1942), the English landscape artist and path-obsessive who loved the chalk-lands of England, especially in snow, and who painted their whorls and tracks in all seasons. When I try to imagine how Edward Thomas saw the Downs, I often think of, or rather I think *in*, the paintings of Ravilious.

~

Ravilious was a watercolourist, engraver and muralist, one of the best-known English artists of the 1930s, a follower of old paths and tracks, a votary of whiteness and remoteness, and a visionary of the everyday. Strangers called him Eric. Friends called him Ravilious. Close friends called him 'The Boy': a Peter-Panish nickname – a charm against ageing, a chrism against death. He was handsome: an angular face, large dark eyes, a sloped nose, dark hair, long fingers always holding brush, pen or cigarette. He liked tennis, billiards, propellers, winter, the shadowlessness of sea light, northerliness, ceramic, boxwood, crystal and ice. Fastidious but also impetuous, he had a habit of putting his head out of train windows and losing his hat to the wind.

He was brought up on England's downlands, and before he fell fatally in love with the ice and light of the far north, Ravilious worshipped the chalk of the south. His childhood was spent in Eastbourne. Up behind the town billowed the South Downs, and on weekday evenings and at weekends, while his father pored over the Old Testament, developing his own annotations to the texts (an intense and private exegesis that lasted for most of his adult life), Ravilious, left alone, began to explore the surrounding countryside. He made expeditions, slept out (tucked under hedges or with the stars for a ceiling), and walked for hours, following the beckoning lines of the Downs: the eye-leading ridges, the meandering streams, and the chalk paths which curled across that landscape. He read *Tom Sawyer* and *Huckleberry Finn*, and dreamt of the adventures to be found down the river roads.

The Downs, with their soft and equalizing sunlight, their pathways and their loneliness, primed Ravilious's imagination. They informed his whole outlook and way of painting, he wrote, 'because the colour of the landscape was so lovely and the design so beautifully obvious'. Through them, he grew to cherish certain landscape characteristics: crisp flowing lines, an aura of detachment from the lived world. This was the terrain – with its combination of human workedness and extreme age – that shaped his temperament and his sensibility, as it differently shaped Thomas's. It bequeathed to both men shades of melancholy, and it also induced the dissociation that tinged the art and personality of both. Ravilious came to possess, in the phrase of one friend, 'a kind of wariness against all allegiances and personal involvements'. Another observed that Ravilious 'always seemed to be slightly somewhere else, as if he lived a private life which did not completely coincide with material existence'. This out-of-kilterness also distinguishes his painting. Viewing his work, one has a sense of looking at two overlaid acetate sheets of the same image, imprecisely matched, or of two intersecting paths that never quite achieve their vertex.

Part of the sense of disengagement that attends Ravilious's paintings has to do with the images of tracks, prints and paths that he repeatedly used: footprints on snow or in mud, left by unseen pedestrians, walkerless paths that entice the eye and the imagination out of sight, promising events over the horizon. Ravilious was obsessed by tracks: he read deeply in the work of Thomas and he revered Samuel Palmer, who wandered the footpaths around his Kent village by dawn, dusk, night and day, and he absorbed Alfred Watkins's *The Old Straight Track* (1927), with its vision of a concealed network of Neolithic trade routes spreading across England and the world. Ravilious's mentor at the Royal College of Art was Paul Nash – another lover of chalk, another follower of the old ways, another artist of the path.

Ravilious walked the chalk paths of the Downs, and he made art of them. In 1929 he engraved the Wilmington Giant on boxwood, for a zodiacal almanac in which the giant features as Taurus: a large white figure crowned by a full moon. In 1934 he painted his own garden path. In 1935 he painted *Chalk Paths*, in which three tracks compete to lead the eye away, while a barbed-wire fence snags the gaze. A 1936 canvas records travellers' caravans stopped by the side of an old road. An undated work, titled *Eastleen Road*, gazes down a Sussex green way. Dozens more paintings are of paths: glimpsed behind waterwheels, out of house windows, from trains; paths crossing fields, leading along cliff-edges or up to the other great chalk figures of the Downs (the Uffington Horse, the Cerne Abbas Giant). In 1937 he visited Gilbert White's Selborne in Hampshire, and walked the holloways of which White had written in his third letter to Thomas Pennant. Ravilious's engraving of a Selborne holloway shows a deep lane, over which the trees are leaning and locking, and the entry to which is guarded by a barn owl in flight. The owl's head is turned out towards the viewer, its eyes quizzical behind its knight's visor of feathers.

The paths of the Downs compelled Ravilious's imagination, and so did the light: falling as white on green, distinctive for its radiance, possessing the combined pearlescence of chalk, grass blades and a proximate sea. If you have walked on the Downs in high summer or high winter, you'll know that the light also has a peculiar power to flatten out the view – to render scattered objects equidistant. This is the charismatic mirage of the Downs: phenomena appear arranged upon a single tilted plane, through which the paths burrow. In these respects the light of the Downs is kindred with another flattening light, the light of the polar regions, which falls usually at a slant and is similarly fine-grained.

The light and the path were Ravilious's signature combinations as an artist. Together they create a unique disharmony. He produced scenes that seem suspended almost to the point of stasis, but that also allude to some future or simultaneous action. The effect on the viewer is one of dissonance: the sensation of occupying a space between two worlds, or even two entirely distinct geometric systems at once.

~

It felt, that day on the Ridgeway, as if we had stepped into a Ravilious canvas. The sense of suspended animation, of action occurring elsewhere. The light levelling the landscape and the path beckoning us through it. Everywhere, the snow was grooved: by the old chalk tracks, by bicycle tyres and tractor wheels, by the lines of our skis and by the prints of dogs, hares, rabbits, pheasants and people. On the declivities we skied past hollow cow-parsley stems and yellowed grass, and we sank into deep drifts around the base of hawthorns, which seemed to grow like crystal: the jag and cross-jag of thorn and black branch against the snow.

Yellow, white, grey, grey-blue: the landscape had been burnt back by the cold to its ashen colours. Here and there were flashes of fire: haw-berries like blood in the hedgerows, the sparks of redwings in flight. Now and then the low sun showed yellow through clouds. Fieldfares clattered in the bushes, plucking haws, throwing their heads back and swallowing them whole at a gulp. Sarsen stones stood about in flocks, with snow on their rounded backs. Buzzards were out in ones and pairs, turning in the sky, looking for the carrion which was more plentiful in such prolonged cold weather. We passed a kestrel hunched on a telegraph post, its head sunk into its shoulders. We passed Bronze Age round barrows and Neolithic long barrows. Two brown hares made an urgent run across a big field, kicking snow from their hind feet. In the canopy of a long thin beech wood, rooks yabbered and called, tossed up into the air and then settled back, as if the wood itself were boiling.

Sometime about mid-afternoon there was a bleak glitter of sun, and shortly afterwards we turned a bend of the Ridgeway and looked across to see, for the first time – in a piece of pure landscape theatre that had not changed for nearly 5,000 years – Silbury Hill rising white in the distance, apparently floating high above the surrounding landscape: another of the flying islands that dot these pages.

For those last short hours of daylight, we moved through a world drained of people and colour. Once, a heron launched itself from low ground to our south, a foldaway construction of struts and canvas, snapping and locking itself into shape just in time to keep airborne, slowing time as it beat away northwards on curved wings.

~

For most of Ravilious's life, the Downs satisfied his landscape needs. Especially in winter, when the beech hangers stood out like ink strokes in a watercolour, they embodied his aesthetic ideal: crisp lines, the fall of pale light on pale land. But as the 1930s wore on, he began to desire an elsewhere, an otherworld. Like many Englishmen before and after him, he came to locate that elsewhere in the far north – the dreamed-of land of the Arctic Circle and the midnight sun, of icebergs floating in water black as lacquer, of the aurora borealis, of spines of grey-blue frosted mountains and the year's last sun shining like foil on the horizon line. Since boyhood, Ravilious had been entranced by the romance of the polar regions. He had read widely in the great books of Arctic exploration and adventure. He collected nineteenth-century editions, maps and images of the far north, including copperplate engravings of the journeys of Barents, Ross and van Heemskerk. The colour white – or if not colour, then tone, or atmosphere, or absence – seems to have possessed a particular power of attraction for him: it was there first in the chalk of the south, and later in the ice of the north.

By the time the Second World War was declared, Ravilious's boreal obsession had deepened. He was restless to travel north, and his chance to do so came with his appointment in late 1939 as an official war artist, which gave him a rank of acting captain in the Royal Marines, and influence over his postings. So it was that, in the last three years of his life, as Peter Davidson has finely written, 'the snow and the snow light on bare hills draw [Ravilious] steadily northwards'.

In May 1940 came the news for which Ravilious had longed. He was to sail with HMS *Highlander* to Norway and across the Arctic Circle. *Highlander* would be supporting the Allied assault on Narvik. 'Goodbye Tush,' he wrote to his wife, Tirzah, 'I'll come back as soon as I can but it is all out of my hands as you can see.'

They sailed for days over good seas, up through the latitudes, the day lengths growing as they ploughed on, escorting the aircraft carrier HMS *Glorious*. Ravilious sat on deck working for hours, or leant on the stern-rail, coatless in the northern sun, watching the wake curdling the sea into cream and green: a white track, a chalk path inviting him to step from the ship's side and stride out along it, back south, back to Tirzah.

Hard sea battles were fought. Ravilious's ship was attacked by plane, mines and submarine. But Ravilious barely referred to these dangers in his letters home. The attacks were offstage events. More important to him was that the sun never fell below the horizon. At 70° 30' 00", he painted the midnight sun, poker-orange above a boreal sea so blue it almost expired into black.

The art Ravilious produced during these weeks was perhaps his finest, certainly his strangest. His images are full of action but devoid of people. They possess a lonely watchfulness: Ravilious the sentinel. The silvered bleakness of the Arctic seems to have entered them, infusing them with a stillness. They are at frost point.

His letters, too, assumed a more oneiric tone than usual. The atmosphere was 'remote and lovely'. When the ship entered fog banks, it was as though they had passed into some 'unearthly existence'. Terns scooted past, dolphins sculled beside the ship, and once they saw an empty upturned lifeboat. He watched German planes drift over, shiny as sixpences in the high zinc sky, and felt briefly as though he had been transformed into a tube of glass, cylindrical and brittle: the effect something to do with being viewed from above . . .

When Ravilious returned from 7,500 miles and four weeks at sea, having witnessed deaths and marvels, he found himself changed. The world seemed more spacious to him, and less consequential. The north was still exerting its pull. Within weeks of getting home he was longing to leave again: to Iceland, then Greenland, then Arctic Russia – Novaya Zemlya, perhaps.

But the War Artists' Advisory Committee asked him to paint the concealment of the White Horse at Uffington, which was being turfed in – millennia after it had been turfed out – to prevent German bombers using it as a landmark or target. They also wanted him to paint the fire engines that had been deputed to spray the chalk roads with black ink, also to prevent them being used as navigation aids by the Luftwaffe.

But then he was posted to Iceland. The timing was far from kind. Tirzah had been hospitalized for an emergency mastectomy, and had returned only a week before Ravilious was due to depart. He should have stayed to care for his family, but he didn't. He bought Tirzah a copy of his second favourite book, Boswell's *Life of Johnson*, and cut it in two with a serrated knife, giving half to Tirzah and packing half himself to take away: proof that they would be reunited. He spoke to a friend about the Iceland trip as fulfilling a long-held desire to explore the outer limits of the physical world.

He flew into Iceland on a calm day in late August 1942. The volcanic mountains, viewed from above, looked to him like lunar craters, casting shadows that were dark and striped as leaves. In a Reykjavik market, Ravilious held and almost bought a narwhal horn. He collected flowers and shells to take back home as tokens of the north. From the capital he made a spine-jolting road journey to Kaldadarnes, an Anglo-American airbase on the east coast of the island: breeze-block barracks, a green corrugated-metal roof and a swell of low mountains behind.

He had only been there a night and a day when a report came in of a missing aircraft out of Kaldadarnes, one of the 269 Squadron Coastal Command: a Hudson Mark III that had disappeared off the coast while engaging a U-boat.

At dawn the next morning Ravilious was shaken awake. A search was about to be launched: three more Hudsons were to fly out and sweep the area in which the first plane had disappeared, 300 miles to seaward. Did Ravilious want to fly as observer, paint the mission, possibly the rescue?

Even as the three Hudsons took off, a storm was brewing. They made their search, found nothing and turned for home, their wings bucking in the turbulence. Radio contact became sporadic between the planes, then non-existent.

Only two of the Hudsons landed again at Kaldadarnes. Ravilious's plane, FH 363, did not. Pilot, navigator, wireless operator, gunner, and an artist who had dreamt as a young boy on the Downs of flying over the northern ice, did not. All five men were lost in a plane looking for a lost plane.

~

Late in the day, David and I entered a deep winter wood of birch, hazel and beech on the crest of a hilltop. Icicles hung from the branches, and the last light condensed in the blebs. Water in a pool in the wood shone black and thick as lithography ink. We crossed an

Anglo-Saxon earthwork, a double dyke that ran east–west. Then we emerged from that high ground and looked down onto the paired summits of Walker's Hill and Knapp Hill, the two rounded chalk hills that form a gateway through which the Ridgeway passes.

And there on the slopes of Knapp Hill, suddenly and gladdeningly, were people again: scores of tobogganers in gaily coloured coats and scarves. Even from a mile away we could see their reds and blues, bright against the snow, and we could hear the cries of the children and the crunch of the toboggans over old snow. We skied down to the low ground between the hills hushing through the snow, which lay so lightly that it plumed off the tips of our skis. When we reached the gateway, we climbed Walker's Hill to the long barrow on its summit, whose contours were encased in crisp layers of ice. Twilight: the sky streaked purple and crimson. The tobogganers on the opposite hill yelled and slid and laughed. A boy in a duffel coat ran down the slope with his arms outstretched. *Lift is created by the onwards rush of life over the curved wing of the soul.*

That unforgettable day held a final surprise. Dark had fallen, and we were driving back in the van. We were only a few miles from the Ridgeway when David pulled out of a side lane onto a fast road. As he did so a large black-pelted animal sloped across the wide snowy verge to our south, moving with the high-shouldered prowl of a big feline, before flowing into the darkness of the hedge. We glimpsed it only for a few seconds. It was far too big for a domestic cat, and had the wrong gait and size for a fox or deer. As David drove off up the road I swung round in my seat to see two great yellow eyes glaring like lamps from the hawthorn and the shadows. 'That was a panther,' I said to David. 'I know, I saw it too,' he said, as he drove on. All the way home we speculated about that dark shape. Later, we would find that there had been many sightings of big black cats in the Marlborough Downs. I wished that we had pulled over and gone back with torches to examine the ground, searching for pug marks in the snow and mud. And then I thought that perhaps it was better – after crossing that otherworldly landscape on that ancient path – to have not proof or disproof, but instead a certain image of uncertain origin: the fierce light of those two eyes scorching out of the darkness.

14

FLINT

Downs storms — The consolations of landscape — Egotism dispersed — Maps of longing & of loss — 'The hill road wet with rain' — Double-penned footfalls — Padders, tramps & hobos — Night on Chanctonbury Ring — Haunting & fear — The Devil's soup & the hairy bikers — The severe Reverend C. A. Johns — Conduplicate, convolute & involute — Tree & bird; root & step — Night on Kingston Down — Dupel & thistledown — Another white horse — The volatility of place — Futile pursuits — Sea-fall at Cuckmere — Glaucous waves — Finding the flints — Inner roads & ghostland.

> The long white roads . . . are a temptation. What quests they propose! They take us away to the thin air of the future or to the underworld of the past.
>
> Edward Thomas (1909)

Footprints in the wet white earth of the path. The ridge of the South Downs I was walking had become a frontier in the landscape, dividing the world into realms of weather, light and colour. Underfoot, the track – of fine chalk, pure enough to write with, pocked by butterscotch flints – was glossy with recent rain. Ahead of me, it ran brightly off over the hills, dipping from sight before looping back up again, softening with distance.

I was walking in a stormlight that made the linseed pulse a hot green, and turned the barely ripened barley fields to red and gold sand. Dark shoals of rooks over the woods, and billows of rain like candle-blacking dropped into water. The Downs are the only high ground in an otherwise flat and low landscape, and this means that, as in the desert or on an ocean, you can sometimes see what weather will reach you hours before it arrives.

For much of that morning I led a charmed life: monsoon-squalls sliding by to east and west. Then, just after noon, a big storm caught me. Yellow sun-flare, dulling to sepia. Rain drilling the earth. The path a river, gathering the water into a torrent that rinsed the chalk white again. A brisk summer hailstorm. Then rain again, so hard and fast that it appeared as cylinders rather than drops, as if I were seeing through reeded glass, and at last sun again and the air re-pristinated. I sheltered in a copse of ash, oak and high-trunked beeches, and ruefully considered Hippolyte Taine's pastoral claim that 'the first music of England' is to be heard in 'the fine patter of rain on the oak trees'. That morning, there was nothing musical to the rain. It was military: weather war.

It was the first of many soakings for the day. During each shower the world bleared and wove. After each shower the sun struck back out and the earth steamed and the smells of the land rose up. Sun-blazed rain-scarps trailed off to the south-east, away over the Channel to make landfall on the French coast. I tried to time my miles between storms, moving from cover to cover. Rain-filled hoof-marks and footprints flashed gold, coined by the sun. I felt lifted, glad to be out and walking. Ahead of me lay more days on foot, and the path insinuating eastwards – in the old and innocent sense of the verb, from the Latin *insinuare*, meaning 'to bend in subtle windings, to curve'.

I'd left early that day from Winchester, planning to follow the ridge line of the South Downs east for a hundred miles or so until it made sea-fall near Eastbourne, where the chalk dipped down underneath the English Channel. I had walked early-day miles past watercress farms and through hangers beneath whose beeches roiled a flak of loose leaves.

My tracking of Edward Thomas had begun on the Icknield Way, and I was ending it back on the chalk again. The Downs were at the centre of his 'South Country', and they were his heartland: the area he lived in and walked on for longer than any other. In December 1906 Thomas – with his wife Helen and their two children, soon to be followed by a third – moved to Hampshire from Kent. Thomas came to know his new country by walking and path-following; he would cover thousands of miles on the Downs in the decade he lived there. They became his landscape of closest acquaintance, consoling him in ways that religion or music consoled others. 'On the ancient tracks above which the kestrel has always circled,' recalled Helen, 'retreading forgotten footpaths and hidden lanes . . . he could throw off his melancholy brooding and be content' (echoes of Albert Camus's half-contemptuous, half-envious remark to his journal that he might write the story of 'a contemporary cured of his heartbreak solely by long contemplation of a landscape'). The paths offered Thomas cover from himself: proof of a participation in communal history and the suggestion of continuity, but also the dispersal of egotism:

Roads go on
While we forget, and are
Forgotten like a star
That shoots and is gone.

Thomas loved the historical synchronicities of the chalk: the ancient path-lines that were echoed in form by yesterday's plough furrows. He liked the evidence of human mark-making and tampering over millennia – tumuli, long barrows, chalk-pits, dew ponds – testifying to a landscape that was commemorative, tending to the consecrated. He wrote down lists of Hampshire and Sussex place names, enjoying the 'wealth of poetry' they possessed. He talked at length with the people he met along the paths of the Downs. And he walked: following lanes to lonely farmhouses or abandoned barns; walking flint-diggers' cartways, smugglers' tracks and hares' paths, generating an elegant typology for the aspects of paths: the 'airy motion' and 'bird-like curves' of those tracks that descend from the ridge-tops down to clay, sand and river; the boustrophedon motion of a path that 'doubles round the head of a coombe'; the long straight line of the Downs paths in which 'a curve is latent'; the 'sheaf of half-a-dozen footpaths worn side-by-side' that ran through fields before narrowing and braiding as a bridge or gate was approached; the 'grassy track[s] of great breadth' that ran under ash trees and 'amidst purple dogwood and crimson-hearted traveller's joy'. Late every summer he would look out for a 'gentleman of the road' who he came to think of as the 'umbrella man', who had been tramping for forty years, and who towed behind him as he walked a perambulator that contained an ebony-handled umbrella and, the first August that Thomas met him, a cabbage. The umbrella man was often to be found camping in the deeper and wilder lanes of Hampshire: under a spreading oak or dark spruce, or in a bay of turf.

Thomas, more than anyone else, had sent me out along the paths, and in the course of my walking I had read my way through much of what he had written – the natural history, the travel books, the letters, the war diary, the poems – and much of what had been written about him. I had come over my years and miles of walking to think of Thomas's writing as a kind of dream-map: an act of cumulative but uncentred imaginative cartography, a composite chart of longing and loss projected onto the actual terrains of his life, and onto the Downs in particular. Thomas knew to some degree, I think, that this was what he was engaged in creating: an ongoing exploration of his interior landscapes, told by means of the traverse of particular places and the following of certain paths.

~

I slept that first night on the Downs in the dubious shelter of a forestry plantation called War Down, tucked into a cocoon-like tent, while the rain slipped down the conifer needles. I have spent more comfortable nights under canvas. But by dawn the rain had stopped, the air was warm and I started early. Thomas's 1916 poem 'Roads', which I was trying to get by heart as I walked, tripped through my mind.

The hill road wet with rain
In the sun would not gleam
Like a winding stream
If we trod it not again.

Wild clematis smoked up the hedgerows. Creepers – bryony, ivy, honeysuckle, bindweed – slinked out along tree branches and hung down over the path like the slipped coils of snakes. Where rain had sluiced the chalk it was slick as silk.

Away to my north-east I could see the shapely high ground that rises above Steep, the village where Thomas and his family lived for ten years in three different houses. The first of these, Berryfield Cottage, sat at the foot of a chalk-land plateau, juniper-dotted and topped with a stand of firs. The house was pleasingly remote: to reach what Helen took to calling 'the outer world', you had to follow a winding lane so deep-sided and dark 'that the entrance to it on the main road looked like the entrance to a tunnel'. At night they could hear wind in the beech hangers, the cough and bark of foxes and owl-hoots. Even there though, in a landscape that brought him pleasure, Thomas couldn't rid himself of his depression. There were whole days of silence in Berryfield Cottage, his head drooping wearily with the effort of being alive, his face sunken and grey under the 'crushing attacks of gloom and wretchedness'. He was sharp and harsh to the children; sharper and harsher to Helen. Nor did the landscape always restore him to himself. One desperate day in the winter of 1908 he took his revolver from a desk drawer, pocketed it and strode out of the house without speaking to Helen. He returned late in the afternoon, unharmed, his shoes caked in mud and leaves, unwilling to speak of what he had been through up on the plateau, his wounding of her having substituted for his wounding of himself.

There were wonderful times in Steep, too, though they were rare. Sometimes he and Helen would sleep the night in the copse at the end of their garden, lying on their backs at roosting hour and watching the patterns made overhead by the birds in flight. At first Thomas tried to help Helen remember the names of the constellations, but she had no desire to learn them, content for the night sky to remain an effect of pure design. When good weather came they would leave the children with a neighbour, put down their work, take their sticks from beside the back door and head off on foot into the countryside. Sometimes they would walk over to Gilbert White's parish of Selborne; sometimes they caught the train to Canterbury and walked the Pilgrim's Way back to Winchester. Once they went to Wiltshire for a fortnight and saw the White Horse at Uffington. Helen thrilled to the atavism of what she called 'the ancient ways', the sense of being connected by footfall to 'history and tradition'. Thomas taught her how to walk differently: 'with [her] body, not only with [her] legs', feeling the landscape as she moved over it.

For Helen, too, each footfall taken in Thomas's company was double-penned, leaving its mark twice: on land and in her memory. 'Every hillside, every wood and meadow, every green lane and steep chalk track' was 'imprinted on my heart for ever [by the] walks that Edward and I took there', she would write after his death.

~

Near Buriton, on the county border with Sussex, I saw a broad-backed figure in the distance on the path. My pace exceeded his and the figure came into focus. A man, short and slim, perhaps fifty years old, his broad back in fact his rucksack. Into net pockets on either side of the rucksack were tucked two battered plastic Coca-Cola bottles, their labels long gone. They resembled boosters on a rocket pack. A pan tied on by its handle clinked against a metal buckle with every pace. It was a long-term wayfarer's pack: messy but efficient. I fell into step alongside him, and we began talking. He was called Lewis. His manner was calm, measured. He wore wire-rimmed spectacles. He'd left home six years previously, he said, after the death of his wife. He had sold his house and decided that he would walk. So he'd walked Britain from top to toe. He'd walked across France, through Spain and over into North Africa, and he had plans for China and the Himalayas. Mostly Britain, though. He lived on the long-distance paths. He woke each day around five o'clock, whatever the time of year, and tried to cover five miles before breakfast. He kept the Coke bottles filled with water.

'Now and then I treat myself to a night in a bed and breakfast,' he said, 'but mostly I just sleep wherever I'm walking.'

He reached behind as he said this, and patted a tent roll on the bottom of his pack. For each major walk, he kept a journal. Always the same kind: red and black cloth-covered, A5, tough enough to be stuffed in a pack. When he had filled one up, he posted it back to his brother who lived in Newcastle. 'He's got three dozen of them now, all lined up on a shelf,' Lewis said. 'One day I'll turn them into a book.'

Somewhere near Amberley a barn owl lifted from a stand of phragmites. We stopped to watch it hunt over the water margin, slowly moving north up the line of the river, pulling a skein of shrills from the warblers in the reeds. It was a daytime ghost, its wings beating with a huge soundlessness. 'You go ahead,' said Lewis to me. 'I'm in no hurry.'

There are two intertwined histories of modern wayfaring. One involves the wilful wanderer, the Borrovian or Whitmanesque walker, out for the romance of the way. The other – a shadow history, darker and harder to see – involves the tramps, the hobos, the vagrants, the dispossessed, the fugitives, the harmed and the jobless, bodging life together as they 'padded' it down the roads. Ten miles a day was the statutory lot of the 'padder'; ten miles a day would eat up the ground. The years in which old-wayfaring flourished in Britain, from the 1880s through to the 1930s, were also key decades in the history of the 'tramp'. The second half of the nineteenth century saw the final breakdown of a guild culture in England which had lasted since the early medieval period, whereby workers would be notified of employment and would walk to find it. Many of the men returning from the First World War came back to England with no job and no prospect of settled work. The life of the road was the only option available to them, and in the twenty years after the war there was a substantial tramping population on the road, sleeping out and living rough. Plumes of smoke rose from copses and spinneys up and down the country, as the woods became temporary homes to these shaken-out casualties of conflict. Their numbers were augmented when the economic depression of the 1930s left millions jobless across Europe and America.

The most heartbreaking moment of Laurie Lee's great book *As I Walked Out One Midsummer Morning* (1969) comes not long after he has left his own valley in the Cotswolds and is dallying over the chalk of Sussex on his way to London. He eats dates and biscuits to keep himself going up, and sleeps by the path: a night in a hayrick, a night in Chanctonbury Ring. The year is 1934, at the height of the depression. Lee is fresh to the road and is just beginning to understand something of the other kinds of people he meets: the odd recreational walker, some long-term professional tramps (who were identifiable because they 'brewed tea by the roadside, took it easy, and studied their feet'). But there were others, Lee noticed, 'all trudging northwards in a sombre procession', who belonged to 'that host of unemployed who wandered aimlessly about England at that time'. These people:

> went on their way like somnambulists, walking alone and seldom speaking to each other. There seemed to be more of them inland than on the coast – maybe the police had seen to that. They were like a broken army walking away from a war, cheeks sunken, eyes dead with fatigue. Some carried bags of tools, or shabby cardboard suitcases; some wore the ghosts of city suits; some, when they stopped to rest, carefully removed their shoes and polished them vaguely with handfuls of grass. Among them were carpenters, clerks, engineers from the Midlands; many had been on the road for months, walking up and down the country in a maze of jobless refusals, the treadmill of the mid-Thirties.

It is a sad and brilliant paragraph, compassionate in its noticing – especially the 'vague' polishing of shoes by men who had once been in jobs where shininess of shoe mattered; a means of symbolically keeping the dust of the road at bay – and it is evocative of these brigades of broken men who walked the land but often fall out of the headier accounts of life on the path.

~

East of Beacon Hill I reached a sustained ridge of chalk. From the woods came the game-show buzzers of jays and crows. Whitebeams marked the path to right and left, with their grey-green upper leaves and their sharp silver unders. I walked through a field of common orchids and pink clover, and ate the clover anthers for their nectar. I passed tombs and memorials of different eras: Bronze Age burial mounds which had once held cremated ashes in pottery vessels; Neolithic long barrows; a wayside shrine to a German airman killed in 1940, which was covered with remembrance crosses, rose petals and flints. Then I emerged out of a dark and yew-rich wood and onto a down that stretched for two miles or more ahead of me. Bleached light, shining grey beech trunks, a tractor ploughing a distant field to corduroy. Grass flickering in the wind, grasshoppers scraping and bowing. White flints scattered across the fields, tumbleweeds of sheep's wool bowling between them.

At dusk I followed a hollowed path that wound up the wooded scarp slope of the Downs east of Storrington. The path's depth spoke of continual foot-passage over centuries, and I liked its design: it moved in round-cornered zigzags, an uphill meander through the trees. There in the forest, night was further advanced. I turned a corner and a badger bustled out of a bank of dog's mercury, stopped, stared at me, its eyes giving a quick green jewel-flash in the dark before it barrelled on downhill along its path, and I followed mine uphill, out of the woods and onto the summit plateau of the Downs, to a place called Chanctonbury Ring, where Lee had slept and where I now wish I hadn't spent the night.

The Ring is a circle of beech trees, planted on a hilltop that had been the site of Bronze and Iron Age fortifications and a Roman temple. In 1760 a young aristocrat from the scarp-foot village of Wiston named Charles Goring decided to add his own layer of history to the Chanctonbury earthworks. He planted beech saplings in a well-spaced circle and, according to one story, then daily carried bottles of water up the slope to irrigate his saplings on that arid downland summit (according to the other story, he got his servants to do this job for him).

Either way, the saplings took and flourished and eventually grew into a cathedral grove. For two centuries, Chanctonbury was the best-known landmark of the South Downs. On one July evening in 1932, 16,000 people boarded specially scheduled Southern Railway trains in London to follow a moonlit walk over a stretch of the Downs, gathering to watch sunrise from the Ring. But then in 1987 the Great Storm blew in and wrecked Chanctonbury. It's now missing most of its main trees, and its interior has reverted to a sprouty scrub of ash and bramble.

Nevertheless, up there that evening it still felt surprisingly remote. Brighton glittered away to the south, like something far-fetched on fire. The Weald to the north was almost lightless. The sky was a tarnishing silver. I rolled my sleeping mat out between two of the remaining beech trees just as dark fell, and took my shoes and socks off. The rabbit-cropped turf soothed my feet, and I wriggled my toes in it, then walked the circumference of the Ring. Nearly back at my starting point, I stepped on some sheep dung and had to spend a few minutes flossing the consequences out from between my toes with bunches of grass. After I'd eaten, I lay down to sleep, placed an ear to the turf and imagined the depths of history the soil held – Neolithic, Iron Age, Bronze Age, Roman, Augustan, down through all of which the beech roots quested. I held that giddying thought for at least half a minute, and then sank into senseless sleep.

I heard the first scream at around two o'clock in the morning. A high-pitched and human cry, protracted but falling away in its closing phase. It came from the opposite side of the tree ring to where I was sleeping. My thoughts were sleep-muddled: *A child in distress? A rabbit being taken by a weasel or fox?* Impossible, though: the sound was coming at least from treetop height. A bird, then; an owl surely. But this was like no owl I had ever heard before: not the furry hoot of a tawny or the screech of a barn owl. I felt a faint rasp of fear, dismissed it as ridiculous. Then another cry joined the first, different in tone: slightly deeper and more grainy, rising at its end; the shriek of a blade laid hard to a lathe. Also more human than avian, also unrecognizable to me, also coming from treetop height. I lay there for two or three minutes, listening to the screams. Then I realized, with a prickling in my shoulders and fingers, that the voices had split and were now coming towards me: still at treetop height, but circling round the tree ring, one clockwise and one anticlockwise, converging roughly on where I was lying. I felt like standing up, shouting, flashing a torch; but instead I lay still and hoped it would all end. The cries met each other almost directly above me, twenty or thirty feet up in the dark. After fifteen minutes they stopped and eventually, uneasily, I fell back to sleep.

It was only once I'd got home that I researched the folklore of Chanctonbury Ring. I now know it to be one of the most haunted places of the Downs. Sussex folklore, mostly from the late nineteeth and early twentieth centuries, is rife with examples of it as a portal to the otherworld. Arthur Beckett in his 1909 *The Spirit of the Downs* had reported that 'if on a moonless night you walk seven times round Chanctonbury Ring without stopping, the Devil will come out of the wood and hand you a basin of soup', in payment for your soul, which sounds like a poor exchange. More energetic variants of the summoning story stipulated that practitioners should circumambulate the Ring seventeen times on a full-moon night while naked, or run backwards seven times around the Ring at midnight on Midsummer Eve. The ghosts that had been summoned in this manner, apart from the Devil, included a Druid, a lady on a white horse, a white-bearded treasure seeker, a girl child, and Julius Caesar and his army. It clearly got crowded up there on busy nights.

I also discovered that many people who had tried to sleep out at Chanctonbury had been forced to abandon the hilltop due to an invisible presence or presences. In the 1930s, Dr Philip Gosse of Steyning declared in his book *Go to the Country* that 'even on bright summer days there is an uncanny sense of some unseen presence which seems to follow you about. If you enter the dark wood you are conscious of something behind you. When you stop, it stops; when you go on it follows.' Most worryingly close to my own experience was a testimony from 1966, when a group of bikers had spent the night at the Ring. Things were quiet until after midnight, when a crackling sound started, followed by the wailing voice of a woman that appeared to move around the circumference of the Ring. The motorcyclists fled, and subsequently complained of physical ailments, headaches and lassitude in the limbs. Reading that, I felt first a shock of recognition and then mild pride that I'd tolerated what had put a gang of hairy bikers to flight.

~

I woke to a kingfisher dawn: orange cumulus in the east and blue streaks in the cirrus cover overhead. I felt headachey and bone-sore, and walked around the Ring looking for any explanation of the night's screams. None. A white chalk path spooled away east-south-east over high downs, so I followed it along Bramber Bank, a sloping shoulder of turf which dips gracefully into the upper valley of the River Adur. For half a mile of the bank, the path was littered with thousands of striped snail shells, *Helix nemoralis*, over which I crunched. In one field, ragwort seethed with cinnabar-moth caterpillars. Another field was pink with bursts of mallow, thrust up from the turf like magician's sprays of false flowers. Tractor tracks swooped and arced between them. The sun was already hot by the time I reached the medieval church of Botolphs, where my friend Rod Mengham – a Downsman by birth and upbringing, and a poet, archaeologist and writer by practice – was waiting in the shade of the tower to walk a few miles with me. I was very happy to see him.

East of the River Adur, the Downs run in three long plateaux, separated by stream and river valleys. On the high point of the first, Edburton Hill, are the earthworks of a motte-and-bailey castle, which in spring and early summer are a knee-high wild-flower meadow. Rod and I stopped there and lounged among the flowers, in a dry westerly wind, talking about Thomas, Ravilious and why I should never have slept in Chanctonbury Ring. A buzzard searched for thermals above the scarp slope, moving over the ground in a swift flapping flight, until suddenly it found an updraft, and one wingtip was buffeted and the bird adjusted and tacked in response, and then its whole body changed posture, its tail and its primaries spreading and its wings bracing, until it was able to ride the heat in an upwards helter-skelter, its wings curved to catch the rising air.

I recognized only a few of the dozens of plant species that made up the meadow in which we were sitting, though Rod could identify more of them: agrimony, wild mignonette, red clover, yellow rattle, marjoram, scabious, knapweed, lady's bedstraw, ash saplings, hawthorn shoots and the odd tall bolt of fireweed. Through them all wandered the string-like stem of bindweed. I'd been trying to learn more of the common English wild flowers using a nineteenth-century handbook called *Flowers of the Field* by the Reverend C. A. Johns, a hugely popular Victorian field guide which Thomas had owned and used. Johns helped Thomas become a fine amateur botanist and a self-taught specialist in the 'fairy flora' of the chalk. Thomas's children had in turn learned the chalk plants so well that when Eleanor Farjeon first visited the family at their home in Steep, the children picked a hundred different species and set her a naming test (with seventy as the pass mark and eighty for honours).

Johns's *Flowers of the Field* pre-dated the concept of user-friendliness. This, for instance, was the Reverend's severe entry for agrimony, a common plant of the chalk, renowned for its healing properties:

> AGRIMONIA (Agrimony) – Herbs with stipulate, pinnate, serrate *leaves* and terminal bracteate spike-like racemes of small yellow flowers; sepals 5, imbricate, persistent . . . carpels 2, 1-ovuled, within the spinous calyx-tube; fruit of 1 or 2 achenes.

I was pressed to think of a description less likely to help me identify agrimony when I saw it. But there was something bracingly Victorian in its presumption of expertise: like reading a washing-machine manual addressed only to professional electricians. There was also a lyrical precision to Johns' accounts. The leaf 'in vernation', he observed, might be:

> *conduplicate*, or folded down the midrib like the two halves of a sheet of notepaper, as in the Cherry; *plaited*, like a fan, as in the Beech; *convolute*, or rolled up like a scroll, as in the Plum; *involute*, with the margins rolled upwards, as in the Water Lily; *revolute*, with them rolled backward, as in the Dock; *valvate*, when they touch one another without overlapping; or *imbricate*, where they overlap like roof-tiles.

Lying there in the meadow, idle and drowsy from the sun, the walk and the druggist's scent of the flowers, with the flies weaving a gauzy mesh of sound above me, I thought that if I fell asleep the bindweed tendrils might lace and sidle around my limbs and I would wake like Gulliver in Lilliput, bound for ever to the ground.

~

Deep at the source of Thomas's melancholy was his double longing for travel and rest, for movement and for settlement. As a young man he had drunk deep of Borrow and felt 'a roving spirit everywhere'. He was gripped by a Yeatsian romance of the way, of the path, in Robert Louis Stevenson's phrase, as a 'white ribbon of possible travel'. '. . . never / Yet of the road I weary,' Thomas wrote in 'Roads', 'Though long and steep and dreary / As it winds on for ever.' This was the aspect of him that took the swift as his totem bird, for their long migrations and their shrill races.

But Thomas also wished to live long and faithfully in a single place. At times – when lying under the whitebeams or when planting herbs and creepers – he experienced the desire to 'take root forever'. The tree (immovable) and the bird (migrant) are among the two most distinctive presences in his writing; the forest (stable) and the path (mobile) its two most distinctive landscape features; and the root (delving downwards) and the step (moving onwards) its two contrasting metaphors for our relations with the world.

Thomas sensed early that one of modernity's most distinctive tensions would be between mobility and displacement on the one hand, and dwelling and belonging on the other – with the former becoming ubiquitous and the latter becoming lost (if ever it had been possible) and reconfigured as nostalgia. He experienced that tension between roaming and homing even as it was first forming. It is a tension I know something of myself. 'It is hard to make anything like a truce between these two incompatible desires,' Thomas wrote in 1909, 'the one for going on and on over the earth, the other that would settle for ever in one place, as in a grave and have nothing to do with change.' 'For . . . years,' noted Helen after he had died, 'Hampshire was his home county.' But then the need to move surged in him again and 'he left Hampshire to enter the army, and never knew a home again'.

~

Before the bindweed could set to work I rose up, and Rod and I continued our journey, stumping eastwards on tired legs, crossing B-roads, car parks and the dry valley of Devil's Dyke, a steep-sided combe carved out of the permafrosted chalk during recent ice ages. By afternoon, high on the longest of the Downs ridges – the Plumpton Plain – I looked longingly up at the buzzards, wishing for wings myself so that I could loft over miles in minutes.

At Kingston, Rod and I parted company. I turned up Jugg's Road, the broad old footpath from Brighton to Lewes that leads onto the summit plateau of Kingston Down, and the path along which fish caught and landed on the coast would be carried over the Downs to the market towns on their north side. I dawdled over the plateau, looking for a place to sleep. I passed dew ponds and tumuli, and a big field mushroom lying upside-down on its cap, its black gills like the charred pages of a book. Eventually, I decided on an area of lush turf, between two gorse bushes that would serve as windbreaks. The turf was rich with bedstraw; a good plant to have as my mattress.

Hundreds of feet above me, skylarks trilled on, the notes of their songs falling like chaff. W. H. Hudson described how on a bright evening in the summer of 1899 he had gone up onto the Kingston Ridge to find the thistles of the Downs shedding their seeds to the wind like a blizzard of 'faintly-seen silvery stars'. It was an extraordinary sight. 'I gave myself up to the pleasure of it,' Hudson wrote simply afterwards, 'wishing for no better thing.' He recalled a similar phenomenon on the South American pampas, when he had gone out riding at night and galloped through head-high drifts of thistledown, his horse shying at this 'insubstantial silver mist' which 'gleamed with a strange whiteness in the dark'. I remembered how, during the Second World War, the summits of the South Downs became strewn with thin strips of metal known as 'dupel', which were dropped by German planes in order to confuse British radar. Thistledown, dupel, songnotes like chaff, slivers of silver, tones, words and scenes starting to shift and smudge . . .

Thomas is often described as a poet of place, but the volatility of place fascinated him more than its reliability. He was compelled by the present-tenseness of nature – the chink of a blackbird in a hedge, the cool of starlight, the feel of a feather's vanes between the fingers – but he was also alert to landscape's instabilities, to the unbidden adhesions of memory that can bind one place to another, to the insubstantial silver mists of association through which we move and within which we see, and to the sudden slides and tricks that the mind can perform upon us even when we think we might be at our truest in the world. Place, in Thomas, frequently operates as the sum total of the locations that have been left behind or have yet to be reached.

This is why reading Thomas's writing is such a dissonant experience. His poems are not harmonious dreams, and while he was acutely sensitive to the consolations of landscape, he also recognized the fractures and queer junctures that can attend our transits. F. R. Leavis rightly described him as working at 'the edge of consciousness': his work is concerned often with suggesting that which is ungraspable or placed beyond reach. 'Many a road and track,' he wrote in a very late poem called 'Lights Out':

That, since the dawn's first crack,
Up to the forest brink,
Deceived the travellers
Suddenly now blurs,
And in they sink.

Blur and sink, blink and slur, for Thomas the past felt fissile, its recovery only partially possible at best. Memory and landscape were both in flux. There is dust on the phonograph needle: voices, if heard at all, reach us through a burr of distortion, or are snatched briefly from the static as we twist the tuning wheel.

In his book *Footsteps* (1985), Richard Holmes compared the biographer's act to 'a kind of pursuit, a tracking of the physical trail of someone's path through the past'. What Holmes realized in the course of his own pursuits was that the footstepping biographer never actually reached his subject; only encountered at best the second-order suggestions of their earlier presence: glimpses of afterglow, retinal ghosts, psychic gossamer. 'You would never catch them,' cautioned Holmes, 'no, you would never quite catch them . . .' I had set out to come to know Thomas by walking where he had walked, but he had mostly eluded me, remaining a Lob-like figure glimpsed now and then at a bend on the path or through a hole in the hedge, still enigmatic. And yet I had learnt so much from the people I'd met along my journeys: people for whom, as for Thomas, landscape was intricately involved with self-perception, and for whom certain places or weathers brought yields of grace. Ian sailing his sea roads, Miguel wandering his forest paths, Steve Dilworth striding from boulder to boulder, Anne Campbell and Finlay out on the moors, Nan Shepherd walking up and into the mountain, Raja roaming the Israel–Palestine anticline, keeping the paths open. This, I thought, had been the real discovery: not a ghostly retrieval of Thomas, but an understanding of how for him, as for so many other people, the mind was a landscape of a kind and walking a means of crossing it.

Above me, swifts hunted the dusk air over the scarp slope. They turned so sharply and smoothly and at such speed that it seemed the air must be honeycombed with transparent tubes down which the swifts were sliding, for surely nothing else could account for the compressed control of their turns. Their flight-paths lent contour to the sky and their routes outlined the berms and valleys of wind which formed and re-formed at that height, so that the air appeared to possess a topology of its own, made visible by the birds' motion.

~

I was woken again the next morning by exulting skylarks. I knew now from skylark experience that sleep was no longer possible, so before dawn I walked down into Lewes and then onto the southern slopes of Mount Caburn, the only major summit of the Downs that outlies the main chain. Purple heads of marjoram thrummed in the warming breeze. I picked up a scabious head and pinches of wild thyme.

Near Glynde, I crossed the Ouse: the river mucky-banked, beginning to loop as it neared its floodplain and the sea. The path climbed again, up onto Firle Down. Teasels were flowering purply-blue, their seed slots arranged in a dense helical pattern upon the seed-head. On one of the teasel-heads a bee was buried face-down in the blue, its legs spread wide in nectar ecstasy, as if floating in water.

Late in the day, tired in the legs, I reached Cradle Hill, into whose eastern slope a great white chalk horse had been cut. Below me the River Cuckmere made its greasy meanders towards the sea. I dropped off the scarp down to the river, and then along the edge of the Cuckmere for two or three miles. The brown river mud was a rich text of bird prints, and my boot marks joined the tracks of heron, cormorant, gull and egret, more densely printed even than the snow I'd walked at night in the winter.

The river water was the colour of milk chocolate. I found and kept an egret wing feather, washing-powder white, and I picked a trail of bryony, its leaves shaped like glossy baroque hearts. Near Exceat a cormorant ducked under the water, its dark shape darting and surging, then popped up with an eel in its beak. The eel flashed and whipped, stiff as a bike chain, gave the cormorant the slip, spun free.

An hour before dusk I stood on the summit of a small chalk bluff, from which I looked down onto Cuckmere Haven, the point at which the river reaches the Channel. It is a wide bay of flint shingle with a shallowly sloping foreshore, formerly guarded by slumping pillboxes. Coastguard cottages perch on the high ground to its west, and to its east the white cliffs of the Seven Sisters are strung out like a line of washed and pegged sheets.

Fledgling little owls made test flights between the branches of sycamores. A pale horse stood motionless in a cropped field, gazing northwards. The tide was high, and for a hundred feet away from the shore the water was the colour of greeny milk. The waves had sluiced chalk from the foreshore and cliffs, and the sea was holding the particles in a glaucous and letterless suspension.

I walked down onto the shore and along the tideline, which was cobbled with flint boulders. Beneath the first of the Sisters, my eye was caught by a clutch of grey flints which lay together like eggs right at the foot of the cliff. I picked them up, one by one, amazed. Each one had a drawing of a creature on it, made in chalk. The style was Lascaux: naïve but fluent in line. A deer, a gull, a hawk, a seal, a human figure. Somebody must have been sitting here that afternoon, using a piece of chalk from the cliffs to draw those figures onto the flints.

I placed the largest of the stones on a flat outcrop of chalk, and then arranged the others above them in decreasing size order. Hawk, on top of seal, on top of deer, on top of human: a simple cairn at the river-mouth, marking my sea-fall and the end of the walk. I looked out over the channel, over the dissolving margin of chalk in the waves. The white ribbon of the path, the snow-white of the flints, the blinding white of the egrets.

~

The same massive chalk deposit that forms the South Downs dips into the English Channel, and then rises again in northern France around the Pas-de-Calais area. During the First World War, much of the fighting on the Western Front took place on a chalk-and-flint landscape: a geological continuation of the same vast Cretaceous deposit that makes southern England.

When Thomas neared the trenches in February 1917, the similarities he discovered between the terrain around Arras and that of the South Downs spooked him: as if he could have turned from the front and walked straight back to the paths of Hampshire. 'I like the country we are in,' he wrote to a friend on 26 February of that year. 'It is open hilly chalk country with great ploughed fields and a few copses on the hilltops. The ruined villages of brick & thatch & soft white stone have been beautiful.' He carried his dream-map of the South Country with him to the front, and studied it often during the ten weeks or so that he survived out there.

'Now all roads lead to France,' he had written in 'Roads', a year before going to war:

And heavy is the tread
Of the living; but the dead
Returning lightly dance:

Whatever the roads bring
To me or take from me,
They keep me company
With their pattering,

Crowding the solitude
Of the loops over the downs,
Hushing the roar of towns
And their brief multitude.

What did take Thomas to France? No means of knowing now unless we improvise, and journey back along his inner roads, into what he once called the 'ghostland' of his past.

15

GHOST

Easter Sunday, 8 April 1917, the eve of the Battle of Arras. Thomas sits on an ammunition crate in his dugout, reading back through his diary. Reeking sack walls. Brown lamplight from a twin wick in a Swan glass chimney. A lid of skim-ice on the water in his mug.

Voices drift in. The men are singing 'Mr John Blunt': *And there came travellers, travellers three / Travelling through the night-oh . . .*

The diary is a Walker's back-loop pocketbook, bound in brown pigskin. There is an entry for the 'bright warm Easter day' just ending: a 5.9" shell had fallen two yards from Thomas as he stood in the forward-command post, but hadn't exploded; the blast from another had scratched his neck. On the final pages he has jotted notes for unwritten poems: 'The light of the new moon and every star'; 'The morning chill and clear hurts my skin while it delights my mind'; 'I never understood quite what was meant by God.'

Outside, the men are singing again: 'It's a Long Way to Tipperary'.

5.30 a.m. is zero hour. The offensive will begin with a creeping artillery barrage – the 'hurricane bombardment', as it's being called – which will prepare the way for the infantry assault on the German lines. Thomas and his battery will supply part of the barrage. For days his gunners have been practising with the new graze fuses, designed to vaporize barbed wire. The timing and aiming of the creep has to be precise: synchronized between batteries, and with the trajectories of each gun carefully calibrated according to its rate of barrel degradation when firing fast and hard, as they all will be tomorrow.

~

Thomas has a long easy gait, rhythmic and swinging. A negligent lope, leisurely but rapid. He has blue eyes (or perhaps they are grey), tawny hair (or perhaps it is sandy, or perhaps just fair) and a fawnishness to his looks. He smells of tweed, peat and tobacco. He has large pockets tailored into his jackets, to carry maps, books and apples. He walks with a stick; hazel, sometimes ash, but holly best of all. He dislikes wearing a wristwatch. He walks usually with one-inch maps, which he consults by tucking his stick under his arm, spreading the map over his large hands, then refolding it and striding on, 'aware of some completely invisible track'. He tends to walk silently, even in company. His friend Eleanor Farjeon, who for years quietly loves him, says that after following a path with Thomas 'you would not walk [it] again as you did before. You would know it in a new way.'

From a young age, he is a compulsive walker, a wandering creature. He's born in Lambeth, south London. His early experiences of walking are suburban: Wandsworth Common, Wimbledon Common. From a young age, too, he is a noticer. He keeps a journal of natural events. He remarks the date of the opening of the year's first violets, he plots the location of birds' nests, he records encounters (a heron taking an eel; a sparrowhawk's berserk pursuit of a starling) and phenomena (clouds that hang like pudding bags in the sky, heat mirages). He's a collector, too, mostly of flowers and eggs. He shins up trees to reach nests, always leaving one egg to encourage another clutch.

He develops an inclusive botanical vision that appreciates weeds as well as wild flowers. He prizes ragwort for the way its flowers show hard as brass. The overlooked and the unnoticed attract him: the 'flowers of rose-bay on ruinous hearths and walls' or 'the long narrowing wedge of irises that runs alongside and between the rails of the South-Eastern and Chatham Railway', almost into the heart of London.

He is introduced to Helen when they're both only seventeen. Helen knows almost immediately that her 'only peace would be to be needed by him', and so it proves to be. Their courtship is conducted mostly through walking. They walk fields and lanes and footpaths together: out at Merton, Richmond Park, Wandsworth Common. She can't at first tell a beech from a birch. She's short-sighted and finds it hard to pick out birds; he teaches her calls and songs so she can know without seeing. They press and label flowers: tormentil, bryony, harebell, bedstraw, milkwort. Thomas gallivants around, showing off his knowledge and ease in country lore. From a copse in Merton he retrieves a compact and mossy chaffinch nest, firm as a ball in the hand. At the Richmond Park heronry he scrambles up a Scots pine to bring down a blue-green heron's egg; a squashed sky-globe.

Helen feels lifted into a new world, doubly intimate with Thomas and with nature. '[I]t seems strange now,' she recalls years later, 'that there was ever a time when I could not recognize the beech's fine-textured skinlike bark, and the set of the trunk and branches like human limbs, and the beautiful curve that the leafy branches make, like a hand opened for giving.' It says much of Helen that she is able to perceive generosity in the form of a branch's curve.

When they first make love on the day of her twentieth birthday, it's inside a leafy glade in a hazel and beech thicket on Wimbledon Common. Thomas weaves her a braid of white bryony and that evening gives her a ring, a fine gold signet ring set with a red stone that had belonged to his great-grandfather, a Spanish sea captain.

They marry in secret, while Thomas is still an undergraduate at Oxford. They move around: lodgings in London, then the lease on a farmhouse in Kent. Their relationship is founded on her absolute love for him. But unconditional love is arduous to give, and even more arduous to receive. It can prompt – as it does in Thomas, over the years that follow – a cruelty on the part of the recipient. Such love, in its willingness to forgive all, in its eagerness to cherish faults as virtues, can come to seem like a declaration of insufficiency on the part of the recipient. You cannot match my love; your love will *always* fall short of mine. Added to this is the realization that the lover who loves you so much *cannot be hurt by you*; that their love is imperishable. Therefore you can try, almost guiltlessly, to hurt them. It becomes a challenge. As Thomas's melancholy tightens on him over the years, as the weasel-bite of his depression locks and deepens, he will hurt Helen increasingly. Her vulnerability, combined with the invulnerability of her love, conspire to encourage his emotional mistreatment of her.

Children come: a son, Merfyn, then a daughter, Bronwen. Thomas is often away from home in body (on long walking tours, researching books) or in mind (present, but writing). He churns out reviews in their hundreds, as well as book-length histories and biographies written to deadline. The work is hard, a bill-paying hackery that leaves him exhausted and despondent. His changes of mood are weather-like, and at times provoked by the weather. Heavy rain can leave him sluiced clean of depression, or more desperately waterlogged. When the black days arrive he lashes out at Helen, criticizing her plainness of mind or her lack of ambition. 'I hate my work,' he writes in a letter, 'I have no vitality, no originality, no love. I do harm.' Helen waits patiently 'to be let into the light again', and meets his cruelty with an unquerying acceptance of his right to be cruel.

So he administers self-punishment through hard walking: a way at once to macerate and to forget himself. Sometimes he leaves the house at evening and walks through the night, coming home haggard near dawn. At times he's settled by this motion; at times only further troubled.

When he's happy? Oh, then the days are fine. The house is filled with stories and rhymes. He sings while he bathes the children. Once they're dried and clothed he lets the children perch on his knees, takes his clay pipe from his mouth and any music that is in him comes forth. His voice is deep and his songs are various: Welsh folk songs, racy and ribald songs, rollicking sea shanties. Song is vital to Thomas: he is involved almost from the start in the English folk-song revival led by Cecil Sharp. He publishes *Poems and Songs for the Open Air*, an anthology of walking ballads and airs. Folk songs and footpaths are, to his mind, both major democratic forms: collective in origin but re-inflected by each new singer or walker. Radical, too, in their implicit rebuke to the notion of private property. He admires 'Sumer Is Icumen in' more than anything by Beethoven. In his poem 'The Path' he will write of an old track to school through the woods that 'wind[s] like silver, trickles on'. It is smudged by moss and leaf-fall, but kept open by the feet of children. The path is a riverbed and the children the water, running 'the current of their feet' over it.

~

They leave Kent and move to Hampshire, to the village of Steep. First to Berryfield Cottage, and then to a house called Wick Green, which is reached by an ancient, deeply worn track, thick with rotted leaves. The track winds through beeches and yews to reach the long, low house, which sits several hundred feet up at the plateau edge and looks across to Chanctonbury Ring and the ridge line of the South Downs, seven miles distant. The house has been recently constructed on Morrisian principles. The planks and beams have been taken from local oaks. The nails, hinges and hasps have been forged in the village, the bricks cast nearby. Native stone has been used for the thresholds. When mists fill the valleys, they feel as if they are in a wooden galleon at sea, creaking in the swell.

Yet for all its magic, they can't fall in love with the house. They have always treated houses as animate, sounding them out for affinities or infirmities of spirit, and have already left one house for its cursedness, another for its tepidity. Thomas tries to settle: he digs a border by the door of his study and plants thyme, rosemary, lavender and old man's beard. But they soon realize that the hostile newness of Wick Green will make it impossible for them to be happy there, sturdy though it stands, magnificent though its position is. It's so high up that the wind shrieks in the gable room, the mists isolate it and the cold gnaws hard. Thomas's depression sharpens. He feels trapped by his work, trapped in his marriage, unhappy in his home. He longs to establish his own route in life.

He reacts to the disappointments of Wick Green by walking. Treading the old paths seems to reduce the complexities of life, as if he has stepped into an archetype or allegory: track, forest, moon, traveller. He wanders far afield, even in heavy rain. Mostly the rain calms him because it deprives him of context. It desirably subtracts some part of him, taking away from him 'everything except the power to walk under the dark trees, to enjoy as humbly as the hissing grass'. Mostly, the 'tender loveliness' of his favourite landscapes offers compensations for his own lacks. At times, though – at the worst times – nature's beauty and exuberance feel to him like accusations. 'I am not a part of nature. I am alone. There is nothing else in my world but my dead heart and brain within me and the rain without.' What he has come to understand, painfully, is that one may too easily take the natural world as companion, friend and salve. Nature can cure but it can also be brutally mute, shocking in its disinterest: the river's seawards run, the chalk's whiteness, the hawk's swivelling stare. But he knows also that the acknowledgement of this refusal of relation might offer its own bracing reward, just as the delusion of response might also serve deep purpose – and that one might not need always to choose the one before the other.

During the Kent and Hampshire years, when Thomas is not walking he is reading about walking. Coleridge and Hazlitt, the nonconformists: path-following as dissent. Bunyan and the Puritan tradition: path-following as obedience. Cervantes and the picaresque, Malory and medieval chivalry, the *Mabinogion* and Wales and Giraldus Cambrensis. Cervantes, he notes approvingly, had 'the sense of roads'. Malory's *Le Morte d'Arthur* 'would have less vitality in its marvel if it were not for the roads'. He enjoys the story of Sir Launcelot, riding 'throughout marches and many wild ways'. Even Shakespeare he finds to be a path-writer who in *Cymbeline* 'gives a grand impression of wide tracts of country traversed by roads of great purpose and destiny'. He absorbs the nineteenth-century romance of the open road in Stevenson's *Songs of Travel*, Borrow's Romany fantasias, the *Rural Rides* of William Cobbett (whose sentences suggest to him the walking swing of an arm or leg) and the work of Richard Jefferies – above all Jefferies, Thomas's hero, whose style 'grew' to his use 'like the handle of a walking stick'; steadying and companionable, the stick taking the hand's mould. Yet Thomas stays sceptical about how one might, in a Rousseauian reverie, mistake walking for a 'primitive act, "natural to man" ', and in this way feel falsely restored to 'a pristine majesty'.

Paths and tracks criss-cross his own work, figuratively and structurally. He writes of winding roads and he writes in winding syntax. He learns these reflexive habits from Hazlitt, who embeds walking as prosody to the depth of grammar. From Hazlitt, too, he learns the epistemological power of the proposition that is made and then part retracted. Again and again in Thomas's imagination, text and landscape overlap: 'The prettiest things on ground are the paths / With morning and evening hobnails dinted, / With foot and wing-tip overprinted / Or separately charactered.' The paths are sentences, the shod feet of the travellers the scratch of the pen nib or the press of the type. He understands that reading and walking expire into one another, that we carry within ourselves evolving maps of the world which are, as Wordsworth put it, '[o]f texture midway between life and books'.

Thomas starts to think, too, about thinking, and the ways in which the physical world might incite in us those kinds of knowledge that exceed cognition. In letters to his friend Gordon Bottomley he describes going beachcombing on the Suffolk coast and finding 'champagne corks, sailors' hats, Antwerp beer bottles, fish boxes, oranges, lemons, onions, banana stems, waterworn timber and the most exquisite flat & round pebbles, black, white, dove grey, veined, wheat coloured'. 'Not one [pebble] but makes me think or rather draws out a part of me beyond my thinking,' he writes to Bottomley. His observation of the difference between being made to think, and being drawn out beyond one's thinking, is tellingly precise; it records the transition from a perception exercised by the self upon the stones to the perception exercised upon the self by the stones.

Nature and landscape frequently have this effect on him: trees, birds, rocks and paths cease to be merely objects of contemplation, and instead become actively and convivially present, enabling understanding that would be possible nowhere else, under no other circumstances. 'Something they knew – I also, while they sang,' he will write of song thrushes in an early poem titled 'March'. He senses that the light-fall, surfaces, slopes and sounds of a landscape are all somehow involved in accessing what he calls the 'keyless chamber[s] of the brain'; that the instinct and the body (the felt smoothness of pebbles, the seen grain of light) must know in ways that the conscious mind cannot. Weather, in particular, is 'integral' to his thinking, as Eleanor Farjeon notices: 'Other people talk about the weather, Edward lived it.' Like Nan Shepherd thirty years later, he recognizes that weather is something we think *in* – 'the wind, the rain, the streaming road, and the vigorous limbs and glowing brain and what they created . . . We and the storm were one' – and that we would be better, perhaps, speaking not of states of mind, but rather of atmospheres of mind or meteorologies of mind.

He is slowly working out a model of thought – no, more than thought, of *self* – not as something rooted in place and growing steadily over time, but as a shifting set of properties variously supplemented and depleted by our passage through the world. Landscape and nature are not there simply to be gazed at; no, they press hard upon and into our bodies and minds, complexly affect our moods, our sensibilities. They riddle us in two ways – both perplexing and perforating us. Thomas knows this to be true because he has felt it on foot, with his feet, and Farjeon again, keenly, senses this: 'he walked with *himself*, with his eyes and his ears and his nostrils, and his long legs and his big hands.'

The challenge, of course, is how to record such experience – apprehended, but by definition unsayable – in language, using the 'muddy untruthful reflection of words'. Poetry is the form of utterance that can come closest; this he knows as a reader. But he has never written poetry, and has little reason to think he can.

~

Over the course of 1913, though, Thomas becomes friends with the American poet Robert Frost. They walk together in the fields and woods near Dymock in Gloucestershire, where Frost is living with his wife and where a group of poets has taken to gathering in order to wander, think and drink. Frost and Thomas tramp almost anywhere they wish 'on wavering footpaths through the fields', sometimes twenty-five miles in a day, discussing poetry, natural history and the coming war. Frost coins a new word for what he and Thomas do: 'talks-walking'.

It is Frost who encourages Thomas to make the move from prose into poetry. He is, Frost tells him, a poet behind the disguise of prose. It's Frost who takes lines from one of Thomas's travelogues and rearranges them as verse, so that Thomas can see what he's been doing all along without knowing it. Frost 'produced . . . the enharmonic change,' Farjeon writes beautifully, 'that made [Thomas] not a different man, but the same man in another key.' Thus retuned, and with such encouragement, his poems start coming – tentatively, experimentally – his first finished on 3 December 1914.

War has been declared, though. The country has changed:

disorganized trains, crowds at the stations, reservists being seen off by flag-waving friends. Thomas is sceptical of cheap nationalism, scornful of pompous martialism. But he is also anxious to fight: to prove his bravery, to defend a landscape he loves, to find the purpose that his life has been so unhappily lacking. Less than a year into the war, he finds himself at a crossroads. Frost and his family have already sailed for America; Frost is encouraging Thomas to emigrate to New England and find work there as a writer and a poet. Frost will help him make his way; they will be safe from the war at that distance. Helen is pleading with him to stay in Hampshire. But the army needs men, and Thomas has felt himself 'slowly growing into a conscious Englishman'. There's no obligation on him to enlist. At thirty-six he's old enough to sit the war out. He's married with children; it remains wholly honourable for family men not to fight. 'He could have been safe, if he had chosen to be,' Farjeon will later write.

It's the greatest decision of his life, and he imagines it as a separation of ways. He spends hours poring over his 'moral map', 'thinking out' his motives, when he 'ought to be reading or enjoying the interlacing flight of 3 kestrels'. On 7 December he begins a poem called 'The Signpost': a figure hesitates at a junction, unable to choose one or other of the paths. 'I read the sign. Which way shall I go?' Now, if only he could take one path and then retrace his steps and take the other . . .

In June 1915 Frost sends Thomas a draft of a poem he has written called 'The Road Not Taken'. It was inspired, obliquely, by the memory of walking with Thomas in the Dymock fields: Thomas's eagerness, his wish to walk every path and his frustration at crossroads, have been transformed by Frost into a finely balanced metaphysical parable. 'Two roads diverged in a yellow wood,' begins the poem:

And sorry I could not travel both
And be one traveler, long I stood
And looked down one as far as I could
To where it bent in the undergrowth;

Then took the other, as just as fair . . .

Thomas is stung, seeing the poem as a parody of his indecisiveness over the question of the war. He interprets it as a spur, feels it as a goad: *Hurry up, man, and make a choice; stop dithering at the junction.* It's a drastic misreading of the poem, but Thomas closes his mind to subtlety. He writes sharply back to Frost. Within weeks he has made his choice. In early July he draws up his will and enlists. On 14 July he passes his medical. The King's shilling is taken: he is Private 4229 in the 28th Battalion of the Artists Rifles, part of the larger London Regiment. He has committed to a route, and the knowledge of its irreversibility reassures him.

Why, really, does he enlist? Impossible to say: another path vanishing back into the distance, another track petering out. One of so many things lost in the creases where the map folds. He doesn't even know himself: 'Several people *have* asked me [why I joined], but I could not answer yet.' To Gordon Bottomley, the best he can do is characterize the decision as 'the natural culmination of a long series of moods & thoughts'. He doesn't even tell Helen in person, instead sending her a telegram from London. 'No, no, no,' is all that she can say, 'not that.'

But he is writing so fast; a life's worth of poems torrenting from him now that he has set his face to France. Verse – from the Latin *vertere*, 'to turn'. He writes nearly sixty poems between enlisting and embarking for the front. Sometimes a poem a day, quick and brilliant: 'Roads', 'When we two walked', 'The Lane', 'The Green Roads'. Some of these poems seem to know more of his own fate than he does; they draw out part of him beyond his thinking: 'the future and the maps / Hide something I was waiting for.'

~

Thomas's first proper posting is to Hare Hall Training Camp in Essex, where he works as a navigation instructor. In spare hours he writes poems, but covertly. He doesn't mind poets knowing he's a soldier, but he does mind soldiers knowing he's a poet. He's surprised by how much he likes aspects of army life: polishing his high trench boots – left hand stuck into the boot, right hand buffing across the toecap – until his own face looms in the shine. Surprised by how he enjoys the unvarying routines: teaching map-reading with a prismatic compass to the men of A Company, taking them out on foot-manoeuvres. Surprised by how much he likes Essex. Surprised by the absence of depression; 'black despair' has given way to 'calm acceptance'.

On top of a hill in Epping Forest he finds a run-down cottage called High Beech, where Helen and the children can live and which he can easily visit when he has furlough. When the snow falls during their first winter there, time slows and modernity retreats. 'It is fine and wintry here,' he writes in a letter. 'The hills look impassable and make me think they must have looked like that 2,000 years ago.'

In early December 1916 a call comes round for volunteers to go straight out to the batteries in France. Thomas is among the first to sign up. On 6 January he comes back to High Beech for his last days of leave before departing for the front. He tries to behave as if nothing is wrong, but Helen can barely function. He studies maps with Merfyn, tries to show Helen how to take a bearing on his prismatic compass; she cries. They're sharp and bickery, then they quarrel openly, then she cries again, and then they are tender together. On the morning of his departure, the snow around the cottage is frozen iron-hard, with the footprints of birds set into it like hieroglyphs. Thomas gives Helen a book into which he has copied out all his poems. 'Remember that, whatever happens, all is well between us for ever and ever,' he tells her. A freezing mist hangs in the air.

Thomas walks away, the hard snow unmarked by his leaving feet. Helen stands at the gate and watches him go until the mist hides him. As he descends the hill, he keeps on calling *coo-ee!* to her, as if he were arriving rather than leaving. She answers him with her *coo-ee!* and they go on like that, call and answer, fainter and fainter.

The day before he's due to sail he hires a bicycle and pedals out from the transit camp in Kent in which he is billeted, to say goodbye to England. It is such a ride! Hedgeless roads over long sloping downs sprinkled with thorns, and covered with old tracks whose routes are marked by juniper. A clear pale sky. A faint sunset, a long twilight.

~

Embarkation: 29 January 1917. Thomas and his men march through the pre-dawn dark to the station. The air very cold, very still. Soldiers stamp their feet. He is one of seven officers commanding 150 men, who will work four 9.2-inch howitzers, and who together make up Number 244 Siege Battery.

The men sing 'Pack Up Your Troubles in Your Old Kit-bag'.

A freezing train to Southampton, where they wait until dusk. Thomas walks to pass the time and stay warm. Inland, an ice-scattered lake, birds diving, a dark wood beyond. Some of the men play rugby on a stretch of waste ground. As the light fails the seagulls seem to float rather than fly.

At 7 p.m. they board the *Mona Queen*, clumping up a sagging gangplank. The sea tumbles. Thomas rests rather than sleeps during the crossing, listens from his cabin to the men laughing and swearing.

Le Havre dock, 4 a.m. Light falling in slabs from the windows of tall pale houses and in arcs from the electric quay lamps. They march through the town in fine falling snow. French sentries: hooded with long loose cloaks and carrying rifles with curved bayonets. Dinner is iron rations, supplemented with cheese and marmalade. They sleep that night in tents, twelve men in each, each with two blankets against the cold. Subalterns sit up late by lanterns in the mess, censoring letters.

Days of waiting, hard clear nights. Troop ships arrive, black stark vessels from the north-west. Hospital trains pull in from the east, carrying men with shocking wounds. At last, on 4 February, they spend cold hours entraining the guns. When the job is done they all sit on bales of cotton on the railway platform and wait for the train to the front.

The men sing 'There's a Long, Long Trail'.

When the train at last arrives some of the men begin shouting in jest, 'All tickets!', 'All tickets please!' Then they fall quiet. At 11 p.m. prompt, the train lurches away and a yell of *HURRAY!* ripples down the carriages. Then silence again, even before they're clear of the bare platform with its trampled snow.

~

The train clacks past Alaincourt, past Amiens and on to Doullens. Thomas looks out of the window at the wooded chalk hills. He's back in the South Country already. Poplars in lines. Mistletoe in the branches. They're on the highest land in northern France and the roads are frozen.

Forwards to Mendicourt, where they billet in part-ruined barns. Enemy planes float over like pale moths, looking serene among the black shrapnel bursts. Thomas rigs up a table on which to do his paperwork. He remembers how one night on the Downs he had gazed up and wondered 'what things that same moon sees eastward about the Meuse'. Forwards again to Dainville along a shell-pocked track, to billets on the Arras road, near a graveyard with three recently arrived residents. Big-gun firing is audible now. There is the distant rickle of machine guns. From an observation post Thomas glasses the snowy broken land. Glinting wires, dead trees. A corpse under a railway bridge. The shell-holes make him think of tumuli and dew ponds. Paths everywhere: duckboard zigzags, wriggling little tracks, and medieval field boundaries now turned into sunken roads used to hide the movement of troops and supplies.

The officers dine on bully, cheese and white wine. Someone has brought a gramophone, its ribbed and flaring trumpet reminding Thomas of bindweed flowers. He writes letters home to Helen, up to five a week, finding it easier to inhabit his marriage lovingly at a distance.

The gramophone plays cheery tunes: 'Wait Till I'm as Old as Father' and 'Where Does Daddy Go When He Goes Out?'

Days pass. Cannonades thud away to the south, over near Ancre. An old white horse works a treadmill, tramping in patient circles. Farmers carry on as best they can. The gramophone plays Gounod's 'Ave Maria'.

Thomas comes to know this landscape as he has come to know all others: by walking and watching. He hadn't expected so much life in such a shattered place. Hare, partridge and wild duck in fields south-east of his guns. Grass just beginning to show green through melting snow. Black-headed buntings talking to each other, rooks cawing. Vegetation flopping over the edge of the trenches: dead campion umbels, rank grass-tangles, clots of thistles.

The gramophone plays 'Dormez-Vous', by the end of which they have all fallen silent.

He writes up the fighting book, sleeps badly. Star shells light up the night. When the big guns fire, he can feel the blasts quivering in his guts. His table and mantelpiece silt up with letters to be censored. One night the artillery falls silent. He can only hear machine guns and rifle shots. He lies, idly, toying with words and rhymes. Rifle and idle, vital and rifle. How odd that rifle fire can feel almost relaxing in comparison to the Berthas. The machine guns sound like someone knocking at a door.

He goes to Arras itself; it reminds him of Bath. White houses, shutters, domes, an empty square. There's so much to recall home and the chalk counties. When sentries challenge him in the street, he answers with the password 'Sussex'. A mad captain takes his men behind the lines to drive partridges into the air, whistling and crying 'Mark over!', as though he were on a field shoot in Wiltshire. A strategic ridge to the west of his position, from which German snipers hunt, is called Telegraph Hill. One day Thomas looks up from his observation post to see kestrels hanging in pairs as they used to over Mutton and Ludcombe hills, except that above the kestrels wheel five planes.

He shifts billet to an abandoned big house, mirrors and paintings still on the wall. In the evenings he reads Shakespeare's sonnets or Frost's poetry. When the guns fire, he and his fellow officers cannot hear each other speak, and gulp like fish, trying to lip-read. He is adjutant to a ruddy colonel, ex-Raj, who refers fondly to the 'confoundedly cheeky . . . old Hun', even as his men are dying.

The gramophone plays 'Peer Gynt', its music drifting through the building.

He begins to experience the world as silent tableaux. German prisoners standing in the mud, one with his hand resting on another's shoulder. A turbaned Indian at a barn door, holding a sheep by a rope around its neck. A line of dark thin trees standing against the bright afternoon sky. One day in early March he sees the Royal Flying Corps lose four planes. The tank of the last burns white as the plane drops from the sky, both pilots scorched to death. The land an exhausted cinder.

The gramophone plays Chopin's 'Berceuse'.

244 Battery moves forward for their first shoot. The men tramp up the road whistling 'It's Nice to Get Up in the Morning' and 'The Minstrel Boy'. Six-inch guns snuffle. The field shells sing. Machine guns spatter. The wind blows the water in the shell-holes into close intersecting patterns, like that of a file's blade.

The gramophone plays 'Allan Water'.

One night, lying in bed, he becomes sure he will die there, by shell-blast, in that big room. It's the first time he has felt real fear – what a place to feel it! Should he die with his clothes on? Should he haul his bed to the window side of the room, or to the chimney side? Should he sleep upstairs where he might fall further if a shell strikes, or on the ground floor where he might be crushed? He has too much time to think: he wants to bite the day to its core. At dawn he listens to the thrushes.

The gramophone plays Ambrose Thomas's 'Mignon Gavotte'.

In March there is snow again, fine snow and a fierce wind. Thomas is working on aerial reconnaissance, using photographs secured by the RFC boys, trying to fit them together into a meaningful pattern. Seen from above – the view of the hawk or the helmeted airman – the trench system resembles an intricate network of paths and holloways, leading from everywhere to everywhere. As well as the photographs he is using flash-spotting and new sound-ranging techniques involving triangulated microphones: all part of the effort to locate and destroy the German gun emplacements, hidden away behind ridges, including those camouflaged from aerial view.

An RFC wireless man reads *The Song of Hiawatha* aloud: 'Down a narrow path they wandered / Where the brooklet led them onward / Where the trail of deer and bison / Marked the soft mud on the margin . . .' Skylarks sing over no-man's-land. There is the noisy parley of starlings, and revolver reports from men hunting rats in the trenches.

He spends dangerous, dull days in observation posts, peering out with his field glasses through a hedge of elder and thorn in which sparrows and blackbirds chink. Action erupts in its casual baffling way, always expected but never anticipated. More of his home life slips from him. He is frustrated by waiting. He feels friendless. The mud sucks at his boots. On the morning of 14 March he is looking out towards no-man's-land when he sees a piece of burnt paper skipping towards him, whisking in the air. No, not paper. A bat, probably shaken from one of the last standing sheds in Ronville. He notices an old grey-green track that crosses no-man's-land, its path still visible even among the devastation. It must once have been a country way to Arras. How hard it is to erase a path. Deep green water has collected in one of the bigger shell-holes, and the skeletons of whole trees can be seen lying there. He writes home to Merfyn, asking him to oil up a bicycle so that the two of them can go out riding together when he returns in the summer.

The gramophone plays 'D'Ye Ken John Peel?'

The military and the natural are so compressed here that it becomes hard to sort the one from the other. When the Huns' guns fire above their heads into Beaurains, the shells come over like starlings returning, twenty or thirty a minute. He sees a great shell-burst stand up like a birch tree. When the larks sing he feels invulnerable. Buried seeds thrown to the surface by explosion and trench digging have resulted in surreal sprays of early spring flowers, growing among bones and mess tins.

~

Word is that the push approaches. Thomas is keen to have a share in the great strafe when it comes. By mid-March, his guns are firing between 400 and 600 rounds a day, mostly at Vimy Ridge. He sights off targets and shell-fall using a lensatic compass, whose degree-plate tipples in the liquid of the instrument's dial.

On 24 March, Thomas goes out to an advance position on the front line at Beaurains. My 'new position, fancy, was an old chalk pit in which a young copse of birch, hazel etc. has established itself', he writes to Helen that day. 'I am sitting warm in the sun on a heap of chalk with my back to the wall of the pit. Fancy, an old chalk pit with moss and even a rabbit left in spite of the paths trodden all over it. It is beautiful and sunny and warm though cold in the shade. The chalk is dazzling. The sallow catkins are soft dark white . . .'

Late March and early April brings a run of clear serene winter mornings, and preparations for the spring offensive. The larks start singing at 5.15 a.m., the blackbirds follow at 6 a.m., the guns shortly afterwards. Thomas and his men fill sandbags for reinforcing their dugouts, readying for battle. Rubin and Smith, the two men with the best voices, sing duets from *The Bing Boys*. Thomas reads *Macbeth*.

Helen writes to an old friend, Janet Hooton – wife of Harry, the man to whom Thomas had dedicated *The Icknield Way*. He's still the poet, even out there, Helen tells Janet proudly, 'delighting in what beauty there is there, and he finds beauty where no one else would find it . . . My eyes and ears and hands long for him, and nearly every night I dream he has come and we are together once again.'

On 4 April they fire all day, 600 rounds dispatched, though almost nothing comes back in return. The artillery makes the air flap, a noise like that of loose sails in a gusty wind. Thomas's feet are constantly wet and cold. Fine green feathers of yarrow fletch the sods on the forward dugout. He reads *Hamlet*.

On the weekend of 7 and 8 April, they line up the heavy guns of the battery out on the old sunken road that runs parallel to the front. The German bombardment is unusually heavy. He composes a letter to Helen:

Dearest
Here I am in my valise on the floor of my dugout writing before sleeping. The artillery is like a stormy tide breaking on the shores of the full moon . . . The pretty village among trees that I first saw two weeks ago is now just ruins among violated stark tree trunks. But the sun shone and larks and partridge and magpies and hedgesparrows made love and the trench was being made passage for the wounded that will be harvested in a day or two . . .

I slept jolly well and now it is sunshine and wind and we are in for a long day and I must post this when I can.

All and always yours Edwy

The gramophone plays 'Death of the Troll'.

~

Easter Monday, 9 April, the first day of the Battle of Arras, begins with a massive artillery barrage from the British – the hurricane bombardment. The air sags and beats with shell-rip. Thomas is in his observation post, watching the shell-fall, directing fire. In the wintry dawn light, behind the creeping barrage, the first waves of troops advance on the German lines.

The morning is a triumph for the British batteries. They disable most of the German heavy guns with their counter-battery fire, and their troops take the German infantry unawares. As the guns slow their fire the British soldiers emerge to shout and dance.

Thomas steps out of the dugout and then leans back into the doorway, to fill and light his clay pipe. Snow and red sun; a ridge sweeping away bare for miles. He has part filled the pipe when a stray German shell drops near him and the vacuum caused by its passing throws him hard to the earth.

His body is unwounded. Beside him lies his clay pipe, unbroken. He has been killed by a pneumatic concussion, his heart stopped still by a violent absence of air. The fatal vacuum has created pressure ridges on the pages of his diary, which resemble ripples in standing water.

~

Helen is sewing and Myfanwy is sitting nearby, filling in the pricked dots on a postcard with coloured wool, making a wild duck to send to her father in France. Out of the window, Helen sees the telegraph boy stop on his bicycle and lean it against the fence. He hands the telegram over. She reads it in silence. He waits to see if a reply is wanted. 'No answer,' she says.

Helen writes to Frost. She cannot tell which tense to use. 'For a moment indeed one loses sight and feeling. With him too all was well and is. You love him, and some day I hope we may meet and talk of him for he is very great and splendid.'

~

The contents of Thomas's pockets are returned to Helen in a box. There is the diary, and inside it a photograph, a loose slip of paper and a creased letter. The letter is from her to him. The photograph is of her. The slip of paper has addresses and names written on one side, and on the other, three jotted lines in pencil:

Where any turn may lead to Heaven
Or any corner may hide Hell
Roads shining like river up hill after rain.

What was Thomas seeing as he wrote those last verses in his Arras notebook? The old ways of the South Country, or the shell-swept support roads that wound to the front? Both, perhaps, folded together, the one kind of path having led in its way to the other.

16

PRINT

Footprints in the mud: two sets of prints, walking northwards. A man and a woman, companionably close, moving together, shore-parallel, at around four miles per hour: journeying, not foraging. This much we know: that the man was around 6' 3" tall, and the woman just under a foot shorter. That the man had a sharp big toe-nail; that the woman had raised arches. That on the day of their journey, some 5,000 summers ago, the sun was bakingly hot, the wind was light and the waves were low. That red deer and roe deer were also out, moving over the intertidal silts, leaving their crisp slots. And that children were there too, a group of children, playing together, mud-larking, making a gaggle of small footprints.

I set my foot by the side of the first print of the man, and then I walk north, keeping pace, and stride with him as he goes, falling into step. Squalls of rain and sun are pushing across the coast. There are rapid tilts of the light. A double rainbow hoops over the sea to the north. White blades are spinning on the wind turbines in the estuary. Far out west, over the Irish Sea, a huge cumulonimbus evolves.

The prehistoric footprint trail appeared a few miles north of Liverpool, on a stretch of coastline known as Formby Point, where the land has preserved what is surely one of the most remarkable archives ever kept. Seven thousand to five thousand years ago, this region was a serrated coastline, cut through by drainage channels and fingers of inlet. Then, as now, a dune barrier had built up, creating an intermittent freshwater–saltwater barrier. Inland of the dunes was a fen carr of alder, birch, willow and scrub oak. A reed-fringed shallow lagoon existed in the intertidal zone, and the foreshore was firm silt. It was a rich territory of mixed habitats, and for this reason it supported a significant population of birds, animals and humans.

When people or creatures traversed the foreshore, they left their tracks pressed into the silt. Over the course of a day – if the sun were strong enough – the silt hardened in the heat, and the tracks were set. Fine sand, blown from the nearby dunes, then filled or coated the imprints. When the tide came in – if it were gentle enough – those sun-hardened, sand-filled tracks were capped with mud. And that set of tracks was compressed as new layers of silt built over it, each of which might – if the conditions were right – also keep a record of passage. In this way, over the course of centuries, thousands of footprint trails were preserved, laid down in the stacked silt strata like a growing pile of pages.

At some point towards the end of the Neolithic period, the coastline began to grow out westwards. First the near-shore silts were covered, then the intertidal lagoon, then the offshore sandbars. The footprints were safely buried beneath this new land. Much later, in the early eighteenth century, vast sandstorms inundated the region, forcing the abandonment of a village and further burying the footprints under dunes. More recently, however, coastal erosion started to bite into the middle of Formby Point. It's here that the underlying Mesolithic and Neolithic silt layers containing the footprints are being uncovered – and then rapidly stripped away.

Presently, when big tides surge at neap or spring, or when a storm blows in from the Irish Sea, the topmost stratum of silt is scoured off to reveal its infaunal predecessor. The sea is reversing the flow of history, lifting pages from the pile of paper, so that even as time moves forwards day by day it also moves backwards year by year. When the sea recedes, a fresh silt surface is exposed – and sometimes this surface will carry the marks of prehistoric foot-journeys. The prints are legible again only for a few days or even a few hours. Each newly revealed layer survives only until the next strong tide or storm, when it in turn is lifted off to uncover the one beneath.

I walk on northwards stride for stride with the man, who is now passing along the shelving edge of a mud-flat. Where the mud-flat angles down to standing water, it resembles the deckled pages of a book. I can see the individual strata of plump brown silt, each an inch or so thick. There are now lines of red-deer and roe-deer prints, the roe-deer hooves sharp and tiny, those of the red deer like big quotation marks. The man keeps walking, and I keep pace.

The Formby silts have yielded an astonishing variety of tracks. The 5,000-year-old prints of wild boar, wolves and dogs have been revealed, as well as those of goats, horses, and red deer whose hooves were up to five inches long – almost twice the size of today's biggest red deer. The potterings of oystercatchers (little wandering tracks, like lines of arrowheads) have emerged, the splay-toed T-prints of a crane padding along with her chicks, and the plate-sized hoof-marks of the aurochs – the giant ungulates that were hunted into extinction in Britain during the Bronze Age, and images of which are painted on the cave walls at Lascaux. A big bull aurochs measured six feet at the withers and eleven feet from muzzle to rump.

Hundreds of human footprint trails have also emerged. Some of these prints have been so crisp that archaeologists have been able to infer the stature, velocity, cadence and speed of the individuals who made them. Most of the walkers were women and children, padding barefoot over the sandy silts, probably engaged in gathering food:

shrimps and razor shells from the sand-flats and pools, and birds' eggs from the shoreline lagoons and creeks. One of them was an adolescent female, possibly pregnant, whose curled toes indicate she may have been finding grip difficult on the slippery ground. Male footprints have been discovered following red- and roe-deer tracks, with deeper imprints and a purposeful line suggesting that the men were running, presumably hunting.

Step for step northwards, keeping to his trail, the wind like a hand in the small of the back, pushing us on. The strong southerly is raising spindrift from the dry sand, long golden snakes that flow loosely across the dunes and through the marram.

The Formby prints are so evocative because they record specific journeys, and they are so mysterious because we know so little of the walkers who left them. Like the daubed handprints on the cave walls at Lascaux, they are the marks of exact and unrepeatable acts – the skin of that palm or this sole was pressed to this cave wall or that beach on this occasion – and in their shape and spacing they remind us of a kinship of motion that stretches back as far as 3.6 million years ago. Other than that, almost nothing is known. Who made these marks that are so particular and so generic? What were they feeling as they left them, in the same centuries that the first pictograms were pressed into Mesopotamian clay with a reed stylus?

To track these tracks, to leave your own prints beside them, is to sense nothing so simple as time travel, a sudden whisking back to the Mesolithic. No, the uncanniness of the experience involves a feeling of co-presence: the prehistoric and the present matching up such that it is unclear who walks in whose tracks. It's this combination of intimacy and remoteness that gives these trails their unsettling power. They are among the earliest texts, from a period of history devoid of recorded narrative. Following them, we are reading one of the earliest stories, told not in print but in footprint.

As I walk, scenes open in my memory from the paths I have followed, coming fast and clear as lantern slides: the green phosphorescent wake of *Broad Bay* as she trundles north to Sula Sgeir, the white paths of the English chalk country, Manus's three-stoned cairn-tracks overflown by gannets, the mirror-line of the Broomway. Bodily recollections surface: the rasp of limestone in Palestine, the slim iron needles of the Spanish pine woods, the sandstone dust of the Black Mountains, so soft underfoot. The remembered senses of spaces small and wide: the beehive shieling set in the open moor of Lewis, the cool interior of the *qasr* near Ramallah, the dark glassy water under a stone arch on the Shiants. And so many people, so many path-followers.

Onwards, northwards, following the ancient footprints. Salt in the breeze, salt in the nose. The great cumulus cloud continues its slow-motion explosion: burly bosses growing out of themselves, volutes and corbels, gullies, seracs and great white bolls. A lateral shear-line at the cloud's base, below which hang black sheets of rain. Northwards, the man and I reach a patch of small footprints: children playing in the mud. Two children are there now, today, jumping about barefoot. Suddenly I feel a tidal pull homewards, to my own children, wanting to keep them safe against harm and time.

The dating of the Formby footprints was achieved by means of a technique known as optically stimulated luminescence. OSL relies on the chronometric abilities of quartz granules. If kept in darkness – if buried in mud, for instance – quartz steadily attracts electrons to itself. Quartz samples are obtained from the site to be dated; they are kept unpolluted by the light and are taken to a laboratory, where they are irradiated by a neon beam. The neon causes the quartz to discharge its hoarded electrons, and the measured rate and quantity of electron discharge gives a reliable indication of the length of time the quartz has been in darkness. A final trail of white stones, marking time, showing the way back.

Images arise, gleaned from the miles on foot. White stones, white horses, flying islands, glowing eyes, mirages, drowned lands, dreams of flying, reversals and doublings, rights of way and rites of way, falcons and maps: the images move as brass spheres in an orrery, orbiting and converging in unlikely encounter. There is a flickering to order; gathered details are sealed by the stamp of the anterior. The land itself, filled with letters, words, texts, songs, signs and stories. And always, everywhere, the paths, spreading across counties and countries, recalled as pattern rather than as plot, bringing alignments and discrepancies, elective affinities, shifts from familiar dispositions. I imagine the Earth seen from an altitude so impossibly great that retrospect is possible as well as prospect, and that the prints of millennia of human walking are visible, the shimmering foil of our species.

Northwards, onwards. One of the prints, a right foot, is beginning to stand above the mud, as if the mark is the impress of another figure standing on the mirror-line, I on the recto and he on the verso.

The mountains of Snowdonia curve away to the south-west, drawing the eye. Anglesey is just visible as a shadow island through the haze. Three rooks strut on the beach ahead; a fourth lands and the group flaps off north. Inland, a sparrowhawk settles snug among alder branches, slyly hidden, orange-eyed. A plastic bag snagged on the marram shivers in the wind. Gulls fly over in Vs and Ws.

I stop by the last footprint, 5,000 years after setting out, my track ceasing where his does. I look back along the track-line to my south. The light tilts again and suddenly the water-filled footprints are mirrors reflecting the sky, the shuddering clouds and whoever looks into them.

GLOSSARY

albedo The proportion of light reflected from a surface.

Anthropocene A recently coined and as yet informal term from geologic chronology that refers to the period of earth history in which human activities have had a significant global impact (*see also* **Holocene**).

anticline A line or axis, geologically speaking, from which strata slope or dip down in opposite directions.

archipelago A group of islands; or a sheet of water or sea in which is scattered a group of islands.

barrow A mound of earth or stones erected over a grave. **Neolithic** barrows tend to be 'long' and lozenge-shaped; Bronze Age barrows tend to be 'round'.

bealach (Gaelic) A pass; a gap or col between two hills.

bleb A bubble of air in water, glass, ice or other substance that is, or was, fluid.

boll A rounded **boss** or knob; a rounded seed-vessel or pod, as in flax or cotton.

boreal Of or pertaining to the north.

boss A protruberance or swelling; a hump or hunch.

brae (Old English) A slope or hillside.

breck A breach, blemish or failing; thus 'Brecklands', the name given to the 'broken' sandy heathlands of south Norfolk.

burn A stream, brook or small river.

carr A bog or fen grown up with low bushes (willows, alders).

chert A form of amorphous silica occurring in several varieties, of which one is flint.

chorten A Buddhist place or object of worship.

coccolith Individual plates of calcium carbonate formed by certain single-celled algae.

cognitive dissonance The experience of holding conflicting ideas or experiences simultaneously.

combe Generally, a hollow or valley. In the chalk-lands of southern England, a hollow or valley on the flank of a hill, or a steep short valley running up from the sea coast. In Cumbria and Scotland, a crescent-shaped scoop or valley in the side of a hill.

corbel Architecturally, a projection of stone jutting out from the face of a wall to support a superincumbent weight. Also, a raven.

Cretaceous Chalk or chalky; also the geological period of generally warm climate and high sea levels extending from *c.*145 million years ago to *c.*65 million years ago. It is associated with a flowering of biodiversity, a massive extinction pulse at its end, and the laying down of huge chalk deposits.

croft An agricultural smallholding.

currach A small boat of wickerwork covered with hides, used in ancient times in Scotland and Ireland. Generally 'currach', or 'curragh', in Ireland and Scotland, and 'coracle' in England.

cursus In terms of **Neolithic** monuments: long parallel banks with outside ditches and squared or curved ends, which run across country, often for long distances. The most famous example in England is the Dorset cursus.

cut for sign In tracking and hunting, to range back and forth across an area of ground looking for evidence of passage.

darshan (Sanskrit) 'Seeing' in the sense of 'beholding a divine vision'.

deckled In book production, having a rough uncut edge.

declivity A downslope (as opposed to an acclivity, an upslope).

dendritic Of branching form, arborescent, tree-like.

dry valley A valley found in chalk or limestone landscape that no longer has a surface flow of water; thought often to have been created after the last Ice Age when melted water eroded the chalk down to the permafrost layer.

dupel Metallic chaff dropped by aeroplanes during the Second World War to confuse radar detection.

eoliths The name given to the earliest worked stones.

erratic In geology, a stray mass of rock, foreign to the surrounding strata, that has been transported from its original site, apparently by glacial action. More generally and adjectivally: wandering, nomadic.

exultation The collective noun for skylarks; almost as good as 'a deceit of lapwings'.

feldspar The name given to a group of minerals, usually white or flesh-red in colour, occurring in crystalline masses (granite, for example, is often composed of feldspar, quartz and mica); *see also* **gneiss**.

floe A sheet of floating ice; a portion of an ice field.

fluting Used to describe the runnel-like ice structures that can form on steep mountain faces under certain weather conditions.

foil The tracks or body impressions of deer and other animals on grass or leaf-covered surfaces.

gansey A dialect version of 'Guernsey', i.e. close-knitted woollen material.

gean Another word for the wild cherry, *Prunus avium*.

gelid Cold as ice.

ghillie (Scots) The person who acts as guide and attendant on shooting or fishing expeditions on an estate.

gill A stream or small river; also a deep cleft or ravine, usually wooded and rocky, following the course of a stream.

gneiss A metamorphic rock composed, like granite, of quartz, **feldspar** or orthoclase, and mica, but distinguished from granite by its foliated or laminated structure.

gnomon The pin or pillar at the centre of a sundial, the fall of whose shadow indicates the time of day.

guga (Gaelic) A young gannet.

gyre To whirl, turn in revolutions, circles or spirals. In its noun form, a whirl, circle or spiral.

haar A wet mist or sea fog.

hanger A wood on the side of a steep hill.

headland The unploughed area at the top of a field, left where the horse, ox or tractor turns.

heel-trail A trail which is followed in the opposite way to which it is made, i.e. against the flow.

helical Having the form of a helix: screw-shaped, spiralling.

hierophany A manifestation of the sacred.

hodology The study of roads and pathways (the word is absent from the *OED*, but usages can be found in Frank Morley's *The Great North Road*, with a speculative reference, on his part, back to D'Arcy Wentworth Thompson, thence to Goethe, thence to Aristotle).

holloway A lane or path that has been grooved down into the surrounding landscape due to the erosive power of, variously, feet, wheels and rainwater.

Holocene The geological epoch extending from the end of the Pleistocene (now globally dated to 11,700 years BP) to the present day; or – for supporters of the **Anthropocene** – to the start of the Anthropocene.

hoodoo A tall thin spire of rock.

immram A wonder-voyage, a sea journey to an otherworld.

infaunal Dwelling within sediment or the substrate of a sea floor.

isobar A line connecting places on the earth's surface at which the barometric pressure is the same.

isthmus A narrow portion of land, enclosed on each side by water and connecting two larger bodies of land; a neck of land.

itinerary A line or course of travel; a book or map describing a line or course of travel.

karst Limestone landscape marked by numerous abrupt ridges, fissures, sinkholes and caverns.

kist (Scots) A chest.

knap To strike or work flint.

kora A circumambulatory pilgrimage whose goal is not arrival but the transcendence, by means of a passage through sacred geographies, of the attachments and inattentions that constrain awareness of a greater reality.

lacustrine Of or pertaining to a lake or lakes; lake-like.

laminated Arranged in layers; of fluids, a series of layers sliding over one another without mixing.

lazy beds A ridge-and-furrow method of arable cultivation. In Gaelic, *feannagan*.

lenticular Lens-shaped (as in 'lenticular clouds').

lias A blue limestone rock, rich in fossils.

ling Sandy heathland.

lithic Of, or pertaining to, stone.

littoral Existing or taking place on or near the shore.

luff To sail nearer to the wind.

lunulae Crescent-shaped marks.

machair (Scots Gaelic) Coastal grassland, usually overlying shell sand and often rich in flower varieties.

mafic Designating the dark-coloured minerals of igneous rocks, which are predominantly ferromagnesian in character.

mani In Tibetan Buddhism, *mani* stones are slates, rocks or pebbles inscribed with the six-syllable mantra '*Om mani padme hum*'.

marram A tough and densely spiky grass which grows on coastal dunes.

massif A prominent range or group of mountains.

megalith A large stone, especially one forming all or part of a prehistoric monument.

Mesolithic The 'Middle' Stone Age. Datings of the Mesolithic period differ depending on location, but in a European context the Mesolithic lasted roughly between the end of the last glacial period and the beginning of **Neolithic** agriculture, or – very roughly – *c.*9000 BC to *c.*4000 BC.

micro-terrains Small-scale aspects and features of a landscape.

misprint An irregular step, or a

failure to **register** in an animal which normally does so.

moraine A mound or ridge consisting of debris that has been carried and deposited by a glacier or ice sheet, usually at its sides or its extremity.

mycelia The network of fine filaments constituting the tissue of a fungus.

nap The texture of a surface, especially concerning the direction in which hair, grass or other fibres are predominantly lying.

Neolithic The 'New' or 'Later' Stone Age, characterized by the use of ground or polished stone implements and weapons, and later by the development of an agricultural rather than a hunter-gatherer lifestyle, with a consequently greater presence of permanent tracks and paths. In a European context, the Neolithic is generally agreed to give way to the Iron Age around 2000 BC (*see also* **Mesolithic**).

oneiric Dream-like.

onomasticon A vocabulary or lexicon of proper names.

orrery A model, usually clockwork in mechanism, designed to represent and perform the relative motions of the earth, moon and planets around the sun.

ortholith A rocky outcrop, or (archaeologically) a stone that has been raised into an upright position.

peninsula A piece of land that is almost, but not wholly, surrounded by water.

peregrini The name sometimes given to early Celtic Christians who travelled widely, often upon the sea, as an expression of religious devotion.

periplus An account or narrative of a circumnavigation or other voyage; a manual of navigation (plural forms being *peripli* or *peripluses*).

petroglyph A rock carving; a sign inscribed on stone.

phragmites A genus of reeds whose members have flat linear leaves and strong erect stems.

Pleistocene The geological epoch spanning the period of the world's recent glaciations, from 2,588,000 years BP to 11,700 years BP.

portolan A set or book of sailing directions, illustrated with charts.

Pre-Cambrian The period of earth history from *c*.4.6 billion years ago to *c*.542 million years ago: around 88 per cent of geological time.

press The means of marking a page with metal or wooden type.

psychogeology The study of the interplay of mind and geology; the shaping of thought by earth and rock.

pugmark The footprint of an animal.

qasr (Arabic) A stone tower.

quill The shaft of a bird's feather, or something – usually a pen – made from it.

reaver A robber or bandit; usually those robbers who raided the Scottish–English border between the thirteenth and sixteenth centuries.

recto The front leaf or upper side of a page of paper (*see also* **verso**).

register The placing of the hind foot into the track made by the forefoot (of, for example, a deer, cat or fox). In a 'clean' register two tracks appear as one.

sarha (Arabic) A walk or wander that leads to some kind of revelation or spiritual renovation.

sarsen A large block or boulder of sandstone found on a chalk down (*see also* **wether**).

scapula The shoulder blade; adjectivally (scapular), having the form of a shoulder blade.

scarp The steep face or slope of a hill.

scree The mass of small stones and pebbles that forms on a steep mountain slope. 'Talus' in American English.

selkie A seal, or in folklore, a spirit that assumes the form of a seal.

selvedge Field boundary, but also the edge of a piece of woven material finished so as to prevent unravelling.

senderismo (Spanish) Walking, hiking or path-following.

serac A bulging tower of ice on a glacier.

shieling A pasture to which livestock are driven for grazing, usually during the summer months; a hut or shelter constructed near such pasture.

sierra (Spanish) A range of hills or mountains, especially those which are sharp or jagged.

sillion The thick curve of soil turned

over by the plough; in ground with a high clay content this 'furrow slice' can appear to shine.

sinter Of particulate materials: to coalesce into a solid mass under the influence of heat without liquefaction.

skerry A small sharp rock island.

slot The track or trail of an animal, especially a deer.

spar In sailing, a general term for masts, booms, yards and gaffs.

stance In the language of droving, a place where drovers would halt their cattle and spend the night.

stramash An uproar, a state of confusion.

stravaig (Scots) To wander aimlessly, unguided by outcome or destination.

stupa A Buddhist monument.

sway The wavering or deviation of tracks from the median line, for example when an animal is tired, injured or heavy with young.

tain The reflective backing on mirror glass which makes reflection possible but limits the viewer's onward gaze.

thwart A seat across a boat.

toponym A place name.

topophilia The love of place, or of a particular place.

tracking In hunting, to follow by the footprints of, or to trace the course or movement of. In cold printing, the action of adjusting the spacing between letters and words.

transhumance The seasonal movement of grazing animals to and from pasture.

trim The most advantageous set of a ship in the water, and/or the most advantageous adjustment of a ship's sails.

tumulus An ancient mound, usually a burial mound.

ungulate Having the form of a hoof; or, of animals, hoofed.

uroboros The circular symbol of a snake or dragon bending round to eat its own tail.

vane The web of a feather.

verso The reverse of a page; the side of a leaf or page presented to the eye when it has been turned (*see also* **recto**).

vertex A junction of two or more lines.

volute Adjectivally, forming a spiral curve or curves.

wadi (Arabic) A ravine or valley which becomes, in heavy rain, a watercourse; the river that runs through such a valley.

wether Boulders of sandstone that lie on top of chalk downs (*see also* **sarsen**).

Wunderkammer (German) A cabinet of curiosities, a treasure chest, literally a 'wonder-room'.

yard The **spar** from which sails are set; the crosspiece of a mast.

zawn (Cornish) A fissure or cave in a coastal cliff.

ziggurat A staged tower of pyramidal form in which each successive storey is smaller than the one below it, so as to leave a terrace all around.

NOTES

List of abbreviations used in the notes

ACP: Edward Thomas, *The Annotated Collected Poems*, ed. Edna Longley (Newcastle: Bloodaxe, 2008)
AIE: W. H. Hudson, *Afoot in England* (1909; Oxford: Beaufoy Books, 2010)
CET: Edward Thomas, *The Childhood of Edward Thomas: A Fragment of Autobiography and the War Diary* (1938; London: Faber and Faber, 1983)
ETGB: Edward Thomas, *Letters from Edward Thomas to Gordon Bottomley*, ed. R. George Thomas (Oxford: Oxford University Press, 1968)
GB: Edward Thomas, *George Borrow: The Man and His Books* (London: Chapman & Hall, 1912)
IW: Edward Thomas, *The Icknield Way* (1913; London: Constable, 1916)
LFY: Eleanor Farjeon, *Edward Thomas: The Last Four Years* (1958; Stroud: Sutton, 1997)
LM: Nan Shepherd, *The Living Mountain* (1977; Edinburgh: Canongate, 2011)
RJ: Edward Thomas, *Richard Jefferies: His Life and Work* (London: Hutchinson & Co., 1909)
SC: Edward Thomas, *The South Country* (London: J. M. Dent, 1909)
SLET: Edward Thomas, *Selected Letters of Edward Thomas*, ed. R. George Thomas (Oxford: Oxford University Press, 1995)
USW: Helen Thomas, *Under Storm's Wing* (Manchester: Carcanet, 1988)
WOW: Tim Ingold and Jo Lee Vergunst (eds.), *Ways of Walking* (Aldershot: Ashgate, 2008)

Epigraphs

Pages
vii *'Much has been written . . . of the road'*: *IW*, p. 13.

vii *'My eyes were in my feet'*, *LM*, p. 46.

Chapter 1: Track

Pages

5 *'All things are engaged . . . print of the seal'*: Ralph Waldo Emerson, *The Complete Works*, ed. Edward Waldo Emerson (Boston, MA: Houghton Mifflin, 1903–4), vol. 4, pp. 261–2.

Chapter 2: Path

Pages

13 *'Always, everywhere . . . symmetrical or meandering'*: Thomas A. Clark, 'In Praise of Walking', in *Distance & Proximity* (Edinburgh: Pocketbooks, 2000), p. 15.

15 *Utsi's Stone*: I am grateful for this detail to Hayden Lorimer, 'Herding Memories of Humans and Animals', *Environment and Planning D: Society and Space* 24:4 (2006), 497–518 (514).

16 *'pointedly condemned . . . female connoisseurs'*: Thomas De Quincey, *Recollections of the Lakes and the Lake Poets*, ed. David Wright (1862; Harmondsworth: Penguin, 1970), pp. 53–4.

16 *'They give me joy as I proceed'*: John Clare, 'Rural Scenes', in *The Poems of the Middle Period 1822–1837*, ed. Eric Robinson, David Powell and P. M. S. Dawson (Oxford: Clarendon Press, 1998), p. 585.

16 *'My left hand hooks . . . a plain public road'*: Walt Whitman, *Leaves of Grass* (1855), in *Walt Whitman: Complete Poetry and Collected Prose* (New York: Library of America, 1982), p. 82.

16 *It is one of the significant differences . . . labyrinth should exist*: It is perhaps the chief paradox of the English footpath network that it came into being chiefly as a result of the Parliamentary Enclosures Acts of *c.*1750–1850. Prior to the Acts, large areas of land were 'common'; as the Acts were passed it became necessary to define the rights and duties of landowners, and the extent of their landownings, by means of hedges and fences (preventing access) and footpaths (designating and permitting, but also implicitly limiting access). Various paths (previously permissive) vanished; new ones appeared (and were protected by bye-laws), but the openness of the landscape, and the freedom to move wilfully within it, was compromised. Thus the legal birth of the footpath system shows it to be on the one hand a function of freedom,

on the other of trammelment. See for a brilliant and impassioned account of this history of access, Marion Shoard, *This Land Is Our Land* (1987; London: Gaia, 1997).

19 *'several books in the Manchu-Tartar dialect . . . no great difficulty'*: this story has had various tellings. I draw here on that given in Herbert Jenkins, *The Life of George Borrow* (London: John Murray, 1912), pp. 94–104. Edward Thomas repeats a version of it briefly but with pleasure in *GB*, pp. 125–6.

19 *'the Horrors'*: Jenkins, *Life of George Borrow*, *passim*; and *GB*, p. 131.

19 *'There's night and day, brother . . . wish to die'*: George Borrow, *Lavengro* (London: John Murray, 1851), p. 156.

20 *'charm of the unknown'*: *AIE*, p. 7.

20 *'the longest walk . . . on record'*: Charles F. Lummis, *A Tramp Across the Continent* (1892; Omaha: University of Nebraska Press, 1981), p. 3.

20 *'going out . . . was really going in'*: Linnie Marsh Wolfe (ed.), *John Muir, John of the Mountains: The Unpublished Journals of John Muir* (Madison, WI: University of Wisconsin Press, 1979), p. 439.

21 *'wildlings'*: Henry Williamson, *Tarka the Otter* (1927; London: Book Club Associates, 1985), p. 142.

21 *'chipped from the breastbone'*: Henry Williamson, unpublished letter to Dennis McWilliam, 11 June 1968. Later in his life Williamson's folk notion of the 'land' soured into a troubling sympathy with fascism.

21 *'thronged by souls unseen . . . man dead'*: John Masefield, *The Poems and Plays of John Masefield* (London: Macmillan, 1918), vol. 2, p. 62.

21 *'slip back out of this modern world'*: *AIE*, p. 14.

21 *'ghost and a ghost-to-be'*: the translation is that given by the American novelist Howard Norman in 'On the Poet's Trail', *National Geographic* (November 2008), 36.

22 *'[a]s if I could look back . . . and their life'*: Richard Jefferies, notebook entry for 1887, quoted by Jem Poster in 'Ghosts: Edward Thomas and Richard Jefferies', *Archipelago* 2 (Spring 2008), 118–25 (118).

23 *'rich & joyful to the mind'*: John Clare, 'Footpaths', in *The Poems of the Middle Period 1822–1837*, p. 317.

23 *'the recesses of the country'*: William Wordsworth, *Guide to the Lakes* (1810; London: Frances Lincoln, 2004), p. 72.

23 *'lines of communication . . . liberty is kept alive'*: William Hazlitt, 'My First Acquaintance With Poets' (1823), in *Selected Writings*, ed. Duncan Wu (London: Pickering & Chatto, 1998), vol. 9, p. 96.

25 *'patient sublunary legs'*: John Keats, letter to John Reynolds, 12 July 1819, in *The Letters of John Keats*, ed. M. Buxton Forman, 4th edn (1931; Oxford: Oxford University Press, 1952), p. 357.

25 *'The earliest roads wandered . . . to keep in motion'*: *IW*, p. 1.

25 *'indelible old roads . . . long-dead generations'*: *RJ*, p. 4.

25 *'potent, magic things . . . over many centuries'*: Edward Thomas, *Beautiful Wales* (London: A. & C. Black, 1905), p. 166.

25 *'one of the great stories of the world'*: *CET*, p. 57.

26 *To Thomas, paths connected real places*: Edna Longley, one of Thomas's shrewdest critics and the editor of the excellent *Annotated Collected Poems*, agrees that 'roads and walks condition[ed] his deepest imaginative structures'; *ACP*, p. 270.

26 *'For untold thousands of years . . . who we were'*: John Brinckerhoff Jackson, 'Roads Belong in the Landscape', in *A Sense of Place, A Sense of Time* (New Haven, CT: Yale University Press, 1994), p. 192.

26 *'enlarge the imagined range for self to move in'*: George Eliot, *Felix Holt: The Radical* (1866), ed. William Baker and Kenneth Womack (Peterborough, Ontario: Broadview, 2000), p. 47.

27 *'I can only meditate . . . works with my legs'*: Jean-Jacques Rousseau, *The Confessions* (1782), trans. J. M. Cohen (London: Penguin, 1953), p. 382.

27 *'so overwhelmed . . . scarcely walk'*: Søren Kierkegaard, *Søren Kierkegaard's Journals and Papers*, ed. and trans. Howard V. Hong and Edna H. Hong (Bloomington, IN: Indiana University Press, 1978), vol. 6, pp. 62–3.

27 *'employ[ing] his legs as an instrument of philosophy'*: Christopher Morley, *Forty-Four Essays* (New York: Harcourt, Brace and Co., 1925), p. 38.

27 *'feeling intellect'*: William Wordsworth, *The Poetical Works of William Wordsworth*, ed. Paul D. Sheats (Boston, MA: Houghton Mifflin, 1952), p. 219.

27 *'Only those thoughts . . . have any value'*: Friedrich Nietzsche, 'Maxims and Barbs', in *Twilight of the Idols* (1888), trans. Duncan Large (Oxford: Oxford University Press, 1998), p. 9.

27 *'Perhaps / The truth depends on a walk around a lake'*: Wallace Stevens, 'Notes towards a Supreme Fiction', in *The Collected Poems of Wallace Stevens* (1955; London: Faber and Faber, 1984), p. 386.

28 *'the skull cinema'*: John Hillaby, 'The Skull Cinema', *New Scientist*, 1 December 1977, 589.

28 *These traces . . . 'footprints', 'tracks'*: Keith H. Basso, *Wisdom Sits in Places* (Albuquerque: New Mexico University Press, 1996), p. 31.

28 *To the Klinchon people . . . used interchangeably*: Allice Legat, 'Walking Stories; Leaving Footprints', in *WOW*, pp. 35–49 (38).

28 *'a mark that remains . . . has passed by'*: Rebecca Solnit, *A Field Guide to Getting Lost* (New York: Viking, 2005), pp. 50–51.

29 *'Are you thinking about . . . Both!'*: Bertrand Russell, *Autobiography* (1967–9; London: Routledge, 1998), p. 330.

29 *'I can't imagine . . . new thoughts within me'*: Ludwig Wittgenstein, in Michael Nedo, ed., *Ludwig Wittgenstein: Wiener Ausgabe Einführung/Introduction* (Vienna and New York: Springer-Verlag, 1993), p. 19.

29 *'carved out of rock . . . wild and cold'*: Thomas A. Clark, *The Hundred Thousand Places* (Manchester: Carcanet, 2009), p. 81.

30 *'clear gray icy water . . . utterly free'*: Elizabeth Bishop, 'At the Fishhouses', in *Elizabeth Bishop: Complete Poems 1927–79* (London: Hogarth Press, 1983), pp. 65–6.

30 *'the depths of reason . . . steps of thought'*: William Wordsworth, 'Essay, Supplementary to the Preface' (1815), in *Prose Works of William Wordsworth*, ed. W. J. B. Owen and Jane Worthington Smyser (Oxford: Clarendon Press, 1974), vol. 3, pp. 82–3.

30 *'each totemic ancestor . . . "ways" of communication'*: Bruce Chatwin, *The Songlines* (1987; London: Picador, 1988), p. 15.

30 *'a spaghetti of Iliads and Odysseys . . . terms of geology'*: Chatwin, *The Songlines*, p. 16.

31 *storytelling was indivisible from wayfaring*: in his fascinatingly intricate book *Lines*, Tim Ingold distinguishes between 'wayfaring' and 'navigation': the navigator plots a course 'before even setting out', such that the journey is 'no more than an explication of the plot', but the wayfarer 'follows a path that one has previously travelled in the company of others, or in their footsteps, reconstructing the itinerary as one goes along'. Tim Ingold, *Lines: A Brief History* (London: Routledge, 2007), pp. 15–16.

32 *'I have long . . . graphically on a map'*: Walter Benjamin, *Selected Writings*, ed. Michael W. Jennings, Howard Eiland and Gary Smith (Cambridge, MA: Harvard University Press, 1999), vol. 2, p. 596.

Chapter 3: Chalk

Pages

37 *'it is about a road which begins . . . had to stop'*: *IW*, pp. vi–vii.

39 *'go ranges of chalk hills . . . against the sky'*: *SC*, p. 2.

40 *'the first . . . plough or wheel'*: Louis MacNeice, 'Autumn Sequel', in *The Collected Poems of Louis MacNeice* (London: Faber and Faber, 1966), p. 422.

41 *It is possible that the entire route is post-Roman*: see Sarah Harrison, 'The Icknield Way: Some Questions', *Archaeological Journal* 160 (2003), 1–22.

43 *'more miles . . . except myself'*: *IW*, p. v.

44 *'travelled along this road till . . . from sea to sea'*: Emslie's notes are published in C. S. Burne, 'Scraps of Folklore Collected by John Philipps Emslie', *Folklore* 26: 2 (June 1915), 153–70.

44 *'dreams . . . under men's feet'*: *SC*, p. 60

47 *'Even when deserted . . . by many signs'*: *IW*, p. 27.

47 *'ghostly . . . roads', 'blind roads'*: *IW*, p. 4.

47 *'It is one of the adventurous pleasures . . . glimmerings'*: *IW*, p. 27.

48 *'the clink, the hum . . . the random singing'*: *ACP*, p. 97.

48 *'shadow-sites'*: for an illuminating discussion of shadow-sites and aerial views, see Kitty Hauser, *Shadow-Sites: Photography, Archaeology and the British Landscape* (Oxford: Oxford University Press, 2007).

49 *'innumerable queer resurrections . . . lost to knowledge'*: Kitty Hauser, *Bloody Old Britain: O. G. S. Crawford and the Archaeology of Modern Life* (London: Granta, 2008), p. 90.

49 *'What is astonishing to the point of uncanniness . . . about their business'*: Hauser, *Bloody Old Britain*, pp. 85–6.

49 *'A white snake on a green hillside'*: *IW*, p. 1.

50 *'The eye that sees the things of today . . . and philosopher'*: *SC*, pp. 151–2.

52 *'several chains . . . mists of morning'*: *IW*, p. 9.

53 *'Thiepval 1915, In Memory of Your Wilhelm . . . To Fritz With Compliments'*: see Nicholas J. Saunders, *Trench Art: Materialities and Memories of War* (Oxford: Berg, 2003), pp. 121–4.

53 *'the continual cracking . . . come up into you'*: Flann O'Brien, *The Third Policeman* (1967; London, Dublin: Dalkey Archive, 1990), p. 90.

54 *'dark beech alley[s] . . . crumbling chalk'*: *SC*, p. 199.

54 *'buried under nettle and burdock . . . bryony bines'*: *SC*, p. 50.

55 *'I could not find a beginning . . . of the Icknield Way'*: *IW*, p. vi.

Chapter 4: Silt

Pages

70 *Doggerland*: The archaeology of Doggerland is well described (briefly) in Laura Spinney, 'The Lost World', *Nature* 454 (9 July 2008), 151–3; and (at length) in Vincent Gaffney et al., *Europe's Lost World: The Rediscovery of Doggerland* (York: Council for British Archaeology, 2009). I draw on both sources.

73 *'ogee . . . line of beauty'*: William Hogarth, *The Analysis of Beauty* (London: J. Reeves, 1753), p. 38.

77 *'could be on the far side of the moon'*: John Burroughs's comment was reported to me by Jules Pretty, and appears in his *This Luminous Coast* (Suffolk: Full Circle, 2011), p. 161.

77 *'soft bluish silvery haze . . . changed to a supernatural'*: *AIE*, pp. 40–41.

77 *'No matter how deliberately . . . live another life'*: Wendell Berry, 'The Rise', in *The Long-Legged House* (New York: Harcourt, Brace & World, 1969), p. 96.

78 *'It is a piece of weakness . . . own natural climate'*: Martin Martin, *A Voyage to St Kilda* (1698; London: Dan Browne, 1753), p. 3.

79 *'Why would anyone want . . . by being in England?'*: Roger Deakin, *Notes from Walnut Tree Farm* (London: Hamish Hamilton, 2008), p. 190.

79 *'An absolutely new prospect . . . King of Dahomey'*: Henry David Thoreau, 'Walking', in *The Works of Henry David Thoreau*, ed. Lily Owens (New York: Avenel, 1981), p. 277. I am grateful to Jos Smith for drawing my attention to the convergence of opinion in these three quotations (Martin, Deakin, Thoreau).

79 *'cognitive dissonance . . . to fail catastrophically'*: see William Fox, 'Walking in Circles: Cognition and Science in High Places', in *High Places*, ed. Denis Cosgrove and Veronica della Dora (London and New York: I. B. Tauris, 2009), pp. 19–29 (20).

Chapter 5: Water – South

Pages

88 *'as by Line upon the Ocean [we] go . . . as the Land'*: John Dryden, 'Annus Mirabilis' (1666), in *The Poems of John Dryden 1649–1681*, ed. Paul Hammond (London and New York: Longman, 1995).

89 *Surface currents, tidal streams . . . between certain places*: see E. G. Bowen,

Saints, Settlements and Seaways in the Celtic Lands (Cardiff: University of Wales Press, 1969), p. 17.

90 *It was the emergence of prehistoric archaeology*: the historiography of the sea roads is valuably discussed in Bowen, *Saints, Settlements and Seaways*, pp. 1–10.

90 *An early breakthrough was made . . . a different vessel*: see O. G. S. Crawford, 'The Distribution of Early Bronze Age Settlements in Britain', *Geographical Journal* 40 (August 1912), 184–97.

91 *In 1932, Cyril Fox published . . . reached Shetland*: see Cyril Fox, *The Personality of Britain* (Cardiff: National Museum of Wales, 1932).

91 *In his superb work on Atlantic cultures . . . sea travel*: see Barry Cunliffe, *Facing the Ocean: The Atlantic and Its Peoples, 8000 BC–AD 1500* (Oxford: Oxford University Press, 2001). Cunliffe's book allows me to speak about the history of the seaways with an authority that is not firstly mine; I draw also on, among other sources, Bowen's *Saints, Settlements and Seaways*, and Peter Davidson's brilliant and compressive essay 'Seven Short Sails', contributed as the epilogue to Pat Law's '7 Short Sails' project. See http://studiolog.heriot-toun.co.uk/7sails/7sails.php

91 *The first sea-road mariners . . . story and drawing*: Cunliffe, *Facing the Ocean*, p. 79.

92 *'poetic logbooks . . . inland kin'*: Kenneth White, *On the Atlantic Edge* (Dingwall: Sandstone, 2006), p. 90; Cunliffe, *Facing the Ocean*, pp. 85–6.

94 *'lost wavelengths . . . of the spirit blow'*: White, *On the Atlantic Edge*, p. 47. See also Hayden Lorimer's fine proposition that at the shore of the sea 'a different order of persons and powers in the world . . . become[s] palpable, taking place through fields of variations, relations, sensations and affects, life felt on the pulse, in the turning of seasons, in mass movements of water and air, in depths and surfaces, inhalations and exhalations, in the quickening and slackening of energies, in the pacing and duration of encounters, in the texture of moods and casts of light, in washes that are biochemical and tidal, and in currents that twine the personal and impersonal, substantial and immaterial'. Hayden Lorimer, 'Forces of Nature, Forms of Life: Calibrating Ethology and Phenomenology', in *Taking Place: Non-Representational Geographies*, ed. Ben Anderson and Paul Harrison (London: Ashgate, 2010), pp. 55–78.

94 *one of Robert Burns's most perfect songs . . . tune*: I am grateful to Peter Davidson for this detail.

95 *Peregrini. . . reached such places*: I have written at greater length about the *peregrini* in the second chapter of *The Wild Places* (London: Granta, 2007), pp. 21–42.

95 *'suddenly began to move . . . quick thinking and poetry'*: White, *On the Atlantic Edge*, p. 38. See also Bowen's mapping of the ancient churches dedicated to the *peregrini* across north-western Europe and Atlantic Britain, in *Saints, Settlements and Seaways*, pp. 51–80.

96 *'metaphor and reality merged . . . over time'*: Cunliffe, *Facing the Ocean*, p. 15.

98 *'affected by isobars . . . hands on helms'*: Ian Stephen, in *Offshore/Onshore* (Edinburgh: Morning Star, 1998), p. 4.

100 *'If it's about anything . . . touch of your people'*: Ian Stephen, 'Southeasterly, Stromness', in *it's about this* (Glasgow: Survivor's Press, 2004), p. 6.

103 *'the grace of accuracy'*: Robert Lowell, 'Epilogue', in *Robert Lowell: Collected Poems*, ed. Frank Bidart (London: Faber and Faber, 2003), p. 838. I take Lowell's line from Gerry Cambridge's fine short appreciation of Ian Stephen, 'All About Shine', which stands as the foreword to Ian's *Mackerel & Creamola: Stories and Recipes* (Edinburgh: Pocketbooks, 2001), pp. 11–15 (13).

105 *In Siberia, the Khanty word . . . 'way'*: I take the detail from Tim Ingold, *Lines: A Brief History* (London: Routledge, 2007), p. 90. Ingold attributes the research to Natalia Novikova, in 'Self-Government of the Indigenous Minority Peoples of West Siberia: Analysis of Law and Practice', in *People and the Land: Pathways to Reform in Post-Soviet Siberia* (Berlin: Dietrich Reimer Verlag, 2002), pp. 83–97. I am grateful also to Tatiana Argounova-Low for our conversation about hodology, and her sharing of research-in-progress on the relationship between roads and narratives in the Republic of Sakha, north-western Siberia.

105 *The Old English* writan *. . . harrowing a track*: I draw here on Ingold's discussion of the relations between text, track and texture in *Lines*, p. 43.

105 *As the pen rises . . . same seam or stream*: see Ingold, *Lines*, pp. 92–3.

110 *'The Shiants . . . the heartlands of Europe'*: Adam Nicolson, *Sea Room: An Island Life* (London: HarperCollins, 2001), pp. 12–13.

111 *'The place has entered me . . . like a stain'*: Nicolson, *Sea Room*, p. 3.

111 *the delusion of a comprehensive totality*: I am grateful for this phrase to Tim and Mairéad Robinson.

111 *'The mind cannot carry away . . . has carried away'*: *LM*, p. 3.

Chapter 6: Water – North

Pages

119 *'In antiquity, Irish scholars . . . intellectual'*: Richard Kearney, *Navigations: Collected Irish Essays 1976–2006* (Dublin: Lilliput, 2006), p. x.

121 *the first record of the* guga *hunt dates to* 1549: see James McGeoch, Catriona McGeoch, Finlay MacLeod and John Love, *Súlasgeir* (Stornoway: Acair, 2010); and John Beatty, *Sula: Seabird Hunters of Lewis* (London: Michael Joseph, 1992). I am grateful to Finlay MacLeod, the McGeoch family and Acair Press for their generosity in making materials available to me concerning Sula Sgeir and the *guga* hunt.

129 *'the bounce of light . . . elaborate counter-physics'*: Ian Stephen, 'Anstruther to St Andrew's Bay, aboard The Reaper', in *it's about this* (Glasgow: Survivor Press, 2004), p. 10.

129 *'long slanting line . . . to tell every day'*: Mark Twain, *Life on the Mississippi* (1883; London: Penguin, 1986), p. 96.

132 'roomy': William James, *The Principles of Psychology* (1890; New York: Holt, 1905), pp. 136–7. James draws on the phrasing of the German physiologist and colour theorist Ewald Hering.

133 *'tin road . . . amber road'*: Kenneth White, *On the Atlantic Edge* (Dingwall: Sandstone, 2006), pp. 29–30.

135 *'Wheeling flights . . . to suck the deck'*: Ian Stephen, 'Groundswell', in *Adrift/Napospas vlnám* (Olomouc: Periplum, 2007), p. 72.

Chapter 7: Peat

Pages

146 *He has devoted himself to the exploration . . . sixteenth century onwards*: see, for instance, Finlay MacLeod (ed.), *Togail Tìr/Marking Time: The Map of the Western Isles* (Stornoway: Acair, 1998); Finlay MacLeod, *The Healing Wells of the Western Isles* (Stornoway: Acair, 2000); Finlay MacLeod, *The Chapels in the Western Isles* (Stornoway: Acair, 2007); Finlay MacLeod, *The Norse Mills of Lewis* (Stornoway: Acair, 2009).

146 *'Sandwalk . . . the thinking path'*: see Janet Browne, *Charles Darwin: The Power of Place* (New York: Knopf, 2002), p. 10; and Rebecca Stott, *Darwin and the Barnacle* (London: Faber and Faber, 2003), p. 69.

153 *'drifts of sparkling bog-cotton . . . commemorate stories and people'*: Anne

Campbell and Jon MacLeod, *A-mach an Gleann* (Stornoway: privately published, 2007).

154 *'a promontory or point . . . narrow neck'*: see the 'Onomasticon' in Richard V. Cox's magnificent *The Gaelic Place-Names of Carloway, Isle of Lewis: Their Structure and Significance* (Dublin: Dublin Institute for Advanced Studies, 2002).

157 *'*Èig*'*: the term is taken from 'Some Lewis Moorland Terms: A Peat Glossary', a document running to four pages and 126 Gaelic terms, detailing the language used in three Lewisian townships (Shawbost, Bragar and Shader) to describe and designate features of the local moorland and peat-banks. Many of the terms are remarkable for their compressive precision; the whole is a deeply moving document. It was compiled between 2005 and 2007 by Finlay MacLeod, Anne Campbell and two others. For a much longer discussion of this document, and the relationship between toponyms and place-intimacy, see Robert Macfarlane, 'A Counter-Desecration Phrasebook', in *Towards Re-Enchantment: Place and Its Meanings*, ed. Gareth Evans and Di Robson (London Art Events, 2010), pp. 106–30.

158 *'Walking barefoot . . . flavour in the mouth'*: *LM*, pp. 103–4.

160 *'During the summer of 1935 . . . became much easier'*: Frank Fraser Darling, *A Herd of Red Deer* (Oxford: Oxford University Press, 1937), p. 27.

161 *'were capable of* insight*'*: I am grateful for the detail of Darling's barefootedness, and for this phrase, to Hayden Lorimer, in 'Herding Memories of Humans and Animals', *Environment and Planning D: Society and Space* 24:4 (2006), 497–518 (500).

163 *'dark of woodland . . . an inner light unveiled'*: Nan Shepherd, 'The Colour of Deeside', *The Deeside Field* 8 (Aberdeen: Aberdeen University Press, 1937), 8–12 (9–10).

Chapter 8: Gneiss

Pages

169 *'I find I incorporate gneiss . . . esculent roots'*: Walt Whitman, *Leaves of Grass*, in *Walt Whitman: Complete Poetry and Collected Prose* (New York: Library of America, 1982), p. 57.

171 *'I have spent my life . . . tribe that doesn't exist'*: personal communication from Steve Dilworth, August 2010.

178 *'stuffed all the way . . . their own'*: Rebecca West, *Black Lamb and Grey Falcon: A Journey through Yugoslavia* (1942; Edinburgh: Canongate, 1993), pp. 335–6.

Chapter 9: Granite

Pages

185 *'Since to follow a trail . . . a return'*: *WOW*, p. 17.

186 *Wherever my grandfather had gone . . . he had walked*: for more detail on my grandfather's remarkable life, see Edward Peck, *Recollections 1915–2005* (New Delhi: Pauls Press, 2005).

186 *'interesting times'*: see Eric Hobsbawm, himself adapting an apocryphal Chinese hex, in *Interesting Times: A Twentieth-century Life* (London: Penguin, 2002).

190 *Illegal droving, mostly by reavers*: I draw here and elsewhere on A. R. B. Haldane, *The Drove Roads of Scotland* (1952; Edinburgh: Birlinn, 2008); the detail about the *via viridis* is to be found on p. 11.

191 *'a lonely grass-grown track crossing the hills'*: Haldane, *The Drove Roads of Scotland*, p. 1.

191 *'The brown sails of the cattle boats . . . roads of Scotland'*: Haldane, *The Drove Roads of Scotland*, p. 222.

192 *'the elementals'*: *LM*, p. 4.

193 *'a traffic of love'*: *LM*, p. xliii.

193 *'does nothing . . . but be itself'*: *LM*, p. 23.

193 *'something moves . . . recounting it'*: *LM*, p. 8.

195 *'far out of her path'*: *LM*, p. xlii.

197 *'bland as silk'*: *LM*, p. 93.

197 *'rooted . . . in . . . immobility'*: *LM*, p. 92.

197 *'the central core of fire . . . the total mountain'*: *LM*, p. 105.

198 *'powerful absence[s]'*: Adam Nicolson, *Sea Room* (London: HarperCollins, 2001), p. 4.

199 *'When standing at the entrance . . . foot of the hill'*: Helen Thomas, 1932 foreword to *The South Country* (Dorset: Little Toller, 2009), pp. 15–16.

199 *'more readily picture the parts . . . principal tributaries'*: Neil Gunn, *Highland River* (1937; Edinburgh: Canongate, 1991), p. 33.

199 *'walking together . . . their own lives'*: John McGahern, 'Country Leitrim: The Sky above Us', in *Love of the World* (London: Faber and Faber, 2009), pp. 19–26 (23).

199 *When the painter John Nash . . . they would travel together*: this story was told to me by Ronald Blythe when I visited him one day at his house in Wormingford, which is reached along a deep-sunk track.

200 *'shin[ing] as red as new-made rock'*: *LM*, p. 76.

200 *'well at the world's end'*: Neil Gunn, *The Well at the World's End* (1951; Edinburgh: Canongate, 1996).

201 *'A mountain has an inside'*: *LM*, p. 16.

201 *'pitching into them . . . the bottom'*, *LM*, p. 25.

201 *'walks the flesh transparent . . . accorded from the mountain'*: *LM*, pp. 106–8.

204 *'Knowing another is endless . . . grows with the knowing'*: *LM*, p. 108.

Chapter 10: Limestone

Pages

212 *Raja had been walking . . . for more than forty years*: the best accounts of Raja Shehadeh's exceptional life and walks are his own, in *Palestinian Walks* (London: Profile, 2007) and also in *A Rift in Time: Travels with My Ottoman Uncle* (London: Profile, 2010).

219 *'an eye for the tracks . . . like catwalks'*: Raja Shehadeh, *Palestinian Walks*, p. 5.

220 *'parched . . . some massacre has been committed'*: William Thackeray, *Notes of a Journey from Cornhill to Grand Cairo*, in *Miscellanies* (1846; Rockville, MD: Wildside Press, 2009), vol. 2, p. 561.

220 *'bleached . . . crunched, gnawed & mumbled'*: Herman Melville, *Journals*, ed. Howard C. Horsford and Lynn Horth (1957; Chicago, IL: Northwestern University Press, 1989), p. 83.

226 *'landswept . . . except the touchable earth'*: John Berger, 'A Place Weeping', *Threepenny Review* 188 (Summer 2009), at http://www.threepennyreview.com/samples/bergersu09.html

Chapter 11: Roots

Pages

235 *'We have been increasingly* on *pilgrimage'*: Edmund Blunden, 'On Pilgrimage in England: Voyages of Discovery', *TLS*, 28 March 1942, p. 156. I am grateful to Alexandra Harris for drawing Blunden's essay to my attention.

235 *'The number of quiet pilgrims . . . a circle from snail shells'*: Václav Cilek, 'Bees of the Invisible – Awakening of a Place', *Artesian* 1 (Autumn/Winter 2008), 27–9.

236 *'there is no road, the road is made by walking'*: Antonio Machado, *Campos de Castilla* (1912; Madrid: Catedra, 2006), p. 223. The translation is by Robert Harvard.

237 *'Bohemia . . . a place within the heart'*: Cilek, 'Bees of the Invisible – Awakening of a Place', 27–9.

244 *'Each of my books records an actual journey . . . an interior path'*: various of the details here are taken from catalogue essays and other writings in Spanish and English by Miguel Angel Blanco, some of which are collected at www.bibliotecadelbosque.net/

244 *'My life has been united . . . seen my destiny'*: Miguel Angel Blanco, 'Trees of Power', at: http://www.bibliotecadelbosque.net/arbolcaido.html

251 *'lost in prayer . . . above the ground'*: Jan Morris, *Spain* (1964; London: Penguin, 1982), p. 130.

254 *'As I watch . . . landscape bristles'*: *LM*, p. 11.

Chapter 12: Ice

Pages

262 *'The power of such . . . invisible magnet'*: Lama Govinda, *The Way of the White Clouds* (1966; New York: Overlook Press, 2006), p. 271.

264 *'I should warn you . . . full of blood'*: Peter Matthiessen, *The Snow Leopard* (1978; London: Harvill, 1996), p. 33.

267 *'When I think of Scott . . . always young'*: J. M. Barrie, *Courage* (London: Hodder & Stoughton, 1922), p. 32.

269 *'Our gates to the glorious . . . adventure and sunshine'*: E. M. Forster, *Howards End*, ed. Douglas Mao (1910; London: Longman, 2009), p. 10.

269 *'sword-light of the Himalayas'*: Matthiessen, *The Snow Leopard*, p. 78.

273 *'The effect of this strange Matterhorn . . . cannot resist it'*: John Ruskin, *Modern Painters* (1843–60; London: George Allen & Sons, 1910), vol. 4, pp. 247–8.

278 *'a rough circle . . . my starting-point'*: *SC*, p. 21.

279 *'the tang of height . . . a good place'*: *LM*, p. 9.

279 *'I believe that I now understand . . . pilgrimage to a mountain'*: *LM*, p. 108.

Chapter 13: Snow

Pages

292 *'the strong paths . . . their settings'*: Christopher Tilley, *The Phenomenology of Landscape: Places, Paths and Monuments* (Oxford: Berg, 1994), pp. 30, 75.

293 *'become more aerial . . . other points of view'*: W. H. Hudson, *Nature In Downland* (1900; Middlesex: Echo Library, 2006), p. 13.

295 *'because the colour . . . so beautifully obvious'*: Eric Ravilious, letter to Peggy Angus, July 1939, in James Russell, *Ravilious in Pictures: Sussex and the Downs* (Norwich: Mainstone Press, 2009), p. 22.

295 *'a kind of wariness . . . personal involvements'*: J. M. Richards, *Memoirs of an Unjust Fella* (London: Weidenfeld & Nicolson, 1980), p. 95.

295 *'always seemed to be . . . material existence'*: John Lake, undated letter to Richard Morphet, quoted in preface to Helen Binyon, *Eric Ravilious: Memoir of an Artist* (Guildford: Lutterworth, 1983), p. 23.

299 *'the snow and the snow light . . . northwards'*: Peter Davidson's brilliant *The Idea of North* (London: Reaktion, 2005), p. 104.

300 *'Goodbye Tush . . . as you can see'*: Eric Ravilious, letter to Tirzah Ravilious, ?30 May 1940, in *Ravilious at War: The Complete Work of Eric Ravilious, September 1939–September 1942*, ed. Anne Ullman (Upper Denby: Fleece Press, 2002), p. 95.

300 *'remote and lovely'*, Eric Ravilious, letter to Helen Binyon, ?30 May 1940, in *Ravilious at War*, p. 93.

300 *'unearthly existence'*: Eric Ravilious, letter to Diana Tuely, ?30 May 1940, in *Ravilious at War*, p. 93.

303 *the paired summits of Walker's Hill and Knapp Hill*: Walker's Hill and Adam's Grave, the nickname of the long barrow on its summit, feature in Thomas's poem 'Lob', about the ghostly Englishman who walks to 'keep clear old paths that no one uses'. *ACP*, p. 77.

Chapter 14: Flint

Pages

307 *'The long white roads . . . of the past'*: *SC*, pp. 108–9.

308 *'the first music of England . . . oak trees'*: this is Peter Ackroyd's account of Taine's 1860 claim, as given in *Albion: The Origins of the English Imagination* (London: Chatto & Windus, 2002), p. 3.

309 *'On the ancient tracks . . . and be content'*: Helen Thomas, preface to Edward Thomas, *The South Country* (London: J. M. Dent, 1909), pp. 13–14.

309 *'a contemporary . . . of a landscape'*: Albert Camus, notebook entry for 29 October 1946, in *Notebooks 1942–1951*, trans. Justin O'Brien (Chicago, IL: Ivan R. Dee Publishers, 2010), p. 217.

309 *'Roads go on . . . That shoots and is gone'*: *ACP*, p. 106.

310 *'wealth of poetry'*: *SC*, p. 4.

310 *'airy motion . . . doubles round the head of a coombe'*: *SC*, p. 148.

310 *'a curve is latent'*: *IW*, p. vi.

310 *'sheaf of half-a-dozen footpaths worn side-by-side'*: *SC*, p. 50.

310 *'grassy track[s] of great breadth . . . traveller's joy'*: *SC*, p. 214.

310 *'gentleman of the road . . . umbrella man'*: *SC*, pp. 185–95.

311 *'The hill road wet with rain . . . If we trod it not again'*: *ACP*, p. 106.

311 *'the outer world . . . to a tunnel'*: *USW*, p. 110.

312 *'crushing attacks of gloom and wretchedness'*: *USW*, p. 113.

312 *'the ancient ways . . . not only with [her] legs'*: *USW*, p. 123.

313 *'Every hillside, every wood and meadow . . . Edward and I took there'*: *USW*, p. 160.

314 *There are two intertwined histories of modern wayfaring*: see R. A. Leeson, *Travelling Brothers* (London: George Allen & Unwin, 1979).

315 *'brewed tea . . . the treadmill of the mid-Thirties'*: Laurie Lee, *As I Walked Out One Midsummer Morning* (London: Penguin, 1969), p. 62.

319 *'if on a moonless night . . . when you go on it follows'*: the folklore of Chanctonbury is helpfully collected by Jacqueline Simpson in her 'Legends of Chanctonbury Ring', *Folklore* 80 (1969), 122–31. See also Arthur Beckett, *The Spirit of the Downs* (London: Methuen, 1943) and Philip Gosse, *Go to the Country* (London: Cassell, 1936).

321 'AGRIMONIA . . . *1 or 2 achenes*': C. A. Johns, *Flowers of the Field* (1851; London: Society for Promoting Christian Knowledge, 1919), pp. 153–4.

322 '*in vernation . . . like roof-tiles*': Johns, *Flowers of the Field*, p. xix.

322 *'a roving spirit everywhere'*: *SC*, p. 182.

322 '*white ribbon of possible travel*': Robert Louis Stevenson, quoted by Duncan Minshull in the foreword to his invaluable *The Vintage Book of Walking* (London: Vintage, 2000), p. xvii.

322 *'never . . . As it winds on for ever'*: *ACP*, p. 107.

323 *'to take root forever . . . to do with change'*: *SC*, p. 161.

323 *'For . . . never knew a home again'*: Helen Thomas, preface to *SC*.

324 *'faintly-seen silvery stars . . . whiteness in the dark'*: W. H. Hudson, *Nature in Downland* (1900; Middlesex: Echo Library, 2006), pp. 1–2.

325 *'edge of consciousness'*: F. R. Leavis, *New Bearings in English Poetry* (1932; Michigan: University of Michigan Press, 1965), p. 69.

325 '*Many a road . . . in they sink*': *ACP*, p. 136.

326 '*a kind of pursuit . . . through the past*': Richard Holmes, *Footsteps* (1985; London: Penguin, 1986), p. 26.

326 *'You would never . . . quite catch them'*: Holmes, *Footsteps*, p. 27.

326 *the mind was a landscape*: I adapt the phrase from Rebecca Solnit, *Wanderlust: A History of Walking* (London: Penguin, 2000), p. 6.

329 *'I like the country we are in . . . have been beautiful'*: Edward Thomas, letter to Gordon Bottomley, 1 March 1917, *ETGB*, p. 278.

329 *'Now all roads . . . And their brief multitude'*: *ACP*, pp. 107–8.

330 'ghostland': *IW*, p. vi.

Chapter 15: Ghost

Pages

333 *'bright warm Easter day'*: *CET*, p. 175.

333 *'the light of the new moon . . . meant by God'*: *CET*, pp. 175–6.

334 *'aware of some completely invisible track'*: *LFY*, p. 6.

334 *'you would not walk . . . in a new way'*: *LFY*, p. 32.

335 *'flowers of rose-bay . . . Chatham Railway'*: *SC*, p. 99.

335 *'only peace would be to be needed by him'*: *USW*, p. 49.

335 *'[I]t seems strange now . . . opened for giving'*: *USW*, p. 36.

337 *'I hate my work . . . I do harm'*: Edward Thomas, note to self dated 9 October 1907 (later discovered by Helen Thomas), *SLET*, p. 44.

337 *'to be let into the light again'*: *USW*, p. 49.

337 *He admires 'Sumer is icumen in'*: *SC*, p. 4.

337 *'wind[s] like silver . . . the current of their feet'*: *ACP*, p. 72.

339 *'everything except the power . . . hissing grass'*: *SC*, p. 275.

339 *'tender loveliness'*: *USW*, p. 152.

339 *'I am not a part of nature . . . the rain without'*: *IW*, p. 281.

339 *'the sense of roads . . . roads of great purpose and destiny'*: *IW*, pp. 6–7.

340 *'grew . . . like the handle of a walking stick'*: *RJ*, p. 179. I draw here and elsewhere on Lucy Newlyn's subtle discussion of Thomas's relationship with Jefferies, Hazlitt and the idea of walking, in 'Hazlitt and Edward Thomas on Walking', *Essays in Criticism* 56: 2 (April 2006), 163–87.

340 *'primitive act . . . a pristine majesty*: *IW*, p. 31.

340 *'The prettiest things . . . Or separately charactered'*: *ACP*, p. 34.

340 *'[o]f texture midway between life and books'*: I borrow the quotation from Newlyn, 'Hazlitt and Edward Thomas on Walking'. The source is William Wordsworth, *The Poetical Works of William Wordsworth*, ed. Paul D. Sheats (Boston, MA: Houghton Mifflin, 1952), p. 145.

340 *'champagne corks . . . wheat coloured'*: Edward Thomas, letter of 15 January 1908 to Gordon Bottomley, *ETGB*, p. 155.

340 *'Not one [pebble] . . . beyond my thinking'*: Edward Thomas, letter of 7 February 1908 to Gordon Bottomley, *ETGB*, p. 157.

341 *'Something they knew . . . while they sang'*: *ACP*, p. 35.

341 *'keyless chamber[s] of the brain'*: *SC*, p. 13.

341 *'integral . . . Edward lived it'*: *LFY*, p. 153.

341 *'the wind, the rain . . . the storm were one'*: *IW*, p. 13.

341 *'he walked . . . and his big hands'*: *LFY*, p. 232.

342 *'muddy untruthful reflection of words'*: *SC*, p. 13.

342 *'on wavering footpaths through the fields'*: Robert Frost, letter to Sidney Cox, 18 May 1914. I am indebted for this detail, and that of Frost's 'talks-walking' coinage, to Matthew Hollis, who quotes it in his outstanding biography of Thomas's last years, *Now All Roads Lead to France: The Last Years of Edward Thomas* (London: Faber and Faber, 2011), pp. 126, 128.

342 *'produced . . . same man in another key'*: *LFY*, p. 56.

343 *'slowly growing into a conscious Englishman'*: Edward Thomas, letter to Jesse Berridge, in *Letters of Edward Thomas to Jesse Berridge*, ed. Anthony Berridge (London: Enitharmon, 1983), p. 74.

343 *'He could have been safe . . . chosen to be'*: *LFY*, p. xix.

343 *'moral map . . . flight of 3 kestrels'*: Edward Thomas, letter to Gordon Bottomley, June 1915, in *ETGB*, p. 129.

343 *'I read the sign. Which way shall I go?'*: *ACP*, p. 37.

344 *'Two roads diverged in a yellow wood . . . as just as fair'*: Robert Frost, 'The Road Not Taken', in *The Poetry of Robert Frost*, ed. Edward Connery Lathem (London: Cape, 1971). I am grateful here to Matthew Hollis, whose discussion of the role this poem played in Thomas's decision to go to war sharpened my sense of its more-than-metaphoric importance. See Hollis, *Now All Roads Lead to France*, pp. 233–9.

344 *'Several people . . . could not answer yet'*: *LFY*, p. 153.

344 *'the natural culmination of . . . moods & thoughts'*: Edward Thomas, letter to Gordon Bottomley, 21 July 1915, *ETGB*, p. 253.

344 *'No, no, no, not that'*: *USW*, p. 153.

345 *'the future and the maps . . . I was waiting for'*: *ACP*, p. 134.

345 *He doesn't mind poets knowing he's a soldier*: *LFY*, p. 218.

345 *'black despair . . . calm acceptance'*: *USW*, p. 158.

345 *'It is fine and wintry here . . . 2,000 years ago'*: *LFY*, p. 191.

346 *'Remember that, whatever happens . . . hangs in the air*: *USW*, p. 172.

348 *'what things that same moon . . . the Meuse'*: Edward Thomas, *The Last Sheaf* (London: Jonathan Cape, 1928), p. 221.

350 *'confoundedly cheeky . . . old Hun'*: *LFY*, p. 253.

352 *'new position, fancy . . . catkins are soft dark white'*: *SLET*, pp. 153–4.

353 *'delighting in what beauty . . . together once again'*: *USW*, p. 204.

353 *'Dearest Here I am . . . All and always yours Edwy'*: *SLET*, p. 165.

355 *'For a moment indeed . . . very great and splendid'*: *USW*, p. 210.

355 *'Where any turn may lead . . . up hill after rain'*: *CET*, p. 176.

Chapter 16: Print

Page

359 *Seven thousand to five thousand years ago*: I draw here and elsewhere in this chapter on the work of, letters from, and conversations with, Gordon Roberts; and on Jennifer Lewis and Jennifer E. Stanistreet (eds.), *Sand and Sea: Sefton's Coastal Heritage: Archaeology, History and Environment of a Landscape in North-West England* (Sefton: Leisure Services, 2008).

SELECT BIBLIOGRAPHY

'We walk for a thousand reasons,' wrote Thomas in 1913, 'because we are tired of sitting, because we cannot rest, to get away from towns or to get into them, or because we cannot afford to ride; and for permanent use the last is perhaps the best, as it is the oldest.' Walking is among our most ancient of practices, and it has been undertaken for an irreducibly complex variety of causes and desires. The literature of walking and paths is extensive and wayward; this bibliography includes a selection of the books, essays and articles that I have read about these subjects, as well as those concerning the book's other broad preoccupations: archaeology, cartography, grief, joy, landscape, metaphor, navigation, orientation, pilgrimage, touch, tracking and toponymy, among others. I have asterisked those works which I have found especially interesting, or to which I am especially indebted for information or inspiration. Asserted facts, suggested details, unattributed uncertainties and explicit lacunae in the two biogeographies of Ravilious ('Snow') and Thomas ('Ghost') may be confirmed or falsified in the appropriate works cited in the notes and bibliography, on the scholarship and memories of which I have closely drawn. All inadvertent errors and deliberate deviations are mine.

~

Abram, David, *The Spell of the Sensuous: Perception and Language in a More than Human World* (New York: Pantheon, 1996)

Abulafia, David, *The Great Sea: A Human History of the Mediterranean* (London: Allen Lane, 2011)

Ackroyd, Norman, and Douglas Dunn, *A Line in the Water* (London: Royal Academy, 2009)

Select Bibliography

Ackroyd, Peter, *Albion: The Origins of the English Imagination* (London: Chatto & Windus, 2002)

Amato, Joseph, *On Foot: A History of Walking* (New York: New York University Press, 2004)

~

Barrie, J. M., *Courage* (London: Hodder & Stoughton, 1922)

*Basso, Keith H., *Wisdom Sits in Places: Landscape and Language among the Western Apache* (Albuquerque: University of New Mexico, 1996)

Beatty, John, *Sula: Seabird Hunters of Lewis* (London: Michael Joseph, 1992)

Belloc, Hilaire, *The Old Road* (London: Constable, 1911)

Benjamin, Walter, *Selected Writings*, ed. Michael W. Jennings, Howard Eiland and Gary Smith, 2 vols. (Cambridge, MA: Harvard University Press, 1999)

——, *Berlin Childhood around 1900* (1938; Cambridge, MA: Belknap, 2006)

Berger, John, 'A Place Weeping', *Threepenny Review* 118 (Summer 2009), at http://www.threepennyreview.com/samples/bergersu09.html

Berry, Wendell, *The Long-Legged House* (New York: Harcourt, Brace & World, 1969)

Beveridge, Erskine, *North Uist: Its Archaeology and Topography* (1911; Edinburgh: Birlinn, 1999)

Binyon, Helen, *Eric Ravilious: Memoir of an Artist* (Guildford: Lutterworth, 1983)

Bishop, Elizabeth, *Elizabeth Bishop: Complete Poems 1927–79* (London: Hogarth Press, 1983)

Blanco, Miguel Angel, *Xunta de Galicia* (Santiago de Compostela: Casa da Parra, 2001)

——, *Die Algen und die Alpen* (Köln: Stefan Röpke, 2002)

——, *Visiones del Guadarrama* (Madrid: La Casa Encendida, 2006)

Blunden, Edmund, 'On Pilgrimage in England: Voyages of Discovery', *TLS*, 28 March 1942, 156

Blythe, Ronald, *Field Work: Selected Essays* (Norwich: Black Dog Books, 2007)

Bode, Steven, et al., *There Is No Road: The Road Is Made by Walking* (Asturia: cajAstur, 2009)

Borrow, George, *Lavengro* (London: John Murray, 1851)

———, *Wild Wales* (1862; Fontana: London, 1977)

*Bowen, E. G., *Saints, Settlements and Seaways in the Celtic Lands* (Cardiff: University of Wales Press, 1969)

———, *Britain and the Western Seaways* (London: Thames & Hudson, 1972)

Browne, Janet, *Charles Darwin: The Power of Place* (New York: Knopf, 2002)

Burne, C. S., 'Scraps of Folklore Collected by John Philipps Emslie', *Folklore* 26:2 (June 1915), 153–70

~

Campbell, Anne, and Jon MacLeod, *A-mach an Gleann* (Stornoway: privately published, 2007)

Camus, Albert, *Notebooks 1942–1951*, trans. Justin O'Brien (Chicago, IL: Ivan R. Dee Publishers, 2010)

*Chatwin, Bruce, *The Songlines* (1987; London: Picador, 1988)

Cilek, Václav, 'Bees of the Invisible – Awakening of a Place', *Artesian* 1 (Autumn/Winter 2008), 27–9

Clare, John, *The Poems of the Middle Period 1822–1837*, ed. Eric Robinson, David Powell and P. M. S. Dawson (Oxford: Clarendon Press, 1998)

*Clark, Thomas A., 'In Praise of Walking', in *Distance & Proximity* (Edinburgh: Pocketbooks, 2000)

——, *The Hundred Thousand Places* (Manchester: Carcanet, 2009)

Clarke, Peter, *The Outer Hebrides: The Timeless Way* (Stornoway: Northampton Square, 2006)

Coles, Bryony, and John Coles, *Sweet Track to Glastonbury: The Somerset Levels in Prehistory* (London: Thames & Hudson, 1986)

Cox, Richard V., *The Gaelic Place-Names of Carloway, Isle of Lewis: Their Structure and Significance* (Dublin: Dublin Institute for Advanced Studies, 2002)

Crawford, O. G. S., 'The Distribution of Early Bronze Age Settlements in Britain', *Geographical Journal* 40 (August 1912), 184–97

*Cunliffe, Barry, *Facing the Ocean: The Atlantic and Its Peoples, 8000 BC–AD 1500* (Oxford: Oxford University Press, 2001)

Curry, Patrick, *Ecological Ethics* (2006; London: Polity, 2011)

~

Darling, Frank Fraser, *A Herd of Red Deer* (Oxford: Oxford University Press, 1937)

*Davidson, Peter, *The Idea of North* (London: Reaktion, 2005)
Davies, Hugh, *From Trackways to Motorways: 5000 Years of Highway History* (Stroud: Tempus, 2006)
Deakin, Roger, *Notes from Walnut Tree Farm* (London: Hamish Hamilton, 2008)
De Quincey, Thomas, *Recollections of the Lakes and the Lake Poets*, ed. David Wright (1862; Harmondsworth: Penguin, 1970)
Driscoll, Rosalyn, 'Aesthetic Touch: Notes towards a Sensual Philosophy of Being', *Artesian* 1 (Autumn/Winter 2008), 39–42
Dryden, John, 'Annus Mirabilis' (1666), in *The Poems of John Dryden 1649–1681*, ed. Paul Hammond (London and New York: Longman, 1995)

~

Eliot, George, *Felix Holt: The Radical* (1866), ed. William Baker and Kenneth Womack (Peterborough, Ontario: Broadview, 2000)
Emerson, Ralph Waldo, *The Complete Works*, ed. Edward Waldo Emerson, 12 vols. (Boston, MA: Houghton Mifflin, 1903–4)
Ennion, E. A. R., and Niko Tinbergen, *Tracks* (Oxford: Oxford University Press, 1967)
Evans, Chris, *Grounding Knowledge/Walking Land* (Cambridge: McDonald Institute Monographs, 2009)
Evans, Gareth, and Di Robson (eds.), *Towards Re-Enchantment* (London: ArtEvents, 2010)

~

*Farjeon, Eleanor, *Edward Thomas: The Last Four Years* (1958; Stroud: Sutton, 1997)
——, *Elsie Piddock Skips in Her Sleep* (1932; London: Walker, 1997)
Finlay, Alec, et al., *Irish (2)* (Edinburgh: Morning Star, 2002)
Fox, Cyril, *The Personality of Britain* (Cardiff: National Museum of Wales, 1932)
Fox, William, 'Walking in Circles: Cognition and Science in High Places', in *High Places*, ed. Denis Cosgrove and Veronica della Dora (London and New York: I. B. Tauris, 2009), 19–29

Frost, Robert, *The Poetry of Robert Frost*, ed. Edward Connery Lathem (London: Cape, 1971)
Fulton, Hamish, *El Camino* (Ortega: Fundación Ortega Muñoz, 2008)

~

Gaffney, Vincent, et al., *Europe's Lost World: The Rediscovery of Doggerland* (York: Council for British Archaeology, 2009)
Garrow, Duncan and Fraser Sturt, 'Grey Waters Bright with Neolithic Argonauts? Maritime Connections and the Mesolithic–Neolithic Transition within the "Western Seaways" of Britain, *c.* 5000–3500 BC', *Antiquity* 85:327 (2011), 59–72
Godwin, Fay, and J. R. L. Anderson, *The Oldest Road: An Exploration of the Ridgeway* (London: Wildwood House, 1975)
——, and Shirley Toulson, *The Drovers' Roads of Wales* (1977; London: Whittet, 1987)
Gough Cooper, Jennifer, *Paths* (Langenbruck: Benteli, 2001)
Govinda, Lama, *The Way of the White Clouds* (1966; New York: Overlook Press, 2006)
Graham, W. S., *The Nightfishing* (London: Faber and Faber, 1955)
Griffiths, Jay, *Wild: An Elemental Journey* (London: Hamish Hamilton, 2007)
Gunn, Neil, *Highland River* (1937; Edinburgh: Canongate, 1991)
——, *The Well at the World's End* (1951; Edinburgh: Canongate, 1996)

~

*Haldane, A. R. B., *The Drove Roads of Scotland* (1952; Edinburgh: Birlinn, 2008)
Harris, Alexandra, *Romantic Moderns* (London: Thames & Hudson, 2010)
Harrison, Sarah, 'The Icknield Way: Some Questions', *Archaeological Journal* 160 (2003), 1–22
*Hauser, Kitty, *Shadow-Sites: Photography, Archaeology and the British Landscape* (Oxford: Oxford University Press, 2007)
——, *Bloody Old Britain: O. G. S. Crawford and the Archaeology of Modern Life* (London: Granta, 2008)
Hazlitt, William, 'My First Acquaintance with Poets' (1823), in *Selected Writings*, ed. Duncan Wu, vol. 9 (London: Pickering and Chatto, 1998)

Hill, Geoffrey, *The Triumph of Love* (London: Penguin, 1998)
——, *The Orchards of Syon* (London: Penguin, 2002)
Hillaby, John 'The Skull Cinema', *New Scientist*, 1 December 1977, 589
Hobsbawm, Eric, *Interesting Times: A Twentieth-century Life* (London: Penguin, 2002)
Hogarth, William, *The Analysis of Beauty* (London: J. Reeves, 1753)
*Hollis, Matthew, *Now All Roads Lead to France: The Last Years of Edward Thomas* (London: Faber and Faber, 2011)
Holmes, Richard, *Footsteps* (1985; London: Penguin, 1986)
Hudson, W. H., *Nature in Downland* (1900; Middlesex: Echo Library, 2006)
——, *Afoot in England* (1909; Oxford: Beaufoy Books, 2010)

~

*Ingold, Tim, *Lines: A Brief History* (London: Routledge, 2007)
Ingold, Tim, and Jo Lee Vergunst (eds.), *Ways of Walking* (Aldershot: Ashgate, 2008)

~

Jackson, John Brinckerhoff, *A Sense of Place, A Sense of Time* (New Haven, CT: Yale University Press, 1994)
James, William, *The Principles of Psychology* (1890; New York: Holt, 1905)
Jenkins, Herbert, *The Life of George Borrow* (London: John Murray, 1912)
——, *The Necessity for Ruins and Other Topics* (Amherst, MA: University of Massachusetts Press, 1980)
Johns, C. A., *Flowers of the Field* (1851; London: Society for Promoting Christian Knowledge, 1919)
Johnston, Devin, *Creaturely and Other Essays* (New York: Turtle Point Press, 2009)

~

Kearney, Richard, *Navigations: Collected Irish Essays 1976–2006* (Dublin: Lilliput, 2006)
Keats, John, *The Letters of John Keats*, ed. M. Buxton Forman, 4th edn (1931; Oxford: Oxford University Press, 1952)

Kierkegaard, Søren, *Søren Kierkegaard's Journals and Papers*, ed. and trans. Howard V. Hong and Edna H. Hong, vol. 6 (Bloomington, IN: Indiana University Press, 1978)

~

*Lakoff, George and Mark Johnson, *Metaphors We Live By* (Chicago, IL: University of Chicago Press, 1980)

Least-Heat Moon, William, *Blue Highways: A Journey into America* (London: Secker & Warburg, 1983)

Leavis, F. R., *New Bearings in English Poetry* (1932; Michigan: University of Michigan Press, 1965)

——, *PrairyErth (A Deep Map)* (Boston, MA: Houghton Mifflin, 1991)

Lee, Laurie, *As I Walked Out One Midsummer Morning* (London: Penguin, 1969)

Leeson, R. A., *Travelling Brothers* (London: George Allen & Unwin, 1979)

*Leigh Fermor, Patrick, *A Time of Gifts* (1977; New York: *New York Review of Books* Classics, 2005)

——, *Between the Woods and the Water* (1986; New York: *New York Review of Books* Classics, 2005)

Leutscher, Alfred, *Tracks and Signs of British Animals* (London: Cleaver-Hulme, 1960)

Lewis, Jennifer, and Jennifer E. Stanistreet, *Sand and Sea: Sefton's Coastal Heritage: Archaeology, History and Environment of a Landscape in North-West England* (Sefton: Leisure Services, 2008)

*Long, Richard, *Selected Statements & Interviews*, ed. Ben Tufnell (London: Haunch of Venison, 2007)

*Lopez, Barry (ed.), *Home Ground: Language for an American Landscape* (San Antonio, TX: Trinity University Press, 2006)

Lorimer, Hayden, 'Herding Memories of Humans and Animals', *Environment and Planning D: Society and Space* 24:4 (2006), 497–518

——, 'Forces of Nature, Forms of Life: Calibrating Ethology and Phenomenology', in *Taking Place: Non-Representational Geographies*, ed. Ben Anderson and Paul Harrison (London: Ashgate, 2010), 55–78

Lowell, Robert, *Robert Lowell: Collected Poems*, ed. Frank Bidart (London: Faber and Faber, 2003)

Lowes, John Livingstone, *The Road to Xanadu: A Study in the Ways of the Imagination* (Boston, MA: Houghton Mifflin, 1930)
Lummis, Charles F., *A Tramp Across the Continent* (1892; Omaha: University of Nebraska Press, 1982)

~

Machado, Antonio, *Campos de Castilla* (1912; Madrid: Catedra, 2006)
*MacLeod, Finlay (ed.), *Togail Tìr/Marking Time: The Map of the Western Isles* (Stornoway: Acair and An Lanntair, 1989)
——, *The Healing Wells of the Western Isles* (Stornoway: Acair, 2000)
——, *The Chapels in the Western Isles* (Stornoway: Acair, 2007)
——, *The Norse Mills of Lewis* (Stornoway: Acair, 2009)
MacNeice, Louis, *I Crossed the Minch* (London: Longman, 1938)
———, *The Collected Poems of Louis MacNeice* (London: Faber and Faber, 1966)
Martin, Martin, *A Voyage to St Kilda* (1698; London: Dan Browne, 1753)
Marsh Wolfe, Linnie (ed.), *John Muir, John of the Mountains: The Unpublished Journals of John Muir* (Madison, WI: University of Wisconsin Press, 1979)
Masefield, John, *The Poems and Plays of John Masefield* (London: Macmillan, 1918)
Matthiessen, Peter, *The Snow Leopard* (1978; London: Harvill, 1996)
McGahern, John, *Love of the World* (London: Faber and Faber, 2009)
McGeoch, James, Catriona McGeoch, Finlay MacLeod and John Love, *Súlasgeir* (Stornoway: Acair, 2010)
Mckee, Eric, *The Working Boats of Britain: Their Shape and Purpose* (London: National Maritime Museum, 1983)
Melville, Herman, *Journals*, ed. Howard C. Horsford and Lynn Horth (1957; Chicago, IL: Northwestern University Press, 1989)
Mengham, Rod, 'Asymmetries in the Bush', *Angelaki* 14:2 (2009), 85–91
*Merleau-Ponty, Maurice, *The Phenomenology of Perception*, trans. Colin Smith (1945; London: Routledge, 1962)
——, *The Visible and the Invisible*, ed. Claude Lefort, trans. Alphonso Lingis (1964; Chicago, IL: Northwestern University Press, 1968)
*Minshull, Duncan (ed.), *The Vintage Book of Walking* (London: Vintage, 2000)
Moore, John, *The Life and Letters of Edward Thomas* (London: Heinemann, 1939)

Moran, Joe, *On Roads: A Hidden History* (London: Profile, 2009)
Moreton, Guy, Michael Nedo and Alec Finlay, *Ludwig Wittgenstein: There Where You Are Not* (London: Black Dog Publishing, 2005)
Morley, Christopher, *Forty-Four Essays* (New York: Harcourt, Brace and Co., 1925)
Morley, Frank, *The Great North Road* (London: Hutchinson, 1961)
Morris, Jan, *Spain* (1964; London: Penguin, 1982)
Motion, Andrew, *The Poetry of Edward Thomas* (London: Routledge & Kegan Paul, 1980)

~

Nedo, Michael (ed.), *Ludwig Wittgenstein: Wiener Ausgabe Einführung/Introduction* (Vienna and New York: Springer-Verlag, 1993)
Newlyn, Lucy, 'Hazlitt and Edward Thomas on Walking', *Essays in Criticism* 56:2 (April 2006), 163–87
*Nicolson, Adam, *Sea Room: An Island Life* (London: HarperCollins, 2001)
Nietzsche, Friedrich, *Twilight of the Idols*, trans. Duncan Large (1888; Oxford: Oxford University Press, 1998)
Norman, Howard, in 'On the Poet's Trail', *National Geographic* (November 2008)

~

O'Brien, Flann, *The Third Policeman* (1967; London, Dublin: Dalkey Archive, 1990)

~

Peck, Edward, *Recollections 1915–2005* (New Delhi: Pauls Press, 2005)
Phelan, Jim, *We Follow the Roads* (London: Phoenix House, 1949)
Poster, Jem, 'Ghost', in 'Ghosts: Edward Thomas and Richard Jefferies', *Archipelago* 2 (Spring 2008), 118–25
*Powers, Alan, *Eric Ravilious: Imagined Realities* (London: Imperial War Museum and Philip Wilson, 2003)
Pretty, Jules, *This Luminous Coast* (Suffolk: Full Circle, 2011)

Pritchett, V. S., *Marching Spain* (London: E. Benn, 1928)
Prynne, J. H., *The White Stones* (Lincoln, Grossteste Press, 1969)

~

*Ravilious, Eric, *Ravilious at War: The Complete Work of Eric Ravilious, September 1939–September 1942*, ed. Anne Ullmann (Upper Denby: Fleece Press, 2002)
Richards, J. M., *Memoirs of an Unjust Fella* (London: Weidenfeld & Nicolson, 1980)
*Robinson, Tim, *Stones of Aran: Pilgrimage* (Mullingar: Lilliput, 1986)
——, *Stones of Aran: Labyrinth* (Mullingar: Lilliput, 1995)
——, *Connemara: A Little Gaelic Kingdom* (Dublin: Penguin Ireland, 2011)
Rousseau, Jean-Jacques, *The Confessions*, trans. J. M. Cohen (1782; London: Penguin, 1953)
Rudd-Jones, Nicholas, and David Stewart, *Pathways* (London: *Guardian* Books, 2011)
Ruskin, John, *Modern Painters* (1843–60; London: George Allen & Sons, 1910)
Russell, Bertrand, *Autobiography* (1967–9; London: Routledge, 1998)
Russell, James, *Ravilious in Pictures: Sussex and the Downs* (Norwich: Mainstone Press, 2009)

~

Saunders, Nicholas J., *Trench Art: Materialities and Memories of War* (Oxford: Berg, 2003)
Sharr, Adam, *Heidegger's Hut* (Cambridge, MA: MIT Press, 2006)
*Shehadeh, Raja, *Palestinian Walks* (London: Profile, 2007)
——, *A Rift in Time: Travels with My Ottoman Uncle* (London: Profile, 2010)
Shepherd, Nan, *The Grampian Quartet* (1928, 1930, 1933, 1977; Edinburgh: Canongate, 1996)
——, 'The Colour of Deeside', *The Deeside Field* 8 (Aberdeen: Aberdeen University Press, 1937), 8–12
*——, *The Living Mountain* (1977; Edinburgh: Canongate, 2011)
Shoard, Marion, *This Land Is Our Land* (1987; London: Gaia, 1997)
Simpson, Jacqueline, 'Legends of Chanctonbury Ring', *Folklore* 80 (1969), 122–31

*Skelton, Richard, *Landings* (Lancashire: Sustain-Release, 2009)
Snyder, Gary, *The Old Ways* (San Francisco, CA: City Lights, 1977)
——, 'Underfoot', *Orion Magazine* (March/April 2009), 46–51
Solnit, Rebecca, *A Book of Migrations* (London: Verso, 1997)
*——, *Wanderlust: A History of Walking* (London: Penguin, 2000)
——, *A Field Guide to Getting Lost* (New York: Viking, 2005)
Spinney, Laura, 'The Lost World', *Nature* 454, 9 July 2008, 151–3
Spirn, Ann Whiston, *The Language of Landscape* (New Haven, CT: Yale University Press, 1998)
Stainer, Pauline, *Parable Island* (Newcastle: Bloodaxe, 1999)
Strassberg, Richard E., *Inscribed Landscapes: Travel Writing from Imperial China* (Los Angeles: University of California Press, 1994)
Stephen, Ian, *Offshore/Onshore* (Edinburgh: Morning Star, 1998)
———, *Mackerel & Creamola: Stories and Recipes* (Edinburgh: Pocketbooks, 2001)
———, *it's about this* (Glasgow: Survivors Press, 2004)
———, *Adrift/Napospas vlnám* (Olomouc: Periplum, 2007)
Stevens, Wallace, *The Collected Poems of Wallace Stevens* (1955; London: Faber and Faber, 1984)
Stevenson, Robert Louis Stevenson, *Essays of Travel* (London: Chatto, 1905)
Stott, Rebecca, *Darwin and the Barnacle* (London: Faber and Faber, 2003)

~

*Taplin, Kim, *The English Path* (1979; Sudbury: Perry Green, 2000)
Thackeray, William, *Notes of a Journey from Cornhill to Grand Cairo*, in *Miscellanies* (1846; Rockville, MD: Wildside Press, 2009)
Thomas, Edward, *Beautiful Wales* (London: A. & C. Black, 1905)
——, *The Heart of England* (London: J. M. Dent, 1906)
*—— (ed.), *The Pocket Book of Poems and Songs for the Open Air* (London: E. Grant Richards, 1907)
——, *Richard Jefferies: His Life and Work* (London: Hutchinson & Co., 1909)
*——, *The South Country* (London: J. M. Dent, 1909)
——, *George Borrow: The Man and His Books* (London: Chapman & Hall, 1912)
*——, *The Icknield Way* (1913; London: Constable, 1916)
*——, *In Pursuit of Spring* (London: Thomas Nelson, 1914)

——, *Collected Poems* (London: Selwyn and Blount, 1920)
——, *The Last Sheaf* (London: Jonathan Cape, 1928)
*——, *The Childhood of Edward Thomas: A Fragment of Autobiography and the War Diary* (1938; London: Faber and Faber, 1983)
——, *Letters of Edward Thomas to Jesse Berridge*, ed. Anthony Berridge (London: Enitharmon, 1983)
*——, *Letters from Edward Thomas to Gordon Bottomley*, ed. R. George Thomas (Oxford: Oxford University Press, 1968)
*——, *Selected Letters of Edward Thomas*, ed. R. George Thomas (Oxford: Oxford University Press, 1995)
*——, *The Annotated Collected Poems*, ed. Edna Longley (Newcastle: Bloodaxe, 2008)
——, *Prose Writings: A Selected Edition*, ed. Lucy Newlyn and Guy Cuthbertson (Oxford: Oxford University Press, 2011–), vols. 1 and 2
*Thomas, Helen, *Under Storm's Wing* (Manchester: Carcanet, 1988)
Thomas, Myfanwy, *One of These Fine Days: Memoirs* (Manchester: Carcanet, 1982)
——, 1932 foreword to *The South Country* (Stanbridge, Dorset: Little Toller, 2009)
Thomas, R. George, *Edward Thomas: A Portrait* (Oxford: Clarendon Press, 1985)
Thoreau, Henry David, *The Essays of Henry David Thoreau*, ed. Lewis Hyde (New York: North Point Press, 2002)
Tilley, Christopher, *The Phenomenology of Landscape: Places, Paths and Monuments* (Oxford: Berg, 1994)
Twain, Mark, *Life on the Mississippi* (1883; London: Penguin, 1986)

~

Watkins, Alfred, *The Old Straight Track* (1925; London: Abacus, 1974)
Watts, Stephen, *Mountain Language/Lingua di Montagna* (London: Hearing Eye, 2009)
West, Rebecca, *Black Lamb and Grey Falcon: A Journey through Yugoslavia* (1942; Edinburgh: Canongate, 1993)
White, Kenneth, *Across the Territories* (Edinburgh: Polygon, 2004)
——, *On the Atlantic Edge* (Dingwall: Sandstone, 2006)
Whitman, Walt, *Walt Whitman: Complete Poetry and Collected Prose* (New York: Library of America, 1982)

Williamson, Henry, *Tarka the Otter* (1927; London: Book Club Associates, 1985)
Wordsworth, William, *The Poetical Works of William Wordsworth*, ed. Paul D. Sheats (Boston, MA: Houghton Mifflin, 1952)
——, *Prose Works of William Wordsworth*, ed. W. J. B. Owen and Jane Worthington Smyser (Oxford: Clarendon Press, 1974)
——, *Guide to the Lakes* (1810; London: Frances Lincoln, 2004)
Wright, Patrick, *On Living in an Old Country* (London: Verso, 1985)

~

Zwicky, Jan, *Wisdom and Metaphor* (Kentville, Nova Scotia: Gaspereau Press, 2008)

ACKNOWLEDGEMENTS

I thank first those who have shaped this book most. Miguel Angel Blanco, Steve Dilworth, Nick Hayes, Finlay MacLeod, Leo Mellor, Jon Miceler, David Quentin, Raja Shehadeh and Ian Stephen have been inspiring companions on and off the path. Peter Davidson, Walter Donohue, Julith Jedamus, Julia Lovell, Rosamund & John Macfarlane and Kate Norbury read versions of the book with invaluable care and attention. My editors Simon Prosser and Paul Slovak, and my friend and agent Jessica Woollard, have been variously patient, encouraging, supportive and editorially brilliant. I have been most fortunate in the people with whom I have worked at Penguin: my copy-editor, Caroline Pretty; John Gray, John Hamilton and Claire Mason, the book's designers; and Anna Kelly, Joe Pickering, Anna Ridley and Ellie Smith.

For help in the walking and thinking of this book, I am very grateful to Bram Arnold, Ivan Bicknell, Ronald Blythe, Anne Campbell, Stanley Donwood, Chris Drury, Richard Mabey, Lily & Tom Macfarlane, Andrew McNeillie, Rod Mengham, Jeremy Noel-Tod, Jules Pretty, Daniel Richards, Gordon Roberts and Tim Robinson.

Thanks are also due, for many kinds of help along the way, to Ruth Abbott, Ellah Allfrey, Tatiana Argounova-Low, Patrick Arnold, Jeff Barrett, Keith Barron, John Beatty, Bella Bigsby, Steven Bode, Tim Brennan, Julia Brigdale, Andrew Brockbank, Amanda Canning, Jonathan & Keggie Carew, Jules Cashford, Adrian Cooper, Jennifer Gough Cooper, Linda Cracknell, Guy Cuthbertson, Jane Davidson, Roger Deakin, Tim Dee, Joan & Beka Dilworth, Sorrell Downer, Robin Duckett, Ed & Will, Martin Elphick, Michael Englard, Chris Evans, Gareth Evans, John Fanshawe, Kitty Fedorec, Alec Finlay, Alan Franks, John Freeman, Robin Friend, Hamish Fulton, Sinéad & Charlie Garrigan-Mattar, Naomi Geraghty, Tom Gilliver, Sophie Gilmartin, Jay Griffiths, Alexandra Harris, Jonathan Heawood, Matthew Hollis, Phil Howell, Michael Hrebeniak, Michael Hurley, Kevin Jackson, Tom King, Patrick Kingsley, Pat Law, Emily Lethbridge, Rachel Lichtenstein, John

Llewelyn, Matt Lloyd, Stephen Logan, Richard Long, Hayden Lorimer, Laurent Loursen, Raphael Lyne, James Macadam, Andy Mackinnon, Malcolm Maclean, Rory Maclean, John MacLennan, Norma Macleod, Sara Maitland, Philip Marsden, Rick Minter, Bob Mizon, Polly Monroe, Janet Moore, Guy Moreton, Ellis Morgan, Colin Myers, Lucy Newlyn, Donald & Lucy Peck, Edward & Alison Peck, Tim Richardson, Chrisella Ross, Diyanne Ross, David Rothenberg, Jasmin & Titus Rowlandson, Pru Rowlandson, Lucia Ruprecht, Jim Rutman, Tom Service, Merlin Sheldrake, Geoff Shipp, Martin Simonson, Iain Sinclair, Michael Skelly, Richard Skelton, Jos Smith, Rebecca Solnit, Anna Stenning, John Stubbs, Kay Syrad, Orla Thomas, Tony Travis, Laurie Tuffrey, Robin Turner, Liesbeth Van Houts, Cristina Viti, Elena Vozmediano, James Wade, Dan Walwin, Stephen Watts, Natalie Whittle, Deborah Wilenski, Christopher Woodward, Ken Worpole and Patrick Wright.

Matthew Hollis and I discovered that for three years we had been following similar paths back into Edward Thomas's life, without ever quite meeting or realizing the other was around. Such footstepping and way-crossing came to seem wholly in keeping with our shared subject, and I remain grateful for Matthew's generosity of spirit. The categorized index, brilliantly composed by Dave Cradduck, was inspired by the work of Richard Skelton and Autumn Richardson, whose Sustain-Release and Corbel Stone presses produce some of the most beautiful books and pamphlets I know.

I am indebted to various institutions: chiefly Emmanuel College, Cambridge, where I have been fortunate to hold a teaching fellowship throughout the writing of this book; also to the Faculty of English in Cambridge, the National Library of Scotland, the Cambridge University Library and the Bodleian Library, Oxford; and differently to *Archipelago*, the *Financial Times*, *Granta*, the *Guardian* and *Lonely Planet Magazine*.

For the granting of permissions I am grateful to: Ian Stephen, Periplum, Pocketbooks and Survivors Press for use of the poetry of Ian Stephen; to John Freeman and *Granta* magazine (where an early version of 'Limestone' appeared); to Andrew McNeillie and *Archipelago* (where an early version of the Ravilious material appeared); to Thomas A. Clark for allowing me to quote from his poetry; to Henry Holt and Co., LLC, and Random House UK, for allowing me to quote from 'The Road Not Taken' (in *The Poetry of Robert Frost*, edited by Edward Connery Latham, © 1969 Henry Holt and Co., LLC); to David Higham Associates and the estate of Louis MacNeice for allowing me to quote from 'Autumn Sequel'; and to the Imperial War Museum for permission to reproduce the photograph prefacing Chapter 15, 'Ghost'.

Acknowledgements

Profound thanks to Richard Emeny, Rosemary Vellender and the Edward Thomas Estate for their support and goodwill, and for their permission to use published and unpublished material concerning Thomas. When quoting from Thomas's poetry I have followed the versions in Edna Longley's *Edward Thomas: The Annotated Collected Poems* (Newcastle: Bloodaxe, 2008). I am grateful to Professor Longley and to earlier editors of Thomas for their work in making available the poems.

All images within the book are mine, save for those which preface Chapter 3, 'Chalk' (© Bram Arnold); Chapter 4, 'Silt' (© David Quentin); Chapter 5, 'Water – South' (© Ian Stephen); Chapter 6, 'Water – North' (© Michael Skelly); Chapter 8, 'Gneiss' (© Steve Dilworth); Chapter 15, 'Ghost' (© Imperial War Museum, image Q 45786, showing opposing trench systems on the Western Front in 1917); and Chapter 16, 'Print' (© Alison Burns). I am grateful to those photographers for allowing me to use their images here. David Quentin's back-cover photograph of me walking the Broomway could not be truer to the book's interest in how we are complicatedly doubled and riddled by the places through which we move.

In 1909 Henry James's novel *The Golden Bowl* was reissued in what is known as the 'New York Edition'. James revised the novel, originally published in 1904, for its new edition and he also contributed a foreword in which he considered the act of self-revision, and the uncanny encounter with the double of your earlier writing self that it involved. In that foreword, he strikingly figures the original writer as a walker who has left tracks in the snow of the page, and the revising writer as a tracker or hunter, following the original print-trail:

> It was, all sensibly, as if the clear matter being still there, even as a shining expanse of snow spread over a plain, my exploring tread, for application to it, had quite unlearned the old pace and found itself naturally falling into another, which might sometimes indeed more or less agree with the original tracks, but might most often, or very nearly, break the surface in other places. What was thus predominantly interesting to note, at all events, was the high spontaneity of these deviations and differences, which became thus things not of choice, but of immediate and perfect necessity.

The snowfield as the blank page, and the tracks as words: here, as so often, walking shimmers into writing and vice versa. One of the talents of the passage is that James holds both sides of his metaphor (snow-plain and page; prints and print) in 'immediate and perfect' balance, so that neither steps forward to dominate the other: rather, they equalize. Visually speaking, it is impossible to pull one aspect of the metaphor into focus and relegate the other to blur. They exist on two planes (plains), but simultaneously. As such, I am reminded of those rare occasions when a white object achieves perfect tuning against snow, defeating the eye's ability to grade and differentiate, so that the object loses its perceptible outline and is absorbed into the snow – or, audaciously, absorbs the snow into it. Which has been tuned to which, or have both been tuned to a new and shared frequency? That rare effect is a conspiracy between observer and two observeds – a coincidental miracle of triangulation.

It is significant that James is interested not in how we might perfectly repeat an earlier print-trail, but in how re-walking (re-writing) is an act whose creativity is founded in its discrepancies: by seeking to follow the traces of an earlier walker or writer, one inevitably 'break[s] the surface in other places'. One does not leave, in the language of tracking, a 'clean register' (placing one's feet without disparity in the footprints of another, matching without excess or deficiency, as an image in cut paper is applied as a sharp shadow upon a wall). James sees our misprints – the false steps and 'disparities' that we make as we track – to be creative acts.

I have, inevitably, followed in the footsteps of many predecessors in terms of writing as well as of walking, and to that end wish to acknowledge the earlier print-trails that have both shown me the way and provoked 'deviations and differences'. The atmospheres, moods and textures of this book arise out of the places through which I have been fortunate to move, but also out of the prose of J. A. Baker, Robert Byron, M. R. James, Patrick Leigh Fermor, Norman MacLean, Cormac McCarthy, John McPhee, Vladimir Nabokov, Martha Nussbaum, Jonathan Raban, Tim Robinson, W. G. Sebald, Nan Shepherd, Rebecca Solnit, Gary Snyder and Colin Thubron; the poetry of Peter Larkin and Colin Simms; the photography of John Beatty, Fay Godwin and Gus Wylie; the art of Chris Drury, Hamish Fulton, Nick Hayes, Kurt Jackson, Peter Lanyon, Richard Long and David Nash; the films of Werner Herzog, Michael Powell and Emeric Pressburger; the music and songlines of Olöf Arnalds, Brahms, the Busch Quartet, Eliza Carthy, Ivor Cutler, The Duke Spirit, Brian Eno, Johnny Flynn, P. J. Harvey, The Kevin Flanagan Quartet, Laura Marling, The Pixies, Schubert, Elliott Smith, The Smiths and Ralph Vaughan Williams; and the thoughts of BLDGBLOG, Fretmarks and Some Landscapes.

INDEX OF SELECTED TOPICS

Headings are arranged alphabetically within each of the selected topics. The topics are arranged in the following order:

ANIMALS, FISH & INSECTS
ARTEFACTS & ARTWORKS
BIRDS
BOOKS, WRITINGS, STORIES & FILM
BUILDINGS & STRUCTURES
COUNTRIES
FLOWERS & PLANTS
IDEAS & PRACTICES
ILLUSIONS & MIRAGES
INSTITUTIONS
ISLANDS
MAPS & MAP-MAKING
MOUNTAINS & HILLS
PATHS & TRACKS
PEOPLE
PLACES
RIVERS & STREAMS
ROCKS, MINERALS & EARTH
SEAFARING, SEA ROADS & VESSELS
SONGS & MUSIC
TOWNS, VILLAGES & CITIES
TREES, WOODS & FORESTS
WEATHER

ANIMALS, FISH & INSECTS
auroch 361
badger 316
birds *see* BIRDS
boar 70
buffalo 14
caterpillars, cinnabar-moth 320
cattle 163, 191, 195, 242, 247
chameleon 229–30
chiru (Tibetan antelope) 265
crickets 254
deer 46, 55, 70, 105, 160–61, 163, 194
  musk deer 282
  tracks/trails 7, 24, 141, 156, 362
dolphins 105, 106, 112–13, 128, 131–2, 300
fox 7, 218
gazelles 220
hare 45, 298, 349
lizards 252
midges 189, 196
moths 163, 176
owls 253
panther 303–4
plankton 134
rabbit 194
  tracks 7, 8
salmon 194
seals 121, 135, 155
sheep 195, 231
  Himalayan blue 264
shellfish/seashells 75, 147–8
  limpets 147–8
Sidi Habismilk (stallion) 18
snow leopard 14, 265n
spiders 163
tracks/trails 7, 8, 9, 24, 76, 141, 156, 272, 298, 327, 362
  Formby footprints 359–64
whales
  minke 106, 128
yak 270
zoo 45, 54, 55

ARTEFACTS & ARTWORKS
Brandt, photograph of Pilgrim's Way 24
Bronze Age 94
cave drawings 53
chalk drawings on flint 328
of Steve Dilworth 169–70, 171–2, 173–6
films *see* BOOKS, WRITINGS, STORIES & FILM
gold lunulae 90, 94
a kist 127, 136, 172
Ravilious, watercolours and engravings 24, 295–7

White Horse at Cradle Hill 327
White Horse at Uffington 312
Wilmington Giant (Long Man of Wilmington) 296

BIRDS
albatross, black-browed 120
avocet 76
buntings, black-headed 349
buzzard 294, 298, 320, 323
cormorant 136, 328
corpses 173–4
crows 257, 316
curlew 76
dipper 189
of the Downlands 294, 298; *see also specific species*
duck, wild 349
eagles 250
  golden 154, 163
eating 127–8, 177
eggs 46
egret 327, 329
falcon 254
feathers 47, 135, 174, 175, 249, 256, 327
fieldfare 298
finches 282
fulmar 109, 121
gannet 109, 120, 127–8, 135–6, 137
  guga hunts 121–3, 135, 178
geese 76
goldfinch 6
grebe 45
grouse 141
guillemot 136, 175
gulls 65, 66, 74, 77, 147
heron 298–9
jay 316
kestrel 219–20, 294, 298
kite, red 256
kittiwake 109
lapwing 179
migration routes 76
owls 163, 294, 328
  barn 314
oystercatcher 66, 67
parakeet 46
partridge 45, 349
  tracks 7
peregrine 76
pheasant 45, 51–2
pigeons 256–7
  snow pigeons 283
puffin 107, 112, 121
raven 141, 272, 279
redwing 298
rook 52, 294, 307, 349
sandpiper 66

skua 135
skylark 37–8, 45, 294, 324, 327, 351
starling 47, 257
swift 294, 326–7
tern 154–5, 300
tits 250
tracks 7, 76, 272, 327
vultures 272
  black 250, 252–3
waders 76
wood pigeon 45

BOOKS, WRITINGS, STORIES & FILM
The Adventure of Bran 95
Afoot in England (Hudson) 77
As I Walked Out One Midsummer Morning (Lee) 315–16
'At the Fishhouses' (Bishop) 30
'Autumn Sequel' (MacNeice) 40–41
'Bees of the Invisible' (Cilek) 235
A Berlin Childhood around 1900 (Benjamin) 32
Bible 19, 145
Black Lamb and Grey Falcon (West) 177–8
'The Blue Men of the Minch' 97
books that choose the reader 239
Campos de Castilla (Machado) 236
A Canterbury Tale (Powell and Pressburger film) 24
Celtic Christian literature 95
Confessions (Rousseau) 27
The Drove Roads of Scotland (Haldane) 191
etymology of books and stories 105
Facing the Ocean (Cunliffe) 91–2
'Fin-Men' 97
Flowers of the Field (Johns) 321–2
Footsteps (Holmes) 326
gannet story 130–31
Go to the Country (Gosse) 319
'The Green Roads' (Thomas) 345
Hansel and Gretel (Grimm Brothers) 15, 25, 48, 144
A Herd of Red Deer (Darling) 160–61
Highland River (Gunn) 199
The Hundred Thousand Places (Clark) 29–30
The Icknield Way (Thomas) 42, 43
'In Praise of Walking' (Clark) 13
Iliad (Homer) 92
islomaniac books 111
La Máscara de Henry Moore 240, 241

Landnámabók (*The Book of Settlements*) 92
'The Lane' (Thomas) 345
Lavengro (Borrow) 19
Leaves of Grass (Whitman) 16
Library of the Forest, Madrid 238–9, 243–4, 245
Life of Johnson (Boswell) 301
Life of the Mississippi (Twain) 129–30
'Lights Out' (Thomas) 325
The Living Mountain (Shepherd) 192–3, 201, 279
Luz Eterna 246
Mabinogion 339
for Manchu translation 19
'March' (Thomas) 341
Massaliote Periplus 92
Le Morte d'Arthur (Malory) 339
Mountains of the Mind (Macfarlane) 188n
Narrow Road to the Far North (Bashō) 14
The Old Straight Track (Watkins) 296
Palestinian Walks (Shehadeh) 213
'The Path' (Thomas) 337
The Path to Rome (Belloc) 20
paths and tracks in 15, 23–4, 25, 48, 143, 144
  Library of the Forest 243–4
The Phenomenology of Landscape (Tilley) 291
Pizarras Espejo de los Alpes 245
Poems and Songs for the Open Air (Thomas) 337
'The Rise' (Berry) 77–8
'The Road Not Taken' (Frost) 343–4
'Roads' (Thomas) 311, 322, 329–30, 345
Romany fantasies (Borrow) 339
Rural Rides (Cobbett) 339–40
Sea Room (Nicolson) 110
sea tales (*immrama*) 95, 97–8
the 'Selkie' 97
'The Signpost' (Thomas) 343
The Snow Leopard (Matthiessen) 264
The Song of Hiawatha (Longfellow) 351
Songs of Travel (Stevenson) 20
The Spirit of the Downs (Beckett) 319
Ian Stephen's poetry 103–4, 135
Sussex folklore 318–19
Tarka the Otter (Williamson) 21
The Third Policeman (O'Brien) 53
Edward Thomas writings 24–5
'Three Knots of Wind' 97
Tibetan Buddhist text 28
Tristram Shandy (Sterne) 52

'Über der Granit' (Goethe) 197
The Voyage of Brendan 95
The Voyage of Mael Duin's Boat 95
'When We Two Walked' (Thomas) 345
Zarzamora virgen 241–2

BUILDINGS & STRUCTURES

Anglo-Saxon earthworks 211, 303
anti-aircraft batteries/pillboxes 71
Avebury earthworks 291
barrows 9, 37, 41, 50, 51–2, 53, 298, 303, 316
Berryfield Cottage 311–12, 338
Bronze Age sites 9, 22, 41, 50, 53, 298, 316
castle earthworks, Edburton Hill 320
cathedrals 244, 256, 257
Eccles Church 71
Fleam Dyke 211
High Beech (cottage) 345, 346
Iron Age sites 9, 41, 49, 54, 317
the Maypole 73–4
Neolithic sites 37, 41, 50, 51, 291, 298, 316
pylons 46
qasrs 218
sea walls 66–7, 68, 72, 76
shielings 142, 143, 152, 153, 161–2, 163, 189
Silbury Hill edifice 291
Torrans (house) 188, 193–5
Wick Green (house) 338

COUNTRIES

America, prairie 'bison roads' 14
Australia 30–31
Bulgaria 186
Canada 28
China 69, 277
  Sichuan Province 261–84
England
  Cambridgeshire 41–2, 159
  chalk country 15, 24, 37–8, 39–55, 159, 291–304, 307–29
  Cumbria 14–15
  Dartmoor 15, 21
  Derbyshire 158–9
  Devon 21
  Dorset 22, 41
  Downs 15, 24, 39–40, 53, 159, 291–304, 307–29
  East Anglia 211
  Essex 345
  Gloucestershire 22, 342
  after the Great War 314–15
  in the Great War 342–7

Hampshire 15, 338–9
silt 59–81
in the snow 5–9, 292–3, 297–8, 302–4
Somerset 62
Suffolk 17, 160, 211
Sussex 32, 40, 295, 315, 316–29
Wiltshire 291–3, 297–9, 302–4, 312
Yorkshire 15
Ethiopia 186
France 329–30, 347–55
Iceland 301–2
Ireland 13–15
Israel 212, 216; see *also* PLACES: West Bank
Italy 186
Japan, farm tracks 14
Netherlands, death and ghost roads 14
Palestine 211–31
Scandinavia 76
Allemansrätten ('Everyman's right') 16
Scotland
access laws 16
gneiss 119
granite 185, 193, 195–7, 200, 202, 203
Highlands 15, 24, 111, 185–205, 279–80, 284–6
mountain paths 15, 284–6
peat country 141–65
Scottish Isles *see under* ISLANDS
seafaring, Outer Hebrides 87–115
seafaring, to Sula Sgeir 119–38
Spain 32, 235, 238–57
drove roads 14
pilgrim routes 14, 32, 235, 238, 242–4, 246–57
Tibet 261, 277
Turkey 187
Wales 15, 25
Black Mountains 159

FLOWERS & PLANTS
agrimony 321
alpine 192, 196, 252
azalea 192, 202
bindweed 51, 54, 311, 321
bog myrtle 190, 202
bougainvillea 214
briar 42
bryony 54, 217, 311, 328, 336
butterwort 190
cherry plum 51
daisies 15
damson 51

dog-rose 42, 51
at Edburton Hill 321
eelgrass 67, 68
ferns 15
gorse 55, 160, 194, 324
heather 160, 190, 202, 285
honeysuckle 311
hyssop 217
ivy 311
jasmine 214
lichen 55, 112, 155
mallow 320
marjoram 217, 321
moss 155, 244, 249
 sphagnum 158, 190
natsch 217–18
ragwort 320, 335
sage 217, 223
samphire 75
sea lavender 75
sundew 190
teasels 327
thyme 217, 327
tormentil 190, 335
yarrow 51

IDEAS & PRACTICES
barefoot walking 158–61
Buddhist 261–2, 276, 283
circumambulation 279
cognition
 knowledge exceeding 340–41
 model of thought and self 340–42
 and walking 27–31
darshan 269
Dreamtime 30
fundamentalist 145
insight 161
map-making *see* MAPS & MAP-MAKING
metaphorical ideas of walking and footfall 26–30
religious *see also (above)* Buddhist 145
 pilgrimage 21, 95, 178–82, 212, 235–6, 242–3, 261–2, 277
 prayer flags 270, 271
rights of way 16
tumo (form of tantric yoga) 276

ILLUSIONS & MIRAGES
in diffused light 68
of the Downlands 293, 297
eyeshine 163
in haze 77
metaphysical hallucinations 77

of a mirror-world 74–5, 200
in mist 155–6
of the Pools of Dee 200
of scale 65, 73

INSTITUTIONS
British and Foreign Bible Society 19
League of Nations 186
Library of the Forest, Madrid 238–9, 243–4, 245
Museum of the Botanical Gardens of Lisbon 239–40
Sierra Club 20
walking clubs 20
War Artists' Advisory Committee 301

ISLANDS
Beechey 266
fabled 95–6
Fortunate Isles 95
Foulness 59, 62
Harris 87, 164–5, 169–82
Hebrides, Outer 87–115, 141–65; *see also specific islands*
Hi-Brazil/Brazil Rock 95–6
Hirta 131
Iceland 301–2
Iona 93n, 95
Island of the Blessed 95
Lewis 15, 87, 96, 97, 98, 100, 114, 115, 121, 133, 138, 141–58, 161–4
North Rona 95, 120–21
Orkney 89, 91, 93, 95, 114
Shetland 89, 91, 93, 95, 120n
Shiants 87, 102, 105–12
  Eilean an Taighe 107, 109
  Eilean Mhuire 106, 107, 113
  Garbh Eilean 107, 113
Sula Sgeir 119–20, 121–3, 135–7, 178
Tory 131–2
Uist 87, 97

MAPS & MAP-MAKING
of Brindled Moor 151–3
chart-reading 123–5
of limpet migrations 148
memories and personal maps 'in the head' 221
of rock formations of the British Isles 38–9
of the Western Isles 146, 164
of the Western Seaways 90–91

MOUNTAINS & HILLS
of the Ala Dag 186
Alps 188, 274
and altitude sickness 274
Ama Dablam 272
Assiniboine 272
Black Mountains 159
Cairngorms 15, 24, 111, 185–205, 279–80
Cantabrian 243
circumambulation of 279
Cradle Hill 327
Croagh Patrick 160
Darling Fell 203
Demirkazik 186
Downs 15, 24, 39–40, 159, 291–304
  Dunstable 53
  Marlborough 304
  South 307–29
Edburton Hill 320–21
Glen Tilt 189
Grey Corries 284–6
Griomabhal 141, 156
Guadarrama 240–41, 244, 246–55
Himalayas 14, 188, 261–85
insides of 201
Kailash 261, 264
Khan Tengri 272–3
Kilimanjaro 188
Kinabalu 188
Kingston Ridge 324
Knapp Hill 303
Matterhorn 272
Minya Konka 261–84
mountain paths 15, 261–86
mountain worshippers 262–3
Palestinian hills 212–14, 220–21
power of 262
pyramidal mountains 273
Pyrenees 244
Rila 186
Silbury Hill 298
Walker's Hill 303

PATHS & TRACKS
animal/bird tracks 7, 8, 9, 24, 76, 141, 156, 272, 298, 327, 362
  Formby footprints 359, 361
and barefoot walking 158–61
'bison roads' 14
border crossings 78
Broomway/'Doomway' 32, 59–69, 72–81
cairned paths 14, 142–4, 149–50, 156–7
Calzada Borbónico 248–9
Camino de Santa Minia 244
Camino Francés 244
Cañada Real 242, 246

Clachan Mhànais ('Manus's Stones') 144, 149–50, 156–7
coffin paths 14–15, 173
consensual nature of paths 17
crofting paths 143
Darwin's 'thinking path' 146
death roads 14
desire lines 17–18
drove roads 14, 190–91, 242, 246, 284–6
European road system 94–5
famine roads 13–14
farm tracks 14
foil 13
Formby footprints 359–64
ghost roads/ghostlines 14, 21
in gneiss country 141, 143
'green track', Isle of Harris 164
as the habits of a landscape 17
holloways 22–3
Icknield Way 25, 31–2, 41, 43–7, 49–55, 291, 308
in Ireland 13–14
in Japan 14
Jugg's Road 324
and the Library of the Forest, Madrid 243–4
the many names of paths 13
migration routes 76
moorland 15, 141–4, 152–8, 162–5
mountain 15, 261–86
Neolithic 40, 296; *see also (below)* Ridgeway
in the Netherlands 14
off-shore 59–81
old paths 47
packhorse routes 15
in Palestine 212–14, 216–31
on peat 141–4, 152–8, 162–5
pilgrim routes 13, 14, 160, 243–4, 261–2
  Camino de Santiago 14, 32, 235, 238, 242–3, 246–57
  Pilgrim's Way 24
'preferential pathways' 228
prehistoric 15
of prose, poetry, stories and art 15, 23–4, 25, 48, 143, 144
Ridgeway 25, 32, 41, 237, 291–3, 297–9, 302–4; *see also (above)* Icknield Way
rights of way 16
rivers as ways 14
Roman roads 42, 90
  Calzada Romano 248–9
Sarn Helen 25
Scotland 14
seaways *see* SEAFARING, SEA ROADS & VESSELS
shieling paths 14, 142–4, 152, 161–2, 163

in snow 6–9, 271–2, 283–6, 292–3, 297–8, 302–3
and Songlines 30–31, 153–4, 215
in Spain 14, 32, 235, 238, 243–4, 246–57
Sweet Track 62
tea routes 269
through terraces 222–3
and Edward Thomas 308–13, 334, 337
wadi paths 219, 227, 228–9
and walkers of note 16, 18, 20, 25, 313–16; *see also* PEOPLE: walkers
way-marking 15

PEOPLE

Aboriginals 30–31, 215
Adomnán, Abbot 93n
Allen, George 49
Arnold, Bram Thomas 237
Arnold, Patrick 62–5
Barrie, J. M. 267
Bashō 14, 21
Basso, Keith 28
Beckett, Arthur 319
Bedouin 231
Belloc, Hilaire 20
Benjamin, Walter 32
Berger, John 226
Berry, Wendell 77–8
Beuys, Joseph 180
Bishop, Elizabeth 30
Bixby, Horace 129
Blake, George 187
Blanco, Elena 239, 240, 245–6
Blanco, Miguel Angel 238–9, 240–42, 243–5, 246–9
Blunden, Edmund 235
Borrow, George 18–20, 23, 25, 236, 243, 322, 339
Bottomley, Gordon 340, 344
'Boxgrove Man' 40
Brandt, Bill 24
Brenan, Gerald 243
Brenhilda 121
Bretons 94
Browne, Thomas 20
Buddhist saints and practitioners 261–2, 276, 283
Bunyan, John 339
Burns, Robert 94
Burroughs, John 76–7
Calvin, John 182
Cambrensis, Giraldus (Gerald of Wales) 339
Campbell, Anne 150–54, 161
Camus, Albert 309
Cano, Melchor 251
Celts 94
Cervantes, Miguel de 339

Chatwin, Bruce 30
Chaucer, Geoffrey 21
Chinese cockle-pickers 61
Chouinard, Yvon 280–82
Cibecue Apache 28
Cilek, Václav 235, 237–8
Clare, John 16, 23
Clark, Thomas A. 13, 29–30
Cobbett, William 339–40
Coleridge, Samuel Taylor 339
Columbus, Christopher 247
Crawford, Osbert 90
Cunliffe, Barry 91–2, 94, 96
Da Gama, Vasco 239
Darling, Frank Fraser 160–61
Darwin, Charles 146
Davidson, Peter 299–300
De Quincey, Thomas 16
Deakin, Roger 22, 79
Dilworth, Alexe 173
Dilworth, Joan 170, 171, 176, 182
Dilworth, Steve 126–8, 164–5, 170–82
Dryden, John 88–9
Durrell, Lawrence 111
Eliot, George 26
Emslie, John 44
Evans, Muir 69
Farjeon, Eleanor 321, 334, 341, 343
Ford, Richard 243
Forster, E. M. 269
Fox, Cyril 91
Fox, William 79
Franz Ferdinand, Archduke 177–8
Frost, Robert 342–4, 355
Fulton, Hamish 243
Galicians 94
Gerald of Wales (Giraldus Cambrensis) 339
ghosts 318–19
Goethe, Johann Wolfgang von 197
Goring, Charles 317
Gormley, Antony 74
Gosse, Philip 319
Govinda, Lama 262
guga hunters of Ness 119–20, 121–3, 135, 136
Gunn, Neil 199, 200
Haile Selassie I 186
Haldane, A. R. B. 191
'Hanging Figure' (skeleton) 169–70, 181
Hardy, Thomas 21–2
Harvey, William 63
Hauser, Kitty 49
Hazlitt, William 23, 339, 340
Hillaby, John 28
Hitler, Adolf 186
Hobsbawm, Eric 186

Hodgkin, Robin 186
Hogarth, William 73
Holmes, Richard 326
Hooton, Harry 43
Hooton, Janet 353
Hudson, W. H. 20, 21, 77, 293, 324
Jackson, John Brinckerhoff 26
James, William 132
Jefferies, Richard 22, 340
Jews of Leopoldstadt 186
Johns, C. A. 321–2
Keats, John 25
Kerouac, Jack 275
Kierkegaard, Søren 27
Kingdon-Ward, Frank 264
Klinchon people 28
Lee, Laurie 243, 315–16
Lloyd, Matt 243
Lockwood, Pilgrim 69
Long, Richard 17, 29, 157
Lowell, Robert 103
Lummis, Charles 20
Macdonald, Revd 147
Machado, Antonio 236
Maclean, Malky 149–50, 157
MacLennan, Manus 144, 149, 150
MacLeod, Finlay 125, 144–9, 154
MacLeod, Jon 153
MacLeod, Norma 145
MacNeice, Louis 40–41
Mallory, George 266
Malory, Thomas 339
Martin, Martin 78
Masefield, John 21
Matheson, James 100
Matthiessen, Peter 264, 269
McDonald, Donald 123
McGahern, John 199
Melville, Herman 220, 228
Mengham, Rod 320, 323–4
Messerschmid, Clemens 227–8, 229–30
Miceler, Jon 263–7, 268, 269, 270, 274, 275, 276, 277, 278–9, 280–81, 282
Milarepa 276
Morley, Christopher 27
Muir, John 20
Myfanwy, Thomas 354
Nash, John 199–200
Nash, Paul 23–4, 296
Nicolson, Adam 110–11, 198
Nietzsche, Friedrich 27
O'Brien, Flann 53
Palestinians 216
Palmer, Samuel 296
Peck, Edward (author's grandfather) 185–8, 192, 197–8, 202, 203–5, 272
Pedro V of Portugal 239

pilgrims 95, 160, 220, 235–8, 243, 257, 261–2, 263
Powell, Michael 24
Pressburger, Emeric 24
Pritchett, V. S. 243
Pytheas 133
Qiang people 270
Qin Shi Huang 69
Quentin, David 66, 68–9, 74, 76, 159n, 188–90, 196, 284–6, 291–2, 302–3
Ravilious, Eric 24, 39, 294–7
Ravilious, Tirzah 300
reavers 190
Red Guards 262
Ridgeway, Rick 280–82
Robinson, Tim 111
Ronan, St 120–21
Ross, Chrisella 149–50
Rousseau, Jean-Jacques 27
Ruskin, John 273
Russell, Bertrand 29
Saigyo 21
Schaller, George B. 264–5
Schmitz, Kim 280–82
Scott, Robert Falcon 266, 267
Scott, Walter 47
Shakespeare, William 339
Sharp, Cecil 337
Shehadeh, Penny 215
Shehadeh, Raja 211–24, 227, 230–31
Shepherd, Anna ('Nan') 24, 111, 158, 163, 192–3, 197, 200, 201, 254, 279
Shotton, Fred 71
Snyder, Gary 264
Sopwith, Thomas 114
Starkie, Walter 243
Stephen, Ian 96–104, 108–9, 113–15, 123–5, 126, 128–9, 130–31, 135, 138
Sterne, Laurence 52
Stevens, Wallace 27
Stevenson, Robert Louis 20, 339
Taine, Hippolyte Adolphe 308
Thackeray, William 220
Thomas, Bronwen 336
Thomas, Edward 24–5, 31, 32–3, 39, 42, 43–4, 47–8, 50, 52, 54, 150, 198–9, 278, 308–13, 321, 322–3, 324–5, 329–30, 333–55
Thomas, Helen 199, 309, 311–14, 323, 335–7, 343, 346, 353
Thomas, Merfyn 336, 346, 351
Thoreau, Henry David 79
Tilley, Christopher 291, 292
Traherne, Thomas 20
Twain, Mark (Samuel Clemens) 129–30

'umbrella man' 310
Vaughan, Henry 20
Verner, Willoughby 250
Vespasian, Emperor 248
Vikings 92
Wade, George 190–91
Watkins, Alfred 296
Waugh, Louisa 216
West, Rebecca 177–8
Westropp, T. J. 96n
White, Gilbert 111, 296
White, Kenneth 92, 94, 95
Whitman, Walt 16
Williamson, Henry 21
wise women/'witches'
of Galicia 244
Wittgenstein, Ludwig 29
Woolf, Virginia 293
Wordsworth, Dorothy 23
Wordsworth, William 16, 23, 27, 340
Wright, Asia 281–2
Wright, Jonathan 280–82
Zalatimo, Basel 224, 225, 226
Zalatimo family 224–6

PLACES *see also* TOWNS, VILLAGES & CITIES
Aird Bheag peninsula 142, 149
Arctic Circle 299, 300–301
Asturias 242
Baile na Cille 147
Bodmin Moor 144
Brindled Moor 151–3
Camus Mol Lìnis 154
Chanctonbury Ring 315, 317–20
Colinda Point 69–70
Cuckmere Haven 328
Devil's Dyke 323
Dogger Bank 71
Doggerland 70–81
Dubh Loch 156
Dymock fields 343–4
English counties *see under* COUNTRIES: England
Fisherman's Head 59
Formby Point 359–64
Fuenfría valley 244, 246–50
Hare Hall Training Camp 345
Havengore Creek 73
Hesperides 95
Ivinghoe Beacon 54–5
Kaldadarnes airbase 302
Lairig Ghru 195–7
Linton Zoo 45
Loch Avon 201
the Maypole 73–4
the Minch 87, 91, 100, 101, 102, 104, 106, 110, 125
Monkton Farleigh Quarry 237
Morecambe Bay 60–61

Ness 121, 123, 138, 145
Orford Ness 211
Outer Silver Pit 71
Plumpton Plain 323
Pools of Dee 200
Puerta de Fuenfría 248, 250
Scottish Highlands 15, 24, 111, 185–205, 279–80, 284–6
Seven Sisters 328
Siberia 105
Spines 70
Therfield Heath 50
Trollamaraig 164
Wadi Kalb 221–3
Wadi 'qda 216–18, 219–20
Wadi Zarqa 227, 230–31
Wakering Stairs 59, 65
West Bank 213–29, 231
Whipsnade Zoo 54, 55
White Peak 158–9
Wimbledon Common 336
Zanskar valley 14

RIVERS & STREAMS
Adur 320
Allt Mor burn 15
Avon 188, 194, 203
Brahmaputra 261
and contact springs 230
Cuckmere 327–8
Dadu 268
Dee 196
Ganges 261
Indus 261
Ouse 327
the river as another world 78
Shannon 199
Shotton 71
Sutlej 261
Tilt 189–90
as ways 14

ROCKS, MINERALS, & EARTH
bog 143–4, 179
boulders 15, 111, 142, 147, 180–81, 249
of the Cairngorm massif 185, 195–7, 200, 203
cairns 15, 111–12, 122, 142, 143, 251, 270, 277, 281–2, 328
Manus's Stones 144, 149–50, 156–7
calcium 194
chalk/chalklands 15, 24, 37–8, 39–55, 159, 291–304, 307–29
chert 229
clay 15, 38, 41, 76, 160
dolerite 111, 175
feldspar 195

flint 40, 94, 146, 214, 229, 307, 316, 328–9
gneiss 96, 102, 111, 119, 120, 137, 141, 162, 180–82
granite 185, 193, 195–7, 200, 202, 203, 240, 246, 248, 249, 251, 252, 253, 272
guide stones 15, 142; *see also (above)* cairns; *(below)* standing stones
henges 291
ice/snow-covered 196, 266–7, 270, 271, 272, 274–86, 292–3, 297–8, 302–3
  glaciers 147, 180, 197
limestone 159, 213, 214, 217, 218, 220, 223, 227, 228, 230
mani stones 270, 277, 278
megaliths 180–81, 291
meteors 32
mica 195, 203
Old Red Sandstone 159
peat 141–65
quartz 157, 180, 181, 195, 203, 363–4
resting stones 14–15
rock formations of the British Isles 38–9
sarsen stones 298
sillion 160
silt 59–81
  footprints in Mesolithic and Neolithic silt layers 359–64
standing stones 142, 143
stupas 277, 278
Utsi's Stone 15

SEAFARING, SEA ROADS, & VESSELS
in Arctic Circle 300–301
boat construction 114–15
Broad Bay 87–8, 100, 101, 106, 107, 113–14
chart-reading 123–5
Colinda 69
Glorious, HMS 300
Heather Isle 135
Hebridean 126, 133–4
Highlander, HMS 300
Jubilee 125–6, 128, 132, 135, 136, 137
language of seafaring 103–4
Mona Queen 347
navigating by the North Star 132–3
Neolithic boats 91
and the night sky 132–4

in Outer Hebrides 87–115
phosphorescent sea 108, 134
seaways set by winds and
currents 14
in the Second World War 299–301
Sula Sgeir journey 119–38
An Sùlaire (*The Gannet*) 101, 107
votive offerings 127
waves 128–9, 155

SONGS & MUSIC
army songs 346, 347
folk-songs 337
'Fraoch à Rònaigh' 97
Gaelic 97
'The Gallant Weaver' (Burns) 94
of the *guga* men of Ness 119–20
'The Road to the Isles' 205
Songlines 30–31, 153–4, 215
Edward Thomas and 337

TOWNS, VILLAGES & CITIES
Aberdeen 192
Arras 329, 333, 349–55
Baldock 50
Barcelona 187
Beaurains 352
Berlin 187
Botolphs 320
Boxgrove 40
Bragar 150
Brion 244
Cercedilla 246
Chengdu 263
Chideock 22
Clothall 50
Detroit 17–18
Dolev 222
Dunwich 72
Eastbourne 295, 308
Geocrab 169–70, 179
Great Chesterford 46
Great Yarmouth 18
Jaffa 216
Kangding 269
Le Havre 347
Letchworth Garden City 50
Lhasa 269
Linton 42, 44–5
Lisbon 239–40
Luton 53
Madrid 238–9
Library of the Forest 238–9,
243–4, 245
Mealasta 142, 154
Norwich 18
Pirton 51
Ramallah 212–15, 219, 222, 231

Ras Karkar 227
Reykjavik 301–2
Rhenigidale 164
Royston 46
Santiago de Compostela 14, 244, 257
Segovia 251, 256–7
Selborne 296, 312
Shawbost 147
sites of former Palestinian villages 221
Skjolden 29
Soissons 53
Steep 311, 312, 338
Stornoway/the Hoil 87, 96, 97, 98, 100, 114, 115, 138, 145, 149
Tarbert 164
Tel Aviv 214–15
Tomintoul 188
Vienna 186
Xian 69
A'yn Qenya 221
Yulongxi 269

TREES, WOODS & FORESTS
almond trees 221
ash 70
beech 7, 293, 302, 316, 338
birch 302
blackthorn 6
Chanctonbury Ring 315, 317–20
dogwood 6
Epping Forest 159, 345
field maple 42
Fuenfría forest 244, 246–8, 250–51
hawthorn 6, 42, 45, 55, 159
hazel 6, 54, 302
juniper 202, 251, 272
lemon trees 214
lime 53
Metasequoia glyptostroboides 194
mountain 192, 247, 250, 252
oak 70
  Himalayan 273
  holm 217
  Quercus petraea 247
and personal 'roots' 244–5
pine 7, 238, 240–41, 247, 250
pollen 254, 255
rhododendron bushes 273
Rothiemurchus forest 202
at Torrans, near Tomintoul 194
trees near the author's Cambridge home 6, 42
War Down 311
whitebeam 316
yew 338

WEATHER
in the Cairngorms 195
and inner mood 336–7, 338–9
mist 65–6, 155–6
rain 223, 307–8, 336–7, 338–9
  and limestone 228
and Ravilious's death 302
snow 5–9, 194, 196, 270, 284–5;
  see *also* ROCKS, MINERALS, & EARTH: ice/snow-covered
  blizzards 195, 281
  cyclones 285
storms 307–8, 317
and Edward Thomas 336–7, 338–9

L E W I S
T H E M I N C H
L I T T L E M I N C H
HARRIS
R O S S
LOCH ASSYNT
SUMMER ISLANDS
LOCH BROOM
LITTLE LOCH BROOM
GAIRLOCH
LOCH TORRIDON
RONA ISLAND
CANNA
EIG
POINT of SLEAT
LOCH SHELL
English Miles.